Praise for *Secularizing Buddhism*

"As Buddhadharma and Buddhist practice are transmitted to the West and as Buddhism engages with modernity, Buddhist ideas, practices, and commitments are adapted and transformed. This fascinating collection of essays by some of the leading scholars of contemporary Buddhism explore the complex interaction of Buddhism with the modern world. This volume will be a valuable resource for practitioners, scholars, and anybody interested in the present and future of Buddhism and in the contributions it can make to our world."

—Jay Garfield, author of
Engaging Buddhism: Why It Matters to Philosophy

"This volume provides a much-needed critical treatment of the multiple 'secularizing Buddhism' processes and projects underway in global Buddhism. Exploring a range of contexts from the Pāli canon to Pure Land Buddhism, the museum to the mindfulness movement, these authors clearly illuminate the complicity between secularization and colonialism, racism, and neoliberalism. *Secularizing Buddhism* makes two important intellectual and ethical interventions: It identifies the ethnocentric, racialized violence that occurs when the secular is constructed as binary other and developmentally superior to the religious. It also suggests how the relationship between the two can be reconfigured in more fluid, dynamic, and context-sensitive ways."

—Ann Gleig, author of
American Dharma: Buddhism Beyond Modernity

"Utilizing but not bound by slippery dichotomies such as secular versus religious, modern versus traditional, and West versus East—taking them instead as 'semiotic pairs' or, to use a more traditional Buddhist concept, as 'nondual'—the essays in this fine collection explore various facets of Buddhism in contemporary society. From mindfulness in the schools to Buddhist art in museums, from controversies over rebirth to 'immanent' Buddhism and more, *Secularizing Buddhism* provides a thoughtful mosaic of our ever-evolving situation."

—Paul L. Swanson, author of
Nanzan Guide to Japanese Religions

Secularizing Buddhism

New Perspectives on a Dynamic Tradition

EDITED BY RICHARD K. PAYNE

SHAMBHALA

Shambhala Publications, Inc.
2129 13th Street
Boulder, Colorado 80302
www.shambhala.com

"Manifesting the Buddha Dharma in a Secular Age" by Bhikkhu Bodhi was previously published in *Buddhism in Dialogue with Contemporary Societies*, edited by Carola Roloff, Wolfram Weiße, and Michael Zimmermann. Religions in Dialogue, vol. 17. Muenster, Germany: Waxmann Verlag, 2020.

Image on p. 56: Printed here in black and white. London (Little Piazza, James Street, Covent Garden): Published according to Act of Parliament & sold by Tho. Worlige painter, 1751. Wellcome Library no. 16433i. https://wellcomecollection.org/works/qfajamnq.

Image on p. 94: Unidentified artist. Standing Buddha, c. 12th century. Wood, 25⁷⁄₁₆ × 8 × 4 ³⁄₁₆ in. (64.6 × 20.3 × 10.6 cm). Ackland Art Museum, University of North Carolina–Chapel Hill. Gift of Ruth and Sherman Lee, 2003.35.4.

Cover art: caoyu36/iStock
Cover design: Daniel Urban-Brown
Interior Design: Michael Russem

9 8 7 6 5 4 3 2 1

First Edition
Printed in the United States of America

♾ This edition is printed on acid-free paper that meets the American National Standards Institute z39.48 Standard.
♻ This book is printed on 30% postconsumer recycled paper.
For more information please visit www.shambhala.com.

Shambhala Publications is distributed worldwide by
Penguin Random House, Inc., and its subsidiaries.

LIBRARY OF CONGRESS CATALOGING-IN-PUBLICATION DATA
Names: Payne, Richard K., editor.
Title: Secularizing Buddhism: new perspectives on a dynamic tradition / edited by Richard K. Payne.
Description: First edition. | Boulder, Colorado: Shambhala, [2021]
Identifiers: LCCN 2020022579 | ISBN 9781611808896 (trade paperback)
Subjects: LCSH: Buddhism and secularism.
Classification: LCC BQ4570.S43 S43 2021 | DDC 294.3/37—dc23
LC record available at https://lccn.loc.gov/2020022579

Contents

Secularizing Buddhism

Editor's Introduction

The title of this volume intentionally avoids an artificial opposition between secular and religious Buddhism. Instead, this collection of essays explores a secularizing process—in other words, an action rather than a fixed object. Framing different approaches to Buddhism in this way dissolves many of the problems, or pseudo-problems, created when two seemingly mutually exclusive categories are applied. Perhaps the most challenging issue is the question of how to define secular and religious, and then attempting to determine which instance of Buddhism fits into which category. Does having regular Sunday morning meetings with chanting make a Buddhist group religious? Why more so than regular Thursday evening meetings with meditation? The realities of Buddhist views, practices, communities, and institutions are much more complex than what such a dichotomy can usefully reflect.

Matching *secularizing*, we also introduce the concept of *traditionalizing*. While some groups move—whether by agreement or by unspoken consent—toward greater degrees of secularity, others do the same but in the opposite direction toward "tradition." At this point, secular and traditional can be understood as two ends of a range, along which any particular Buddhist group might be located at any particular time. The final qualification, "at any particular time," reflects another complicating factor for understanding this development of Buddhism in the twenty-first century. No group is static, and attempts to keep it from changing can result in tensions and misrepresentations, both personal and institutional.

There are three pairs of matching categories that are considered in this collection: (1) secular and religious, (2) modern and traditional, and (3) Eastern and Western. None of the six concepts involved in these pairings have an objective referent. There are no objects that one can point to and say "this is religion" and "that is secularity," or "this is tradition" and "that is modern," or "this is Eastern" and "that is Western." At best one can engage in stipulative definitions—that is, pointing at something as an instance of what one means by the category—though that is itself fraught with intellectual challenges. What is one pointing to when one points to *the* Catholic Church as an instance of religion? And, to highlight the difficulty, what is one pointing to when one points to *a* Catholic church as an instance of religion?

The process of understanding something unfamiliar necessarily works on the basis of existing understanding. Generally what happens is that the characteristics of a familiar category are extended to the new, unfamiliar category by analogy—though vanishingly rarely in the self-conscious manner of a formalized argument by analogy such as these:

1. Catholicism and Buddhism are alike.
2. Catholicism is a religion.

Therefore, Buddhism is a religion.

And in doing so, there are unlimited opportunities for more specific characteristics of one to be attributed to the other on the basis of the analogy.

1. Catholicism and Buddhism are religions.
2. Catholicism teaches priestly poverty.

Therefore, Buddhism teaches monastic poverty.

Natalie Quli has discussed the construction of traditional and modernist around the dichotomy of Western and Eastern in the

academic study of Buddhism. The relationships drawn are complicated by different ways that the terms are juxtaposed, including by
the rhetoric of "preserving tradition." As Quli says,

> [The] simplistic model of Asian versus Western, traditional ver-
> sus modernist, repeats the stereotype of a passive Asian and
> an active Westerner, perpetuating the researcher's inclination
> to "save" Asian (and by extension, Asian American) Buddhism
> from the West. Others have used this dichotomy of the pas-
> sive Asian/modernist Westerner to promote a new, supposedly
> "culture-free" form of Buddhism in the West that is unlike that
> traditional, conservative Asian Buddhism against which they
> paint it.[1]

Using the verb forms "secularizing" and "traditionalizing" reflects
the view that the primary terms structuring this collection are also
not simply oppositional to one another but can best be understood
as poles of a dialectic. At the same time, this intentionally allows
for a play of ambiguity, in that "secularizing Buddhism" can be
understood as either "to make Buddhism secular" or as "that kind
of Buddhism whose proponents promote a secular interpretation."

Although individual contributions may employ the oppositional
categories, juxtaposing different views helps us to avoid creating
two artificial entities, secular Buddhism and traditional Buddhism.
If traditional and secular are conceptualized as two distinct and
separate categories of Buddhism, then it is all too easy to interpret
them as static and autonomous. Instead of being static, the two are
dynamically related to one another. At the level of concepts, secular
and religious, or modern and traditional, or Eastern and Western
are each conceived in opposition to one another—that which is the
one is that which is not the other, and vice versa.

The three dichotomies—secular/religious, modern/traditional,
Western/Eastern—have served rhetorical purposes privileging one
interpretation of Buddhism over other interpretations for a century
and a half. It is the intent of this collection to sensitize readers to the
ways in which these dichotomies are deployed and enable readers

to critically consider for themselves the values these dichotomies implicitly promote in the discourse of secularizing Buddhism.

Why "Secularizing Buddhism"?

The concept of the secular is perhaps one of the most overtheorized categories in the study of religion. This introduction first seeks to wend our way through this dark and tangled conceptual wood so as to provide readers with some landmarks by which to orient themselves to the individual contributions collected in the main body of this work.

One of the fundamental distinctions in how the term "secular" is used is whether it is used to identify a characteristic of modernity—that is, a historical process that is in large part taken for granted as an inevitable development of society. That conception usually then points to conditions in the nineteenth century, such as the creation of the technologies of industrialization, relocation of formerly agrarian people in the process of urbanization, the rise of a concept of social governance that linked geography, language, ethnicity, culture and legitimacy of political authority in the form of the nation-state, and the rise of an increasingly global capitalist system with its ideological support of neoliberalism becoming the taken-for-granted idea of the human condition. In many instances, these changes are cast as inevitable and beneficial developments, a view of history as progress and improvement.

Distinct from this historical conception of the secular as an inevitable social force is an older political conception of actively separating political and religious institutions. This points even further back historically to the eighteenth century, and the idea of the separation of church and state. Many people understand this separation as the means by which religious conflicts, most importantly the religious wars in Europe that lasted two centuries—from the early sixteenth to the early eighteenth century—were brought to closure by giving religion its "proper" place in the personal realm, and keeping it out of the realms of politics and economics.

Both of these usages, historical and political, tend to valorize the secular positively. This in turn contributes to the active program of reinterpreting Buddhism that is the subject of this collection. In general, "secular" is identified with the modern (historical) and the progressive (political). But every concept is deeply enmeshed with other concepts, particularly the oppositional pairings that give it its sharpest contrasts. In the case of the secular, that conceptual opposite is the traditional.

Secular is symbolically paired in opposition to traditional. Where "secular" carries a connotation of "modern," in contemporary discourse "traditional"—as in the phrase "traditional Buddhism"—is "a qualifier that harkened a bygone era when religion was the primary source of social morality and religious ethics were livable in all aspects of life."[2] While for some this evinces nostalgia for an idyllic, harmonious past now lost, for others it produces a sense of authoritarian control from which we need to be free. No matter the response, it is doubtful that this construct of traditional religion was ever the norm in the Christian West, and it is even more dubious that this image of religion as the primary source of morality and ethics permeating all aspects of life is an accurate representation of Buddhist history. However, it is the set of connotations that are evinced when the opposition between secular and traditional is deployed in the present-day construction of secular Buddhism.

A secularizing rhetoric has been part of the European and American understanding of Buddhism since the latter part of the nineteenth century. More recently, however, forms of secularized Buddhism have become increasingly institutionalized, identifying themselves under capitalized labels such as Secular Buddhism,[3] Secular Dharma,[4] Pragmatic Buddhism,[5] and Pragmatic Dharma.[6] As of 2020, these institutional forms remained relatively informal regarding such matters as membership and leadership, some apparently being primarily virtual associations, even before the time of the Covid-19 pandemic. As the founders of these secular Buddhist institutions pass, however, transmission of authority will become an issue. Classic sociology of religion suggests that the charisma of a now-absent founder may contribute to the creation of more formal institutions, so that authority can be transmitted and institutional continuity itself maintained.

But this present moment of transition from informal to formal is an important phenomenon in itself, whether viewed from the perspective of individual practitioners or from the perspective of the academic study of religion and Buddhist studies. Bringing together a variety of perspectives from members of the Buddhist community who have actively reflected on these changes is intended to provide a snapshot of this moment, but a snapshot that is multidimensional in nature—what is happening is more complex than any one author can adequately represent.

Secularizing Buddhism Has Had Several Different Motivators

Many of the factors motivating these developments are located in the Buddhist modernist revisioning of Buddhism "for the modern world," particularly on the model of late-nineteenth-century liberal Protestantism. One aspect of liberal Protestantism derives from the theology of Jesus's return and the transformation of the world— that is, millennialism, and specifically the ordering of tribulation, second coming, and millennium. The most common theology in conservative, evangelical Christianity today is that of premillennialism, in which the order is tribulation, second coming, and then the millennium. Postmillennial theology on the other hand taught that it was incumbent upon believers to create the ideal conditions of the millennium here and now in order to facilitate the second coming. Known as the Social Gospel, this belief led to several religiously motivated social reform movements, each having the goal of perfecting society so as to bring about the second coming of Jesus. In addition to general support for social justice and worker's rights, the Social Gospel was manifest in institutions such as settlement houses (the first being Toynbee Hall, Whitechapel, established in the East End of London in 1884) which provided services to the poor and to immigrants. Other expressions were the organization founded as the Young Men's Christian Association (now YMCA) in 1844 and the enactment of Prohibition through the passage of the Eighteenth Amendment to the US Constitution in 1919 (repealed by the Twenty-First Amendment in 1933).

While always complexly involved with many other dimensions of social organization, such movements as the abolition of slavery, women's suffrage, prohibition of alcohol, and the civil rights movement were also motivated by this liberal Protestant postmillennial theology. As a believer it was incumbent upon the individual Christian to contribute to making the world a better place so that Jesus would return, which created the association between religion and social engagement.

All six paired concepts—secular, religious, modern, traditional, East, West—are social constructs, and as such have a history. They are also deployed as rhetorical strategies—being able to use the concepts and control the meanings of the terms actively structures the conceptual framework under which the process of secularizing Buddhism proceeds. One example of this is the debate over whether Buddhism is a religion or a philosophy of life or a system of ethical self-improvement. Early in the history of Buddhism in the United States and Europe, Buddhist proponents claimed that it was not a religion—thus protecting themselves from direct confrontation with established religions. Conversely, the assertion that Buddhism is not a religion, meaning that unlike Christianity it could not offer eternal salvation, was also meant as an insult. Much of this rhetoric, both positive and negative, remains active today.

Conversely, there is not only a protective power but also a kind of social status to be found by saying that Buddhism is a religion. This was made evident in an analogous argument in favor of the phrase "Buddhist theology." The argument was that theology is not only widely employed but is also a highly respected category of intellectual endeavor, and to use the phrase "Buddhist theology" would garner for that project the same kind of authority and respect granted to "theology," which when used without a qualifying adjective refers to Christian theology.[7] The same kind of status claim has been made when asserting that Buddhism is a religion. Gil Fronsdal, in his essay in this collection, points out a different aspect of this claim, however, which is that for him personally, Buddhism has the same feel, or fulfills the same function, as other people ascribe to their religious identity. In other words, Fronsdal implicitly defines religion functionally, rather than as some set of dogmatic beliefs and authoritarian hierarchies as do some contributors to the secularizing discourse. Rather than concretizing Buddhism into reified categories of one kind or another—whether religion, philosophy of life, or lifestyle choice—this collection is intended to reflect the instability of "Buddhism" in the present. Like all socially constructed entities, instability has been its character since the formation of the category "Buddhism" as a "world religion" in the nineteenth century.[8] Two metaphors provide ways to think about this collection as more than individual contributions. These are the metaphors of landscape and of overdetermination.

If we think of the current situation as a landscape, then what we are pointing out first is features of that landscape. Of particular importance are those that serve as landmarks, allowing us to find our way around the landscape, to know where we've been, and where we're going, and how, if necessary, to get back to where we were. Of course, a landscape—whether physical or conceptual—is not a static thing but is instead itself in constant change—often with layers building up on top of existing layers. Secondly, therefore, to explore a landscape also implies considering that which lies under the surface—for a conceptual landscape, this means a kind of cultural geology. In other words, examining the secularizing of Buddhism involves unearthing the complexes of cultural concepts that support the claims being made. Why are certain claims about the nature of Buddhism, whether secularized or not, being framed in particular ways? How does that framing interact with the existing cultural assumptions of the intended audience? These dynamics are of course not unique to Buddhism in the present. They are the dynamics that have been at work across the entire history of the Buddhist institution and at each point that the teachings have entered a new cultural context. It is also a natural process in the sense that of course people understand something new by reference to that with which they are already familiar. In particular it is the well-entrenched cultural concept that religious and secular constitute two clearly separate and oppositional forms that underlies the landscape of this discourse.

Distinguishing the Secularizing of Buddhism from Buddhist Modernism

Buddhist modernism is a descriptive category, grouping together a number of different phenomena, both in Asia and the West, and stretching across the last century and a half. It is rooted in Asian resistance to colonialism and in Western responses to the rise of science as an explanatory system displacing religion, together with an increasing awareness of religious diversity.[9] Such resistance "generated the need for anticolonial national movements to reformulate their own collective representations in terms of the dominant Western paradigms."[10] Buddhist reformers recast local forms of Buddhist praxis in the mold of "religion," and in doing so they adopted not only models of organization but also the values of liberal Protestant thought widespread in England and the United States at the end of the nineteenth century. Buddhist modernism "has been shaped by an engagement with the major discourses of Western modernity— science, Romanticism, and liberal Protestantism—and is marked by a number of distinctively modern values such as individuality, democracy, pluralism, and the privileging of meditation experience as the core of the tradition."[11] Natalie Quli provides a summary list of twelve interrelated features of Buddhist modernism that are said to derive from the influence of the West:

1. the extolling of reason and rationality,
2. a rejection of ritual, "superstition," and cosmology,
3. an understanding of doctrine and text as more authentically

Buddhist than practices such as relic veneration or Buddha-name recitation,

4. laicization and democratization,
5. a valorization of meditation and an optimistic view of nirvana, culminating in the hitherto unprecedented widespread practice of meditation among the laity,
6. an ecumenical attitude toward other Buddhist sects,
7. increased status of women,
8. interest in social engagement,
9. the tendency to define Buddhism as a philosophy rather than a religion,
10. a return to the "original" teachings of the Buddha, particularly as ascribed to the Pāli canon,
11. a focus on text, and
12. rejection of "spirit" or "folk" religion…as mere cultural accretions (introduced through the process of decay) to be separated from the rational core of Buddhism.[12]

As we are using the terms here, Buddhist modernism is distinct from the secularizing of Buddhism. Buddhist modernism is an ideological framework, while the secularizing of Buddhism is a movement—there are no leaders proclaiming Buddhist modernism, only scholars using the term to identify a complex of mutually supportive ideas and to describe the changes in Buddhist institutions and teachings over the last century and a half. In contrast, there are active proponents advocating the secularization of Buddhism, and building institutions and networks.

Again, "secularizing Buddhism" is not meant to identify a kind of Buddhism but rather a process or dynamic that is at work in present-day Buddhism. Since the reader may be expecting clear delineation between two equal categories, and feel confused and distressed by what appears to be a lack of clarity, it is worth reiterating that we are looking at a dynamic process that is continuing to change—the instability of "Buddhism" mentioned above. While much of present-day European and American Buddhism can be described as instances of Buddhist modernism, the process of secularizing Buddhism has a much wider reach. Although counter to the idea that modern and secular and Western necessarily go together, secularizing is also part of Buddhist traditions that are not *prima facie* modernist. One example, the modern Japanese group Soka Gakkai, shares such key characteristics with secularizing as an anticlerical attitude—it is a lay organization with lay leaders that has formally broken with the monastic institution that had been its initial source of legitimation. At the same time, its main practice is chanting a mantra before a thirteenth-century mandala of the names of buddhas and bodhisattvas important in the Lotus Sutra written in a medieval style of Japanese calligraphy in expectation of fulfilling one's wishes—a practice that a strongly secularizing attitude would no doubt find nothing more than superstitious.

Another instance is Fo Guang Shan, which, although originating in Taiwan, is now an international organization located in what has been called "global Buddhist China." This is the range of expatriate communities whose members increasingly identify as Chinese rather than as being from some specific "locality (be it the People's Republic of China [PRC], Hong Kong, Taiwan, Singapore, or the diasporas of Southeast Asia and worldwide)."[13] Used in this sense, "being Chinese" is a relational concept rather than an identifier of an "ethnic essence" of some kind. It refers instead to an imagined collectivity that allows people at a diasporic temple to use the parlance of "we Chinese," whatever their national origin.[14] While there is this expansive sense of a global Buddhist China, the kind of Buddhism being propagated is Han, the dominant ethnic group within contemporary China. In China issues of modernization began at the end of the nineteenth and beginning of the twentieth century—for example, with the work of Taixu (1890–1947); see the chapter by Charles B. Jones in this volume. Buddhist modernism, however, includes developments throughout the Buddhist world. In Japan many of the movements that are known as "new religions" (*shin shūkyō*, those originating from around the beginning of the nineteenth century), as well as the "new new religions" (*shin shin shūkyō*, those originating after 1970), are either founded by lay Buddhists or have a strong lay leadership—the move away from monastic leadership being a marker of a secularizing trend. Similar modernizing movements, such as the Mahasi Thathana Yeiktha in Burma/Myanmar, originated in South and Southeast Asia as well.

The Contributions

The following brief summaries provide the reader with information about each contribution, and also highlight connections between them, giving a sense of how they work together collectively. The creation of secularized forms of Buddhism, particularly in the form of lay-oriented and lay-led, is a global phenomenon dating from the nineteenth century. Developments in Asia have, however, largely not operated in a cultural context structured by the oppositional binary of secular versus religious. Advocacy for a secularized version of Buddhism, in this strong sense of a version defined in opposition to its hypothesized religious opposite, has largely, though not entirely, been a project of white convert Buddhists. Similarly, resistance to this movement has taken place largely, though not entirely, in the white convert community. The contributors to this collection are themselves already contributors to that discourse, though they do not represent the full range of views and voices on these issues.

Sarah Shaw

Sarah Shaw introduces her essay with an overview of the development of Buddhist modernism as an interaction between internal pressures and international ones. The internal pressures were toward the modernization of Buddhism in Thailand, Burma, and Sri Lanka, which were similar to those we've noted above that were taking place simultaneously in China and Japan. The international pressures were created by colonialism—and, we should add, Christian missionizing. This complex interaction, both push and pull, created a form of Buddhism "tailored to fit modern global expectations." It is this version of Buddhism that was effectively ready-made for secularizing.

Shaw sees this development as consistent with Buddhism's long history of adapting the teachings to differing social, cultural, and linguistic situations. She argues that secularized forms of mindfulness practice have provided relief for problems ranging from depression and suicidal thoughts to anxiety and otherwise uncontrollable rage. These techniques "have, undoubtedly, proved beneficial." She further argues that most importantly such secularized practices give the individual agency for their own well-being, instead of fostering dependence on medical interventions. Personal empowerment can be seen as the positive dimension of Ron Purser and Kathleen Gregory's concerns regarding passivity and splitting, respectively.

However, Shaw goes on to point out a problematic equation by which science, rationality, truth, and secularism are identified with one another. And she points out that this compound has become a belief system to which is implicitly attributed the same authority as has been to religion. In this light, she makes an important analogy between colonialist interpretations of Buddhism in the nineteenth century and contemporary secularizing interpretations. Shaw maintains that secularism has an important practical contribution: "It suggests ways toward a common consensus that give effective and respectful grounds for interaction, as a kind of orthopraxy, between different groups." She goes on to ask, however, whether as a belief system there is not a danger that secularism is "becoming our new orthodoxy."

David L. McMahan

In his contribution to this collection David L. McMahan focuses on secularity as the shared view of the present day, the mood or sensibility. This is more contextual for the process of secularizing Buddhism than the more frequent and often contentious question of specific beliefs, such as the beliefs in rebirth and karma that Jackson examines in this volume.

McMahan discusses this shared context in terms of the kind of subjectivity that has arisen in European and American culture from the time of René Descartes's formulation of the self as an exclusively mental conscious awareness. Secular subjectivity is the sense of being an "individual," the atomic sense of self as an autonomous agent, only responsible to oneself. McMahan goes on to trace this way of conceiving of oneself into more recent theorists, including analyses that point to the constant reconstruction of the self, particularly through consumption, a dimension of the personal that connects with Ron Purser's discussion in this volume. From a variety of perspectives—including, we can note, the neurosciences—the idea of the fully autonomous individual sense is increasingly seen as a fiction.

McMahan's discussion of secular subjectivity brings our attention to the shared personal conditions of modernity and postmodernity, calling into question one of the common polarities found in popular treatments of Buddhism in the West—that is, the polarity between immigrant and convert, in which immigrant is identified with a kind of premodern traditionalism, while convert stands as a marker for modern or what we might call "post-traditional" Buddhism. Yet as McMahan indicates, while the effects of the transition from modern to postmodern are not globally uniform, they are still the conditions of present-day members of Buddhist institutions whether those originated among immigrant communities before the end of the nineteenth century, or came via immigrant teachers from Japan or Tibet in the 1960s and '70s, or were embraced by techno-Buddhists after the turn of the millennium.

McMahan outlines two alternative versions of mindfulness that respond to this sense of being a fragmented, and fictional self. One is as a means to reinforce the autonomous self, while the other moves to a more Buddhist conception of the self as an ongoing self-construction. (Self-help Buddhism is outside the scope of McMahan's discussion. But as a consumerized form of Buddhism, it reinforces a dualistic self-conception by splitting the self as autonomous agent from the self as a social fiction subject to change and improvement. It motivates adherents by asserting that their fictional, social selves are inadequate in one way or another. Simultaneously, however, the fictional self is represented as unstable in that people are encouraged to be autonomous agents able to recreate themselves in new and putatively more satisfying ways.)

Funie Hsu

With the urgency that accompanies societal violence against minorities, Funie Hsu shows that secularizing is not a value-neutral, context-free process. A secularized Buddhism erases race and religion, both markers for the despised Oriental Other, as irrelevant to the "True Dharma." Managing race and religion in this fashion allows command over the teachings, not only expropriating Buddhist meditative practices but also not-so-covertly shifting authority away from Asians and into the hands of white converts.[15] The rhetoric that portrays a secularized Buddhism as universal and scientific serves to make the social and cultural context of a secularized Buddhism invisible. Hsu's main focus is the introduction of secularized mindfulness into public schools. This same analysis, however, can be extended to any institutional location—hospitals, prisons, business, government, the military—where a denatured version of meditation is presented as simply a secular, universal, inclusive, and scientific mental practice that brings calm and eases distress.

Locating a secularized mindfulness meditation practice in its historical, social, and cultural context and noting the racialized character of the process that has created it, does not directly call its efficacy into question. A critique easily leveled against such analyses is to point to "the evidence" that mindfulness practice is beneficial. While often anecdotal, such evidence also invokes scientific research as proof that the idea of a cultural location is in fact irrelevant. That strategy, however, is itself part of the neoliberal worldview that focuses on the individual in isolation—erasing not only the Asian and Buddhist origins of the practice but also the Western and white context of its present iteration. Claiming that "efficacy" trumps culture and history is, in other words, another act of imperialistic violence.

Pamela Winfield

A fraught topic in the Western Buddhist world has been the decontextualization of meditation in the form of secular mindfulness. Is mindfulness significantly different from Buddhist meditation as suggested by Shaw (this volume)? Or are the differences matters simply of cultural style? By turning to the effects of displacing objects from Japanese Buddhist temples and relocating them into the secular context of an art museum, Pamela Winfield provides a unique perspective on the issues of decontextualization enabled by the secular versus religious divide.

She sees the space of museums as potentially fruitfully ambiguous. The objects curated can be understood as instances of aesthetic vision and technical skill, deepening and enriching our own aesthetic sensibilities. At the same time the legacy of museums as displaying the spoils of imperialism can also be the focus of attention. Both discourses intentionally recontextualize objects, though one in a discourse of "timeless" aesthetic values and the other in a discourse of historical power relations.

Winfield points out that "the European separation of the sacred from the secular was a necessary precondition of the historical development of Buddhist 'art' in the modern museum"—and that this binary was exported to a modernizing Japan in the nineteenth century, where temples began the process of creating their own museum spaces for the display of items outside of their former ritual contexts. The treatment of objects as symbols of the dharma meant that they lost their presence as powerful embodiments of the dharma.

Highlighting the multiple ways in which museums can display objects, Winfield suggests that multiple purposes can be served, contributing to both aesthetic and historical awareness. And since contemporary society museums themselves function as quasi-sacred public spaces, objects displayed may also be "reconsecrated"—presented as preserving a sacred reality that may also speak to people in the present.

Thinking about these issues in relation to my own experience, I was reminded of an exhibit at a museum in San Francisco as an instance of "reconsecrating" art. It was a goodwill attempt to give museumgoers a better understanding of the significance of the mandala. The display comprised five mandalas, the central one horizontally and then in the four cardinal directions an additional four mandala hanging vertically—the four being the directional bodhisattvas of the main deity in the horizontal central mandala. In that sense the mandalas were accurate but displayed in a "postmodern" way unlike any conceivable traditional usage in an actual temple setting—reconsecrated, but according to the sensibilities of the museum curators. In another instance a museum showing an exhibit of Buddhist art from Southeast Asia invited a local and internationally famous meditation teacher, who "explained" the art in terms of psychological categories, while the gift shop sold miniature vajras mass-produced in China as souvenirs.

Charles B. Jones

Charles B. Jones's essay on the early twentieth-century Chinese monk Taixu opens up our consideration of the relation between secularizing and modernizing by making both categories more complex. As discussed elsewhere in this introduction, a modernizing impulse to reinterpret Buddhism does not always mean the same thing in different historical or social contexts.

The image of Buddhism as having human happiness as its central concern is widespread. The plausibility of that image depends on the idea that having happiness as the goal of one's life is natural, and indeed this idea is itself a long-standing part of Western values—perhaps being traceable to the "hedonic calculus" of Jeremy Bentham (1747–1832). Lacking Bentham's utilitarian rationale, however, in the mid-1980s undergraduates in my Introduction to Philosophy classes overwhelmingly replied "happiness" when asked what their goal in life was. Contrast this with Taixu's vision of the human condition. Taixu divides human needs into two categories, those of this life and those of the next. In this life people need security and material resources, while in the next, bliss and immortality. The rationale employed in much of the secularizing rhetoric is itself, therefore, not a matter of "human nature" but rather one of cultural context.

Like many contributors to the project of secularizing Buddhism, Taixu appropriated modern science—for example, identifying Uttarakuru as a planet in our solar system. Uttarakuru is a mythic realm of great material abundance. In the Abhidhamma literature, for example, the Buddha is said to have gone there for alms during his time teaching the Abhidhamma to the gods so that he did not need to return to our human realm. Taixu's equation of Uttarakuru with a planet in our solar system no doubt seems quaint by the standards of the present day. This problem, however, has always plagued the science and religion discourse. Claims of truth or authority based on explaining religious teachings, whether Buddhist or Christian, by reference to scientific theories have inevitably lost credibility when once-current scientific theories become outdated by more recent scientific developments. The emphasis on the scientific in present-day secularizing rhetoric is simply the most recent instance of a strategy stretching back over a century and a half and is equally subject to becoming outmoded by future scientific developments.

Kate Crosby

Examining the modern history of Buddhism, Kate Crosby provides a more complex image both of the meaning of secularizing and traditionalizing and of the modernist image of Theravāda Buddhism. The background for these modern developments is European colonialism. Crosby marks the beginning of modern Asian history with the mid–nineteenth-century Opium Wars between the Qing dynasty and Britain. This conflict disrupted China's influence in Southeast Asia, and further colonial wars in Burma and Sri Lanka further destabilized the region. The exercise of colonial power included the movement of Muslim laborers into formerly Buddhist societies, setting the foundations of contemporary Buddhist Islamophobia.

Such changes led Buddhists to fear for the future of Buddhist traditions of thought and practice (Pāli *sāsana*), and both to conservative, traditionalizing movements, and to modernist, secularizing ones in Southeast Asia. Crosby demonstrates that both traditionalizing and secularizing movements draw on the same rhetorical strategies of corruption and purification. "The difference between the responses lies in what is identified as corruption and where its source is detected." If the source is identified as Western culture (that is to say, colonialism), then the *sāsana* is to be purified of modernizing corruptions. However, if in keeping with the Protestant historiographic rhetoric of decadence the source of corruption is an increasing decay of the original purity of the founder's teachings, then developments between that originary moment and the present are to be cast aside.

Looking at the traditional meditation practices (*boran*), which have been displaced by insight and mindfulness, Crosby points out the historical connection between meditation and sciences, such as embryology and chemistry. This connection was integral, since *boran* meditation is a holistic practice unencumbered by the Cartesian mind-body dualism that pervades contemporary Western discussion of meditation. Crosby also introduces us to modern heresy trials, enforced by the government of Myanmar. A court system was created to adjudicate accusations against citizens of teaching contrary to the *dhamma* (*adhamma*) or of engaging in practices contrary to the rules of the order (*avinaya*).

These aspects may sit uncomfortably with the modernist image of Buddhism as a "tolerant, relativist, and scientific religion, or even nonreligion." Consequently, Crosby notes, "Those who share an interest in the genuine teaching of the Buddha may be looking at mutually unrecognizable visions of the dharma."

Bhikkhu Bodhi

Bhikkhu Bodhi introduces his essay with a brief overview of the conditions that converted Buddhism from an exotic interest of a small minority of individuals beginning in the late nineteenth century into a major religious tradition in the West from the 1960s on. Foremost among these conditions are the displacement of traditional Christianity by existentialism and psychotherapy, contributing to the view that relief from the distress of modern life was to be sought via the mind. Particularly conducive to this change was the appeal of Buddhism as a nontheistic tradition, as well as the resonance between Westerners grounded in the presumptions of modernity and Asian modernizers of Buddhism.

Bodhi presents what he identifies as "Traditional" and "Secular" forms of Buddhism as end points on a range, rather than as two mutually exclusive forms of Buddhism. The former accepts the conception of human life defined by rebirth and suffering, the cessation of which is nirvana. The latter focuses on an understanding of human existence as natural and not necessitating belief in rebirth or its cessation. Instead liberation is interpreted as liberation from greed, hatred, and delusion. The most predominant form of Buddhism in the present-day West is, however, neither of these two, but the orientation that Bodhi calls "Immanent Buddhism."

Rather than either accepting or actively rejecting the cosmology of rebirth, immanent Buddhism remains agnostic on this and other issues. Indeed, the debate over whether rebirth is essential to defining a Buddhist, as discussed by Roger R. Jackson (this volume), is seen as irrelevant to the immediacies of living in the present world. Bodhi sees immanent Buddhism as manifest in much of the Western Vipassana, or insight meditation, movement, mentioning Gil Fronsdal (see essay in this volume) specifically as representative of what Bodhi is calling immanent Buddhism. Bodhi goes on to evaluate these three forms of Buddhism in light of the question as to whether they are equally viable vehicles for maintaining and promoting the teachings of the Buddha in the twenty-first century.

Arguing for a cautious approach to revising the teachings to match our modern preconceptions, Bodhi does not disparage the practical utility of Buddhist teachings and practices for existential benefit. However, he argues that training programs taking such an approach are best understood as deriving from Buddhism rather than being a new evolutionary stage in the development of Buddhism.

Philippe Turenne

Philippe Turenne's essay is a close examination of the way that Stephen Batchelor has gone about creating his own version of secular Buddhism. Arguing that "ignoring dissonant voices leads to isolation," Turenne suggests that Batchelor's critiques of traditional Buddhism need to be taken seriously, rather than simply being dismissed out of hand. Turenne also argues, however, that taking the issues that Batchelor raises seriously does not mean accepting Batchelor's solutions.

A fundamental issue with Batchelor's work, according to Turenne, is that he is slaying straw men. In Turenne's estimation, Batchelor "targets an artificial, often unfair representation of how certain doctrines and practices are held." At the same time, while Batchelor critiques traditional Buddhism as being committed to an exclusive orthodoxy, Turenne considers Batchelor to be creating his own exclusivist understanding of what constitutes proper belief. Turenne highlights how Batchelor's own intellectual commitment to discard anything that is "metaphysical" in favor of a purely pragmatic reinterpretation of the buddhadharma means that a majority of Buddhist practices and teachings are discarded. They are replaced with a version of mindfulness practice, not as it is described in Buddhist literature but rather in its modernist rendering as "bare awareness."

Perhaps most critically, Bachelor's own ideological commitments determine his representation of Buddhist history. The image of the Buddha's "original teachings" that Batchelor describes is determined not by historical research but by Batchelor's own presumptions and beliefs. Batchelor is not simply presenting a new interpretation of the buddhadharma but is instead representing his own interpretation as the authoritative original word of the Buddha. Turenne, in other words, identifies the fundamental contradiction of Batchelor's project. On the one hand, Batchelor claims to be presenting an interpretation of Buddhist praxis that is accessible and useful in our present world—that is, an interpretation molded in response to contemporary concepts, categories, and concerns. On the other hand, Batchelor wants to be able to claim that this is not an interpretation, and certainly not his own idiosyncratic interpretation, but rather that it is the true, original, authentic, and pure teachings of Śākyamuni Buddha. Batchelor does not attempt to resolve this contradiction, but rather shifts between the two views as needed to advance his claims rhetorically.

Ron Purser

Ron Purser calls attention to the neoliberal socioeconomic context within which the secularizing of Buddhism is taking place. He points out that neoliberalism is not simply a matter of how economic transactions are handled but includes a set of values regarding the character of human existence that mold our social interactions and judgments as well. Neoliberal ideology is largely invisible because it has become the taken-for-granted underlayment of present-day Western society.

Individualism has been claimed to be both the strength of Western culture and its weakness. According to Purser the secularizing of Buddhism integrates individualism as the sole locus of agency—which, in corporate settings that promote forms of secularizing Buddhism, becomes the idea that if someone is unhappy, they need to fix their attitude, not the conditions of employment. The individual is understood to be the autonomous agent of their own well-being and, further, to be fully able to affect that well-being. In such a context, it is the individual who is responsible for their own happiness, and its absence is their own failing.

The dichotomy between secular and religious also entails the distinction between public and private. As an individual, private activity, mindfulness is an ambiguous activity, secularized in its ideology and social location, but quasi-religious in its private application. Purser points out how that private application further inculcates neoliberal values into the individual, creating a condition of "governmentality," the process whereby the individual integrates as their own the values of the larger society—that is, those of neoliberal ideology. A person no longer needs to be governed, but governs themselves to remain within the socially accepted values and actions.

As also noted by Kathleen Gregory (this volume), there is an irony about the way that secularized mindfulness encourages practices of self-mastery that require the dualistic division of the self into subject and master. Not uncommonly, this personal mastery is extended into a kind of idealism, evident as Purser points out in the slogan "to change the world, change ourselves." The larger consequences of this kind of passivity are what Purser, following Lauren Berlant, calls "cruel optimism," continually committing one's time and affective energy to "working on oneself," or "self-care," in the pursuit of goals, such as personal perfectionism, that can never be accomplished.

Kathleen Gregory

Kathleen Gregory begins by noting the emphasis on the individual, psychological self that characterizes secularized mindfulness. In doing so she asserts an important theoretical claim that informs the balance of the essay—"religious" and "psychological" function not in opposition to one another but rather in a dynamic relation to one another. This is a cautionary tale about how psychologizing and neurologizing the self, at the basis of much of secularized mindfulness, can be counterproductive, because those interpretations of the self foster a dualistic self-conception in the practitioner.

In her exploration of the way in which meditation is deployed in the formation of the self, Gregory explores three of the paradoxes of the modern mindfulness movement. First, while teaching that one should hold a nonjudgmental attitude, judgments about the adequacy of one's practice and progress reinforce a negative attitude toward oneself. Second, constantly paying attention can contribute to heightened vigilance and anxiety. Third, focusing on the present moment is promoted as the means of achieving some future goal. Cumulatively these reinforce the divided self, which in the therapeutic culture becomes the manipulative self who is working to better the inadequate self. This is the "instrumental attitude" in which meditative practices are employed by the self as instruments to improve the self.

While the therapeutic culture, which envisions the self as inadequate or dysfunctional, is the ground, these contradictions are more specifically created when the instructions for practice are confused with guidelines for living. Gregory shows that in our secularized present we experience ourselves as psychologized beings. This self-understanding, however, need not limit our understanding of our own potentials.

Roger R. Jackson

In 1997 *Tricycle* magazine sponsored a debate between Robert Thurman and Stephen Batchelor regarding the teaching of rebirth and its function in the belief system of present-day Buddhists. Simply, the question was this: Does one have to believe in rebirth to be a "real" Buddhist? Deploying ethical, epistemological, and practical arguments, Thurman argues for the doctrine's literal truth and its centrality to contemporary Buddhists, while Batchelor maintains that not only is it not essential for us, but it may not have been for the Buddha, either, and is best understood not literally but figuratively.

Prompted by Batchelor's claim, Jackson goes on to examine the place of the rebirth doctrine in premodern Buddhist traditions, beginning with the Buddha represented in the Pāli canon and the Indic-language *āgamas* found in Chinese translation. He considers various claims to the effect that the "earliest" Buddhist texts do not emphasize rebirth, but he finds these claims problematic and argues that the overwhelming evidence of the early canonical texts points to the centrality of the concept. He goes on to consider the classical arguments for rebirth by the seventh-century Indian philosopher Dharmakīrti and to describe briefly some of the ways in which rebirth figures prominently in other premodern Asian Buddhist cultures. It is clear, says Jackson, that most premodern Asian Buddhists took rebirth literally and seriously.

Turning to modern Buddhism, Jackson offers a brief history of nineteenth-century approaches to rebirth by a variety of European and American intellectuals, including German philosophers, American Transcendentalists, and various Theosophists. He then focuses on the period after World War II, when Buddhism began to make serious inroads in the West, examining the influence of "Beat" Buddhism and various strains of Zen, Theravāda, and Tibetan Buddhism, which reveal a range of attitudes to rebirth, from literal acceptance to overlooking it almost entirely. He pays particular attention to philosophical debates and discussions, including recent critiques of Dharmakīrti's arguments, attempts to reconcile traditional Buddhist claims with the findings of modern science, and discussions of the reliability of "empirical" evidence for rebirth through past-life memories or other paranormal experiences.

Jackson concludes by exploring a number of possible ways forward for modern Buddhists grappling with rebirth, from fundamentalist literalism, to neotraditionalist reinterpretation, to modernist demythologization, to secularist eschewal of the idea altogether, arguing for an "as-if agnosticism" that remains noncommittal on the literal truth of the rebirth doctrine but embraces the cosmology of which it is a part for its psychological, existential, and aesthetic value.

Gil Fronsdal

At the opening of his contribution to this collection, Gil Fronsdal introduces a topic having widespread relevance to our discussion of secularizing Buddhism—that is, an individual's self-identification. Fronsdal discusses his own difficulties with identity in terms of the modern history running from Theravāda, Vipassana, and Mahasi Sayadaw lineage to insight meditation, as well as his personal history, which includes years of training in Zen. This background informs his aversion to the label "secular Buddhist," despite the affinity he feels with aspects of that identity. Fronsdal's ambivalence about adopting the label for himself no doubt reflects the concerns of many contemporary Buddhist adherents who feel that their connection with Buddhism has a religious quality to it.

Rather than "secular," Fronsdal describes his own conception of the dhamma as "naturalistic"—that is, a dhamma that does not require belief in any supernatural forces or beings. This is, however, just the kind of scientific naturalism that Bhikkhu Bodhi argues against in his own contribution to this collection, labeling Fronsdal's style of Buddhism "immanent Buddhism."

Instead of rejecting all labels, Fronsdal does feel that labels have a value, particularly as a means of making one's location clear. He explains that "by identifying myself as a naturalistic Buddhist within the Theravāda Buddhist tradition, I am letting people know that, while my teachings are based on and accountable to the ancient scriptures of Theravāda Buddhism, I have a naturalistic perspective, orientation, or interpretation of these scriptures." At the same time, he avoids claiming that he is representing "the actual teachings of the Buddha as presented in these texts—a task that no discerning person can confidently do given the complicated historical origin of the surviving records." Perhaps most controversially, Fronsdal lets go of the idea that nirvana is "a transcendent, unconditioned dimension of reality."

Fronsdal sees the precursors of his own conception of a naturalistic Buddhism in the "humanistic Buddhism" of Taixu, discussed by Charles B. Jones in this volume, and also in the modern interpretations of Theravāda by the Thai monk Buddhadasa. As a scriptural source, Fronsdal points to *The Book of Eights* (Aṭṭhakavagga) as evidencing a naturalistic understanding of the dhamma.[16] He finds that this text avoids a sharp distinction between the means and the goal. (As an aside, we note that this is an idea that is explicitly developed in tantric forms of Buddhism.)

Richard K. Payne

In the concluding essay to this collection Richard K. Payne specifically focuses on a theme mentioned in passing by several of the contributors—the dynamic of polarization between the concepts of religious and secular. Treating these concepts as mutually exclusive opposites means that the significance of each is defined by the other, or what is known as a semiotic pair. Semiotic pairing means that the two are necessarily bound to one another.

In other words, the creation of a secular Buddhism is not an independent development moving beyond preexisting kinds of Buddhism, but rather it simultaneously creates its opposite, a religious Buddhism. The conceptual associations—that is, the semiotics— extend to include not simply secular and religious but also modern and traditional, and Western and Eastern. These oppositions are further projected onto the categories of immigrant and convert. As David L. McMahan explains in his essay in this volume, "The binary of religious and secular does not refer to some objective state of things in the world but is a historically particular way of dividing things up, of constituting human subjects, and of framing institutions like public schools, governmental organizations, and the courts."

As pointed out by Natalie Quli,[17] this interconnected complex of ideas is grounded in European and American imperialism, and the biasing stereotypes employed in the justifications of imperialism. In these stereotypes, East is a marker of all that is "naturally" feminine, weak, and submissive, and in need of a dominating organizing authority. That allowed West to stand for, and its inhabitants to see their culture as, masculine, strong, and powerful, and as providing the dominating organizing authority needed and indeed desired by the subject peoples. (Although today identified with the work of Edward Said, an important source for understanding these dynamics is the work of the earlier theorist Franz Fanon.)

Payne traces several of the strands of rhetoric supporting the secularizing discourse, including ones which go back to the Reformation, and more proximately to liberal Protestant thought from the end of the nineteenth century. Many of the beliefs and values held by proponents of a secularized Buddhism are simply part of popular religious culture, despite Buddhist flourishes and claims of privileged access to the true, original, and pure dharma of Śākyamuni Buddha. Because those beliefs and values are so widely shared in popular religious culture, they seem to simply be the way things are—that is, the beliefs and values are treated as natural and unproblematic—while anything else is unnatural and requiring explanation, or explaining away.

The Intent of This Collection

The intent of this collection is "critical" in the sense of attempting to look closely at the ways in which particular sets of ideas are used, including their background in Western religious and philosophical culture. It is not criticism in the sense of making an overall negative value judgment. Some readers may mistake a critical approach as being an implicit accusation of inauthenticity. Claims of authenticity or accusations of inauthenticity are simply strategic moves for the acquisition of power. This collection is not, therefore, a project about authenticity—it is not the goal here to either promote or to discredit the movement toward a secularized Buddhism. Rather, the intention is to contribute toward a deeper understanding of its characteristics and sources by highlighting a range of topics and views, contributing to a maturing discourse on the dynamic process of secularizing trends in Buddhism.

1 | Has Secularism Become a Religion?

Some Observations on Pāli Buddhism's Movement to the International Stage

SARAH SHAW

Tensions arising from people of diverse backgrounds and religions living together are ancient. King Aśoka, who was from Pāṭālipu-tra in Magadha (present-day Patna), was the Indian emperor of the Mauryan dynasty (268 BCE–232 BCE) and one of the earliest political leaders to envision peaceful coexistence among different religious groups. His empire stretched on a west-east axis from present-day Afghanistan to the Bay of Bengal and on a north-south axis from southern Nepal to Karnataka. He had been, according to legends, a cruel and tyrannical ruler, intent only on increasing the extent of his territories. But after a particularly vicious attack on the Kaliṅga people, in which one hundred thousand people were massacred, the remorseful Aśoka apparently became a Buddhist. In a series of rock edicts, he proclaimed a new way of living, a modus operandi for the disparate groups that lived together within his domain. Describing himself in the third person as Devanampriya Priyadarsin ("beloved by the gods, the humane one"), he outlined codes of peaceable coexistence, to which he hoped those in his domains would subscribe:

King Devanampriya Priyadarsin honours men of all religious communities with gifts and with honours of various kinds, irrespective of whether they are ascetics or householders.

But the Beloved of the Gods does not value either the offering of gifts or the honouring of people so highly as the following, viz. that there should be the growth of the essentials of all Dharmas among men of all sects. And the growth of the essentials of Dharma is possible in many ways. But its root lies in restraint in regard to speech, which means that there should be no extolling of one's own sect or disparagement of other sects on inappropriate occasions and that it should be moderate in every case even on appropriate occasions. On the contrary, other sects should be duly honoured in every way on all occasions.

If a person acts in this way, he not only promotes his own sect but also benefits other sects. But if a person acts otherwise, he not only injures his own sect but also harms other sects.

Truly, if a person extols his own sect and disparages other sects with a view of glorifying his sect owing merely to his attachment to it, he injures his own sect very severely by acting in that way.

Therefore restraint in regard to speech is commendable, because people should learn and respect the fundamentals of one another's Dharma.

This indeed is the desire of the Beloved of the Gods that persons of all sects become well-informed about the doctrines of different religions and acquire pure knowledge.

And those who are attached to their respective sects should be informed as follows. 'The Beloved of the Gods does not value either the offering of gifts or the honouring of people so highly as the following, viz. that there should be a growth of the essentials of all Dharma among men of all sects.'... And the result of their activities, as expected by me, is that the promotion of each one's sect, and the glorification of Dharma.[1]

A dharma here is a teaching and also a code of conduct, a system of aligning oneself in one's life that is in accordance with dharma as law, or principle. Derived from the Sanskrit word "to bear," it is a way of life as much as a belief system or a doctrinal affiliation. For Buddhists, their dharma is to live according to the five precepts and the eightfold path. Aśoka's vision of peaceful cohabitation certainly offers an early ideal of how various religious groups can live in harmony together. Perhaps one of the most humane and enlightened figures associated with the need for tolerance in the midst of plurality, he could be said to be the first secularist, in one of our more modern uses of the term: the promotion of mutual respect among religious groups in a polity based on values shared, irrespective of creed.

We do not have the historical information to know how this played out in practice and whether his policies proved workable. Potential issues may have arisen, for instance, from his assumption that within all dharmas there is a shared ethical framework that permits interaction with those who follow other dharmas of different kinds. But despite such questions, Aśoka's edicts, which are all that we really know of his life and works, demonstrate an openness to the ways of life and belief systems of others that is admirable.[2] His idea that tolerance and a willingness to engage actively with other religious groups benefits all concerned demonstrates how early Buddhists made their own attempts at what we now call secularism, in terms of tolerance toward the practice of differing religious beliefs. The statement that in criticizing other traditions, or dharma, one is demeaning one's own is a nuanced and astute reading of potential problems that can arise amid diversity and plurality. It is a statement worth reflecting upon in one's own daily contacts and discussions, whatever one's religion or code of conduct.

Aśoka's edicts show how one early Buddhist considered the problem of various belief systems and religious traditions living and working together. We will come back to indigenous Buddhist systems later. But how does this play out in our modern debate about secularism and, specifically, what is sometimes termed the "secularization" of Buddhism? Before considering this, it is worth reflecting on the term itself.

Secularism

Vocabulary is important, for words can arouse quite different associations for different readers. This is particularly the case with the terms "secular," "secularization," and "secularism," which carry different meanings in different contexts. The word *saeculum* is the Latin for a period of one person's lifetime, or a generation, of a hundred years—and hence of the times. In the Christian church it is associated with the coming and going of ages, and hence, usually, worldly matters. The social reformer and radical thinker George Jacob Holyoake (1817-1906) coined the term "secularism" in 1851, to describe a means of social interaction and discourse that was independent of religion but did not challenge its domain. Developing late eighteenth-century views of rationalist interchange, he did not reject religious belief but suggested (in his *English Secularism*) rather a questioning of issues "which can be tested by this life"—words not unlike the recommendations of the Buddha.[3] While secularism still retains specific meanings in Christianity, it has come to mean different things in different contexts. Most of us, however, probably understand it as an operation on a neutral ground, whereby there is a separation between affairs of spirituality and belief from codes of behavior and interaction in the world. We should bear in mind, however, that secularism is defined with interesting variations even in modern dictionaries: "the doctrine that morality should be based solely on regard to the well-being of mankind in the present life, to the exclusion of all considerations drawn from belief in God or a future state" and "the view that national education should be purely secular,"[4] becomes elsewhere "the belief that religion should not be involved with the ordinary social and political activities of a country,"[5] to the "belief that religion should have no place in education,"[6] and then what is potentially an active opposing force to the espousal of a particular religion: "indifference to, or rejection or exclusion of, religion and religious considerations."[7] The problem is compounded in political contexts. Secular states and governments vary greatly in their application of the term, from France, to Turkey, to India. All share a broad premise that religious beliefs and affiliations should have nothing to do with the workings of the state, but how that is understood differs in complex ways. In a general sense, however, in matters of social interchange and governance, secularization is a process whereby such traditions self-consciously work within a remit of the separation of state and religious tradition. Those movements that are considered secular identify themselves as operating within principles that do not pertain to any specific religion but can be applied more universally.

As can be seen, we are already in an area fraught with questions. To what extent does separation involve rejection? Does secularization potentially undermine spiritual practice and what we term "religion"? Before we consider this, let us look at some background, and the curiously close relationship that Buddhism has had with secularism over the last hundred and fifty years.

Buddhism in Asia from the Nineteenth Century

Buddhism was first introduced on the global stage, as opposed to its homelands of Asia, in the mid- to late nineteenth century.[8] It was around this time that the term "secularism," and what it indicated, also became popular. From the end of the nineteenth century, within what were mostly Buddhist countries, the need for some steps toward what was considered a rationalist scientific approach, suitable for modernity and international exchange, was deemed necessary for acceptability and survival. Colonialism and increased travel, commerce, and diplomacy with Europe and the United States had a significant impact on this reevaluation throughout Asia, in various ways, according to specific context. Different Buddhisms, which may not have seen themselves as being particularly related to one another, varied in the way they introduced themselves to the West.

The Chan traditions, known as Seon in Korea and Zen in Japan, were in great measure adapted for Western consumption through the greatly creative endeavors of the Kyoto School and thinkers like

Nishida Kitarō (1870-1945). Though these largely Japanese exponents were not primarily intent on such a goal, their deployment of, for instance, Kantian theory and the application of the terms and arguments of Western philosophical discourse introduced their traditions to a larger international audience—as, of course, did the later writings of D. T. Suzuki (1870-1966).[9] Tibetan Buddhism took a slightly different approach. Before the diaspora and the seismic events of the Chinese Cultural Revolution of the 1950s and '60s, Tibetan Buddhism was largely communicated through an appeal to its mysterious, colorful, and decidedly nonsecular origins with the work of proponents such as Alexandra David Neel (1868-1969).[10] Now that has changed, as great efforts have been made to address a genuinely global audience through engaging in dialogue with Western science, principally under the auspices of the Fourteenth Dalai Lama.

Pāli Buddhism, the cluster of traditions that privilege the "three baskets" of the Pāli canon, has had a slightly different history, and throughout the twentieth century often self-consciously exercised an appeal to the intellectual and the scientific.[11] The Buddha was promoted as a rational teacher; devotional Buddhist customs and traditions came to be regarded as accretions. As Peter Skilling notes, "There are many Buddhas, and, among them, the 'rational Buddha' is powerful in the present age."[12] Since the nineteenth century a number of Western colonialists had formed strong links with the traditions in Southeast and South Asia.[13] Late nineteenth-century reforms in Thailand, Burma, and Sri Lanka attempted to present Pāli Buddhism in a way that would render it more palatable to Westerners. Pressures also came from within. So the reforms of King Rama IV (Mongkut), who wished to restructure and revitalize the sangha, with or without Western comment, made radical changes with the Dhammayut monastic traditions. Other changes implemented by the king tended to be on what he regarded as modernist lines.[14] Certain apparently rationalist elements of Pāli Buddhism came to be those most widely promoted, both within and outside Southeast Asia. The nineteenth-century Vipassana movement, emanating from Burma (Myanmar), was a key factor in the transmission of Pāli Buddhism, thus ensuring that forms of practice were disseminated that made less overt recourse to the emotional or to ritual, appealing instead more directly to the cognitive and, sometimes, intellectual aspects of Buddhist theory and practice. Some elements of this transmission were undoubtedly triggered by international pressure. Others were internally derived and included, for instance, a desire to override perceived imbalances within the meditative teachings.[15]

While this overall trend may be primarily attributed to colonialist influences, other factors, sometimes associated with a perceived need for internationalism but also pertaining to local particularities, contributed.[16] As Kate Crosby has demonstrated, by the latter half of the twentieth century dramatic changes within the meditative teachings common to Southeast Asia had ensured that promotion of the new Vipassana schools had become predominant.[17] Abroad, the Ambedkar movement saw the conversion of many Indian untouchable groups to this largely reform school. Indeed, some of the aims of early Vipassana movements—the greater participation of the laity in meditative practice, a more "rationalist" approach to meditation, and the emphasis on what are regarded as scientific and intellectually interesting elements of Buddhist practice—were indeed achieved. By the late twentieth century, bookshops at all South and Southeast Asian airports were selling manuals for the laity on meditation, largely in insight-based traditions. So from without and from within, South and Southeast Asian Buddhism made deliberate adaptations toward secularism throughout the twentieth century. European models of education, social and political structuring, and an emphasis on "scientific" understandings of Buddhist principles meant that indigenous mores and ancient doctrines were somewhat tailored to fit modern global expectations.

Toward the Secular

At some point, in that tidal shift and meeting together of currents that occurs sometimes in popular discourse, whereby new ideas meet other ones and merge as if within one wave, this process of rationalization became associated with what we term "secularism," and the perceived need for secularization. Buddhism, for its apparent rationality, has suited well the wish for a separation between affairs to do with religion and those to do with state and social interchange. With a creativity and inventiveness that are often the hallmark of Buddhism's evolution—for adaptability has from the earliest days been a key feature of Buddhist development—there have been all kinds of strands of various new forms of Buddhism, framed in what are described as secular terms.[18] In addition, ideas have been transmitted in what we understand as secular disciplines, such as psychology, absorbing Buddhist techniques and, perhaps only occasionally, some Buddhist theory too.

The Buddhist groups that have in some way worked with this have shown a careful and compassionate adaptation to the expectations of modern society. The movement toward what is termed "secularization" reflects a flexibility of method and doctrine that emerges at various points in Buddhist history. The teaching is said to be *akāliko*: suitable at any time. To take a contemporary example, the Massachusetts-based Secular Buddhist Association has a practical and encompassing website (https://secularbuddhism.org) that attempts to reformulate Buddhist terminology and practice in terms easily accessible for Western practitioners, a project inspired in large part by the writings of Stephen Batchelor.[19] Jack Kornfield and others in the Western Vipassana movement, through their strong experiential and practical teachings, have attracted many people to Buddhist practice who might not otherwise have engaged.[20] This sense of freshness and sensitivity to the zeitgeist of the times has often been evident in the way Buddhism adapted in different contexts and new terrains, and those practicing in Buddhist traditions have historically chosen to find new terminology, express the teaching in different ways, and find new outlets in which awakening and the path to awakening can be expressed.[21] The process of meshing with traditions in different areas, and adaptation to the demands of new generations, is an ancient pattern of Buddhist evolution.

Indeed Robert Sharf has argued that the extraordinary success of the Chan movements in medieval China was based on an appeal to the laity, the "quick" nature of returns on meditative practice, and a non-text-based, popular form of mindfulness practice. These factors are strongly comparable to those of the modern, and now global, insight and mindfulness traditions.[22]

The Mindfulness Movement

In academic, nonaffiliated disciplines we can see the most obvious manifestation of adaptation of Buddhist technique and principle in the mindfulness movement. The various schools and systems associated with this trend are too often unfairly criticized either for being too Buddhist or not Buddhist enough; too Western or not Western enough; or too scientific or not scientific enough. Success breeds criticism; but the critiques that are a necessary response in the wake of a mass movement do not undermine the validity of the methods employed. Here, the mindfulness movements have also acted with considered deliberation. Secularist principles have been a necessary part of the absorption of mindfulness in mindfulness-based cognitive therapy (MBCT) and mindfulness-based stress reduction (MBSR) programs in the West. Put simply, "For mindfulness to be approved it needed to look as scientifically based as possible."[23] Constant reference to the Buddhist foundations of mindfulness would exclude those who are, as many are now, wishing to be helped by therapies but uneasy about using a "religious" solution to problems that are experienced in daily life.[24]

Such psychological therapeutic systems and methods of mindfulness have, undoubtedly, proved beneficial—for example, when these methods have been applied with those suffering from severe depression. They have combated suicidal tendencies and the kind of despair that leads to self-destructive behaviors.[25] In a more general sense, people who thought they faced a lifetime of depression and anxiety find that such methods help them to cope and, in some cases, enjoy life again. Specific clinical applications, from

adaptations based on sound clinical study, have also helped sometimes isolated groups suffering from various disabilities. Children
with Asperger's syndrome have been taught means of managing
outbursts of anger through simple and easy-to-learn body mindfulness techniques, such as remembering the soles of their feet
when they start to feel anger; thus they have started to learn, for
themselves, how better to control their emotions.[26] Various forms
of cognitive mindfulness training have, as with other transmissions,
been adapted from early techniques, and have made significant
impact on, for instance, some physiological conditions such as cardiovascular disease.[27]

Some radical differences in intention and delivery between the
mindfulness movements and the Buddhist traditions need to be
clarified, as both sides would probably agree. But the mindfulness
movement is sometimes criticized by Buddhists themselves for
changing the use of the word "mindfulness," a term previously used
in the mid-part of the twentieth century for Buddhist discourse. In
using the term "mindfulness" secular clinical disciplines did change
the Pāli *sati*—a little. Here, we need to remember that such shifts
in usage were there in Buddhism too, sometimes, where a particular method required them. So the famous term "nonjudgmental
direct observation,"[28] and some associated terms derived from the
Vipassana traditions, such as "bare attention," did possibly slightly
shift the emphasis of *sati/smṛti* away from some of its applications
in meditation, the Abhidhamma, and indeed in ethical discourse.[29]
In traditional Buddhist practice, mindfulness would be considered
to include, for instance, ethical awareness, a sense of mindfulness
of others as well as oneself, and has a strong association, in Pāli
Buddhism, with the divine abidings—how one applies mindfulness
in a compassionate or equanimous way, to oneself and others.[30]

Instructions for bare attention and nonjudgmental observation
are, however, useful for a particular kind of meditational observation, at a particular time. Given the often very different parameters of modern clinical contexts, the translation of these Buddhist
elements into secular psychology has proved effective. And recent

trends within therapeutic traditions, in part from pressure from Buddhist thinkers and psychologists and in part from clinical observation and investigation, are accommodating other features associated with traditional mindfulness too. Given the success of the associated psychological movements, and indeed those within the Buddhist tradition that have espoused comparable terminology and situate themselves as secular Buddhist ways of practice, shifts in terminology look like a natural development. Technical terms often change meanings in different contexts; and we have just seen ways that a small change of wording, in different dictionaries, affects how one understands terms we all somehow feel we vaguely understand, like "secularism" and "secularization." How much more is this the case for a key Buddhist term, which has, even before the twentieth century, sometimes been interpreted with different emphases and stresses at different times, and in different settings and genres, within Buddhism itself?

Perhaps just as significant is the fact that such inspirational adaptation of basic principles of mindfulness practice, both within the psychological professions and among Buddhist groups that use the term "secular" in their descriptions, do something else as well, which is unquantifiable but equally groundbreaking. They place the means to effect change in oneself back to where it should belong, from a Buddhist standpoint: with the volition and aspirations of the practitioner, who can learn, with teaching, training, guided assistance, and group work, ways that discard or minimize medical interventions and medication and provide hope where there was not a realistic reason for optimism before. (For critiques of this emphasis on individual agency, see Gregory and Purser in this volume.) While methods are still in early stages of adaptation and evidence is not yet conclusive regarding all conditions, with the mindfulness movement too there has been a welcome shift toward the acceptance of what is, in essence, a modification of nineteenth-century Vipassana techniques. MBCT and other methods have been sensitively and compassionately adapted to suit a society where the overall acceptance of new treatments requires scientific verification in clinical study, accompanied by the use of language that meshes with the discourse of contemporary psychological and therapeutic interchange.[31]

Rethinking Secularism

But would it be right for us to fail to examine something else, something that we may be taking as an assumption? For is there not a curious process, which has occurred almost imperceptibly over the last hundred years, whereby, to put it in simple terms, secularism = rationality = science = truth? Has secularism, once intended as a practical means of separating the affairs of state from private belief and practice, now become itself a kind of religion? At some point, the incoming currents of secularism and secularization met those of science and rationalism and some ideals inherited from the eighteenth century. The wave produced by this confluence, which has swept through twenty-first-century discourse, can be seen as a force for great good. It has produced immensely helpful insights and new ways of working. And, just as waves pull back a little when the tide comes in, it seems inevitable that criticisms and demands for modification in, for instance, our understanding of terms such as "mindfulness" should emerge. Here, of course, one needs to be conscious too of the force of sometimes violent countertrends, such as, for instance, religious extremism and fanaticism. Careful and respectful work will not always find acceptance or integration. Acceptance of the mindfulness movement and its tenets does, however, seem to be an incoming tide, and ideally one that will exercise more, not less, appeal in the future.

But is it always right that secularism has somehow become conflated with something we, perhaps just as nebulously, call these days "science"? For secularism seems to have subtly moved on from its first formulation in 1851, perhaps to something closer to the *Merriam-Webster* definition quoted earlier: "indifference to, or rejection or exclusion of, religion and religious considerations." Or, in Aśokan terms, as something which potentially opposes other dharmas. So in becoming a prime touchstone of the West's belief systems, is secularism starting to assume for us, perhaps unconsciously, the authority of a kind of belief system itself, a way of understanding the world that is an implicit religion in terms of possessing doctrines, codes of conduct, institutions, and indeed its own occasional fanatic? No one can turn back the tide, and it is not the intention of this essay to suggest we should. But Buddhism gives us notable precedents: rather than assuming that we need to "-ize" Buddhism in some way, we can find much to draw on in the tradition itself. Somewhat free of the cultural assumptions of an Anglophone world and originating in India well before the colonial age, early Buddhist doctrine, social policy, and psychology often dealt with many of the same problems that we confront now. It seems that Pāli Buddhism can offer quite a bit beyond simply the teachings on mindfulness as we move to what is, apparently, an increasingly secular global discourse.

Tailoring the Buddhist Teachings to the Needs of the Time

It may be helpful to refer to ancient Buddhist texts, where such issues are raised in different ways, for the Buddha himself set the precedent for this willingness to reformulate tradition and articulate it in new ways. Deeply creative, he encouraged resourcefulness and applicability to changed circumstances from the outset. As Graham Dixon observes in his study of the finely balanced tact with which early Buddhisms were transmitted and traveled, "Coercion sits uneasily within a tradition which insists on exploration and personal transformation."[32] Just as those who in our own time are explaining, reformulating, and analyzing Buddhism in secular terms, the Buddha seems, from the evidence of the texts, to have taken some pains to acknowledge ways of practicing meditation that preceded Buddhism, where they were helpful, and integrate them into his own teachings.[33] He adapted his teachings to specific individuals, drawing new similes and analogies that referred to their way of life, and expressed the teaching in terms they would understand.[34] He taught a graduated path, and his teachings on meditation are, from what we can see in the texts, pitched to suit the inquirer or the audience. At different times, he would give different teachings to various people, depending on their level of attainment.[35] So to his son, Rāhula, he taught elements practice when the boy was not yet ready for the meditations on the foul that Sāriputta wanted to teach him; at a later time the Buddha gives different teachings, when the boy is clearly ready to take the step to become awakened himself.[36] One key feature of the Buddha's teachings is that they are often tailored to the specific individual, the stage of their development, and what would be useful to that person at that time. In other instances, the Buddha employed language and concepts that were typically used, often by brahmins, and changed their meaning. The threefold knowledge of the brahmins becomes, for instance, the threefold knowledge of Buddhism.[37] Indeed he seems to have done this with the very word "mindfulness," which, from the evidence of the Pāli texts, he changed from the meaning of "remembering"—as in the Sanskrit word *smṛti*—to a meaning that also involves sustained, ethical awareness of the present moment and of the world as it is experienced by the practitioner.[38]

As the Buddha did so, however, he did not forfeit basic Buddhist understanding, but rather infused common concepts with new meaning to enable Buddhism's accessibility. In early Buddhism, mindfulness, for instance, includes ethical discrimination. But the Buddha did not suddenly "go religious"—as is indicated, for instance, by his use of the famous gatekeeper image, which suggests ethical discrimination is included as part of mindfulness. Here, mindfulness is compared to a wise and experienced gatekeeper of a border city, who knows, from experience, what to let in and what to exclude. He notices, observes—and discriminates.[39] Some discernment is needed to be mindful; it is not just passively aware. How one is mindful, and what one is mindful of, is also important. The *anussatis*, a term often translated as "recollection," but which

more literally means "repeated mindfulness," involve actively bringing to mind various topics or areas of awareness that are likely to
bring happiness and purpose in daily life: the Buddha, the dharma,
the sangha, morality, generosity, the happiness of the gods, death,
the body, the breath, and the bringing to mind of peace.[40] Most of
these are not particularly biased toward any religious affiliation;
rather, they are regarded traditionally as ways of cheering the mind,
by occasional attention to objects that enliven it, still it, or bring
peace.[41] Oddly enough, even mindfulness of death is felt to have
a good effect on the mind, if conducted with other practices. How
one extends awareness is key: in one early text, the instruction to
practice loving-kindness (mettā) in daily life is described as a "mindfulness."[42] An association between happiness and ethical behavior,
a link not always highlighted in modern psychological discourse,
is also stressed, as in this explicit statement in the Kālāma-Sutta:

> Kālāmas, when you know for yourselves: "These things are
> unwholesome, these things are blameworthy; these things are
> censured by the wise; and when undertaken and observed, these
> things lead to harm and ill, abandon them."... Kālāmas, when
> you know for yourselves: "These things are wholesome; these
> things are blameless; these things are praised by the wise; these
> things, if accepted and undertaken, lead to welfare and happi-
> ness," then you should live in accordance with them.[43]

These are not particularly religious elements, though they may be
so: they acknowledge differences between people and their needs.
Yet, in their association of mindfulness and well-being with a common ethical ground, and the suggestion that one can actively arouse
within one's own mind factors associated with mindfulness that
contribute to happiness, they find a common, and easily understood, discourse to describe them.

While considering the subject of this essay, and secularization
as a process, I realized something was troubling me. Does Buddhism always need something "being done" to it? We are now

rightly wary of the colonialist impulses of the nineteenth century. But are we sometimes doing something comparable, in assuming, in a progressivist manner, that Buddhism somehow needs to be made acceptable for its principles to be applied in what we term a modern secular society? Are the very parameters of secularism, based so deeply on late eighteenth-century enlightened thinking, occasionally themselves becoming a little constricting? Can they marginalize other, equally important aspects of Buddhist doctrine and practice?

As we consider this, it also seems to me we need to be careful that other approaches to Buddhist practice and the development of the mind are seen as worthy, and not berated by other Buddhists. Aśoka's edicts are a good precedent in this. The Buddha clearly saw the need for different temperamental needs and approaches, hence the variety of method and practice explicitly sanctioned within the *nikāyas*.[44] Those of a Sāriputta temperament might prefer to delineate each stage of meditative attainment in precise detail, in a manner that may be seen more developed in the Abhidhamma or some insight traditions.[45] Others, however, like Moggallāna, follow a more intuitive practice route, found in more *samatha*-based lines, of a path through *jhāna* development.[46] There were clearly strong predilections of all kinds among early Buddhists.[47] We certainly find such diversity in Buddhisms today. Indeed, my teacher, L. S. Cousins, felt that this very capacity to accommodate and integrate different approaches was one of the most significant contributions of the historical Buddha to spiritual practice.[48]

Secularism within Buddhism

In 1958, Christmas Humphreys said "a definitely Western form of Buddhism must in time emerge";[49] his words now could apply to international, not just Western, Buddhisms. The tendency to think in terms of secularism—that is, rational, scientific, and pragmatic terms—is admirable, but perhaps needs some reminders. For Buddhism itself has its own traditions too of this kind. Early Buddhism addressed problems concerning how to live with various groups outside one's religious community, and it provides non-Western models of what we could call secularism, in the sense of an amicable working within secular society on terms that are not doctrinally objectionable within its own context.

We have seen this with Aśoka, an early anticipation of what it is like to think in pluralistic terms. As the Kaliṅga edict (Rock Edict 13) states, "The chief conquest is not that by war, but by dharma." Whether he implemented this, we do not know, but Aśoka's sentiments are expressed in the *Mahāsudassana-Sutta*, where the Buddha in an earlier life ruled as a *dhammarājā*, a just king.[50] Monarchies are not necessarily prized now. But the brahmins, sometimes criticized by the Buddha, are in one early set of verses praised for their onetime code of conduct, which was not specifically Buddhist but ensured their own happiness and that of those around them. In the *Brāmaṇadhammika-Sutta*, the Buddha describes brahmins at a time when they had no cattle, gold, or wealth but guarded the holy life "as a treasure." Then, he says, they were invulnerable: "They praised the holy life, and virtuous conduct, uprightness, mildness and austerity, meekness and non-violence, and forbearance."[51] These qualities suggest applicability in any context—perhaps something akin to the dharma that Aśoka attributes to many people, and which he says all traditions must respect.

What could very precisely, within modern terms of peaceful coexistence, be described as a secular way of life may be found not only in canonic but also in literary products of the Buddhist tradition. In the *jātaka*s, we see stories where the aspirant Buddha, the *bodhisatta*, works through many lives to develop the ten perfections of generosity, morality, renunciation, wisdom, vigor, forbearance, truthfulness, resolve, loving-kindness, and equanimity. In taking the bodhisatta vow, to find a way to discover and teach the eightfold path to others,[52] he developed qualities that anyone, in any tradition, can hope to find for themselves too. The "wisdom" of the jātakas is not the salvific wisdom described in the final life of the Buddha, as insight into the three marks of existence, impermanence, unsatisfactoriness, and non-self, though it does not exclude it. The bodhisatta is an aspirant to buddhahood, at a time when there is no Buddha, so cannot know and teach a full eightfold path. The wisdom demonstrated by him in the jātakas, often at times where there is no Buddhist dharma, is more worldly, and more universally applicable: it is that of a sea captain, capable of steering his passengers to safety in stormy waters,[53] or a shrewd and conscientious merchant, who ensures everyone in his caravan crosses a wilderness safely, with good returns.[54] Throughout these stories, the creative wisdom and skill-in-means (*upaya kusala*) in devising ways to ensure the welfare of others, as well as solving problems, is not framed in Buddhist terms at all: when the bodhisatta is a chief minister in the court, for instance, he devises strategies to avoid war, to promote others' welfare, and to solve detective-story puzzles, in constantly resourceful exercises that avoid harm and bring happiness and safety to those around. But, because there is no Buddhist teaching, these are described in entirely nonreligious terms.[55] The jātaka stories, precisely because they are so often set at a time when there is no Buddha, and no Buddhism, have to be "secular" in their formulation.

Buddhism comes into being and falls away too; the bodhisatta and others are, in the stories, usually born at times when there is no Buddhist teacher to guide them. These tales offer models of a nonaffiliated—or perhaps more accurately, universalist—means of acting well in the world. Beings—monkeys, hares, elephants, brahmins, untouchables, priests, and kings—act skillfully or badly in them. They experience the effects of good karma, and the effects of bad, too.

The Buddha, unusually for his time, ignored caste in his monastic orders, and he also does so in explaining the laws of karma, unlike his Brahmanic counterparts. And throughout the stories there is an assumption: that it is possible to act in the world while developing factors that bring well-being and good, to oneself and others, without necessarily "being a Buddhist."

Taught throughout the jātaka stories to often woefully inadequate kings, the ten principles of kingship offer features that are not particular to any religion and could be applied to rules of good governance anywhere.[56] The *dhammarāja* is a ruler who governs by means of, and with, dharma. The "just king" acts in accordance with dhamma, or dharma, in the sense of "law." In ancient Indian praxis and doctrine, the word—whether in Pāli or Sanskrit—has connotations of duty, law, and personal responsibility, as well as principle, in the sense that each being has his *svadharma*, or particular duty to fulfill. The list of ten qualities of a just king are presented as a series of ethical, social, and moral duties, applicable to any governing body, any constitutional code, or, by extension, any individual. "Dharma" here has underlying connotations not only of the teaching, in the Buddhist sense, but of the things one must do if one occupies a particular role in one's present lifetime, like the dharmas described by Aśoka in his rock edicts.[57] The ten are as follows:

1. *dāna*: generosity
2. *sīla*: the moral or ethical behavior of keeping the five precepts (of not killing, stealing, practicing sexual conduct likely to cause harm, lying, or letting oneself become intoxicated)
3. *pariccāga*: renunciation
4. *ajjava*: straightness (Skt. *ārjava*, to *ṛju*, to *uju* in Pāli)
5. *maddava*: softness; often, with straightness, found related to *mudutā*,[58] the softness of mind and body present in skillful consciousness
6. *tapa*: self-restraint
7. *akkodha*: the absence of anger; loving-kindness
8. *avihiṃsā*: the absence of harm; compassion[59]
9. *khanti*: forbearance
10. *avirodhana/avirodha*: gentleness; the absence of obstruction[60]

This seems to me a good list that is indigenous to South and Southeast Asia, entirely "secular" in its articulation, and, of course, formulated before colonialism or the need to situate the tradition in terms of, or in relationship to, the post-Enlightenment secular-religious divide. These ten duties of a king represent some rather helpful guidelines for those in positions of power and authority, which appear to be compatible with most of the world's religions as well as secular institutions. The list of the ten perfections cited above, to which this seems in some way akin, is likewise not specifically Buddhist. Unlike the ten principles of kingship of a king, the ten perfections are never mentioned in full in the early canonical verses and are therefore considered to be later. They also, however, offer an aspiration, or an ideal, that does not require any adherence to Buddhism as a tradition.

A Continuing Dialogue

Buddhism, adaptive as it is, has considered from its beginnings many of the social and psychological problems that concern us now. For if secularism is given excessive precedence, we need to be careful about where we assign authority for the health of our mind. Many people who come to the Buddhist group with which I am involved, and I am sure this applies to other groups too, say when they start meditation that they want something "secular"; they do not want "the trappings," or "Buddhism as a religion." Some retain this feeling, whether they prefer not to chant or offer devotions, or whether they are closely involved with another spiritual tradition, such as Christianity. But many do go on to appreciate chanting, devotion, making offerings, and the sense of refuge in the triple gem of the Buddha, dharma, and sangha, as forms of practice in themselves. They notice they arouse mindfulness, direct the mind to the meditation, and encourage a willingness to let go of problems and hindrances. They "go" for refuge, or in some cases "understand" the refuge: the Pāli verb *gacchāmi* allows both meanings.[61]

At some point there is a need to trust and, perhaps, take a leap in the dark. The refuges are to help us with that. We may articulate these refuges in terms that could also be regarded as secular: the Buddha as the fully awakened state of mind, the highest potential for a human being, whose seeds are present in ourselves; the dharma as the teaching of the graduated path that leads to this awakening; and the sangha, variously understood as being those who have attained this awakening or the orders of monks and nuns, or the community at large, of those who are following the same path. These, to many Buddhists, are what really ensure our balance and health in following a Buddhist practice. They offer three, interdependent reference points: the Buddha, a graduated teaching that can be re-created and reformulated, and a community to safeguard the development of the other two.[62] As refuges, these three elements restore one another, and support each other.

But many are drawn to Buddhism precisely because of the devotional, the sense of the mysterious, and the numinous, which is there for those who wish it. Should such people wait to have their tastes sanctioned by scientific study on chanting or devotional practices in the name of what has become something of a secular imperative? Their love is intuitive and arises to them from a different kind of knowing. For this is where there is a real problem area in issues concerning this subject. Secularism has a real excellence: it suggests ways toward a common consensus that give effective and respectful grounds for interaction, as a kind of orthopraxy, between very different groups.[63] Is it in danger, however, of becoming our new orthodoxy?

Awe and humility are strange things, but they need to be there and cannot be measured. For the possibility that we can find awakening, with the help of the three refuges, is awe-inspiring, and oddly humbling too. It is important to measure, for all sorts of purposes: to compare, graph, tabulate, assess, and quantify. But the "divine abidings" (brahmavihāras) in Buddhism are defined by the fact they are immeasurable (appamāṇa); they cannot be experienced or understood in full without an openness to the infinite and to the large, whether in time, in past and future buddhas and bodhisattvas, or in space, in infinite universes. It is this which is to many so mysterious and inviting about the Buddhist path—the sense of something much greater than oneself, or one's society, or even a group of societies. The infinite manifoldness of things around is, in the end, a transcendent teaching. The desire for transcendence is, it seems to me, a human impulse, unacknowledged sometimes within secularist discourse. One Christian friend said she found mindfulness teaching very helpful. For her, she said, mindfulness of the infinite is really what heals, and gives her life meaning. A sense of transcendence for her was not an added extra to activities in daily life: it is something that can inform all she does.

A sense of awe, and of the infinite, is part of the healing of the Buddhist path too. The full extent of mindfulness encompasses this, and allows that possibility in daily life, and all dealings.[64] The Buddha once taught an old man, Piṅgiya, who said his path was one of devotion. The Buddha sanctioned his chosen route.[65] The Buddha might not have taught that path to everyone, but if it worked, he encouraged it; where another meditator is excessively dependent, he tells him to look to himself.[66] Secularism has proven itself an effective way of breaking down old barriers and of allowing communications between groups that may not have been easy before. It has also prompted many people to follow Buddhism and explore it more. But do we need to be careful where we finally assign real understanding of what contributes to our health of mind? While secularism is not considered a religion, sometimes it feels a bit that way. At the time of the Buddha, we are told, only high priests had the means of sustaining the sacred texts and teachings.[67] Other people had to rely on them for their perpetuation, for the performance of rituals, and for spiritual authority. Like others, I often talk of "they," as in "they have found that…" or "they have proved that…" We do not need to reject the impulse to investigate external validation for Buddhist methods and techniques. Scientific, well-grounded research is encouraging, often framing Buddhist technique in modern technical terms and situating it in often highly specialized disciplines. But I have noticed we are increasingly regarding those that conduct research as "they," our arbiters of all things to do with the mind, as if they must be the only ones who can really understand the path to happiness and recovery (however that is articulated). In my experience scientists, mindfulness researchers, psychologists, and psychotherapists are not high priests, and would not want to be!

Holyoake's original formulation of secularism accommodates the free practice of religion, without intervention. At some point, however, Western society somehow conflated science, reason, enlightened thinking, and truth. Something called "religion" seems to challenge this and is thus identified as a threat. For something to be real these days it needs to have a good scientific backing. But the very word "secular," in its Latin meaning, suggests changing times and new generations; secularism is by definition one mode, for our time. It is not the only, or indeed a transcendent one. Over the last few decades, secular academic findings, often fused with a rationalistic, scientific worldview, seem to be gaining ground in domains that we used to see as nothing to do with secularism at all. Peter Skilling has recently noted how universalism was deeply embedded in early Buddhist inscription and text: it is framed as the wish for ourselves and others to find happiness and freedom, and it informs the Buddhist approach to a sensibly balanced transmission in many languages, together with the promotion of tolerance, shared cultures, and new technologies.[68]

Acting within this universalist approach is what Buddhist groups are undertaking now, and academic disciplines working with Buddhist techniques and doctrines are doing so too. If we are to stand our ground in Buddhism, with the three refuges, we need to remember that Buddhism has always done this kind of thing, and that in this process there is, in the end, no "they." Faith is not the same as belief; having faith does not involve opposing the practices and beliefs of others, or insisting on one's own rightness, either. It is possible to be deeply religious and passionate yet respectful. The Buddhist path is apt, inviting (*ehipassiko*), and leads onward (*opanayiko*); there is also a community, to help us find it.[69] The teaching is to be known directly by the wise (*paccattaṃ veditabbo viññūhi*). It is an ornament, as Buddhaghosa indicates, on one's own, not on another's, head.[70] By being mindful of these protections and the larger perspective they offer, Buddhism can, where it is needed, continue to encourage secularism and secularization but still genuinely allow "all dharmas to flourish."

BIBLIOGRAPHY

Pāli texts

Pali Text Society editions. Except where otherwise stated, each work is cited by volume number, where appropriate, and page number—for example, AN 2.324; Vibh 234.

AN	Aṅguttara Nikāya
DhS	Dhammasaṅgani
DN	Dīgha Nikāya
It	Itivuttaka
Ja	Jātakatthakavaṇṇanā (Individual stories cited by number in the collection: eg. J 1).
Mv	Mahāvaṃsa
MN	Majjhima Nikāya
SN	Saṃyutta Nikāya
Sn	Sutta Nipāta (cited by verse number)
Ud	Udāna
Vibh	Vibhaṅga
Vism	Visuddhimagga (cited according to Ñāṇamoli translation)

Ahemaitijiang, Nigela, Xiaoyi Hu, Xuan Yang, and Zhuo Rachel Han. "Effects of Meditation on the Soles of the Feet on the Aggressive and Destructive Behaviors of Chinese Adolescents with Autism Spectrum Disorders," *Mindfulness* 11 (2020): 230–40.

Appleton, Naomi, and Sarah Shaw. *The Ten Great Birth Stories of the Buddha: The Mahānipāta of the Jātakatthavaṇṇanā*. Chiang Mai, Thailand: Silkworm Publications, 2015.

Batchelor, Stephen. *Secular Buddhism: Imagining the Dharma in an Uncertain World*. New Haven, CT: Yale University Press, 2017.

Bluck, Robert. *British Buddhism: Teachings, Practice and Development*. London and New York: Routledge, 2006.

Bodhi, Bhikkhu. "What Does Mindfulness Really Mean? A Canonical Perspective." *Contemporary Buddhism* 12, no. 1 (2011): 19-39.

———. *The Numerical Discourses of the Buddha: A Translation of the Aṅguttara Nikāya*. Somerville, MA: Wisdom Publications, 2012.

———. "The Transformations of Mindfulness." In *Handbook of Mindfulness*, edited by Ronald E. Purser, David Forbes, and Adam Burke, 3-14. Cham, Switzerland: Springer International, 2016.

Brazier, David. "Mindfulness: Traditional and Utilitarian." In *Handbook of Mindfulness*, edited by Ronald E. Purser, David Forbes, and Adam Burke, 63-74. Cham, Switzerland: Springer International, 2016.

Cousins, L. S. "*Samatha-yāna* and *Vipassanā-yāna*." In *Buddhist Studies in Honour of Hammalava Saddhātissa*, edited by Gatārē Dhammapāla, Richard Francis Gombrich, and Kenneth Roy Norman, 56-68. Nugegoda, Sri Lanka: Hammalava Saddhātissa Felicitation Volume Committee, University of Jayewardenepura, 1984.

———. "Theravāda Buddhism in England." In *Buddhism into the Year 2000: International Conference Proceedings*, 141-50. Bangkok and Los Angeles: Dhammakaya Foundation, 1994.

Crosby, Kate. *Traditional Theravāda Meditation and Its Modern-Era Suppression*. Hong Kong: Buddha-Dharma Centre of Hong Kong, 2013.

———. *Esoteric Theravada: The Story of the Forgotten Meditation Tradition of Southeast Asia*. Boulder: Shambhala Publications, 2020.

David-Neel, Alexandra. *Magic and Mystery in Tibet*. London: Souvenir Press, 2007. First published 1929.

Dixon, Graham. "Assertion and Restraint in Dhamma Transmission in Early Pāli Sources." *Buddhist Studies Review* 32, no. 1 (2015): 99-141.

Gethin, Rupert. "On Some Definitions of Mindfulness." *Contemporary Buddhism* 12, no. 1 (2011): 263-79.

Gombrich, Richard F. *How Buddhism Began: The Conditioned Genesis of the Early Teachings*. London and Atlantic Highlands, NJ: Athlone, 1996.

Greenberg, M. T., and Mitra, J. L. "From Mindfulness to Right Mindfulness: The Intersection of Awareness and Ethics." *Mindfulness* 6, no. 1 (2015): 74-78.

Harvey, Peter. *An Introduction to Buddhism: Teachings, History and Practices*. 2nd edition. Cambridge, MA: Cambridge University Press, 2013.

———. "Mindfulness in Theravāda Samatha and Vipassanā Meditations, and in Secular Mindfulness." In *Buddhist Foundations of Mindfulness*, edited by Edo Shonin, William Van Gordon, and Nirbhay N. Singh, 115-37. Cham, Switzerland: Springer International Publishing, 2015.

Holyoake, George J. *English Secularism: A Confession of Belief*. Chicago: Open Court Publishing, 1896.

Humphreys, Christmas. "Zen Comes West." *Middle Way* 32, no. 4 (1958): 126-30.

Klaus, Konrad. "On the Meaning of the Root *smṛ* in Vedic Literature." *Wiener Zeitschrift für die Kunde Südasiens* 36 (1992): 77-86.

Kornfield, Jack. *Living Buddhist Masters*. Santa Cruz, CA: Unity Press, 1977.
——. *A Path with Heart: The Classic Guide through the Perils and Pitfalls of Spiritual Life*. Revised and updated edition. London: Rider, 2002.
Loucks, Eric B., Zev Schuman-Olivier, Willoughby B. Britton, David M. Fresco, Gaelle Desbordes, Judson A. Brewer, Carl Fulwiler. *Mindfulness and Cardiovascular Disease Risk: State of the Evidence, Plausible Mechanisms, and Theoretical Framework*. Current Cardiology Reports 17, no. 12 (2015): 112.
"Mindfulness." NHS (website). https://www.nhs.uk/conditions/stress-anxiety-depression/mindfulness/.
Ñāṇamoli, Bhikkhu, trans. *The Path of Purification of Buddhaghosa (Visuddhimagga)*. 5th edition. Kandy: Buddhist Publication Society (Vism trans.: this edition cited by section heading), 1991.
Norman, K. R. *The Group of Discourses (Sutta-Nipāta)* II. Oxford: Pali Text Society, 1995.
Olivelle, Patrick. *Dharmasūtras: The Law Codes of Ancient India*. Oxford: Oxford University Press, 1999.
——. *Language, Texts, and Society*: *Explorations in Ancient Indian Culture and Religion*. New York: Anthem Press, 2011.
Rhys Davids, T. W. *Dialogues of the Buddha*. Volume 2, Sacred Books of the Buddhists. London: Froude, 1910.
Russell, Tamara A. and Gerson Siegmund. "What and Who? Mindfulness in the Mental Health Setting." *BJPsych Bulletin* 40, no. 6 (2016): 333–40.
Samuel, Geoffrey. "Mindfulness Within the Full Range of Buddhist and Asian Meditative Practices." In *Handbook of Mindfulness*, edited by Ronald E. Purser, David Forbes, and Adam Burke, 47–62. Cham: Springer International Publishing, 2016.
Sharf, Robert H. "Mindfulness and Mindlessness in Early Chan." In *Meditation and Culture: The Interplay of Practice and Context*, edited by Halvor Eifring, 55–75. London: Bloomsbury, 2015.
Shaw, Sarah. *Buddhist Meditation: An Anthology of Texts*. London: Routledge, 2006.
——. *The Jatakas: The Birth Stories of the Bodhisatta*. New Delhi: Penguin, 2006.
——. *Introduction to Buddhist Meditation*. London: Routledge, 2009.
——. *Mindfulness: Where It Comes From and What It Means*. Boulder: Shambhala Publications, 2020.
Sircar, Dineschandra C. *Inscriptions of Aśoka*. Calcutta: Indian Publication Society, 1956.
Skilling, Peter. "The Buddhist Cosmopolis: Universal Welfare, Universal Outreach Universal Message." *Journal of Buddhist Studies* 15 (2018): 55–80.
Skilton, Andrew and Choompolpaisal Phibul. "The Old Meditation (boran

kammatthan), a Pre-reform Theravāda Meditation System from Wat Rat-chasittaram; The Piti Section of the kammatthan matchima baep lamdap." *Aseanie* 33 (2014): 83–116.

Smith, Rodney. *Touching the Infinite: A New Perspective on the Buddha's Four Foundations of Mindfulness*. Boulder: Shambhala Publications, 2017.

Taylor, Jim L. *Forest Monks and the Nation State: An Anthropological and Historical Study in Northeast Thailand*. Institute of Southeast Asian Studies, 1993.

Tiyavanich, Kemala. *Forest Recollections: Wandering Monks in Twentieth-Century Thailand*. Honolulu: University of Hawai'i Press, 1997.

Williams, Mark, John D. Teasdale, Jon Kabat-Zinn, and Zindel V. Segal. *The Mindful Way through Depression: Freeing Yourself from Chronic Unhappiness*. New York: Guilford Press, 2007.

A portrait of a young man, William Taylor, looking in a mirror.
Thomas Worlidge, 1751.

2 | Buddhism and Secular Subjectivities

Individualism and Fragmentation in the Mirrors of Secularism

DAVID L. MCMAHAN

Consider two works of art featuring mirrors. The first, by Thomas Worlidge (1700–1766), a British painter and etcher, is titled *A Portrait of a Young Man, William Taylor, Looking in a Mirror* (1751). The etching is precisely what its title promises: a man looking into a small hand mirror, which reflects his puffy visage and buoyantly coiffed hair. It can be viewed as an apt emblem of the European Enlightenment, whose philosophers promised to develop the methods that would hold man and nature up to the mirror of empirical investigation and rational analysis, rendering clear and distinct representations of them. Nothing else appears in the work but the young man, his mirror, and his reflection.

Another quite different mirror-themed work is a series conceived in 1965 by the Japanese artist Yayoi Kusama (b. 1929) called Infinity Mirror Rooms.[1] In one, a viewer stands in a room whose walls are mirrors reflecting uncountable numbers of lights receding in all directions. Although a smallish room, it seems enormous, indeed infinite, and includes multiple images of the viewer herself. People around the world wait in line for hours to stand in these rooms and experience themselves enveloped in countless lights and objects multiplied throughout unlimited space.

If Worlidge's image was compelling in the eighteenth century for its resonance with the Enlightenment ideal of the mirror of nature and the promise of clear and accurate representation of the autonomous, independent individual, Kusama's image is more resonant with our own era and its fragmentation, its consciousness of the vastness of the cosmos, and its hope for some significance—some reflection of ourselves—in that vastness. We might consider the two images to represent two archetypal ways of considering—or perhaps experiencing—oneself in the world. One, a coherent sense of selfhood, distinct from the world and clear to itself, still echoes in our time in calls for authenticity, self-realization, individualism, identity, thinking for oneself. The other represents a contemporary sense of multiple, displaced, disembedded, vertiginous subjectivity, more difficult to pin down, more disorienting, and perhaps frightening, but also potentially expansive and ecstatic.

These images illustrate competing versions of secular subjectivity. Although the Infinity Mirror model is more recent, the hand mirror model is by no means a relic of the past. We might instead see the contemporary era as marked by a tension between the two. In what sense are they secular, and what might they have to do with secularizing or secularized Buddhism?

Secularity and the Secular Buddhist

One way to approach the issue of secular Buddhism is to ask questions such as the following: *Should* Buddhism be secularized? Is secularized Buddhism authentic? Does it strip away too many essential elements? Rather than weigh in on the merits and defects of a secularized Buddhism, I want to think through some issues involving how two long, variegated traditions—Buddhism and modern secularism—converge. Often when people speak to the issue of secular Buddhism, they speak in terms of explicit beliefs. Do we believe in the possibility of rebirth as a hungry ghost? In a hell realm? In a cosmos centered on Mount Meru? In evil spirits that can be fended off through Buddhist rituals? The fewer things like this we believe, the more secular our Buddhism, one might say. These questions play an important role in secularizing Buddhism, especially because one common use of the term "secularism" today involves explicit beliefs. But I'd like to think about the ways in which what we might call "secularity"—the pervasive, naturalistic zeitgeist of the times, the dominant discourse of modernity, the ideology of public discourse—structures not just explicit beliefs but more subtle ways of being in the world and experiencing oneself. I then want to further consider how secularity selectively draws forth and transforms particular elements of Buddhism.

Secularity in this sense is not only a matter of explicit beliefs that constitute a naturalistic worldview but also a complex of intuitions, practices, and sensibilities that structure lived experience in the late-modern world. It functions as a kind of background ideology that is so pervasive it often goes unnoticed. It is tied inevitably to particular political projects (the separation of church and state), particular configurations of the self (an independent, subjective self confronting an objective world of neutral facts), and, indeed, particular notions of what is religious and what is secular (religion as having to do primarily with beliefs, internal experience, emotions, and the secular having to do with rationality, public discourse, and politics). The binary of religious and secular does not refer to some objective state of things in the world but is a historically particular way of dividing things up, of constituting human subjects, and of framing institutions like public schools, governmental organizations, and the courts. As a sociopolitical project, secularism itself is rooted in an attempt to separate out the activity of rational individuals deliberating in the public square from "religion," which is conceived as a matter of private, individual belief. This paradigm is deeply rooted in the European Enlightenment, with its valorization of reason, choice, activity, personal autonomy, and individualism, not to mention its historical framing of these virtues as the properties of "the West," while "the East" was often associated with the irrational, the mysterious, the feminine, the passive, and the collective. In ways that Buddhists should understand, the religious and the secular are not mere facts in the world, but, like many (all?) binary oppositions, they are coconstituted, intertwined, and culturally and historically contingent. Religion and secularity, in other words, are interdependently arisen, recently invented ways of configuring the world and constituting our experience. Nevertheless, if secularity is, in fact, the dominant zeitgeist of much of the developed world, it has already deeply structured the way many Buddhists practice their tradition. In fact, Buddhism made headway in Europe and North America in large part by being framed as aligned with secular, scientific orientations and eschewing things that were typically associated with "religion" and, especially, "superstition." In other words, much Buddhism today, whether it claims the mantle of "secular Buddhism" or not, is already secularized to a great extent.

Particular elements of the zeitgeist of secularity have served as "magnets" that have drawn forth and transformed certain specific elements of Buddhism—especially the doctrine of non-self (*anātman*), dependent origination or interdependence (*pratītya-samutpāda*), and certain meditative practices. These elements of Buddhism, I suggest, have been transformed and embodied by modern people in ways that both embrace and attempt to ameliorate certain aspects of modern secularity as a lived experience. More specifically, they attempt to negotiate the tension between the two modes of modern secular subjectivity suggested by our two mirror-themed works of art: the sense of selfhood as singular, independent, and autonomous and the sense of fragmentation of the self into multiple identities.

Secular Subjectivities

Here is a brief story about the experience of selfhood in the modern West, how it developed and changed, and how it prepared the ground for particular versions of Buddhism to emerge. It is a ridiculously abbreviated and too-neat story, and we could fill a book with caveats and attempts to nuance it, but we can't, so here it is. The Age of Enlightenment promised a kind of narrative clarity about the self. Descartes claimed to isolate the soul definitively—"I am nothing but a thinking thing." At its best, the soul, or self, had "clear and distinct" ideas. The discovery (or creation) of this self was part of a larger "subjective turn" in the West, through which attention turned inward as never before in European history. The subjective turn entailed attempts to systematically account for the faculties of mind and body—nail them down and establish once and for all just what the soul of man (yes, man) and its faculties was and its place in the universe.

The Enlightenment thinkers proposed that rationality was the essence of the self, and through stepping away from the emotions and relying solely on reason, one could make moral choices and live a good life. Romanticism countered this notion by insisting on the centrality of emotion, of passion, of deep interiority, of getting in touch with nature and the divine through interior exploration. Although they seem opposed, these two versions of selfhood were complementary and shared the notion of the autonomous individual whose judgment could, and should, transcend social convention and conditioning and be the sole author of itself. We can characterize these visions of selfhood as "secular" not because they necessarily rejected God or divinity altogether but because they shifted emphasis from dependence on God to self-determination and individual autonomy.

Charles Taylor argues that a distinctive characteristic of this newly constituted modern self is that it is "buffered" rather than porous. That is, the modern West inaugurated a firmer boundary between the self and objects than had existed in the premodern, enchanted world. In the enchanted world, he claims, this boundary was porous, and people were more vulnerable to the influences of external things—gods, spirits, and demons—directly. Objects were charged with inherent meaning: black bile was not just a physical cause of melancholy as a mental state—it *was* melancholy. Sand from a sacred place could have beneficent, healing effects. This is not just a matter of beliefs but of a deep-rooted way of experiencing and interpreting oneself and the world. Think also of the significance of dreams or hearing voices in a lot of ancient literature: one heard God's voice; or maybe it's that of a demon.

Today, although many people still gather sand from sacred sites, see ghosts, and hear voices, most of us experience such things within the framework of a bounded self—the mind, the inside— more distinct from the external world. If I see a ghost, I wonder if it might be an eruption of my unconscious, a repressed memory, a hallucination, or the result of a chemical imbalance. I might explain any beneficent effect of sacred sand in terms of the effect it has on my mood; or perhaps it's a kind of placebo effect.

In the buffered self, the mind is the locus of all meaning, and the external world in itself is the blank slate for the projections of meanings. This framework also makes for the possibility of dis-tancing oneself from the manifestations of the mind and treating them as objects—observing, controlling, and disciplining them.[2] The point is that the autonomous individual of the Enlightenment philosophers was a theoretical expression of something that was also taking shape on a more phenomenological level among many people in the West. If Descartes's "thinking thing" was a dry phil-osophical abstraction, it was (if Taylor is right) also refracted in the ordinary experience of "buffered selves," who, encouraged by educational and institutional structures, began more and more to conceive of and experience themselves as enclosed, self-contained beings with private minds separate from the world.

If it is true that a novel sense of subjectivity gradually emerged in the modern period, we might characterize "late modernity"—the latter half of the twentieth century up through the early twenty-first century—as a period when this sense of the autonomous, buffered self begins to fray at the edges. Countless examples from philoso-phy, art, literature, sociology, psychology, and religious studies offer insights into this. I only present a few gleanings.

The social theorist Anthony Giddens marks "late" or "high"

modernity as a period of increased disembeddedness from traditional social orders in which people's roles are more rigidly defined. Rather than being embedded in a family, community, social order, and cosmos that gives a de facto meaning to their lives, people in the conditions of late modernity are increasingly thrown back upon themselves to continuously figure out and construct who they are. The self, in other words, becomes a "reflexive project":

> Transitions in individuals' lives have always demanded psychic reorganisation, something which was often ritualised in traditional cultures in the shape of *rites de passage*. But in such cultures, where things stayed more or less the same from generation to generation on the level of the collectivity, the changed identity was clearly staked out—as when an individual moved from adolescence into adulthood. In the settings of modernity, by contrast, the altered self has to be explored and constructed as part of a reflexive process of connecting personal and social change.[3]

Such conditions, Giddens argues, create increased uncertainty and doubt, as well as a sense of the fragility of one's narrative of the self: "A self-identity has to be created and more or less continually reordered against the backdrop of shifting experiences of day-to-day life and the fragmenting tendencies of modern institutions."[4] In premodern times, Giddens argues, people's identities were, to a great extent, determined by gender, family, clan, lineage, and so on. Today some of these factors are still important; however, people increasingly must actively construct identities through "lifestyles," consumer choices, and interaction with many abstract systems, such as the educational system, the health care system, and the ubiquitous economic system of global capitalism. One must continually construct and revise one's identity in multiple contexts, repeatedly adapting and creating a "narrative of self"—a coherent life story that appears to maintain itself throughout time. According to Giddens, the splintering of the self, and the energy-consuming struggle to maintain a sense of narrative coherence, can lead to a disorienting sense of fragmentation, uncertainty, doubt, and the looming threat of personal meaninglessness.

Zygmunt Bauman extends some of Giddens's insights on the malleability of the self in modern times. He characterizes our contemporary period as one of "liquid life" in which conditions change at such a rapid rate that predicting the future on the basis of the past becomes increasingly difficult and, therefore, anxiety-producing. It is a period in which people, rather than having an identity given to them at birth based on being embedded in family, community, and nation, must create their identities in an ad hoc fashion. Baumann highlights the differential effects this situation has on people in different socioeconomic strata:

> At the top [of the social hierarchy], the problem is to choose the best pattern from the many currently on offer, to assemble the separately sold parts of the kit, and to fasten them together neither too lightly (lest the unsightly, outdated and aged bits that are meant to be hidden underneath show through at the seams) nor too tightly (lest the patchwork resists being dismantled at short notice when the time for dismantling comes—as it surely will). At the bottom, the problem is to cling fast to the sole identity available and to hold its bits and parts together while fighting back the erosive forces and disruptive pressures, repairing the constantly crumbling walls and digging the trenches deeper.[5]

Identity must be constantly constructed, reconstructed, and maintained in large part through consumption of items—cars, phones, decor, clothing—of limited life and temporary value in conferring cultural capital. The self itself then comes to feel tenuous, fleeting, unstable, and thus continually in need of scrutiny and reform, while the external world is reduced to having primarily instrumental value. Individuality, rather than a given of our nature, as assumed by both the Enlightenment and Romantic thinkers, is an endless task to be achieved through lifelong struggle amid dizzyingly rapid change. For Baumann, achieving individuality, therefore, is an *aporia*—an irresolvable contradiction—in a society that requires uniqueness and yet has undercut the social bonds of community that would confer any sense of stable identity. Thus, Baumann claims, "The struggle for *uniqueness* has now become the main engine of *mass* production and *mass* consumption."[6] Identity is perpetually hybrid, unstable, unfixed, yet always promised. And yet the construction of identity through career and consumer choice remains a privilege for those who can afford it, while those in less-privileged sectors of society remain stuck in assigned, imposed, overdetermined identity.[7] No one escapes "liquid modernity"; however, the affluent global, "de-territorialized" citizen learns to ride the waves of rapid change while the underprivileged struggle with the risk of constantly being left behind, bereft of economic and cultural capital.

The psychologist Kenneth Gergen adds to this picture the ways that "technologies of social saturation"—primarily media technologies—have contributed to the sense of self-fragmentation:

> Emerging technologies saturate us with the voices of human-kind—both harmonious and alien. As we absorb their varied rhymes and reasons, they become a part of us and we of them. Social saturation furnishes us with a multiplicity of incoherent and unrelated languages of the self. For everything we "know to be true" about ourselves, other voices within respond with doubt and even derision. This fragmentation of self-conceptions corresponds to a multiplicity of incoherent and disconnected relationships. These relationships pull us in myriad directions, inviting us to play such a variety of roles that the very concept of an "authentic self" with knowable characteristics recedes from view. The fully saturated self becomes no self at all.[8]

As we are bombarded with ever-increasing social contexts, the languages of the self inherited from modernism and Romanticism—the knowable, rational, autonomous individual and the passionate soul with a deep interior—begin to recede. If, in the past, a sense of relatively stable selfhood was created by embeddedness in tight-knit communities with relatively stable roles, the "saturated self" confronts countless others—physical, fictional, virtual—and is called upon to respond to each, creating a sense of subjectivity characterized by "a plurality of voices all vying for the right to reality."[9] The world of rapid travel and instant communication has created, Gergen argues, a situation in which "we are bombarded with ever increasing intensity with the images and actions of others; our range of social participation is increasing exponentially." In this world, "we no longer experience a secure sense of self," and "doubt is increasingly placed on the very assumption of a bounded identity with palpable attributes."[10]

> Social saturation brings with it a general loss in our assumption of true and knowable selves. As we absorb multiple voices, we find that each "truth" is relativized by our simultaneous consciousness of compelling alternatives. We come to be aware that each truth about ourselves is a construction of the moment, true only for a given time and within certain relationships.[11]

Gergen dubs the "infusion of partial identities through social saturation" the "populated self," a cacophony of images and voices representing disparate possibilities of selfhood that are constantly displaced by others. This condition is not merely a matter of self-concepts but also of activities and investments of time and energy. One effect is what he calls "multiphrenia...the splitting of the individual into a multiplicity of self-investments."[12] The expansion of relationships leads to the "vertigo of the valued," in which each context of interaction entails new things to value, desire, and choose, until life becomes a vertiginous swirl of beckonings and demands.

We shouldn't be so naive as to think that this collage of late-modern subjectivities amounts to something all-encompassing or universal. Although there is little doubt that the symptoms they describe have gone global, they may be refracted quite differently in different cultural, class, or gender contexts, and may even be relatively absent in some. There is also reason for some skepticism about Taylor's distinction between "porous" and "buffered" selves. People today still hear the voice of God and experience various enchantments and mysteries that many educated people have relegated to the "premodern" past but that are still quite alive today. No doubt, further nuancing is needed, but for now let's hazard the generalizations that, first, the modern world brought forth not just new ideas of individualism but also a felt sense of experiencing the world in a more bounded way, as an individual mind separate from an objective world; and second, that the conditions of late modernity have encouraged a sense of subjective fragmentation that disrupts the sense of the modern autonomous individual, as well as more "premodern" embeddedness in communities. Most pertinent to Buddhism in the West, these phenomena were likely familiar to those who have been responsible for bringing Buddhism into North America and Europe as a live option throughout the late twentieth century. Whether they have been Japanese immigrant Zen priests, Tibetan refugee lamas, or educated and spiritually curious European Americans, those who have shaped modern Buddhism have either experienced or been keen observers of this new mode of secular consciousness.

So the picture that coalesces from these authors about contemporary modes of subjectivity in the West is that the "modern self"—with its valorization of self-reliance, individual autonomy, and freedom from the external coercion—is splintering. In hindsight, it was always deeply flawed as a theory, but as an ideologically driven phenomenological sense of self, it attained a kind of provisional actuality as a coherent constellation of habits, dispositions, and sensibilities. Therefore, its fragmentation in the face of some of the above factors forms a part of the architecture of late-modern anxiety, stress, and malaise. There is, therefore, a tension at work in late-modern secular subjectivity, especially in the West: the modern construction of the self-sufficient, self-responsible, free agent separate from the objective world, isolated and buffered—a lingering centripetal force of Enlightenment individualism—exists in tension with a centrifugal sense of internal fragmentation, media saturation, rootlessness, and disembeddedness. The late-modern secular subject, with the Enlightenment inheritance still part of the background understanding of individualistic personhood, is disturbed when that understanding is shattered daily by the forces of fragmentation. The man looking at his singular reflection in the hand mirror begins to see his image distort, double, triple, then explode into an infinity of images, some of himself, some of others, all scattering into a dizzying array of lights expanding to infinity.

How is it, then, that various strands of Buddhist thought and practice weave their way into this picture and create a further chapter in the story? How are certain elements of Buddhism envisioned as either accommodating this sense of subjectivity or offering ameliorative, transformative possibilities for its ills?

Tensions: Creative and Conflictual

The secularization of Buddhism is a process more complex than "Buddhism" being imported into "Western culture." Different selected threads of Buddhisms around the world have been reconfigured and woven into the fabric of a globalized secular modernity (which is itself really an extended family of modernities and secularities, not all of which are "Western"), while other threads have been ignored. How could it be otherwise? So rather than list the various solutions and possibilities that Buddhism may offer to the tension between individualism and fragmentation I've outlined above, I confine myself to considering some secular interpretations of particular Buddhist ideas and practices: the ideas of non-self and interdependence, and the modern practices of meditation. I am not suggesting that these ideas and practices stand on their own as true and efficacious per se, and therefore provide solutions to the conditions I've identified. Rather, I am looking historically at how these social conditions (along with others) have created a space for certain Buddhist ideas and practices and have drawn them forth out of their home contexts and into new habitations of late-modern secularity.

Fragmented Selves and Non-Self

The most obvious place to begin is with the Buddhist insistence on the absence of an independent, enduring, and unchanging self (*ātman*). Given the received notions of modern Western selfhood rooted in the Enlightenment and Romanticism, the prospects for the doctrine of non-self (*anātman*) in the West would seem dim. But non-self functions in particular ways when drawn into the gravitational orbit of late-modern secular subjectivity and its chaotic liquidity, media saturation, instability, disembeddedness, and fragmentation—not to mention the nostalgia for the stable self-responsible agent of the Enlightenment.

If Giddens and Bauman are right that many people in late modernity are disembedded from the social forces that once provided a ready-made identity and that, instead, we must now constantly ask, "Who am I?"—that identity is not given and so requires a continuing task of constructing a stable, narrative self—then certain interpretations of *anātman* become, for some, a compelling way of navigating this reality. If we have never had a coherent, stable, permanent self to begin with, then attempting to construct one is not only unnecessary but futile. Better to recognize the fluid, malleable nature of consciousness, be aware of how various "selves" rise and fall depending on diverse causes and conditions, and learn to skillfully guide the process. This approach might serve to mitigate the anxiety of trying to anchor a stable sense of selfhood amid the whirlwind of ever-changing conditions of the late-modern period. If the bad news for the modern autonomous self is that it was a fiction to begin with—something that Western philosophy, psychology, neuroscience, and social science increasingly agree upon—the good news is that a rich, meaningful, and ethical life is available in its absence. If the fragmenting forces of late modernity have shattered the illusion of a fixed self, *anātman* provides a way of rethinking subjectivity in its absence.

The doctrine of *anātman* claims that, in the face of the constant flux of plural selves "vying for the right to reality," as Gergen puts it, that none actually has such a right. In a time of the multiplication of self-images and the frantic attempts to ground one of them in reality, refiguring subjectivity as non-self admits that such grounding will never happen and, moreover, that abandoning the attempt is part of the solution to the problem. And yet there is the possibility of agency and intention outside the confines of the isolated, autonomous self. *Anātman* introduces a way to imagine navigating the tensions between, on the one hand, the Cartesian notion of the bounded, autonomous self and, on the other hand, the lived experience of fragmentation, saturation, and permeability of the self. The autonomous self, it suggests, is a fiction. We are a combination of various processes coming together under the influence of past actions that color, constitute, characterize the present. Yet we have agency, in each moment, for further directing this complex process, our own stream of consciousness, in more wise and compassionate directions. We are neither wholly determined by the past, nor fully free from it.

Two Poles of Mindfulness

Reimagining subjectivity in this way is intimately intertwined with secular adaptations of Buddhist meditative practices. If the splintering of subjectivity into multiple selves, commitments, and projects constitutes a uniquely modern anxiety, what new uses and transformations of mindfulness emerge in the space created by these conditions? First, we can see mindfulness as the detached observation of these "selves" and their activities, which may desubstantialize them, decrease anxiety, and lessen the feeling of being trapped by them or overwhelmed by their mercurial flux, allowing room for critical reflection on the process. Rather than fleeing the modern burden of hyperreflexivity that Giddens outlines, meditative practices plunge the practitioner into the process in order to observe and reconfigure it. Mindfulness promises to harness the fragmented sense of self, cull it into a manageable, intention-directed stream of consciousness, and conjure a sense of steadiness—even resoluteness—out of the infinitely plural phenomenological continuum.

Given this, though, meditative practices might gravitate toward either of two poles. They might be used to shore up the "buffered self" and reassert the lost sense of autonomous selfhood. Popular culture in the United States and Europe (and increasingly around the world) tells us that we, indeed, have a self that we need to discover, and to discover it we need to look within. When we discover who we are, we must be true to that self, casting off socially conditioned influences to emerge as a truly free, autonomous self-contained being. Some Buddhist-derived approaches to mindfulness implicitly take this approach, using contemplative methods originally designed to undermine the perception of a fixed, permanent self instead to reinforce the individualism so deeply rooted in Western culture. They attempt to strike back against fragmentation by using meditation to reaffirm the integrated, singular individual— the man in the mirror. In this sense, meditation, mindfulness, self-monitoring, and self-observation have the potential to exacerbate the sense of individual isolation, separation from the world, and even narcissism. These interpretations of mindfulness tend to be either purely introspective or instrumental, offering either private psychological comfort or increasing one's effectiveness at doing whatever one happened to be doing anyway. If mindfulness is a tool to enhance the efficiency of the autonomous self, then it can, in the current context, simply reinforce a sense of isolated individuality, to which instrumentalized, decontextualized, commercialized, and corporatized applications of mindfulness become an appendage.

But the other pole of interpretation retains something more substantive from the Buddhist tradition and uses contemplative methods to deconstruct the singular identity, to recognize the radical impermanence and multiplicity of conscious experience, and to open up the buffered self—not to the spirits and demons of old but to a renewed sense of connection and interwovenness with the world. This approach might mitigate the forces of fragmentation not by retreating to a doubly bounded and isolated subjectivity but by admitting the open, fluid, multiple nature of human consciousness and its intimate relatedness to other individuals, to community, to the physical objects in our lives, and to the natural and built worlds we inhabit.

There is, therefore, a tension between two poles of interpretation of modern, secular mindfulness practices: at one pole is mindfulness as a private matter, a matter of personal experience and psychological health or instrumental efficiency; on the other is mindfulness as an awakening to a more urgent sense of connectedness with others, which in turn may foster particular ethical sensibilities. How are these approaches secular? They are all interfused with secularity insofar as they take for granted the value of *this* world instead of striving for another. They mostly accept the modern naturalistic worldview, which shifts attention away from otherworldly aims—eternal bliss in nirvana, rebirth in the pure land—in favor of this-worldly projects. One pole is constituted by a combination of the various elements of Buddhism—self-discipline and karmic responsibility, for example—with the picture of the autonomous self derived from secular modernism and neoliberalism, with its emphasis on free choice, self-responsibility, independence, and self-determination. The other combines other elements of Buddhism—compassion for all sentient beings, interdependence or (in some cases) oneness of self and world—with a greater emphasis on a political, social, and ecological ethic emphasizing systemic suffering and care for the world and other beings. Secularity, with its shift to this-worldly concerns, provides the scaffolding for both poles of this continuum, and the many possibilities in between.

Secularity and Interdependence

These reimaginings of subjectivity through the idea of non-self, as well as the contemporary interpretations of mindfulness I've mentioned, are intimately related to modern articulations of the classical Buddhist doctrine of interdependence. The resurgence and rethinking of the ancient doctrine of dependent arising (*pratītya-samutpāda*) is perhaps inevitable in today's world, in which interconnectivity is the undeniable blessing and curse of the age.

Contemporary interconnectedness allows the grandmother in Taiwan to talk in real time to her grandson in Evansville, Illinois, and the carpet buyer in Los Angeles to put money in the pocket of the sweatshop owner in Pakistan. It allows feminism, white nationalism, lithium batteries, and CO_2 to pervade the globe with ease and speed unimaginable even a generation ago. Modern notions of interdependence extend to the cosmic realm, as humanity gets used to the recently discovered fact of the near-unimaginable vastness of the universe. It is no wonder that people wait in line for hours to stand in Kusama's Infinity Mirror Rooms in order to feel the expansive sense of themselves and their world in countless reflected images mingling and trailing off into endlessness. Art reviewers have noticed the relevance of Kusama's Infinity Mirror Rooms to Buddhism. In his review of one such installation, Michael Venables suggests that it invokes the Buddhist doctrine of emptiness and Thich Nhat Hanh's "interbeing," a popular modern articulation of the doctrine of dependent arising:

> Thinking about Kusama's art, I find the Buddhist concept of "emptiness" to be useful. First, we are all uncertain expressions of a world that is passing. It begins with your own realization of the great cloud of dots, of which you are a part: your own "emptiness of essence."... Might this be something akin to Thich Nhat Hanh's "interbeing"? An affirmation of the inter-connectedness of the essence of all things?... It's the experience of infinity, in an instant of time. A sense of place in what seems like the chaos of our modern world. It's a feeling of hope, of connecting the Kusama dots that can bind us all together.[13]

Venables's drawing together Kusama's Infinity Mirror Rooms with Nhat Hanh's formulation of interbeing gestures toward a particular modern understanding of interdependence as a way of reenchanting the world. Nhat Hanh's descriptions of the cloud in the paper (the cloud produces rain, which waters the tree, which provides material for the paper) or the mutual dependence of roses and garbage (the rose depends on decomposing material to nourish it, then it dies and becomes compost for other plants) provide mundane examples of how things exist in a vast process of mutually interdependent events. We too are a part of this process of the cosmos producing innumerable forms, says Nhat Hanh, transforming into each other in a vast web of interconnected life: "I" am not this limited form but the entire process—the entire ocean and not merely this one temporary wave.[14] Such images take the mundane things of life and weave them together in ways that strive at once to gently obliterate the fixed, independent self of the Enlightenment and ease the frenetic fragmentation of the saturated self through mindfulness. Or perhaps ease *into* that fragmentation and reinterpret it as communion with all things. Nhat Hanh's interbeing takes the raw ingredients of secular cosmology and infuses them with wonder by imagining the reopening of the isolated self into the cosmos, a reintegration into the alienated world, an expansion of the I into all things. But he offers nothing to transgress the basic foundations of the normative discourse of naturalistic secularity—no rebirth in the traditional sense, no heavens or hells, no miracles but mindfully walking on the earth. His unbuffering of secular subjectivity invites in no demons or gods or voices from other worlds. Just clouds, paper, roses, garbage, stars, planets, and each other.

Modern interpretations of interdependence like this take the splintered and decentered and reconfigure it as expansive and grand. They negotiate ways in which the fraying of the self-contained individual, with its scattering across so many spheres of activity, obligation, and meaning, can be called to order as a beautiful, expansive interwovenness with the cosmos. Rather than experiencing the world as a network of hostile forces aligned against an individual self, on the one hand, or as an overwhelming array of ever-splintering selves, on the other, one is invited to imagine all things as contiguous with oneself. Your current form is just one of many that you will take. The "you" that you think is you is not you—the real you is everything. Nhat Hanh's cosmos is not a cold, lifeless, indifferent world receding into nothingness but a living process tossing up form after form in a playful, creative, infinite process. Such a view offers a reenchanted cosmology that affirms the truths of scientific naturalism, with its webs of life and complex systems, giving them a glow of mystery and wholeness.

If modern articulations of interdependence like Nhat Hanh's are enchantments of the secular interdependence, they are also secularizations of earlier Buddhist models. In fact, Kusama's are not the first infinity mirrors to emerge from Asia. A second-century Indian Buddhist text, the *Gaṇḍavyūha Sūtra*—part of the vast *Avataṃsaka Sūtra*—is an orgy of visionary imagery designed to disrupt the ordinary sense of self, space, and time through the infinite multiplication of images. In its climax, the main character, a pilgrim named Sudhana, encounters a great enlightened being, Samantabhadra. Rather than having a conversation, Sudhana gazes at him and sees that there are universes "as infinite as the sands of the Ganges" in each of the pores of his skin. In each universe, Sudhana sees an image of himself.[15] Later, in China in the sixth and seventh centuries, the Huayan Buddhist philosopher Fazang attempted to boil down the narrative to a single image: reality is like a candle in a room with opposite-facing mirrors. Everything reflects and interpenetrates everything else, while still remaining distinct. Every individual contains the whole, and the whole is dependent on each individual. Another image used in Huayan Buddhism has become popular in recent ecological discussions: Indra's net—a net expanding out infinitely with a multifaceted reflecting jewel at each juncture. Each jewel in the net contains the mirror image of all the other jewels, while that single jewel is likewise reflected in all the others.

How is it that such images are drawn into the sensibilities of secular subjectivity and transformed by its hopes, fears, and anxieties? Like modern mindfulness, the Infinity Mirror model of self and world has two possible poles of interpretation. First is an aestheticized version of interdependence, focusing on wonder and comfort, blunting the soft edges of gritty physicality, shedding a soft-focus light on the harsh realities of death, illness, aging, and vulnerability to the capriciousness of the world. In this sense it may be comforting but potentially anesthetizing of the reality that Buddhism itself has insisted we should look at squarely—remember the grizzly descriptions of the interiors of bodies and of corpses in the cremation ground in Buddhist meditation literature.

The other pole, however, holds additional possibilities. If the valorizing of wonder pushes human agency in the direction of passivity (things are beyond my personal control; death and suffering aren't so bad; or, perhaps, everything works together for a grand, cosmic good, so accept and surrender to it), other interpretations insist on ethical, social, and political implications. They urge action. It is no wonder that Indra's net has become a recurring image in ecological and social thought, where it is a potent symbol for the densely interconnected biosphere or the fraying social fabric, both under threat. Shake one part of the net and the reverberations are projected throughout its entirety, like coal smoke from China reaching Alaska or ethnic nationalism in the United States resonating with similar movements throughout Europe, spreading like wildfire across the internet.

Here the vision of intertwinement of self and world tends not (or at least not only) toward passive wonderment but also toward a heightened sense of ethical, social, and political responsibility. Infinite interconnectedness as an ethical imperative entails a recognition that all actions reverberate into the wider world. It opens up attention to what some have called "systemic suffering" perpetrated by the webs of interactions inherent in the globalized economic and political spheres. It encourages reenvisionings of right livelihood to include, for example, the consumer choices of the wealthy and their effects on the lives of the poor and disenfranchised. Some contemporary Buddhist authors encourage a sense of empathy that fosters imagining oneself as the other, as all others—as everything—and taking responsibility for the world as one would a part of one's own body, a body extending infinitely outward.[16]

If I am right that there are tensions—creative and conflictual—between these different approaches to non-self, meditation, and interdependence, then underlying these tensions is perhaps the fundamental tension between versions of Buddhism as mainly a private matter—a matter of personal experience and psychological health—and Buddhism as more active and engaged in the monumental social, political, and ecological problems of the present age. This is not a stark, binary choice, and there is a spectrum of possibilities in between. Someone might simply use mindfulness for reducing stress, for example, but also be an avid political activist. But all of these approaches I've mentioned are interfused with secularity insofar as they take for granted the value of *this* world instead of striving for another.

Conclusion

In his influential book *Philosophy and the Mirror of Nature* (1979), Richard Rorty describes the aspiration of modern philosophy and science to be a "mirror of nature," a "final language" that directly reflects and gives a definitive account of things as they are.[17] That ideal of the mirror of nature still survives today, mainly in the sciences, but in many ways it has given way to a funhouse mirror, where truth is harder to nail down, and competing versions of every conceivable thing multiply endlessly in ever-proliferating internet worlds. If there was ever a time when Thomas Worlidge's young man could gaze into his hand mirror and rest content in the singular vision of an uncomplicated individual self, that time has passed. Today we have multiple identities—personal, professional, legal, political, virtual. They are reflected back at us, in chaotic rapid-fire, in pixilated screens. Meanwhile, the secular cosmology that has emerged recently depicts humans as brief, accidental, and fragile wisps of living matter in an infinitely vast, impersonal universe. The "strategy" of many Buddhists and Buddhist sympathizers in allowing Buddhism to speak to this situation has been to infuse selected Buddhist ideas, practices, and images into secular discourse, with the hope that they will whisper a sense of wonder within confusion, invoke fractal order out of fragmented chaos, and assert responsibility in the face of powerlessness. It remains to be seen whether these bits of Buddhism will be subsumed and tamed by secularity's more rapacious elements—commodification, commercialization, and trivialization—or will have a significant transformative effect on the ethos of secularity itself.

BIBLIOGRAPHY

Bauman, Zygmunt. *Liquid Life*. Cambridge, UK: Polity Press, 2005.

Cleary, Thomas, trans. *The Flower Ornament Scripture: A Translation of* The Avatamsaka Sutra. Boulder: Shambhala, 1993.

Gergen, Kenneth. *The Saturated Self: Dilemmas of Identity in Contemporary Life*. New York: Basic Books, 2000.

Giddens, Anthony. *Modernity and Self-Identity: Self and Society in the Late Modern Age*. Stanford, CA: Stanford University Press, 1991.

Kaza, Stephanie. *Green Buddhism: Practice and Compassionate Action in Uncertain Times*. Boulder: Shambhala Publications, 2019.

Loy, David. *Ecodharma: Buddhist Teachings for the Ecological Crisis*. Somerville, MA: Wisdom Publications, 2019.

Macy, Joanna. *World as Lover, World as Self: Courage for Global Justice and Ecological Renewal*. Berkeley, CA: Parallax Press, 1991.

Nhat Hanh, Thich. *Peace Is Every Step: The Path of Mindfulness in Everyday Life*. New York: Bantam, 1991.

Nhat Hanh, Thich. *The Heart of Understanding: Commentaries on the Prajñaparamita Heart Sutra*. Berkeley, CA: Parallax Press, 1988.

Rorty, Richard. *Philosophy and the Mirror of Nature*. Princeton, NJ: Princeton University Press, 1979.

Taylor, Charles. *A Secular Age*. Cambridge, MA: Harvard University Press, 2007.

———. "Buffered and Porous Selves." The Immanent Frame (website), September 2, 2008. https://tif.ssrc.org/2008/09/02/buffered-and-porous-selves/.

Venables, Michael. "Review: 'Yayoi Kusama: Infinity Mirrors'—Of Dots and Emptiness." *Medium*, July 25, 2017. https://medium.com/future-technology-and-society/review-yayoi-kusama-infinity-mirrors-dots-and-a-sense-of-emptiness-f6ebf8bf363e.

3 | American Cultural Baggage

The Racialized Secularization of Mindfulness in Schools

FUNIE HSU

In her widely circulated piece on Asian American Buddhist youth, "We're Not Who You Think We Are," the writer Chenxing Han reflects, "It saddens me that many Asian Americans—myself included—are reluctant to 'come out' as Buddhist....Sometimes this reluctance arises from a fear of being discriminated against or stereotyped."[1] In writing about Han's article on his *Angry Asian Buddhist* blog, the late Aaron J. Lee, who wrote under the pseudonym arunlikhati, noted that her statements "resonated with me particularly."[2] Han's sentiments ring painfully true for me too. As one who was raised in an Asian American immigrant Buddhist household, the path to publicly identifying as Buddhist was fraught with uncertainty and U-turns, having experienced several episodes of overt racial-religious discrimination during my youth in conservative Orange County, California. In a 2012 blog post recalling the anti-Asian sentiment that led to the murder of Vincent Chin, Aaron referenced the brutal killing of Vietnamese American Buddhist Thien Minh Ly by a white supremacist in Orange County.[3] I was taken aback at the mention of Ly. His murder occurred at my high school, while I was a student. I vividly remember sitting in one of my morning classes when an announcement was made over the

PA system about a body on the tennis courts and police being on the scene. When it was later revealed that the individual was an Asian American Buddhist, my suspicions about the violence embedded in our social marginalization were confirmed. I did not know then that these deeply embodied feelings were telling the (continued) history of Asian American Buddhist exclusion in America.

The feelings of fear described by Han have been instilled through the historical reality of Asian racial and religious exclusion in America. As Duncan Ryuken Williams, Jane Iwamura, Joseph Cheah, and others have documented, the history of Japanese American incarceration,[4] Orientalist representation,[5] and white supremacy[6] has long marginalized Buddhists—who have, and continue to be, of majority Asian descent—as un-American. The more recent proliferation of Buddhism among non-Asian practitioners in the US has popularized the religion in the mainstream, but this growth often still functions within a framework of racial othering for Asian American Buddhists where our practices are shunned as merely cultural adornments. The historical racial-religious marginalization, both from the dominant mainstream and white Buddhist cultures, has structured an internalized shame for many Asian American Buddhists who have picked up on the not-so-subtle hegemonic critiques of Asian and Asian American Buddhisms as "heathen," "idolatry," "superstition," and "cultural baggage": code words for "foreign." For Asian American Buddhists, our religion has been invoked as a threat to continually argue that we do not belong.

The secularization of Buddhism in America is an extension of this exclusion. Though individuals may be drawn to secular Buddhism for myriad reasons and intentions, the structure of secularization, as Vincent Lloyd argues in *Race and Secularism in America*, is not neutral. Rather, it is a "process by which race and religion are excluded or managed."[7] To be clear, I am *not* arguing that individuals participating in secular forms of Buddhist practice are inherently racist. I *am* asserting, however, that the secularization of Buddhism is mediated by power, and this power has functioned to preserve hierarchies through the process of religious exclusion. In this regard, secularization speaks directly to the historical rejection of Asian American Buddhists as un-American elements. It also names the contemporary mechanism that continues this marginalization. Thus, the secularization of Buddhist practices, specifically mindfulness, must be read in the context of Asian racial and religious exclusion in the United States. As a religion, Buddhism is racially marked as a superstitious threat. Examining the secularization of mindfulness in the context of public schools illuminates how the discourse of universality and science filters out that threat, protecting the white mainstream of society. It also highlights how the racialized secularization of mindfulness upholds the neoliberal domination of education that has come to characterize the contemporary era of schooling. Moreover, the impulse to secularize mindfulness reveals a legacy of American cultural baggage about Buddhism and Asia, or as Joseph Cheah describes it, "Orientalized Buddhist baggage,"[8] that is mapped onto secular mindfulness programs in schools.

Secularization of Mindfulness in Schools as Racial-Religious Management

The status of public-school operations during the Covid-19 pandemic era has been a source of much contention and instability. Despite the uncertainty, one increasingly popular feature of contemporary schooling in the twenty-first century has remained a constant in many districts. Whether in person or online, secular mindfulness practices, often referred to as simply "mindfulness," have been integrated into the curriculum at schools across the United States. As a June 22, 2020, EdSource article explains, "The exercise of quiet breathing and focusing on the present moment, mindfulness is a way to become aware of one's emotional state and usher in a sense of calm."[9] Such secular depictions of mindfulness bear promises of a much desired tranquility, thus, the pandemic has turned an already growing movement to incorporate mindfulness into schools into a seemingly urgent task for many school districts.

This turn toward secular mindfulness programs to help students navigate the increasing structural insecurities in America has been an upward trend in schools from coast to coast. The Los Angeles Unified School District "hopes all teachers eventually undergo training in mindfulness and other stress-reduction techniques" and offered a summer school class for all students on mindfulness and staying fit.[10] Ohio congressman Tim Ryan has made a concerted effort to advocate for mindfulness in schools and beyond, gaining the moniker, "the mindful politician."[11] Public schools in New York have turned to mindfulness to combat the increasing stressors impacting the lives of young students and teachers.[12] A study on the 2017 National Health Interview Survey data found that the use of meditation by children ages 4–17 years old in the US increased from 0.6% in 2012 to 5.4% in 2017.[13] The definition of meditation used in the survey includes Buddhist meditation and secular mindfulness. It is important to note, though, that within the public schooling context, mindfulness must be presented as a secular project to ensure a separation between church and state.[14] This legal concern has been a central factor in the spread of mindfulness's scientific secularization in schools.

Though secular mindfulness is often framed around the language of inclusion and universality (via the vocabulary of science), it often deploys an exclusionary negation and/or trivialization of mindfulness's Buddhist framework in order to assert secular inclusion and a scientific rationality to promote its mainstream acceptance. This management of, and distancing from, Buddhism draws from the history of Asian American Buddhist marginalization. For Asian American Buddhists, the secularization of mindfulness often maintains the idea that our religious beliefs are superstitious, dangerous, and have no place in the American public sphere. Thus, while secular mindfulness is valued as a bodily practice (here I allude to the popular Orientalist conceptions of mindfulness as necessarily sitting meditation and to the disciplinary mechanisms of governmentality and biopower described by Michel Foucault and commonly applied in the neoliberal context), its Buddhist framework (and, thus, its Asian association) is not validated as part of the body politic. In this light, we can see that the secularization of mindful-ness functions as racial-religious management to perpetuate Asian American Buddhist "foreignness" and exclusion.

While some secular mindfulness programs might attribute the roots of mindfulness to Buddhism, Oren Ergas and Linor Hadar have observed the emergent pattern of an "'apologetic' statement" in the literature on school-based mindfulness programs that attempts to excuse and manage the practice's association with Buddhism.[15] They cite the following example for consideration, "[M]indfulness originates from Buddhist philosophy, but the practice has been secularised and adapted to Western society in programs such as mindfulness-based stress reduction for adults."[16] That such pro-grams present secularization as penitence for mindfulness's ties to Buddhism demonstrates more than an impetus to uphold the disestablishment clause of the US Constitution. Rather, it highlights the American cultural baggage that has positioned Buddhism as simultaneously exotic and dangerously foreign.[17]

In the example statement above, Buddhism is presented as sim-ply a philosophical tradition in order to elide its religious basis—a maneuver, like secularization, that is infused with racialized dimen-sions of power. "In reality," Scott Mitchell explains, "Buddhism is a religion, complete with all the aspects and depth that implies and the respect a great world religion deserves."[18] While the apologetic statement reduces Buddhism to a philosophy, it also employs the conjunction "but" to perform a secular distancing, evidencing the perception of a persistent taint of religious otherworldliness that requires cleansing.[19] "Proponents of mindfulness meditation and other Buddhist-inspired practices," Mitchell notes, "have positioned themselves as level-headed advocates of practices whose benefits, they claim, are proven by science. It's not hard to imagine that this secular–scientific turn is in part an attempt not to be tarred by the popular stereotype of Buddhism as cultish and downright weird."[20] The depiction of secularization as a necessary process for adapting mindfulness "to Western society" locates this religious otherworldliness in an Orientalized East, and displaces Asian American Buddhists—who have long established Buddhism in the

US and practiced various forms of mindfulness—from the space of the "West," rendering us foreign. Statements like these, with their embedded value judgments and racial-religious implications, instruct a reluctance among young Asian American Buddhists to claim their religious identities, as Han observed. In this regard, the secularization of mindfulness reinforces stereotypical tropes about Buddhism, Asia, and Asian Americans. It leads Asian American Buddhists to anticipate the hegemonic cultural baggage of others and, often, to keep our religion private in order to remain safe from scrutiny and violence.

Science and Universalizing

Science and the language of universalism function as the dominant forms of secularization for mindfulness programs in schools. The popularity of Jon Kabat-Zinn's Mindfulness-Based Stress Reduction (MBSR) has served as a foundation for many of these programs. Thus, MBSR's focus on science as a means to secularize by extracting the "universal applicability" of mindfulness is similarly emphasized in adapting mindfulness for the schooling context.[21] Highlighting the privileging of the scientific paradigm, the "evidence-based yoga and mindfulness program,"[22] Yoga 4 Classrooms, advises yoga and mindfulness educators seeking funding under the 2015 federal Every Student Succeeds Act (ESSA) to "Use science to make the case for yoga and mindfulness in schools."[23] The use of the discourse of science in relation to Buddhism and Buddhist practices is not new. In fact, Asian Buddhist modernists in the nineteenth and early twentieth centuries similarly employed the vocabulary of scientific rationality and universality. Of critical difference, however, is the context of European colonization and Christianizing that the early Asian Buddhist modernists were responding to. Given the circumstance, asserting the scientific basis of Buddhism was a means of survival and continuation in the face of racial-religious colonial domination. Indeed, the insight meditation tradition emerged as a decolonial act against British rule in Burma.[24]

The contemporary turn toward science as a means to secularize mindfulness depicts an entirely different social and political dynamic in the US—one that is imbued with maintaining the racial superiority of whiteness and the Protestant status quo (crucial pillars in the continued settler colonial occupation of Indigenous land). The very need to secularize mindfulness for mass appeal reveals the American cultural baggage of racial-religious hierarchy upon which Asian Buddhist immigrants were constituted as inferior others who required salvation. As Candy Gunther Brown details, "Until the late twentieth century, yoga and meditation remained culturally marginal in the United States. Nineteenth-century Christian missionaries described yoga and meditation for Western audiences as evidence of 'heathen,' 'superstition,' and need of the gospel."[25] With the increasing popular interest in Asia during the post-war period, science emerged as a salvific force by which to wash away mindfulness's association with heathen elements and make it suitable for "Western society." Thus, the "universal applicability" of mindfulness was unleashed from the superstitious container of Buddhism and made appropriate for, and appropriate-able by, schools.

The appeal of universalism in the context of the United States speaks to a long-held belief in its seemingly democratic ideals, beliefs that have fostered an exceptional self-image of the nation and its citizens. The declaration that "all men are created equal," which sounded our call for independence in 1776, invoked a universalism that belied the blatant hierarchies that justified chattel slavery. The language of universalism, therefore, has been utilized to express an imagined equality that is exclusionary at its very foundation. This power dynamic persists in the contemporary discourse of universalism. Angela Davis critiques what she calls the "tyranny of the universal" in relation to the right wing rally cry "All Lives Matter," which attempts to repudiate the validity of Black lives by subsuming it under universal whiteness.[26] Thus, though universalism may engender American democratic sensibilities of inclusion, its rhetorical use often signals a process of exclusion. Such is the case with the secularization of mindfulness for use in public schools.

Here, I would like to make very clear that in making connections between the deployment of universalizing rhetoric I am not drawing parallels between Asian Americans and Black Americans. The circumstances of (ongoing) racialization are distinct for each community. Neither am I saying that individuals who practice secular mindfulness are necessarily ideologically aligned with the All Lives Matter belief system (in fact, I believe that concern with parsing individual behaviors often functions to distract from the actual systemic issues at hand). What I am saying is that the "universal" has been used as a marker by whiteness to assert and maintain the privileges of whiteness, and that in schools, this can be seen in the discourse of secular mindfulness as universal inclusion.

The strong desire to couch mindfulness within secular terms facilitated by the paradigm of science is often articulated as a matter of universal inclusion, both in regards to upholding the separation of church and state, and in relation to making mindfulness available to a wider audience of diverse beliefs. However, since the structure of secularization is one of exclusion and management, as Lloyd points out, it renders any resulting inclusivity in name only. Secularizing mindfulness to advance diversity in schools then justifies the continued exclusion of Buddhist practice and the Asian bodies who are tied to such practice through both individual commitment and/or familial inheritance and the cultural baggage of American Orientalist imagination. The following "Recommendation for Integrating Mindfulness in the Classroom" detailed in a working paper entitled, "Mindfulness in the Classroom: Learning from a School-Based Mindfulness Intervention through the Boston Charter Research Collaborative," demonstrates the manner in which secularization is asserted as a means to achieve inclusivity, yet functions to normalize the primary marginalization of Buddhism and Asian American Buddhists:

> Ensure that mindfulness is integrated with a secular approach. At least in secular schools, it is important for educators to use and teach about mindfulness in a way that neither promotes nor discourages the religious beliefs (or lack of beliefs) of teachers or

students. The primary goal of mindfulness is to enhance well-being by developing one's attention, and thereby, reduce stress, acknowledge and accept one's range of emotions, and engage better with others (as opposed to advancing or inhibiting any particular set of beliefs). Be inclusive in the way that mindfulness is taught. Make sure not to use any objects associated with any particular religion and make sure to never limit or invalidate the belief systems of others. Furthermore, given the central aim of mindfulness as a means to improve well-being, its effects should continue to be held to the same rigorous, scientific evaluation standards as any other practice. Therefore, it is important to be up to date and responsive to any evidence that may emerge which challenges the claims of the effects of mindfulness.[27]

As we see, the recommendation is quite explicit in its assertion of secularity as a technique of inclusion. Stressing that mindfulness should be taught "in a way that neither promotes nor discourages the religious beliefs (or lack of beliefs) of teachers or students," the recommendation is framed with the Free Exercise Clause of the First Amendment in mind. However, in urging secularity, it already discourages the religious beliefs of Buddhists by discounting Buddhism's foundational development of mindfulness within the framework of the eightfold path. It is this Buddhist framework that programs like MBSR have explicitly drawn and simultaneously *distanced* from. While MBSR and some school-based mindfulness programs might make reference to the historical relationship of mindfulness to Buddhism, the aggressive secularity within the above recommendation structures an outright exclusion of any mention of the religion and its influence in developing the practice. In fact, there is no mention of Buddhism or the Asian traditions that maintained Buddhism and mindfulness in Asia and the US in the entirety of the working paper. As the writer Leah Lakshmi Piepzna-Samarasinha has noted, "It's like Asian cultural practices—yoga, meditation, tantra— aren't really Asian according to Western non-Asian folks, because it's as if on some level they can't think of Asian cultures as real places, real cultures, real people."[28] Secular inclusion, therefore,

is predicated upon a historical and continued Orientalized exclusion of Buddhism and the history of Asian American Buddhists,
and it cloaks ongoing domination in the language of democracy.

Though there is no explicit acknowledgment of Buddhism in
the document, there is constant reinforcement of the need for its
exclusion as a foreign element that threatens democratic inclusion, and thus, our nation. The instruction to "Make sure not to
use any objects associated with any particular religion and make
sure to never limit or invalidate the belief systems of others," as a
matter of inclusivity, for example, is a clear allusion to the bells,
chimes (or singing bowls as they've been popularized), and other
accoutrements from Buddhist practice that have often been used
to adorn secular mindfulness with an air of authenticity. It is a
mark of distinction that when utilized by white secular mindfulness
teachers often enables them to walk the delicate balance of "exotic
discovery," "scientific validity," and "diversity/inclusion"; but when
used by Asian and Asian American Buddhist practitioners labels us
as superstitious idol worshippers at worst and (foreign) Oriental
monks at best. Here, however, the use of such religious artifacts is
seen as skirting too close to Buddhism and is therefore denounced
in the name of inclusion. That Buddhism is named and yet remains
nameless in the working paper demonstrates the American cultural
baggage that views it as a dangerous, lingering threat—one that
seems to perpetually haunt the values of the nation and its democratic creed, thereby justifying the American proclivity for viewing
it with constant suspicion.

Just as Buddhism is visible in its invisibility, the phantom of
whiteness is likewise present in its inconspicuousness. The racial
hierarchy embedded within the recommendation is masked by the
lens of scientific objectivity, which positions white privilege and
power as "expertise" and as all-knowing. The idea that mindfulness is secular is just as much socially constructed as the religion
from which it derives (here, I'm referring to the social and cultural
practices that shape all religions and not to any judgment of Buddhism's truthfulness). What does and does not constitute secular
(or religion, for that matter) in the US is shaped by structures of

hegemonic power such as white supremacy and, increasingly, what the Rev. William Barber II and Jonathan Wilson-Hartgrove refer to as Christian Nationalism.[29] The reliance on "rigorous, scientific evaluation standards" to evidence mindfulness's effectiveness in producing desired results in well-being reveals an attempt to naturalize the socially constructed nature of secularization and conceal the elements of whiteness and hegemonic Christianity at play. Additionally, the democratic inclusivity offered through the scientific secularization of mindfulness arranges inclusion only so much as it fits within the broader structure of white-dominant settler colonial occupation and systemic anti-Blackness, excused by techniques appropriated from Asia. Thus, secular mindfulness's invocation of inclusion, once again, maintains histories of ongoing exclusion.

Racialized Secularization and Neoliberal Education

Moreover, in asserting that mindfulness is secular, the implication is that it is a culturally neutral technique, much like we view science. Declaring that the primary goals of mindfulness are quantifiable measures of well-being demonstrates the argument about the role of scientific objectivity. Hence, recognizing any tie to Buddhism would sully mindfulness with the bias of religion and the aura of seemingly superstitious and otherworldly Asian cultures. What results is a logic that frees mindfulness up for appropriation, where anyone can lay claim to its development, brand themselves experts, and oversee its adaptation in schools. As I have previously argued, secular, scientific mindfulness "renders Buddhist practice suitable for mass consumption in the neoliberal educational marketplace of public schools."[30] Secular mindfulness's focus on measurable effects, stress reduction, and academic productivity readily lends itself to neoliberal appropriation since the neoliberal structure of schooling prioritizes efficiency, quantifiable outcomes, and quick, tangible results. The language of science that secular mindfulness is couched within is therefore not only a means to distance from the contamination of foreign religiosity but also a method to further establish, and achieve, the metrics that drive neoliberal education. Thus, "secular mindfulness education's intention of cultivating student well-being is circumscribed within neoliberalism's economic imperative."[31]

In explaining the funding structure of the Every Student Succeeds Act in regards to opportunities for integrating yoga and mindfulness in the classroom, Yoga 4 Classrooms explains, "The first two categories of these grants are highly focused on promoting student health and well-being through initiatives that support mental health, physical health, and social-emotional learning." The program then goes on to note how "the ESSA grant guide for Title IV funding specifically lists 'schoolwide positive behavioral interventions' as a fundable activity."[32] Here, at least two important functions of secular mindfulness in neoliberal schooling are revealed. First, well-being is often tied to notions of behavioral management and intervention. Second, mindfulness as a corrective advances the neoliberal strategy of reframing structural issues as individual concerns. As David Forbes details, "Within neoliberal culture stress becomes decontextualized and interpreted as personal failure of the individual to successfully adapt to the demands of productivity or of being a team player."[33] Utilizing secular mindfulness to promote well-being as a "positive behavioral intervention" normalizes the neoliberal individuation of systemic inequalities and places the burden of reform upon the bodies of students and teachers. It is no coincidence that this individualizing process of isolation mirrors the internalization of shame experienced by many Asian American Buddhists as a consequence of historical exclusion and secular marginalization.

Forbes further explains that teaching mindfulness in schools at the individual level "may be helpful to students' self-development and experience."[34] "However," he cautions, "without a critical take on the context in which they are promoted, teaching individualistic skills such as mindfulness can mask the actual conditions of schooling, including adverse ones that give rise to stress, and divert any critical analysis of the cultural, social, and moral factors that contribute to one's well-being or lack of it."[35] As this chapter demonstrates, I am in strong agreement with the need for a critical take on secular mindfulness in schools. I urgently contend that such critical interpretations must explicitly address the manner in which secular mindfulness not only produces individuated, self-governing bodies for the reproduction of wage labor but also relies on the foundational racial-religious alienation of Asian American Buddhists—the very exclusion that made possible the appropriation of mindfulness as a neoliberal mechanism of self-discipline.

Conclusion: Free from Fear

To develop critical understandings of school-based secular mindfulness is not to dismiss the value that some people have found in such practices, nor to diminish the efforts of educators to reduce student suffering (as a former elementary school teacher, I greatly appreciate the importance and difficulty of this work). Instead, a robust interpretation of the secularization of mindfulness draws much needed attention to the systems of domination that have employed our bodies to sustain oppression through mechanisms of internalized racial-religious shame and neoliberal self-regulation. Moreover, critical analyses of secularization reveal the cultural baggage of the US in regard to Buddhism, demonstrating how its outward projection onto the racialized bodies of Asian American Buddhists is a reflection of the United States' longstanding Orientalizing and exclusionary history. Making this dynamic of power more visible releases Asian American Buddhists from the constant assault of hegemonic alienation. The cultivation of this critical awareness relieves the suffering of individuated fear. Thus, the "mindful" interrogation of secularization facilitates the long overdue public recognition of Asian American Buddhist presence and belonging in the US.

BIBLIOGRAPHY

Barber II, William, and Jonathan Wilson-Hartgrove. "The Unveiling of Christian Nationalism." *Herald Sun*, January 27, 2018. https://www.heraldsun.com/opinion/article196961234.html.

Black, Lindsey I., Patricia M. Barnes, Tainya C. Clarke, Barbara J. Stussman, and Richard L. Nahin. "Use of Yoga, Meditation, and Chiropractors Among U.S. Children Aged 4–17 Years." US Department of Health and Human Services, Centers for Disease Control and Prevention, *National Center for Health*

Statistics Data Brief, no. 324 (November 2018). https://www.cdc.gov/nchs/
data/databriefs/db324-h.pdf.

Boyce, Barry. "The Mindful Politician: Why Tim Ryan is Promoting Mindfulness in Washington." *Mindful*, April 3, 2019. https://www.mindful.org/the-
mindful-politician-why-tim-ryan-is-promoting-mindfulness-in-washington/.

Cheah, Joseph. *Race and Religion in American Buddhism: White Supremacy
and Immigrant Adaptation*. New York: Oxford University Press, 2011.

Davis, Angela. "Angela Davis in Conversation with Astra Taylor: Their Democracy and Ours." Interview by Astra Taylor. *Jacobin*, October 13, 2020. Video,
1:12:49. https://www.youtube.com/watch?v=6ScF2GeTUsY.

Ergas, Oren, and Linor L. Hadar. "Mindfulness in and as Education: A Map of
a Developing Academic Discourse from 2002 to 2017." *Review of Education*
7, no. 3 (2019).

Forbes, David. "Mindfulness and Neoliberal Education: Accommodation or
Transformation?" In *Weaving Complementary Knowledge Systems and Mindfulness to Educate a Literate Citizenry for Sustainable and Healthy Lives*,
edited by Malgorzata Powietrzynska and Kenneth Tobin, 145–58. Leiden,
Netherlands: Brill Sense, 2017.

Gunther Brown, Candy. *Debating Yoga and Mindfulness in Public Schools:
Reforming Secular Education or Reestablishing Religion?* Chapel Hill: University of North Carolina Press, 2019.

Gutierrez, Akira S., Sara B. Krachman, Ethan Scherer, Martin R. West, and John
D. E. Gabrieli. "Mindfulness in the Classroom: Learning from a School-Based
Mindfulness Intervention through the Boston Charter Research Collaborative." *Transforming Education* (January 2019). https://www.transformingedu-
cation.org/wp-content/uploads/2019/01/2019-BCRC-Mindfulness-Brief.pdf.

Han, Chenxing. "We're Not Who You Think We Are," *Lion's Roar*, May 15, 2017.
https://www.lionsroar.com/were-not-who-you-think-we-are/.

Harris, Elizabeth A. "Under Stress, Students in New York Schools Find Calm
in Meditation." *New York Times*, October 23, 2015. https://www.nytimes.
com/2015/10/24/nyregion/under-stress-students-in-new-york-schools-find-
calm-in-meditation.html.

Hsu, Funie. "What is the Sound of One Invisible Hand Clapping? Neoliberal-
ism, the Invisibility of Asian and Asian American Buddhists, and Secular
Mindfulness in Education." In *Handbook of Mindfulness*, edited by Ronald
E. Purser, David Forbes, Adam Burke, 369–81. Switzerland: Springer, 2016.

Iwamura, Jane Naomi. *Virtual Orientalism: Asian Religions and American Popular Culture*. New York: Oxford University Press, 2011.

Jones, Carolyn. "California Schools Turn to Mindfulness to Help Students Cope
with Stress." EdSource, June 22, 2020. https://edsource.org/2020/california-
schools-turn-to-mindfulness-to-help-students-cope-with-stress/633956.

Lee, Aaron J. "We're Not Who You Think We Are." *Angry Asian Buddhist*, July 6, 2016. http://www.angryasianbuddhist.com/2016/07/were-not-who-you-think-we-are/.

——. "Don't Forget Vincent Chin." *Angry Asian Buddhist*, June 23, 2012. http://www.angryasianbuddhist.com/2012/06/dont-forget-vincent-chin/.

Lloyd, Vincent W. "Introduction: Managing Race, Managing Religion." In *Race and Secularism in America*, edited by Jonathon S. Kahn and Vincent W. Lloyd, 1–19. New York: Columbia University Press, 2016.

McMahan, David L., and Erik Braun. "From Colonialism to Brainscans: Modern Transformations of Buddhist Meditation." In *Meditation, Buddhism, and Science*, edited by David L. McMahan and Erik Braun, 1–20. New York: Oxford University Press, 2017.

Mitchell, Scott. "Yes, Buddhism Is a Religion." *Lion's Roar*, November 19, 2017. https://www.lionsroar.com/yes-buddhism-is-a-religion/.

Piepzna-Samarasinha, Leah Lakshmi, "small island: on being a decolonial sri lankan buddhist for a just peace." *Buddhist Peace Fellowship*, October 8, 2013. http://www.buddhistpeacefellowship.org/small-island-on-being-a-decolonial-sri-lankan-buddhist-for-a-just-peace/.

Williams, Duncan Ryuken. *American Sutra: A Story of Faith and Freedom in the Second World War*. Cambridge, MA: Harvard University Press, 2019.

Yoga 4 Classrooms. "About Yoga 4 Classrooms." Accessed Oct. 23, 2020. http://www.yoga4classrooms.com/about-yoga-4-classrooms.

——. "Funding Yoga, Mindfulness and SEL Using ESSA and Title IV Grants," August 29, 2018. http://www.yoga4classrooms.com/yoga-4-classrooms-blog/funding-yoga-mindfulness-sel-essa-and-title-iv-grants.

4 | Curating Culture

The Secularization of Buddhism through Museum Display

PAMELA D. WINFIELD

In the Asian galleries of the Ackland Museum of Art at the University of North Carolina-Chapel Hill, there is a decapitated and amputated silhouette of a standing Buddhist figure. It is headless, handless, and footless. It is nameless as well, since it has lost any iconographic attributes that might indicate its specific identity within the Buddhist pantheon. Its missing head and limbs may have been violently removed during the purges of the nineteenth century, when Japanese ultranationalists tried to promote a "pure" State Shintō orthodoxy devoid of any supposedly foreign Buddhist influence. Or the appendages may simply have been detached and sold separately in the early twentieth century for added commercial profit on the global antiquities market. The figure was part of the private collection of Sherman E. Lee (1918-2008), an eminent scholar, curator, and professor of Asian art history who began teaching at UNC-Chapel Hill in 1983 and who donated the statue to the university's study collection upon his retirement in 2003.

The freestanding and beautifully sculpted block of a body stands approximately two feet tall. Its technical sophistication and refined proportions are typical of Japan's classical Heian period (745-1192). Its fluid robes are rendered through exquisitely carved wooden drapery that outlines a bare male chest and the contours of an implied body beneath the rippling, undulating surface. Its columnar trunk is made from a single block of wood, which exemplifies the so-called one-tree method that characterizes early Heian period sculpture. Little wooden pegs also jut out from its side to the spectator's left. These pegs are the only enduring remnants of its tongue-and-groove construction technique for attaching a separately sculpted body part, which demonstrates the so-called assemblage, or parquetry, method that was typical of later Heian period statues. This is an ideal figure for discussing both sculptural techniques.

Today this statue stands on a floodlit pedestal against the Ackland's Asian gallery walls, and it is studied primarily for its style and form, not necessarily its enlightened identity, doctrinal significance, or ritual role, which have all been lost. The figure silently teaches how classical Japanese Buddhist sculpture in Japan was carved and constructed. Its presence stresses the technical skill, not the devotional purpose or once-imagined soteriological power of the image. Without its head, hands, or feet, with no face or identifying handheld attribute, it is a shell of its former self. There is no salvific agency attributed to it any longer, nor any ritual-functional significance imputed onto it. It has become a *thing* in this museum. It is a beautiful thing, but a thing nonetheless.

This object serves as a fitting starting point for our discussion of the secularization of Buddhism in the modern museum. How should we view such artifacts today, especially in the museum context? How did this process of aesthetic objectification take place, and what are the ethical ramifications of this secularization process for us as museumgoers? Should we take images like this only at face(less) value, as teaching tools for understanding the technical sophistication, material value, and conservation needs of aesthetic artforms? Or should we view them as a point of departure for deeper, hidden histories of colonial exploitation, displacement, and appropriation, which have robbed them of their ritual contexts, doctrinal symbolism, devotional allure, and situated power formerly accorded to them by adherents? Is it possible to simply enjoy the aesthetic pleasure and historic significance of beautifully made Buddhist icons, or must we feel guilty, as our presence in the modern Euro-American museum validates and perpetuates our own complicity in the colonial culture of voyeuristic consumption?

This essay will argue that both perspectives are possible, and indeed appropriate, approaches to the study of Buddhist imagery in the modern museum context. On the one hand, the hermeneutic of suspicion allows us to critique the modern categories of the sacred versus secular that allowed early American collectors to turn powerful religious icons into aesthetic artforms. These well-intentioned individuals nonetheless appropriated and domesticated the exotic Other under the purported secular space of their neoclassical museum roofs. On the other hand, however, the hermeneutic of charity recognizes that such pure, binary categories of sacred versus profane never exist fully in toto, and that the modern museum can alternately be perceived as a pseudo-sacred space. Here, in the hybrid space of the temple museum in particular, the dichotomies of sacred versus secular, icon or art can be mediated, and the museum can be appreciated for its role in cultural preservation and transmission (as opposed to blatantly commercialized Buddhist garden ornaments, for example). This essay concludes that the Buddhist icon in the museum context occupies a middle ground that is constantly being negotiated by multiple actors, be they institutional curators, religious adherents, academic audiences, or the general public at large.

Rationale

This topic is worthy of our sustained attention because it offers a critical yet nuanced analysis of the role of museums in the modern Euro-American understanding of Buddhism. It contributes to the discourse of secularized, psychologized, and commodified Buddhism by considering aestheticized and objectified images of Buddhism as well. By shifting the focus away from texts and translators, and by retraining our attention onto images and institutions, we gain a clearer picture of what contemporary Buddhism literally *looks like* in the museum context.

To help focus attention on the functional dynamics of a world-wide phenomenon, this chapter looks specifically to Japanese Buddhist imagery in Eurpean-style museums as a case study. Japan is a particularly instructive example of larger religio-artistic shifts and movements throughout the world, because its rapid transition to a modern industrialized nation-state is so easily pinpointed. It took only fifteen years to dismantle the military dictatorship of the shogunate that had supported Buddhist institutions for centuries (Commodore Matthew Perry arrived in Tokyo Bay with American gunboats in 1853, and Japan's Emperor Meiji was restored to the throne as a Prussian-style constitutional monarch in 1868). After that, from 1868 to 1872, it only took four more years of overt Buddhist persecution and fire sales of temple treasures to mark the beginning of modern museum collections of Buddhist "art." These museums appeared not only in Europe, America, and Japan but also, ultimately and ironically, back in the temple compounds themselves. The liminal status of objects in these temple treasure-houses, therefore, ultimately calls into question the original ideological split between sacred and profane that characterized the earliest collections of Buddhist "art" in the nineteenth century.

The Ideology of Sacred versus Secular

Conceptually speaking, the European separation of the sacred from the secular was a necessary precondition for the historical development of Buddhist "art" in the modern museum. Both David L. McMahan and Richard K. Payne discuss this separation in their chapters in this volume. From the perspective of intellectual history, in order for devotional Buddhist icons to become merely beautiful *things,* the Euro-American conceptual split between private "religious" and public "secular" spheres had to be imported into Japan.[1]

Previous to foreign influence, Japanese Buddhism had always

functioned in the public sphere. The separation of private religion from public government was completely anathema to the ancient ethos of ritual statecraft that ensured "the pacification and protection of the family-state."[2] State-sponsored monasteries and convents, Buddhist rituals for the emperor's and the shogun's health, and government-regulated ordinations and temple budgets to ensure agrarian prosperity were the norm throughout Japan from roughly the seventh through nineteenth centuries. Buddhist imagery was part and parcel of Japan's public policies for homeland security and national health care. A temple's main image was often consecrated through large public eye-opening ceremonies, in which the artist drew or incised a pupil into the eyes of the image as a final animating act of creation. These public ceremonies ritually transformed inert figures into living images[3] that held the imputed capacity to heal, make rain, protect the state, pacify vengeful spirits, prevent calamities (earthquakes, pestilence, famine, and other disasters) and cause many other "this-worldly" benefits. The founder of esoteric Buddhism in Japan, Kūkai Kōbō Daishi (784–835), for example, claimed that the esoteric teachings that were depicted in painted mandalas were "as useful to the nation as walls are to a city, and as fertile soil is to the people."[4] In particular, throughout the Edo period (1600–1868) when the capital was located in Edo (present-day Tokyo), Buddhist temples functioned as direct organs of the state, receiving government support in exchange for their role as instruments of census collection and social control. The shogunate used Buddhist temples to keep tabs on local households through the compulsory family registration system, and to enforce an official anti-Christian policy through the temple certification system. The very notion of a special "religious" sphere of compartmentalized activity that was somehow set apart from other everyday "secular" concerns was a wholly modern and foreign bifurcation for Japan.[5]

Given these preexisting conditions, the word for "religion" never even existed in Japan before the western European powers arrived. A new word literally had to be invented to fit this completely new and foreign conceptual category. As a result, in the context of larger nineteenth-century attempts to standardize a new national Japanese language, numerous scholars, linguists, and authors experimented with a series of two-character compounds until they finally translated the foreign concept of "religion" as "sect-teaching." Once established in the lexicon and in the cultural imaginary of Japan, however, "religion" was defined as private belief, influenced in large part by Christian missionary activity that also began making inroads during this period. Freedom of religion was guaranteed in the Meiji Constitution as long as it remained in the private sphere; as soon as it began to encroach on public order and stability, however, the state was justified in suppressing it, as it did with many so-called New Religious Movements (NRMs) at the time.[6] By apposition, "the secular" referred to public and universally held civic values and activities such as politics, economics, social structures, gender roles, public education, and other sectors such as sport and leisure. Large-scale public Buddhist ceremonies did continue throughout the Meiji period, especially to commemorate sectarian founders' memorials, but domestic and funerary Buddhism truly came into its own as part of the private sphere during this period.[7] Eventually, the political ideology of State Shintō slotted into the secular category, as it was understood to be a form of civic religion or patriotic devotion to the new Japanese nation.

Church-State symbiosis

Sacred	Secular
(Private)	(Public)
Christianity	State Shintō (civic religion, patriotism),
Domestic Buddhism	[Buddhism]
NRMs	Politics, economics, social structures,
	gender roles, public education, etc.

In the realm of visual culture, the new modern secular ideal rejected the depiction of "religious" figures as a result of a principally Protestant animus against representational and specifically anthropomorphic imagery that smacked of idolatry. The salvific power of Buddhist icons was consequently dismissed as mere superstition by modernizing elites, but Buddhist "art" as defined by Euro-American ideals could be appreciated for its technical skill, precious materials, impressive provenance, historical significance, and well-preserved condition. Within this imported bifurcated conceptual scheme, Buddhist icons could be stripped of their "religious" significance and could be reclassified according to their "secular" aesthetic value.

This process was part of what Richard Gombrich and Gananath Obeyesekere first labeled as "Protestant Buddhism,"[8] or what Bernard Faure has called the "modern gaze,"[9] which could reduce a ritually empowered and empowering icon in its temple context into a mere piece of "art." Empowered figures were thus emptied of their perceived apotropaic, thaumaturgic, or soteriological powers and instead were held up as mere symbols of the dharma or quaint vestiges of a once-powerful pantheon that had been relegated to the realm of mythology for our optical consumption and pleasure. This process of aestheticizing the icon did a certain colonizing violence to the Buddhist image on its own terms. Japan was never fully colonized by foreign powers in the political, economic, or military sense—but to the beleaguered Buddhist temples of the early Meiji period, the technical distinctions between political and cultural colonization were largely immaterial. In the disenchanted world of the modern, the living power of the Buddhist icon could be reduced to the aesthetically pleasing contours of forms, much like the wooden body on display in the Ackland Museum collection today.

Of course, the very notion of a supposedly universal canon of beauty was a historically contingent Western European Neoplatonic social construction and was thus appealing to the foreign colonizer-collectors. Universalism in this sense could reject and neutralize the power of particularism by dissolving and domesticating all foreign colonized cultural expressions into the same sterilized, reductionistic sphere. Since the outward form, color, line, texture, and other formal compositional elements of the Euro-American notion of "art" could be appreciated by anyone in the world, essentially defined as fellow adherents of Euro-American values who justified their own collections with such universalist claims, it didn't matter where the objects were located or where they originally came from. At the time, private collectors often displayed their acquired objects by mixing and matching them according to their own socially constructed aesthetic sensibilities, not necessarily according to today's curatorial standards of regional or historical provenance. The Barnes collection of European art in Philadelphia is the most famous example of this idiosyncratic approach to installing art (for example, interspersing Impressionist paintings with medieval arms and armor to create visually pleasing patterns on the wall). In terms of Asian art displays, likewise, the Peacock Room for Asian ceramics created by James McNeill Whistler and Thomas Jeckyll (reinstalled at the Freer Gallery in Washington, DC) and the Guimet Museum's Buddhist Pantheon in Lyon and Paris also present side-by-side collected works with vast geographical, historical, material, functional, and doctrinal differences. This kind of universalizing, ahistorical aesthetic was typical of late nineteenth and early twentieth century display strategies.

Moreover, the idea of world art in a public, secular museum could put a patina of respectability and charity on the violent appropriation of colonized cultures. Just as early natural history museums at the time showcased the sanitized beauty of brutal safaris, so too did early Western art museums showcase the trophy spoils of Euro-American adventurer-collectors abroad. Both types of museums presented the fascinating yet also somewhat threatening exotic Other in a safe space, where it could be examined with admiration or aversion or both. As James Dobbins remarks, "In their most generous moments, museumgoers in the West treated such objects as aesthetic treasures from far-off lands. But in more condescending moments, they looked upon them as exotic artifacts from a strange religion."[10] The process of aestheticizing the Buddhist Other and emplacing it within the controlled confines of the European-style art museum domesticated it and made it accessible for elite Euro-American consumption and edification. At the same time, thanks to the philanthropic largesse of well-meaning but patronizing donors, art museums could also educate the masses who didn't have the means to go on the same kind of grand world tours as the elite collector-donors did. The rationale behind the free entrance day at the Metropolitan Museum of Art in New York, for example, was that sheer exposure to great works of world art would inspire the poor to pull themselves up by their own bootstraps and join in the great capitalist system of science, art, and industry.[11] The ideological foundations for the respectable and charitable modern art museum were born.

Historical Movements: Persecution

Historically speaking, the process of secular museumification in Japan unfolded in three steps, from persecution to preservation and then to paradox. That is, the initial persecution of Buddhism from 1868–1872 triggered the second movement to preserve Japan's Buddhist imagery in both foreign collections and through the Japanese National Treasure system. Then, paradoxically, there was a third feedback phenomenon in the twentieth century, as Buddhist temples in Japan began constructing temple museums or "treasure-houses" to display the material elements of their ritual culture as "art," mirroring the very secular institutions that plundered their temple treasures in the first place over a century and a half before.

After America forcibly opened Japan to foreign trade, some traditionalists in the 1850s wanted to "revere the emperor and expel the barbarians," but other pro-Western modernizers embraced these foreign ideas, along with European fashions and meat-eating, as part of the country's rapid evolution toward what they considered to be "civilization and enlightenment." Initially, this rapid modernization process occurred at the expense of Buddhism.

In the context of exploitative trade agreements with the Western European powers, the sudden and complete withdrawal of government support for Buddhist temples after the Meiji Restoration of 1868, and the popular iconoclastic cries to "abolish Buddhism and destroy Shakyamuni [Buddha]," thousands of forcibly laicized Buddhist priests in Japan were forced to sell off their temple treasures.[12] In addition, from 1868 to 1872, the new Meiji government passed a devastating series of edicts that forcibly separated a purportedly pure Japanese Shintō state orthodoxy from a supposedly foreign and contaminating Buddhist tradition that had arrived in Japan from India via China and Korea thirteen centuries previously. These edicts were soon overturned, and Buddhism rallied and eventually recovered from this four-year period of overt persecution. However, its weakened influence in the public sphere and its desperate selling off of Buddhist icons to Euro-American collectors marks a watershed moment in the roughly 150-year-old history of secularized Buddhism both in the West and in Japan.

In the early Meiji context, therefore, traditional Buddhist creators of Buddhist images or icons were considered to be in a class or category of their own and viewed as outdated and antimodern. Artificially separating religion from all other spheres of public life, and artificially setting Buddhism apart from State Shintō meant that Buddhist icons occupied a discrete category that was essentially unrelated to the public sphere or to other universally held civic values of the modern nation-state. It is for this reason that in the 1870s, for example, the zealous modernizer and vice minister of Kyoto, Makimura Masanao (1834–1896), ordered stone buddhas to be used as construction materials and displayed a particularly sacred "hidden Buddha" icon in the secular space of his prefectural office.[13] It is also for this reason that traditional Buddhist iconography and production techniques were not taught in the new Tokyo School of Fine Arts that opened its doors to students in 1889. It only taught European-style fine art, as opposed to decorative or applied arts and crafts, as the philosopher Nishi Amane (1829–1897) first distinguished in his systematic science of beauty in the 1870s.[14]

The normative influence of European art and artistry became so pervasive in the early Meiji period that the great lineage holder of decorative folding screens, Kanō Hōgai (1828–1888), worked in collaboration with the leading American collector and preservationist, Ernest Fenellosa (1853-1908), to help conserve the traditional Japanese-style of painting called *nihonga* (lit. "Japan-painting"). But even this style of decorative painting slotted into the "secular" category, as its painted subjects were primarily "nonreligious" landscape or social scenes. "Religious" themes and artists were not even part of the conversation.

Preservation

Given the extreme conditions of the early Meiji period, American expatriate collectors such as Fenellosa and his fellow Bostonian William S. Bigelow (1850-1926) acquired a vast treasure trove of Buddhist imagery. At the time, they were genuinely concerned with the preservation of the Japanese Buddhist artistic tradition but were also simultaneously benefiting from the economic hardship of the forcibly laicized Buddhist priests. In 1910, Bigelow installed their Japanese consultant and colleague, the scholar Okakura Kakuzō (also known as Okakura Tenjin), as the first curator of their Asian collection at the Museum of Fine Arts in Boston. Their core collection was later augmented by the bequests of future generations of great American collectors of Japanese Buddhist "art" and calligraphy, such as Mary Griggs Burke (1916-2012), Sylvan Barnett (1926-2016), and William Burto (1921-2013), among others.

Other significant early collectors of Buddhist "art" in America during this period were Charles Lang Freer (1854-1919), whose Chinese collection is still housed today in Washington, DC. The Sri Lanka collection created by Ananda Coormaraswamy (1877-1947) is still held at the Los Angeles County Museum of Art. The controversially sourced Chinese collections from Langdon Warner (1881-1955) at Harvard's Fogg Art Museum, as well as Warner's Japanese collection at the Nelson-Atkins Museum in Kansas City, Missouri, were notable additions to other central and Southeast Asian collections of Buddhist imagery in America.[15]

Concurrently in Europe, while Russian, British, and German collections of Buddhist "art" expanded, the French industrialist and avid world traveler Émile Guimet (1836–1918) was commissioned in 1876 to study the religions of the "Extrême-Orient" (East Asia), and he acquired an equally impressive collection of Chinese and Japanese Buddhist objets d'art for his eponymous museum in Lyon in 1879. He moved his Musée Guimet to Paris ten years later, where his core collection of Buddhist materials was joined in 1912 by Tibetan works courtesy of Jacques Bacot (1877–1965). In 1927, the Musée Guimet added a collection of manuscripts from Dunhuang provided by Paul Pelliot (1878–1945) as well as works from the Trocadéro Museum of Indochina. Other additions included objects from excavations in Afghanistan (in the 1920s), Khmer Cambodia (in 1936), and the Louvre's entire Asia collection, gained in exchange for the Guimet's Egyptian collection (in 1945).[16] By the mid-twentieth century, the aesthetic objectification of once-powerful Buddhist icons was complete, and the "museumification" of Buddhist art in Europe and America was already well established.

In addition to exporting its Buddhist images to European and American museums, Japan itself began to "museum-ify" its religious heritage back at home. In a feedback loop typical of the era, the once iconoclastic Meiji government began to preserve what it considered to be the new nation's historic and artistic treasures.[17] In 1872, the year that the devastating edicts suppressing Buddhism were rescinded, the government began the process of establishing its first national museum in Tokyo.

The idea for such an institution originally derived from Euro-American historical museums, which, at the time, primarily meant natural history museums. However, as Japanese study tours abroad increased with international exhibitions and world fairs, the Japanese were exposed to a wide range of Euro-American art museums.[18] For example, the Louvre Museum was established in 1793, well before the 1867 Exposition Universelle in Paris, which saw the first official Japanese delegation at a world fair.[19] The Victoria and Albert Museum in London was established in 1852, well before the 1885 Colonial and Indian Exhibition that incidentally inspired the 1885 Gilbert and Sullivan Orientalist musical, *The Mikado*. And the Art Institute of Chicago was established in 1879, well before the 1893 Columbian Exposition that famously hosted the World Parliament of Religions. Here, Zen Master Shaku Sōen (1860-1919), his assistant D. T. Suzuki (1870-1966), and Anagarika Dharmapala (1864-1933) favorably introduced Buddhism to their Protestant American hosts as a nontheistic, nonimagistic, and nonritualistic practical philosophy, arguably constituting another watershed moment in the secularizing process of Buddhism in the American cultural consciousness.

Meanwhile back in Japan, at the great Tōdaiji temple in the ancient capital of Nara, the Meiji government sponsored the first exhibition of over one thousand Buddhist works of "art" from nearby Nara temples in 1887.[20] Five years later in 1882, the National Museum in Tokyo acquired from the Imperial Household Collection 319 objects from the ancient Nara temple of Horyūji, which Hōryūji had "gifted" to the emperor in exchange for temple renovation funds. Beginning in 1884, the government conducted occasional surveys and inspection tours of temple and shrine treasures "that demonstrated an ideal, universal aesthetic."[21] In 1895, the Nara National Museum opened its doors (though its famous Shōsōin collection of eighth-century materials would not be added until 1914), and the Kyoto National Museum followed two years later in 1897. By the turn of the century in Japan, therefore, the museumification of Japanese Buddhist "art" was complete.

This process was aided by official Japanese government policy. In 1897, the Meiji government passed the Ancient Temples and Shrines Preservation Law, which categorized its tangible cultural patrimony according to the European model that focuses on masterpieces. It designated its most ancient temples and historically significant Buddhist icons as National Treasures or Important Cultural Properties at the municipal, regional, or national levels.[22] In addition, artists, calligraphers, performing artists, and folk craftspeople could also be classified as Living National Treasures or, more formally, as Preservers of Important Intangible Cultural Properties. A series of other laws protecting historic, scenic, or natural monuments as well as the "cultural landscapes" of social life throughout Japan's long history ultimately resulted in the 1950 Law for the Protection of Cultural Properties, which is still today administered through Japan's Agency for Cultural Affairs. This reclassification and sub-ordination of "religious imagery" under the invented category of government-regulated secular "cultural properties" mirrors the ideological assumptions of early Euro-American aesthetes and is indicative of the larger shifts of Japan's modernization process.

Paradox

A recent twist in this process is the development of temple muse-ums, which paradoxically reinforce the aesthetic ideology of the very institutions that exploited the Buddhist temples' misfortune a century and a half ago. This phenomenon of displaying temple treasures certainly draws upon the annual airings of Kyoto's great Zen temple collections in the fall and spring, as well as other trav-eling picture shows with guided explanations that began in the Edo period for temple fundraising and reputation-raising purposes.[23] However, beginning in the twentieth century, Japanese temples began constructing dedicated temple museums or "treasure-houses" that adopted and emplaced modern museological princi-ples and practices within the temple compound for the first time.[24] If the nineteenth century transferred the temple out to the museum, then the twentieth century transported the museum back into the temple grounds.

For example, the Reihōkan sacred treasure hall at Kōyasan mon-astery in Wakayama prefecture (est. 1921) and the Hōmotsukan treasure hall at Tōji temple in Kyoto (est. 1963) were the first to "museumify" the arts of esoteric Shingon Buddhism. Elsewhere, the Hōmotsukan treasure hall at Sōjiji temple in Yokohama (est. 1974, in honor of Keizan's 650th death anniversary) and the small three-room temple galleries at Eiheiji temple in Fukui (est. 2002, in honor of Dōgen's 750th death anniversary) museumified the arts and artifacts of Sōtō Zen Buddhism.

These temple museums foreground the objects' historic importance to the sect and their prestigious provenance (for example, letters or calligraphy from the emperor, shogun, or feudal lords). They also note the precious materials, aesthetic value, calligraphic flourish, technical sophistication, and pristine condition of the objects. The explanatory texts accompanying these works also occasionally include doctrinal explanations and artist information, when known.

Like any art museum, modern temple museums systematically research and catalog their objects according to international museum standards, employ modern lighting designs, and utilize temperature and humidity control devices in modern or postmodern architectures and display cases. This is in contradistinction to the less consistent but still fairly effective light and temperature control of the traditional Japanese storage warehouse. In addition, the display strategy of temple museums is to exhibit isolated objects on a rotational basis according to their material format, display requirements, and chronological age. As a result, curators sequentially display all the handscrolls together, or hanging scrolls, or freestanding sculptures, or decorative arts, and so on, organized according to their period dates. By contrast, the in situ mixed-media altar arrangements of Buddhist temples assemble a cacophony of forms from all time periods all in the same space: a central Buddha image may be surrounded by lesser deities, painted murals, hanging mandalas or scrolls, suspended gilt bronze banners with bells, ritual implements, offertory tables, incense burners, ancestral tablets, wooden fish drums and metal gongs, red felt runners along tatami mat floors, painted coffered ceilings, and all the other *materia liturgica* for the ritual adornment of the sanctuary.[25]

Perhaps most importantly, the functions and intended audiences of these two kinds of institutions differ significantly, even if they now occupy the same temple grounds. The modern treasure hall (Hōmotsukan) is designed to preserve the material tradition for the future and to educate the general public. It requires no initiation other than an entrance fee and no faith commitment other than a tourist's general interest in checking off the must-see highlights. The temple's in situ altar display, by contrast, is designed by insiders for insiders to inspire devotional acts, provide a visual focus and a presiding deity for ritual activity, and elicit temple donations through offertory boxes before each image. (This latter convention is not a modern invention, but was already present in the Edo period, as evidenced by temple financial registers like the one at Zenkōji convent).[26] It is meant for adherents, or potential ones, drawn in by what Lindsey Jones calls the allure of the spectacle.[27]

Afterword: The Japanese Temple Museum as a Hybrid Space?

A notable exception to this distinction between museum and altar display is the Reihōkan museum at Kōyasan, which conflates the two modes by emplacing offertory boxes in front of particularly famous Heian-period statues. These powerful esoteric deities have been moved to the museum for conservation purposes, but visitors to the Kōyasan complex continue to toss in coins, bow before the statues, and offer a silent prayer for health, or safety, or perhaps success with college admissions examinations, before moving on to the next image. In theory they offer five-yen (go-en) coins, since in Japanese "five yen" and "good luck" are pronounced in the same way.

This kind of ritual activity replicates the kind of behavior that regularly occurs in temple settings all across Japan, and it embodies the kind of deeply conditioned muscle memory that Catherine Bell has called a "socially instinctive automatism of the body."[28] As a result, at the Reihōkan, the institutional distinction between temple and museum is a porous and ill-defined one. The mixed signals of offertory boxes and explanatory wall copy creates a kind of hybrid space in which ritual activity may or may not take place, and in which the Buddhist image may or may not be viewed in a particularly reverent or worshipful light.

To theorize this phenomenon, Sally M. Promey has observed that "aestheticization, with all its apparent neutralizations, actually often respiritualizes both secular and religious objects, articulating them back into new domains of animation and understanding."[29] This means that the secularization process of Buddhism through museum display may not always be unidirectional; it may sometimes be elliptical, returning back in on itself to reanimate and reinspire devotion, albeit in an altered environment. As Fabio Rambelli has likewise observed about Buddhist images in modern museums,

> This relocation of images is done in order to preserve them and enhance their sacredness, but it results in a radical redefinition of their semiotic and cultural status.... And yet, selecting sacred objects and displaying them as part of processes of cultural redefinition (either positive or negative) may at times result in the resacralization of those images and even of the entire religious system associated with them.[30]

This resacralization of Buddhist imagery may also arguably be taking place in the renowned Gallery of Hōryūji Treasures that opened to the public in 2000. This pavilion, next to the Tokyo National Museum in Ueno Park, was designed by the great architect Taniguchi Yoshio (b. 1937) to house more than three hundred objects from the famous seventh-century temple Hōryūji. Taniguchi writes of his atmospheric design,

> Out of a desire to respect both the sublime works to be displayed and the natural setting, I made it my goal in designing the new Gallery of Hōryūji Treasures to create on the site an environment of a kind that has become all too rare in present-day Tokyo— that is, an environment characterized by tranquility, order, and dignity...creating a space that establishes a special relationship between visitors and the exhibited works.[31]

Paradoxically, via the process of creating and populating unique museum spaces with deconsecrated, decontextualized, and deanimated visual and material objects, the museum has become rean-

imated and reenchanted with all the displaced power of what we
formerly recognized as "religion." Perhaps, as Jeff Wilson writes
of secularized Buddhist meditation and mindfulness-based stress
reduction (MBSR), "The intention and approach behind MBSR
[like museum displays] were never meant to exploit, fragment, or
decontextualize the dharma, but rather to recontextualize it."[32] As
a result, the secularization of Buddhism through museum display
has certainly done damage by ripping the icons from their ritual
settings, but it has also preserved those images and sometimes
consciously reframed them as sacred objects, especially within the
temple museum context.

The temple museum phenomenon takes on new levels of self-
conscious self-constructions with the advent of temple museums
dedicated to the charismatic founders of early-twentieth-century
religious movements. The museum dedicated to the life and ministry of Rev. Nikkyō Niwano (1906–1999) of Risshō-Kōseikai (est.
1938) is a case in point. This is a masterfully orchestrated museum
journey that takes the visitor through Niwano's early life and education, his association with Miyoko Naganuma, his devoted study of
the Lotus Sūtra, his split from the Nichiren-based Reiyūkai group,[33]
and his tireless interfaith efforts for world peace, which led to the
eponymous Niwano Peace Prize and his many accolades. But it is
in the final galleries of the hall that the so-called "secular" aspects
of his life are, paradoxically, emphasized. The most memorable
elements for this author, at least, were the everyday photographs
and "contact relics" such as his working desk and swivel chair, his
reading glasses and television set. His lengthy kimono, long walking
stick, and a frosted glass silhouette of his tall slender figure remind
the visitor of his bodily frame and his basic common humanity.
This museum is a hagiographic homage to a deeply religious man,
but it uses anthropological museum techniques to humanize and
normalize him at the same time. It is self-consciously a shrine to
the master and simultaneously a very modern memorial museum.

To unpack these kinds of examples, we must dismantle the diametrically opposed categories of sacred versus profane, and rather

consider the two as intimately connected. Seen in this transformed light, the Ackland Museum figure is not just a *thing*, but rather, a liminal figure. It always was and still is a material object, but once it was sculpted, ritually empowered, and worshipped as an enlightened figure for centuries, its wooden form became transformed into an enlightened body. Then after its modern dismemberment and dislocation into an American museum, it now occupies a liminal status, as both a material and physical body, as both a tree and a Buddha. Buddhist doctrines have long taught that insentient objects can and do preach the dharma by their very nature, and that even insentient grasses and trees can become a Buddha. Perhaps, then, this fancy block of wood has always already been enlightened and enlightening, regardless of its appearance in nature, or in a temple, or in a museum environment. Perhaps art, or enlightenment itself, only exists in the "true dharma eye" of the beholder.

BIBLIOGRAPHY

Bell, Catherine. *Ritual Theory, Ritual Practice.* New York: Oxford University Press, 1992.

Bernstein, Andrew. *Modern Passings: Death Rites, Politics and Social Change in Imperial Japan.* Honolulu: University of Hawai'i Press, 2006.

Eliade, Mircea. *The Sacred and Profane: The Nature of Religion.* New York: Houghton Mifflin Harcourt Press, 1959.

Faure, Bernard. "The Buddhist Icon and the Modern Gaze." *Critical Inquiry* 24, no. 3 (1998): 768-813.

Forbes, Roy Tetsuo. "Schism, Orthodoxy and Heresy in the History of Tenrikyō: Three Case Studies," master's thesis, University of Hawaii, 2005.

Garon, Sheldon M. "State and Religion in Imperial Japan, 1912-1945." *Journal of Japanese Studies* 12, no. 2 (1986): 273-302.

Graham, Patricia J. *Faith and Power in Japanese Buddhist Art, 1600-2005.* Honolulu: University of Hawai'i Press, 2007.

Hakeda, Yoshito. *Kūkai Major Works.* New York: Columbia University Press, 1972.

Isomae, Junichiro. "Deconstructing 'Japanese Religion': A Historical Survey." *Japanese Journal of Religious Studies* 32, no.2 (2005): 235–48.

Jones, Lindsay. *The Hermeneutics of Sacred Architecture: Experience, Interpretation, Comparison.* Vol. 2: *Hermeneutical Calisthenics: A Morphology of Ritual-Architectural Priorities.* Cambridge, MA: Harvard University Center for the Study of World Religions, Harvard University Press, 2000.

Josephson, Jason Ananda. *Inventing Religion in Japan.* Chicago: University of Chicago Press, 2012.

Kaminishi, Ikumi. *Explaining Pictures: Buddhist Propaganda and Etoki Storytelling in Japan.* Honolulu: University of Hawai'i Press, 2006.

Lee, Sonya S., ed. *Journal of the History of Collections: Special Edition: Ideas of Asian in the Museum* 28, no. 3 (November 2016).

Levine, Gregory. *Daitokuji: The Visual Cultures of a Zen Monastery.* Seattle, WA: University of Washington Press, 2006.

Lockyer, Angus. "Japan and International Exhibitions, 1862-1910." In *Commerce and Culture at the 1910 Japan-British Exhibition: Centenary Perspectives,* 27–34. Leiden, Netherlands: Global Oriental/Brill, 2013.

Marra, Michael F. "The Creation of the Vocabulary of Aesthetics in Meiji Japan." In *Since Meiji: Perspectives in the Visual Arts of Japan, 1868-2000,* edited by J. Thomas Rimer. Honolulu: University of Hawai'i Press, 2016.

Mitchell, Matthew. "Beyond the Convent Walls: The Local and Japan-wide Activities of Daihongan's Nuns in the Early Modern Period (c. 1550-1868)." PhD diss., Duke University, 2016.

Oakes, Julie Christ. "Japan's National Treasure System and the Commodification of Art." In *Looking Modern: East Asian Visual Culture from the Treaty Ports to World War II,* edited by Jennifer Purdle and Hans Bjarne Thomsen. Chicago: Center for the Art of East Asia, University of Chicago with Art Media Resources, 2009.

Promey, Sally, ed. *Sensational Religion: Sensory Cultures in Material Practice.* New Haven, CT: Yale University Press, 2014.

Rambelli, Fabio, and Eric Reinders, *Buddhism and Iconoclasm in East Asia: A History.* London and New York: Bloomsbury Academic, 2012.

Schopen, Gregory. *Buddhist Monks and Business Matters: Still More Papers on Monastic Buddhism in India.* Honolulu: University of Hawai'i Press, 2004.

Taylor, Charles. *A Secular Age.* Cambridge, MA: Harvard University Press, 2007.

Thomkins, Calvin. *Merchants and Masterpieces: The Story of the Metropolitan Museum of Art.* New York: Henry Holt, 1989.

Watsky, Andrew M. *Chikubushima: Deploying the Sacred Arts of Momoyama Japan.* Seattle: University of Washington Press, 2003.

Wilson, Jeff. *Mindful America: Meditation and the Mutual Transformation of Buddhism and American Culture.* New York: Oxford University Press, 2014.

5 | Establishing the Pure Land in the Human Realm

CHARLES B. JONES

In a 1968 monograph, the eminent Harvard religious scholar Holmes Welch described Venerable Taixu (1890-1947) as "the most important figure in the history of modern Chinese Buddhism."[1] A tireless advocate for Buddhist renewal, Taixu worked hard to reform a monastic system widely viewed as parasitic and corrupt, sought ways to keep Buddhism relevant to the changing needs of a rapidly modernizing nation, and helped organize Buddhists into national and international associations for the pursuit of common goals. As a conceptual foundation for these reforms, he generated the vision of "Buddhism for human life" (*rensheng fojiao*) to counter the religion's primary occupation with funerals and memorial services or "Buddhism for the human realm" (*renjian fojiao*) as a way to focus energy on the needs of human beings rather than on making offerings to spirits and deities. Nowadays both of these terms are commonly rendered into English as "humanistic Buddhism." Within this overall framework, we find his proposal for the establishment of "the pure land in the human realm" (*renjian jingtu*), an idea he laid out most extensively in his 1926 essay "On the Establishment of the Pure Land in the Human Realm" (*Jianshe renjian jingtu lun*; hereafter referred to as "essay").

Scholars have generally assumed that this essay's main purpose is to redirect Buddhism from escapism to engagement and to exhort Buddhists to focus their efforts on the problems of the present world rather than on the search for rebirth in a buddha land after death. However, when one reads this essay along with Taixu's other writings and speeches on Pure Land, one notices that they are not so narrowly focused and that they mix the modern and the traditional in sometimes awkward ways. The latest astronomy blends with premodern Buddhist cosmology; long scriptural citations occupy a great deal of space; the "human realm" turns out to include mythical places such as the paradisiacal northern continent of Uttarakuru and several buddha lands in addition to the present world; he nowhere discourages the aspiration for rebirth in either Amitābha's Pure Land or in the Tuṣita Heaven with Maitreya; and so on. This chapter will bring the full range of subjects addressed in this pivotal essay up for discussion by giving a more complete summary than has been available heretofore;[2] it will then give a précis of previous Western scholarship on it. The conclusion will show that Taixu is a transitional figure and that his image as a modernizer or secularizer came from Western observers rather than from his Chinese audience.

Summary of Taixu's Essay

Section One

Taixu opens his essay by stating that human beings have two basic needs: (1) security of life and resources in the present world, and (2) "immortality and bliss" after death. While Buddhism does discuss ways of obtaining the former, the latter is provided by belief in the Pure Land of Amitābha (p. 356).[3] People attempt to gain security of life by extending their lifespans and having children; they try to acquire security of resources by establishing households, nations, and other social and political structures (pp. 356–57). The mythical northern continent of Uttarakuru, which Taixu identifies as a planet within the solar system, serves to fulfill these desires, a point he illustrates with a very long quotation from the "Chapter on the Continent of Uttarakuru" from the *Sutra on the Arising of Worlds*[4] (pp. 357–71). Taixu seems to think that since Uttarakuru lies within our solar system, it might one day serve as a place where beings may achieve security of life and resources in a future rebirth gained by the good karma of Buddhist virtue. He also inserts notes into the quotation to show that people can create a paradise on Earth similar to Uttarakuru through technology. However, Taixu acknowledges that even in Uttarakuru a life that lasts a thousand years comes to an end, and Buddhism teaches the possibility of rebirth in the Pure Land of Amitābha as a way to attain the second human need, immortality and bliss. In support of this, he quotes a lengthy description of the Land of Bliss from the *Larger Sukhāvatī-vyūha-sūtra* (pp. 372–82).[5] Taixu thus admits that improvements made in the present human world provide benefit only while people are alive and that Buddhists must still think about what happens after they die.

Section Two

Section 2 is titled "Problems of Contemporary Humanity,"[6] and in it Taixu describes all of the difficulties that vex humankind in three broad categories: (1) disasters of the natural world, (2) problems internal to the self (that is, psychological problems), and (3) societal problems. After listing some examples of each, he says this: "In Uttarakuru one is removed from the problems of the natural world and of society, but problems based in the self remain. Only in the Pure Land of Amitābha does one escape from all suffering. That is why it is called 'Utmost Bliss.'"[7] He goes on to describe all the groups and interests whose competition leads to the savage and murderous struggles of the modern world. In a clarion call for Buddhists to help cleanse the present world of these problems, he says, "Please! Take up the Buddhist slogan 'turn the five evils into the five virtues'[8] as counsel for everyone who has a mind to wake up!"[9]

Taixu follows this call with another very long quotation from the *Larger Sukhāvatī-vyūha-sūtra* in which the Buddha Śākyamuni exhorts the bodhisattva Maitreya to work diligently to quell wrong-doing and suffering in the present human world (pp. 384-91).[10] In the sūtra, just before the quoted passage, the Buddha told Maitreya that he will attain rebirth in the western pure land through this virtuous practice, but Taixu takes up the passage at the part in which the Buddha describes the five sufferings of the present world. Toward the end of the passage, the Buddha declares that a single day and night of practice in the present world equals a hundred years of practice in the western pure land, because in that ideal environment with a Buddha to teach one and no distractions, such practice comes more easily than in this world.

Another quotation follows that Taixu ascribes to Laozi's *Dao De Jing* but which actually comes from another early Daoist text, the *Liezi*. The quotation states that human beings regard others as human if they have a human body even if their minds are animal-like, while beings who do not have a human form are considered inhuman even if they have the mind of a sage. To illustrate, the text mentions several ancient sage-emperors who had serpentine bodies or the heads of oxen and others who had human bodies but acted brutishly.[11] Immediately after this citation, Taixu provides a chart upon which he arranges all the beings within the Buddhist cosmos and the Chinese political world so that the reader can distinguish superior beings from inferior (pp. 392-93). Its purpose is to correlate human beings of the present world to all the various levels of rebirth:

> Those who extend their strength to monopolize power to their own benefit and the detriment of others—these are the barbarians and *asuras*! Those who amass capital for their own enrichment, eating the substance of others to fatten themselves—these are the animals and beasts! Those who form the majority, whose capital is coerced, who labor without sufficient food or clothing—are they not the hungry ghosts? Those multitudes who live under force and pressure and cannot speak or act freely—are they not the denizens of hell? Contemplating this in silence, the kind of world this human realm is and what manner of doings one finds

in this human world, can you not feel an outpouring of grief, and do tears of sorrow not fall?[12]

Section Three

Next comes section 3, "The Establishment of a Pure Land in the Human Realm".[13] After briefly describing six utopian schemes from both East and West—such as Laozi's rustic community, Thomas More's *Utopia*, Christian and Hindu ideas of heaven, and so on (pp. 395-96)—Taixu lists the "ingredients" (*chengfen*) needed for a Buddhist pure land in the present world. First, this world must have the three treasures: Buddha, dharma, and sangha, which Taixu reinterprets as aspects of enlightened humanity to be realized in this world. The Buddha turns out to be our own rational minds when turned from defilement to enlightenment. From this basis in the mind, the present human realm manifests as Buddha, dharma, and sangha:

> Now we are intelligent and can imagine and remember. This is the Buddha hidden within our nature. Inside, we have the body and its faculties and the cognizing mind; outside is the container world and the nation. These internal and external factors give rise to body, speech, and conduct, and this forms the basis for the dharma. The Buddha's enlightenment turns all the dharmas, the dharmas accumulate and manifest as the Buddha revealed in the mind. They come together as the body, the household, the nation, the masses, as humanity, and as the immeasurable beings throughout the universe; this is our innate faculty for the sangha.[14]

While the meaning of this is a bit obscure, Taixu follows it by saying that failure to embody the three treasures within ourselves and our societies leads to rebirth in samsara and that it is only in a human rebirth that we may achieve the Pure Land in the Human Realm through cultivating Buddhist practices (p. 397).

The subsection called "The Dharma of Safeguarding the Security of Life and Property"[15] begins by stating that security is a prerequisite for establishing the pure land here and now. This may be done in a "radical" way (*zhiben zhi fa*), meaning one may either attain rebirth in Uttarakuru or fundamentally transform one's present society, or by "superficial" measures (*zhibiao zhi fa*). The two superficial measures are (1) establishing a transnational Buddhist association dedicated to charitable and relief work or (2) performing esoteric rituals to "diminish calamities, augment good fortune, and quell the resentments of devils," as well as repentance rituals to "turn misfortune into good fortune." He concludes, "If we could practice these methods for addressing both root and surface using both exoteric and esoteric means, then the causes and conditions would harmonize and no one would be unable to maintain security."[16]

The next subsection is titled "Concrete Means for Establishing [the Pure Land in the Human Realm]."[17] Here Taixu provides a detailed charter for a utopian Buddhist community to be constructed on Mount Putuo or on a secluded, forested mountain purchased with government assistance. At its center, Taixu envisioned a monastic compound with about one thousand resident monks and nuns. The compound would include halls and liturgical spaces for each of the eight schools of Chinese Buddhism, and Taixu especially desired that clerics in the Esoteric Hall practice rituals for the aversion of disaster and the quelling of demons every day (p. 402).

Around this compound, he planned three concentric rings of lay family dwellings. Families who had taken the three refuges would occupy the outermost ring, and they would receive the smallest allocations of farmland. The next ring would offer larger tracts to be distributed to those families that had taken the five lay precepts.[18] Those who had undertaken the ten virtuous deeds.[19] would live closest to the central monastic compound and receive the largest plots. Each of these zones would have schools and a police force. The remainder of this section stipulates the community's form of government and methods for electing officials (pp. 399–403). The next section, called "Universal Ingathering,"[20] is fairly brief and details ways in which this Buddhist community would interact with the wider world, both by making its facilities and services available to everyone from world government representatives to private families, and by sending missionaries and teachers out to share the fruits of their study and practice abroad (p. 404).

Section Four

Section 4, "The Pure Land in the Human Realm and Eternal Life and Bliss,"[21] begins by pointing out that even for those dedicated to building up the Pure Land in the Human Realm, life still comes to an end and people must still prepare for their postmortem fates.

> The Pure Land in the Human Realm is limited to safeguarding life and property by the three refuges and the ten virtues, and to keeping the three refuges and the ten virtues by safeguarding life and property. Although one may extend life, life still comes to an end and one dies. Since we believe that the mind-consciousness goes on and takes on another body and does not revert to oblivion, we must therefore arrange for the "mark of consciousness that continues to be embodied" a stable and appropriate basis in order to avoid the danger of going from delusion to delusion while bobbing up and down in samsara. Having already laid down the good roots of the Pure Land in the Human Realm by the three refuges and the ten virtues, we must add on the practice of invocation and transfer of merit to gain ascent and rebirth in the Pure Land of the inner court [of Maitreya] or of the [Pure Land of] Utmost Bliss [of Amitābha] in the next life.[22]

In order to provide a scriptural warrant for both of these pure lands, Taixu first quotes from the *Sutra on the Contemplation of Maitreya's Ascent to the Tuṣita Heaven Preached by the Buddha*[23] (pp. 405-13), and then from the *Shorter Sukhāvatī-vyūha-sūtra* (*Foshuo Amituo jing*, T. 366) (pp. 413-15). Each citation is quite extensive, and each gives a detailed description of the magnificence of Maitreya's and Amitābha's pure lands followed by instructions on the practices that lead to rebirth in them after death. However, he relativizes all of the lands of which he has spoken thus far (impure lands, the Pure Land in the Human Realm, the inner court of Maitreya, and the Pure Land of Amitābha) as mere manifestations of the ultimate reality, which he calls the "true suchness buddha-nature pure land" (*zhenru faxing jingtu*). All beings have the inherent mind of awakening (*juexin*), but their minds are tainted in particular ways, leading them to either the five destinies or the Pure Land in the Human Realm in this life, and to attain rebirth in the inner court or the western pure land thereafter. Even the latter two manifestations involve some small degree of lingering delusion; the ultimate goal, buddhahood, brings with it the realization of the true suchness pure land, which contained all the others all along (pp. 415-16).

Section Five

Section 5 is called "One's Own Vows of Compassion and Acts of Charity as the Starting Point."[24] It begins by exhorting readers to generate their own vows of compassion, noting that vows mark the point of departure for the creation of any pure land, human or celestial (pp. 416-17). As an example, Taixu quotes in full the forty-eight vows set forth by the bodhisattva Dharmākara by which he arrayed the splendors of the western pure land of utmost bliss (pp. 417-22). Following this, he remarks that vows need to be upheld by offerings. He supports this with another quotation from the *Larger Sukhāvatī-vyūha-sūtra* that describes the innumerable offerings that Dharmākara gave while pursuing buddhahood. With a short verse exhorting readers to work for the benefit of all by purifying a buddha land, the main text ends (pp. 422-24).

The Appendix

An appendix called "Creating the Pure Land in the Human Realm"[25] (pp. 424-30) contains the text of a lecture Taixu gave in 1930. While the foregoing text mixed calls for practical social action with highly traditional elements of Buddhist thought, this section seems more thoroughly modern. Gone are the sutra citations and the expressions of concern for the afterlife; gone also are the plans for a specific local utopian community and the esoteric rituals for the welfare of the nation. Instead we find here four sections dealing solely with social action to improve the present world in order to create the pure land in the human realm, not in a distant future when Maitreya will descend and attain buddhahood here, but in a nearer future and as a result of human effort.

The first part describes the five turbidities (*wu zhuo*)[26] that make our present world an impure land and acknowledges that Buddhism accepts the notion of pure buddha lands that lie elsewhere, perhaps in the form of other planets. However, it goes on to say that pure lands are accomplished by the practice of virtue; they do not just appear spontaneously. The mind of each individual is the root, and purification through discipline and virtue will lead to the goal. Right action directed toward good deeds provides not only for the establishment of a buddha land in the distant future but also the good society in the nearer term (pp. 425–27).

Second, given the centrality of the mind and the constant transformations of consciousness that give rise to the phenomenal world, there is no need to abandon this world and seek purity elsewhere in the same way that many Chinese citizens of his day thought that migrating to America would solve their problems. Instead, Taixu points out:

> Even if this present land is neither good nor stately, if everyone works to purify their own minds and accumulate the causes and conditions, then, moving forward bit by bit over the long haul, this defiled and evil human realm can be transformed into a magnificent pure land. There is no need to leave this human realm and look for a pure land somewhere else. This is why it is called the Pure Land in the Human Realm.[27]

Third, in order to put forth appropriate effort, one must go beyond the delusions of both the optimists and the pessimists. The first believe the world is already good and in no need of change, while the second do not believe it can be improved by any means. When one learns that everything happens through causes and conditions, then one gives up false doctrines of creation by a sovereign God and pure materialism, both of which deprive human beings of their ability to change things. Realizing that things arise as transformations of mind, then one will realize that the purification of the mind is an effective way to improve society (pp. 428–29).

Fourth, how does one proceed? The first necessity is government involvement. Just as one needs the government's forces to put down bandits, one needs the government's aid in working for social progress. After that, the founding of the pure land in the human realm requires industry to provide the requisites of life, education to form character and teach skills, the arts to raise industry from mere technology to new levels and elevate thought, and then morals to guide and direct the application of industry, education, and the arts. When all of these are combined with Buddhism's understanding of the formative power of the mind and its push toward liberation, then society can move to implement the pure land in the human realm (pp. 429–30).[28]

The Evolving Western Understanding of Taixu

Taixu's image as a Buddhist modernizer and a secularizer congealed early among Western observers because that was the aspect of his activities and publications that drew their attention. Traditional Pure Land practice and modernization did not mix in their minds, so they either ignored Taixu's involvement in the former or claimed that Taixu was not sincere about it. The Norwegian missionary Karl L. Reichelt, for example, met Taixu in the mid-1920s and observed his activities for some years. He knew that Taixu's missionary chapel in Hankou had an image of Amitābha in it and that its gatherings included long stretches of group buddha-recitation practice (*nianfo*), but he ascribed this to Taixu's desire to duplicate the successful methods of the Christian missionaries and his determination that the Chinese masses wanted it: "[Taixu], who actually had little use for the ways of faith and worship, found it expedient to use this method as a preparation with the crowds."[29] The last chapter of Reichelt's *The Transformed Abbot* is a brief biography of Taixu that reports only his early revolutionary activities and his later efforts to modernize Buddhism.[30]

The Presbyterian missionary Frank R. Millican gives a similar report of his interactions with Taixu. In 1923 he reported that in conversation with Taixu he pointed out that Buddhism had no savior figure to help human beings. In response, Taixu said there was indeed such a figure in Buddhism, but he "did not seem to be very strong on this point....Emphasis on faith in another as a means of salvation as we find it in the writings of...adherents of the Pure Land Sect is conspicuous by its absence from the writings of [Taixu]."[31] Clarence Hamilton, a philosophy professor in Nanjing, saw Taixu unexpectedly at Mount Lu around the same period. Hamilton reports that Taixu had no use for religious images but kept them "because he believes it is necessary for the common people to have some image to which they can turn their thoughts."[32] All these religious interlocutors stated that Taixu's use of Pure Land images and practices was a sham that he tolerated only because it was expedient for attracting "the masses" and "the common people."

Paul Callahan, the earliest secular academic writer to report on Republican-era Buddhism, also placed exclusive emphasis on Taixu's role as a modernizer in a 1952 report on the reformer's activities. Callahan's focus on Taixu's modernization program was so single-minded that he ignored even the counterevidence that appeared in his own report. For example, in delineating Taixu's reform program, Callahan noted that besides encouraging social engagement, restructuring the sangha, land reform, and so on, Taixu also advocated use of buddha images to encourage the masses, esoteric rituals, and *nianfo* ("muttering of prayers and names of the Buddha"[33]), and he reproduces a report stating that Taixu preceded one of his public lectures with an "impressive act of worship."[34]

Even so, he concludes: "To one versed in traditional Buddhism, such a program seems rather un-Buddhistic, a far cry from the 'other-worldliness' usually associated with Buddhism."[35]

Even with these prior studies available to them, most Western scholars first became aware of Taixu's importance through the work of Holmes Welch, who devoted a chapter of *The Buddhist Revival in China* to him.[36] In this work, Welch portrays Taixu primarily as an ineffective organizer and modernizer. While acknowledging (briefly and citing Reichelt) that Taixu's ministry included "pure land" elements, Welch contends that Taixu was not sincere about it but rather that he grudgingly included it as a sop for ignorant followers who knew nothing better.[37] Welch's characterization dominated the Western understanding of Taixu's role in Buddhist modernism for a long time.

Don Pittman, in the first monograph-length study of Taixu, retained this interpretation. His summation of Taixu's "On the Establishment of the Pure Land in the Human Realm" omits all references to traditional Pure Land and Maitreyan themes and focuses primarily on the plan for a Buddhist mountain community. In his conclusions, Pittman lists Joseph Kitagawa's three hallmarks of modern religion, the second of which is an abandonment of otherworldly or postmortem paradises in favor of work in the present world, and he states that Taixu meets this description: "[Taixu] understood the significance of human existence, emphasized the attainment of buddhahood within this world, and rejected the givenness of the social order in favor of building a pure land on earth."[38]

A 2012 doctoral dissertation by Eric Goodell and a 2017 monograph by Justin Ritzinger have expanded our understanding of Taixu and shown him to be a much more complex character than the earlier studies indicated. Goodell makes note of the influence that Taixu's grandmother's practice of buddha recitation had on him[39] and the importance of early experiences in meditation. He grants that Taixu recognized Pure Land as one of the eight schools of Chinese Buddhism[40] and that after 1928 Taixu softened his criticism of more traditionalist forms of practice in an effort to smooth his relationships with older influential monks.[41] However, for Goodell, Taixu remains a modernizer whose tolerance of traditional practices was merely tactical:

> The elimination of the deva vehicle also involves the "faithful masses" of faithful Buddhists. Taixu was not so much interested in reducing the influence of the incense-offering Buddhists, but rather in demonstrating to new Buddhists that their understanding of Buddhism was more genuine, and unrelated to the more traditional type. In this connection, Taixu's [book] *Humanistic Science* disparages the devotional masses who see buddhas and bodhisattvas as gods and seek heavenly rewards.[42]

Ritzinger is much more expansive in the matter of Taixu's devotional life. His book shows that Taixu nurtured a lifelong devotion to Maitreya and sincerely sought to gain rebirth in the Tuṣita Heaven when he died. He promoted Maitreya worship when he could and provided Maitreya devotional liturgies for his followers within the institutions that he founded.[43] We have seen this already from Taixu's declaration in his essay that, even after years of social engagement, one must still face the fact of one's inevitable death and prepare for one's future rebirths. Ritzinger's assessment of Taixu's feelings regarding Amitābha Pure Land practice is somewhat ambiguous, however. Was Taixu content to let Buddhists conduct practices leading to rebirth in Sukhāvatī rather than the Tuṣita Heaven, or did he simply resign himself to its inevitability given its long tradition and overwhelming popularity? In the next section, we will take a closer look at the relationship between the two practices, but let us conclude this section by seeing what effect previous scholarship has had on the wider academic understanding of Taixu.

We can see the effect of these trends in specialized scholarship when we look at the work of researchers who do not focus on the study of Taixu in particular but cite the above works for their own research in modern Chinese Buddhism. By and large they have adopted the prevailing view that Taixu was strictly a modernizer who deplored traditional Buddhist practice. Here are just two examples among many. Richard Madsen, in his book *Democracy's Dharma*, says, "Monks like Tai Xu strove to interpret Mahayana Buddhism in this-worldly terms. Instead of hoping to go to some heavenly pure land after death, Buddhists should place their hope on making this world a pure land by devoting themselves to eliminating social suffering."[44] David Schak's synopsis of Taixu's thought is similar:

> Socially engaged Buddhism grew out of the teachings of a very influential monastic, Ven. Taixu (1890-1947). Ven. Taixu was very dissatisfied with the state of Buddhism. He wanted to move it away from its dependency on funerals, rituals to appease spirits and repeating Amithaba's [sic] name to earn merit for others and ensure their rebirth in the pure land. He also hoped to make this world into the pure land by working in and improving society. Buddhism, he argued, needed to concentrate on accumulating merit in this life.[45]

What seems common to all these analyses is the tendency to split the Republican-period Buddhist world into two opposing camps: traditionalist monks and the "Buddhist masses" or "common people" on one side, and the reformers and modernizers on the other. Left out is a middle group of monks and laymen who were educated and prosperous members of modern urban society but still desired to participate in more traditional practices such as Pure Land. Brooks Jessup has shown that even as they agreed with reformers that the Buddhist clergy needed reconstruction and went about setting up their own lay Buddhist societies in Shanghai, such organizations included sutra chanting and *nianfo* as daily practices.[46] Thus, I would contend that Taixu never needed to make elimination of such practices part of his modernization program, nor did he need to deploy them disingenuously simply to gain the support of "the masses." Urban Buddhist laypeople wanted them, and, as seen in Taixu's essay and in the missionary reports of his activities, he was happy to provide rationales for them. We must conclude that while Taixu wished to modernize Chinese Buddhism, he did not necessarily want to secularize it.

Sukhāvatī versus the Tuṣita Heaven

Taixu's essay "On the Establishment of the Pure Land in the Human Realm" seems to give roughly equal space to both Amitābha and Maitreya. When he first moves from the topic of securing life and property in the present world to that of providing for one's postmortem fate, he inserts a long citation from the *Larger Sukhāvatī-vyūha-sūtra* describing the physical attributes of the Western pure land.[47] He then returns to the problems of this present world, following this with another long quotation from the same sutra. Up to this point, he appears to be favoring the Amitābha cult while ignoring Maitreya.[48] But it is not that simple. While it is true that this second quotation comes from a classic sutra of the Pure Land tradition, the section he quotes shows the Buddha Śākyamuni addressing Maitreya and praising him for his long-standing efforts to succor beings in the present world. While a more traditional Pure Land devotee might think Taixu is emphasizing the cult of Amitābha here, in fact Taixu is cleverly using the text to focus on Maitreya and this-worldly compassionate action.

After this, he returns to his plans for improving life and establishing a Buddhist utopia and does not come back to the subject of future rebirths until much later. Only then does he finally bring up practices conducive to rebirth in a buddha land. He begins with the possibility of joining Maitreya, providing a long citation from the *Sutra on Maitreya's Ascent to the Tuṣita Heaven* (T. 452). The passage presents a description of Maitreya's abode in the inner court of the Tuṣita Heaven and the practices that lead to rebirth there.[49] He follows this immediately with another long passage from the *Shorter Sukhāvatī-vyūha-sūtra* (T. 366) that describes the splendors of the western Pure Land of Amitābha.[50]

That is all that Taixu says about postmortem matters in this essay. It ends soon thereafter, but not before Taixu has rooted the purity of both the Tuṣita Heaven and Sukhāvatī in the human mind and exhorted his readers to follow the examples of both Maitreya and Amitābha insofar as they constructed their paradises by long *kalpas* of compassionate action on behalf of others. One cannot see a clear preference for either cult here. If anything, the traditional Pure Land focus on Amitābha has an edge over the cult of Maitreya, at least to judge by the amount of space devoted to each. When he does juxtapose them, he seems interested only in presenting them as two equally viable options.

This appears to be consistent with Taixu's other writings. For example, in a text titled "Chan, Tiantai, and Huayan Flowing Back into Pure Land Practice,"[51] Taixu presents both Maitreya practice and traditional Amitābha practice as two possible methods of attaining rebirth in a pure land. He does take time to explain why the cult of Maitreya is not as popular as that of Amitābha: it had few texts in circulation and few advocates, and it received unfair criticism from authors favoring Amitābha. He goes on to say that Maitreya has greater affinities with denizens of our world and his inner court is closer, being also within the present *sahā* world, or "world to be endured." He does *not* declare that Maitreya practice is superior to Amitābha practice; he merely seeks to elevate Maitreya practice to the same level: "Thus, the lack of currency of this practice is not a matter of superior versus inferior or difficult versus easy; it is just that after the Tang there were few practitioners and few advocates."[52]

Reevaluating Taixu's Buddhist Modernism

A master narrative that has persisted for too long (and to which I confess I have contributed) depicts Taixu as a modernizer who, by propounding humanistic Buddhism[53] and articulating the goal of building a "pure land in the human realm," sought to replace backward, traditional, and otherworldly Buddhist practice with a modern, socially responsible, scientific, and this-worldly orientation. As Scott Pacey put it, "One of the most important contributions to twentieth-century Chinese Buddhism came in the form of his 'pure land in the human world' (*renjian jingtu*) concept in 1926—the notion that rather than focusing on attaining rebirth in the pure land, this world itself could be 'purified' by making Buddhism the basis of individual and social life."[54]

A careful reading of Taixu's "On the Establishment of the Pure Land in the Human Realm" and related texts reveals no such agenda. While it is true that Taixu promoted modernization in many areas— education, the organization of the sangha, and a pivot away from traditional gentry in favor of the urban middle class—he never sought to displace practices that tended to the believer's postmortem fate. Justin Ritzinger is surely correct in identifying Maitreya worship as Taixu's own preferred practice, but I see less evidence that he tried to promote it publicly to the exclusion of other practices. A look at the essay under examination shows that he wanted all the traditional schools of Chinese Buddhism represented in his mountain utopia, and if anything he stressed esoteric ritual as the practice that would benefit the nation most.

As to the shibboleth that Taixu was being disingenuous when he spoke approvingly of traditional Amitābha worship, addressed it in writing, and tolerated its practice in his establishments merely as a concession for "the masses," I would point out that whatever his personal attitude and regardless of what he said to confidantes in private settings, his legacy consists in the writings he left, and these present an apparently honest concern for the afterlife and promote rebirth in the pure lands of both Maitreya and Amitābha.

In the end, Taixu remained much more of a traditional Buddhist and maintained more premodern beliefs than Western scholarship has been willing to acknowledge. His modernization project was adaptive: he wanted to make Buddhism address the situations and needs of modern society. It was also inclusive: he wanted to add more by way of concern for the public good and political involvement than perhaps had been the case previously. He did not want to subtract anything or replace the traditional with the modern. He wanted a rebalancing that would make efforts at social reform compatible with the pursuit of venerable Buddhist goals such as enlightenment or rebirth in the pure land.

In the public square, Taixu's voice competed with many thinkers and social engineers whose reform plans were wholly secular and who gave religion no positive role to play in China's future. Several Western observers, sharing the view that religion could only retard progress toward social reform, sometimes expressed the view that Taixu's more progressive proposals, if implemented, would not make Buddhism relevant once again but instead would spell its end. That is why it is important to read Taixu's works carefully, for only by doing so can we see that he was a modernizer but not a thoroughgoing secularist. Future scholarly treatments of Taixu should therefore cease portraying him one-sidedly as a modern figure who wanted to abolish the traditional. We should see him more appropriately as a transitional figure who initiated the modernization process that is still ongoing today.

BIBLIOGRAPHY

Callahan, Paul E. "T'ai Hsü and the New Buddhist Movement." *Harvard University Papers on China*, no. 6 (1952): 149–88.

Fo shuo Amituo jing, T. 366.

Fo shuo guan Mile Pusa shangsheng doushuaitian jing, T. 452.

Fo shuo qishi yinben jing, T. 24.

Giles, Lionel, trans. *Taoist Teachings from the Book of Lieh-Tzu*. London: Murray, 1912.

Goodell, Eric. *Taixu's (1890–1947) Creation of Humanistic Buddhism*. PhD diss., University of Virginia, 2012.

Hamilton, Clarence H. "An Hour with T'ai Shu, Master of the Law." *Open Court* 42 (1928): 162–69.

Inagaki, Hisao, and Harold Stewart, trans. *The Three Pure Land Sutras*. 2nd ed. Berkeley, CA: Numata Center for Buddhist Translation and Research, 2003.

Jessup, Brooks. *The Householder Elite: Buddhist Activism in Shanghai, 1920–1956*. PhD diss., University of California–Berkeley, 2010.

Jones, Charles B. *Taixu's "On the Establishment of the Pure Land in the Human Realm": A Translation and Study*. New York: Bloomsbury Academic, 2021.

Larger Sukhāvātī-vyūha-sūtra (Fo shuo wuliangshou jing), T. 360.

Madsen, Richard. *Democracy's Dharma: Religious Renaissance and Political Development in Taiwan*. Berkeley: University of California Press, 2007.

Millican, Frank R. "T'ai-hsü and Modern Buddhism." *Chinese Recorder* 54, no. 6 (1923): 326-34.

Pacey, Scott. "Taixu, Yogācāra, and the Buddhist Approach to Modernity." In *Transforming Consciousness: Yogācāra Thought in Modern China*, edited by John Makeham, 149-69. New York: Oxford University Press, 2014.

Pittman, Don A. *Toward a Modern Chinese Buddhism: Taixu's Reforms*. Honolulu: University of Hawai'i Press, 2001.

Reichelt, Karl Ludwig. *The Transformed Abbot*. Translated by G. M. Reichelt and A. P. Rose. London: Lutterworth, 1954.

Ritzinger, Justin. *Anarchy in the Pure Land: Reinventing the Cult of Maitreya in Modern Chinese Buddhism*. New York: Oxford University Press, 2017.

Shorter Sukhāvatī-vyūha-sūtra (Foshuo Amituo jing), T. 360.

Taixu. "A Statement to Asiatic Buddhists." *Young East* 1 (1925): 177-82.

———. "On the Establishment of the Pure Land in the Human Realm" (*Jianshe renjian jingtu lun*). In his *Taixu dashi quanshu*, vol. 24, 349-430. Taipei: Shandao Temple Sutra Distribution Center, 1956.

Welch, Holmes. *The Buddhist Revival in China*. Harvard East Asian series 33. Cambridge, MA: Harvard University Press, 1968.

Xu, Muzhu, Jinhua Chen, and Lori Meeks, eds. *Development and Practice of Humanitarian Buddhism: Interdisciplinary Perspectives*. Hualien, Taiwan: Tzu Chi University, 2007.

6 | The Shared Origins of Traditionalism and Secularism in Theravāda Buddhism

KATE CROSBY

A couple of years ago, on hearing that I was in town to give a lecture on Buddhism, a fellow customer at a teashop in central Dunedin, New Zealand, unlocked her phone to show me a photograph she had taken on a recent holiday to Thailand. The screen displayed one of the famous images of that epitome of scientific thinking, Albert Einstein, hand raised to write on a blackboard, face turned to look back at the viewer. Beneath, in both English and Thai, was one of the several quotations on Buddhism misattributed to Einstein: "Buddhism has the characteristics of what would be expected in a cosmic religion for the future: It transcends a personal God, avoids dogmas and theology..."[1] Though now tarnished by the wider broadcasting of news about the Rohingya situation, Buddhism has long had good press as a tolerant, relativist, and scientific religion, or even nonreligion, sitting easily within modern secular society, or alongside other beliefs. I did not have the heart to inform my fellow tea-drinker that the lecture I was due to deliver was on the subject of the ultratraditionalist heresy trials, backed up by the power to impose long prison sentences, that have been held in Myanmar (formerly Burma) since the late twentieth century.

These two extremes both have their origins in changes to Buddhism that took place in the late nineteenth and early twentieth centuries. The story of the engagement between Theravāda Buddhist intellectuals and Western sympathizers in modernizing Buddhism is well known. Geoffrey Samuel summarizes the effect: "The Buddhism which resulted was, one could say, pre-adapted for its incorporation in secularized form into the Western therapeutic context a century later in forms such as Mindfulness-based Stress Reduction and Mindfulness-based Cognitive Therapy."[2] Here I shall examine some of these interactions within their Asian context. What interests me here is that, within Theravāda Buddhism at least, the developments that made the secularizing trajectory possible also informed traditionalizing trajectories. Moreover, some of their most notable contrasting features were made possible not by opposing responses to crisis, but by shared responses.

The this-life focus of the revival of meditation at that time, which would facilitate its transition into fully secularized contexts as "mindfulness," is a prime example of a single response reflecting very different goals. The new emphasis on meditation during the colonial period was in origin a radical traditionalism stemming from a millenarian turn to origins and rigorous practice by Buddhists confronted with signs that the end of the *sāsana* was nigh. The word *sāsana* is the closest Pāli word to what we now term "Buddhism." It literally means "teaching" or "dispensation" and refers to the teaching by a particular Buddha—in our case the historical Gotama Buddha—as well as to the texts, conduct, and institutions that maintain the presence and accessibility of that teaching. The disappearance of the sāsana is believed to be attended by breakdown in social norms, natural calamities, disease, and warfare. The purpose of focusing on meditation in the face of such indications was to attain in this life the supramundane states that culminate in nirvana (Pāli *nibbāna*), while such attainments were still possible, while the sāsana was still intact.

Here I shall explore how these and other developments, whether to be seen as traditionalizing or secularizing, played out in the Theravāda world of the nineteenth and twentieth centuries. The essay culminates with a discussion of the Burmese monk Shin Ukkaṭṭha (1897–1978) and his associates, which illustrates how these different responses affected the everyday lives, religious beliefs, and the successes and failures of individual Buddhists. This will allow us to see the complex interplay as well as conflicts produced by the various modernizing, traditionalizing, and secularizing trajectories taken by Buddhist teachings in the colonial and postcolonial Theravāda world.

Responses to Fears of Buddhism's Decline

Fears of the demise of the sāsana have repeatedly reshaped Buddhism, perhaps most famously in the case of thirteenth-century Japan. Natural disasters and Mongolian invasions created conditions that eventually led to Japan's distinctive discarding of traditional monastic roles and a widespread concern with rebirth in the "pure land" heaven of a nonhistorical Buddha. In the early modern period, the signs of the imminent demise of the sāsana in the Theravāda world came in the form of the devastating wars and other major upheavals caused by European colonialism. The next life became deemphasized not because it was no longer believed in or because people became agnostic, a distinctive feature of secular Buddhism, but because of anxiety that this current life might be the very last in which progress on the path would be attainable during Gotama ("Gautama" in Sanskrit) Buddha's dispensation.

For Theravāda Buddhists, rebirth in a pure land was not considered an option—it relied on the concept of multiple coexistent buddhas, each with their own buddha field where it is possible to achieve enlightenment now, if reborn there. According to the Abhidhamma, the body of literature that explains and explores the Theravāda understanding of reality and causality in detail, there is only one Buddha at a time. Once the sāsana of Gotama, the buddha of our era, dies out, Theravāda Buddhists have to await the arrival of the future Buddha Metteyya ("Maitreya" in Sanskrit) for any hope of salvation. Acts of merit could be and were performed with the aim of rebirth in Metteyya's presence, as at previous periods of crisis, but the unraveling of karma is hard to fathom or control. Rebirth in any of the animal and hell realms, or even divine realms, of Buddhist cosmology, could disrupt this plan. There was no guarantee of being reborn as a human at that critical time and only humans are able to benefit fully from a Buddha's teaching. The now is therefore extremely precious.

This-life emphasis in Asian Buddhism of the late twentieth century may be associated with greater social mobility under new political and economic models as well as the broader hegemony of modern science and secular discourse, but the impact of those influences came later. I shall show that even where Buddhists during the colonial period radically rethought traditional cosmology and rebirth in the light of Western "science"—another move that facilitated secularization—they did not discard rebirth in its entirety or in identical ways.

The correlation between science and Buddhism, another feature associated with secular Buddhism, is—I shall also show—not new or unique to the modern period. As might be expected, the universal truth of the dharma was inevitably regarded by adherents as concordant with scientific truths, especially before the science-religion divide that necessitates the question of their relationship came to the fore in the nineteenth century. We can see from patterns of practice how in the premodern period even meditation, today commonly regarded as a mind science, was influenced by sciences now classified as pertaining primarily to the physical realm, such as chemistry and pharmacy. Such technological aspects of premodern meditation ceased to be recognized when local culture throughout the Theravāda world was reformed by the newly hegemonic Western sciences. The label "magic" is often applied to technology now outdated or no longer recognized, a consideration to bear in mind in the traditional-secular discourse. Science is itself in flux. Even much of the science with which early modern apologists sought to align Buddhism is now largely discarded.[3]

All this means that while secular Buddhism in its current forms is new, some of the factors that shaped changes in Buddhism in the modern period were not. In Theravāda, as in Japan, we can detect previous crises in earlier centuries. In the Theravāda world, these produced precursors to modern responses such as the turn to traditionalism, particularly through textual fundamentalism, and the rise and universalization of meditation.[4]

The Destabilization of the Nineteenth and Early Twentieth Centuries

It is tempting to see Buddhism as a timeless religion. This view fits the internal narrative of an eternal dharma, particularly within Theravāda, which is seen by its adherents as preserving the earliest, most orthodox form of Buddhism. It is reinforced by the global accessibility of texts dating back millennia that are so practical and psychologically astute that they continue to appeal to new generations both in and beyond the Buddhist fold.[5] Modern methods of meditation are recognizably related to practices advocated in early Buddhist canons. We can easily forget the crises undergone by Buddhism and that some of the correspondence between modern and early result from a turn to origins stimulated by global developments of the nineteenth century, especially the collision between European expansionism and Asian cultures. These encounters set in motion both the traditionalizing and secularizing developments that ensued.

The nineteenth-century Opium Wars fought by the British to defend their addiction-inducing trade, itself aimed at reversing Britain's trade deficit, destabilized China, disrupting Chinese influence in Southeast Asia and ultimately ushering in modern Asian political history. Britain also fought the three Anglo-Burmese wars over the same century, displacing the Buddhist kings of the Tonbaung dynasty, and in 1815 they took Kandy, the last stronghold of royal patronage of Buddhism in Sri Lanka. Similar colonial expansion was under way by other European powers. France was the most notable presence in the Theravāda region in this period, competing with Britain for cultural, economic, and political influence, eventually colonizing the region now primarily comprising Vietnam, Cambodia, and Laos.[6] In its imposition of economies of extraction through the establishment of monocultures and plantations, along with the resulting displacement of peoples and mass migration of workers to feed it, the colonial machine induced disease epidemics and famine—small wonder that Buddhists saw in these events signs of the long-predicted decline of the sāsana, which brings with it apocalyptic warfare, disease, and social chaos.[7]

The imposition of Western medicine and education, in part to justify colonial wars and land grabs as the necessary route to "progress," in part to man the colonial machine, further expanded the scope of colonial dominance of the physical realm. This disrupted traditional roles, career paths, and hierarchies, including for the Buddhist monastic community (sangha), which had been the primary provider of literacy and other forms of prestige education in both religious and temporal specializations, including medicine. Temporary ordination, residence at monastic complexes, and participation in the variety of training available at different monasteries had long been a stepping-stone in the careers of many. Monasteries had acted as landlords and held important management roles, including management of the water technologies so crucial for irrigation, such as the magnificent tanks that had for two millennia supported the highly productive rice cultivation of the Sri Lankan dry zone. Monasteries marked trading points along river and land navigation systems. Educational, economic, and medical reform during the colonial period changed this. Changes in education, and to some extent medicine, were often mediated by Christian missionaries who, even when not officially representative of colonial policy, were enabled by it.[8] These missionaries were funded from home by narratives of superiority, progress, and salvation that made them actively antagonistic to Buddhism. Some also received funding from Buddhist sponsors keen to keep up with new, secular knowledge, with King Mindon of Burma (r. 1853–1878) providing land

and finances for missionary schools. King Mongkut (1804–1868, r. 1851–1868), one of the most influential reformers of Theravāda Buddhism, had received secular education from Christian missionaries while a Buddhist monk.[9]

The disruption of Buddhist involvement in the physical realm and the fabric of society, coupled with attacks on its doctrines and teaching, led to an emphasis on Buddhism's superiority in the realms of the spiritual or psychological. This shift corresponded with the division between matter and mind (or psyche) in Western thinking. This division was itself a response in Europe to the challenges that new scientific discoveries, such as the heliocentric model of the universe, had presented to literal interpretations of the Bible. Ultimately this division would lead to a specifically Western evaluation of religion: the spiritual as a personal matter, allowing for the subjective turn at the individual level and the separation of religion and state at the political level within the context of colonial governance.

British policies of noninterference in religion, regardless of initial promises of protecting and privileging the place of Buddhism, unwittingly opened up a space for Buddhist revival movements. If religion was an area in which the government would not intervene, then it was the realm in which the fight against colonialism could develop. If the colonial administration would not step in to ensure the patronage of Buddhist institutions and the purity of Buddhist teachings, and no Buddhist king could be found to take on this role, then it would become the duty of everyone. If monasteries were disinvested of their land or the tithes due them, monks would need to rely on close day-to-day relations with lay supporters. All these factors contributed to closer monastic-lay relations, a broadening of responsibility and religious activity for laypeople, and Buddhism as an expression of emerging national identities. Concern for Buddhism's survival became increasingly intertwined with matters of identity, economy, and politics. In contrast to the Western view of religion as a private affair, for Buddhists it was a communal, collective responsibility, another divide that lies behind the current traditional-secular dichotomy.[10]

Meanwhile, the colonial recovery of the lost Indian Buddhist land-scape through surveys, archaeology, and textual research, which as it evolved relied on collaboration between Westerners and erudite Buddhists, was informing a sense of Buddhism's global reach and connectivity. This would inform the universalism of Buddhism as a shared meeting point between not only Buddhists but different thinkers and activists, with India as the main hub. At the same time, the simplistic narrative of Islam as the primary agent for Buddhism's historic disappearance in India that emerged with this rediscovery would have ongoing implications for the presence of Islamophobia within Buddhism, present in both secularizing and traditionalizing responses to the anxiety to protect Buddhism from further decline. That narrative should be seen in the context of colonial rivalry with Islam and Islamic powers both close to home, with the Ottoman Empire, and in colonial territories globally. Yet it informs one of the characteristics of modern, nationalistic Buddhism, which, in its quest to defend a Buddhism regarded as under threat, employs a rhetoric and encourages violence greatly at odds with Buddhism's reputation for tolerance.

Compassion, Tolerance, and Science: Higher Civilizational Values

Defenders of Buddhism in the colonial period highlighted the Bud-dha's teachings of loving-kindness, compassion, and tolerance, while making claims that Buddhism was based on rationality and science. These two aspects—the emotional and ethical positivity and the rationality—were offered as evidence of higher civilizational values. These features were contrasted to the cruelty and irratio-nality that Buddhists and their supporters associated with Chris-tianity against the backdrop of colonial despotism. In examining this discourse from the Buddhist side, we can see that Christianity is totemic in that it represents colonialism. This applies to other religions, such as Hinduism and Islam, when they were the religion of workers introduced by the British to run the colonial machine, a historical development that still shapes Theravāda chauvinism among both traditionalist and otherwise more secular practitioners today.

Influential in the spread of the claims that Buddhism was tolerant and scientific was the Pānadura debate of 1873, held between Buddhists and Christians in the small town of that name in southwest Sri Lanka. It was won for the Buddhist side by Migettuwatte Gunananda, who primarily focused on the attribution of omniscience to God and the Buddha respectively. Toward the end of his arguments he declared, "The great doctors of the science of medicine…the originators of ethics, the propounders of that important and wonderful science astrology, by which even the date of death of a man could be accurately foretold…always invoked the aid of Buddha and extolled the praise of him and of his religion, in every one of their works."[11] This argument made sense to a Sri Lankan audience: scientific manuscripts at the time would begin with homage to the Buddha, reflecting their cultural context. Astrology was the basis for decisions in daily life, from when and whether to get ordained as a monk, to whom to marry, to when to make a journey. One and a half centuries later, scientific works, even in Sri Lanka, rarely open with homage to the Buddha, and Buddhist modernists and secularists are unlikely to refer to astrology as a science, yet the discourse validating Buddhism with reference to scientific truth continues.[12]

Having made brief references to the Christian God's intolerance and predilection for blood throughout his arguments, Gunananda finishes his oration by characterizing Buddhism as follows: "[It] inculcated the purest morality and urged the necessity of self-denial, self-sacrifice and charity. It encouraged peace. It tolerated all religions in its midst."[13]

Science and Compassion as Themes in Global Buddhist Discourse

Gunananda's successful rhetoric attracted the cofounders of the Theosophical Society (established in 1875), Colonel Henry Steel Olcott and Madame Helena Blavatsky, to its cause. Theosophy played a major role in shaping global understandings of Buddhism.

Widely regarded as the most significant proponent of Buddhist modernism and nationalism in Sri Lanka, Anagarika Dharmapala (1864-1933) had attended the Pānadura debate as a boy. He also witnessed the arrival of Blavatsky and Olcott in Sri Lanka six years later, developing relationships with both of them that were significant in both his public and private religion.

The scientific claims made for Buddhism not only resonated with their own antagonism to establishment Christianity but also triggered the interests of the Theosophists because of their quest to find the scientific religious truth underlying all religion. The fashionable science of the day was Charles Darwin's evolutionary theory, which at this time, in the form of social Darwinism, provided justification for the devastating wars of colonial expansion. Evolutionary theory led Theosophists to challenge traditional Buddhist cosmology in ways that would pave the way for its rejection in secular Buddhism. The physical layout of Buddhist cosmology, with continents radiating from central Mount Meru, and layers of heavens and hells above and below, was already being challenged by the heliocentric model of the universe and by the increased mapping of the globe. Now the notion of rebirth within that cosmology was also challenged by the Darwinist belief that the human embodiment was the highest possible stage of evolution for a living being. Regress to lower states was impossible. The influential *Buddhist Catechism* published by Olcott in 1881 just over a year after his first visit to Sri Lanka includes the following question and answer: "Q. Does Buddhism teach that man is reborn only upon our earth? A. As a general rule that would be the case, until he had evolved beyond its level."[14] Here, rebirth is not denied, but lower rebirth is.

The close relationship between the Theosophical Society and Buddhist revivalists grew. Theosophists funded some of Anagarika Dharmapala's projects to reduce poverty in Sri Lanka, promote Buddhism, and regenerate Buddhist sites in India. These funders included wealthy Western individuals such as the Hawaiian heiress Mary Foster (1844-1930), who was apparently impressed by advice Dharmapala had given her to deal with her short temper,[15] as well as local Theosophists in India, who often hosted the Theravāda monks sent there. Engaging in the discourse of enquiry and competitive debates between followers of multiple religious, philosophical, and political persuasions, these monks returned with critical and international perspectives, inspired also by the growing Indian independence movement. The colonial structures that oppressed Buddhism also facilitated a network of interactions that enabled the emergence of a Buddhist response shaped by new perspectives.

While not an obvious feature of modern Sinhalese chauvinism, the notion of Buddhism as a religion of compassion and tolerance was very important to Anagarika Dharmapala, not just as a claim to civilization superiority, but for its practical application to people's lives. Gunananda's initial observations of the Christian God as cruel were expanded on by the American spiritualist J. M. Peebles in his introduction to a book containing a translation of the Pānadura debate that he published in 1878. Peebles had witnessed the debate, showing the initial English report to Olcott and Blavatsky on his return to the United States, thus inspiring them to make the contact with monks in Ceylon that would prove so productive.[16] A section titled "The Moral Influence of Buddhism" in Peebles's introduction opens with testimony to the savagery and cruelty of Christians. First he offers the details of a recent bullfight in honor of a royal wedding in Spain "where Christian men, dressed like savages, shake crimson rags at bulls to madden them for the bloody fray!" and in response to which ensuing gruesome scenes of suffering, the "Christian ladies of Roman Catholic Spain cheered and waved their handkerchiefs." He continues with descriptions of the commonplace violence in London taken from reports in the *Times* newspaper.[17] While Theosophist financial backing enabled Dharmapala to set up the Mahabodhi Society in 1891 with the aim of reclaiming Buddhist sites in India and creating a global Buddhism, his mission to establish a Buddhist monastery in the United Kingdom was aimed at converting the British to Buddhism so that they would become less cruel.[18] This led to the first Asian Buddhist mission in Europe, established in 1926 in Ealing at "Foster House," named in honor of its main benefactor. The secularizing and ecumenical leanings of this establishment, today the London Buddhist Vihara in Chiswick, still mark it out from more recent Sri Lankan temples. While the London Buddhist Vihara eschews the pantheon of gods that populate more traditional Sinhalese Buddhist religiosity, as does secular Buddhism, the newer temple at nearby Kingsbury actively accommodates it with a shrine to the most popular gods.[19]

Antisecular Responses in Burma

The Mahabodhi Society and growth of Theosophy contributed to an emerging Buddhist network in India that drew Theravāda monks from Sri Lanka, mainland Southeast Asia, and the Chittagong region of Bengal (now part of Bangladesh). Some Arakanese and Burmese monks went to run newly established monasteries and service revived pilgrimage sites. One of these was Shin Chandra (1876-1972), sent to Bodh Gaya as a novice after Olcott and Dharmapāla visited Arakan. Chandra oversaw the mass conversion of the Ambedkarite Dalits (former "untouchables") to Buddhism in 1956, in order to take them out of the caste system. Other monks pursued an international education, beginning with the study of English, an activity precluded them in Burma.

The difficulty of learning English as a Burmese monk related to the Burmese resistance against British attempts to use the country's twenty thousand monasteries, which had until the British time been the main source of Burma's impressively high literacy rates, to teach English and secular subjects.[20] Relevant to this resistance is that Burma, like Sri Lanka, had already implemented Buddhist reforms in the eighteenth century. Those reforms had sought to exclude monks from teaching temporal—we might now say secular— subjects such as medicine, martial arts, carpentry, and astrology, which had in fact for centuries been taught in monasteries. We can see these earlier reforms not just as a response to concerns about the decline of the sāsana but also as attempts to restrict and disrupt the power of monasteries and bring them under centralized control, promoting Buddhist factions loyal to those seeking to gain or maintain power. Theravāda history offers many instances where criticism that monks were insufficiently pure was used by rival monasteries or temporal powers to wrest positions of power, donated lands, tithes, and bonded laborers from the monasteries, not to mention to recruit into service young and able-bodied men defrocked from the monkhood. Narratives of purification have repeatedly taken place within contexts of political and economic crises. One effect of this history of crisis and purification is that the so-called secularization of Buddhism may in fact bring Buddhism back into an involvement in the temporal world that was traditionally present before such a reform. To label one activity secular and another traditional assumes separate spheres of engagement between the spiritual and temporal that may in fact be of recent origin. An example of this is the currently controversial use of meditation to enhance military performance, on the assumption that this is a new development, even though meditation and martial engagement have a long history in Buddhism itself, including in Theravāda.[21]

Yet with reforms of the previous century in both Sri Lanka and Burma, the saṅgha was pulled in different directions, criticized both if monks did not engage in the broader service of society and if they did. With the Burmese looking back to the eighteenth century as a high point of Buddhist union and purity, the British attempt to co-opt the monasteries for secular education was resisted using the rhetoric of defending the sāsana from corruption. Traditional learning in subjects such as canonical and commentarial texts became more popular, with new organizations dedicated to their pursuit and examination. The Abhidhamma, regarded both as the highest formulation of Buddhist truth and as the first section of the Pāli canon to disappear when the sāsana declines, alongside meditation as the primary means of personal transformation, became a particular focus of study and practice among monks and laypeople alike.[22]

Meditation as Mind Science

Influential in the popularization of meditation was the monk Ledi Sayadaw (1846–1923), whose emphasis on *vipassanā*, insight meditation, as a fast track to enlightenment in these uncertain times, paved the way for the later uptake of vipassanā-based practices as mind science. Ledi relegated meditation practices aimed at *samatha* "calming" outcomes, more associated with the physical realm, to lower down on the scientific scale and a lower priority. This neatly circumvented the colonial dominance of the physical realm, contributed to the claim of Asian superiority of the mind and would make it possible to practice meditation in shorter periods, adaptable to the routine of a layperson. While the practice of Buddhist-derived meditation in secular contexts globally is rarely associated with the Abhidhamma, Ledi's innovation in meditation was accepted within Burma because of his previously established expertise in the field of the Abhidhamma.

While Ledi's focus on personal transformation in this life facilitated its uptake in secular contexts, it should not be mistaken for a rejection of traditional cosmology. His most famous work in Burma, an extensive Abhidhamma commentary, affirms the traditional teaching that one may see omens of one's future destiny in the different realms of *saṃsāra* before one dies.[23] We can see how these themes developed in subsequent decades. Shwe Zan Aung (1871–1932), who had worked in the colonial administration, bridged the two worlds, drawing on the expertise he had gained studying under erudite Burmese monks to provide several of the first English translations of Abhidhamma texts, published by the Pali Text Society in the early twentieth century. In 1918, in an article titled "Buddhism and Science," Shwe Zan Aung writes, "Psychology is the stronghold of Buddhism. Buddhist psychology is at once complete and comprehensive, providing a place for every possible form of thought known or unknown in Western psychology." At the same time, he explicitly responds to the prevailing assumption that Buddhists lack expertise in materiality, by pointing out the detailed discussion of the subject in the Abhidhamma. At the same time, he explains away the problem of Buddhist cosmology, which had been challenged by Western science, as an allegory rather than something Buddhists literally believed.[24]

The Direction of Reform in Thailand

The Burmese rejection of secularization of the monastic curriculum and corresponding emphasis on the Abhidhamma and meditation is in marked contrast to the development of monastic education in neighboring Thailand. There King Mongkut's experience of secular education from Christian missionaries led him, his sons, and grandsons to actively engage with Western education, technology, sciences, economics, and military training. In the ensuing radical reform of education and Buddhism, Thai Buddhist education was increasingly secularized. Mongkut claimed to be discarding centuries of corruption by returning to the original teachings and practices of the Buddha when, as a monk, he (Mongkut) established a new monastic lineage, the Thammayut. While this rhetoric may have reflected his personal belief and a desire to protect Buddhism from decline, his understanding of what was original was shaped by both personal aptitude and the scientific and religious discourse of the time. In contrast to neighboring Burma, the Abhidhamma and meditation, both requiring lengthy apprenticeship to gain expertise, fell by the wayside.[25] The types of meditation that were approved were those simplified and authorized in line with the texts and commentaries of the *Sutta Piṭaka* section of the Pāli canon, which—unlike the Abhidhamma—provide doctrine and teachings in more accessible narrative form. The significance of meditation was radically deemphasized, especially once Mongkut was king. He and his successors used the loyal Thammayut as an administrative tool for consolidating power over newly centralized Thailand, strengthening its position against the threat of French and British encroachment.

Intertwining Traditionalizing and Secularizing Tendencies

Both responses, the antisecular and prosecular, while in part politically motivated were also an attempt to protect the sāsana from corruption. The difference between the responses lies in what is

identified as corruption and where its source is detected. Is secularization corruption and is the West a corrupting influence? Or
is corruption already to be found in the development of practice
within Buddhist cultures over the centuries, in the commentaries
going back to at least the fifth century, or even in the formation
of the canonical texts themselves? Modern secular Buddhists for
the most part take the latter position: that where a canonical text
or body of literature does not align with modern secular notions
of truth, it must be a corruption, not what the Buddha originally
taught. This willingness to discard inconvenient canonical texts,
anathema to traditionalist Buddhists, can be seen in contemporary arguments about the ordination of nuns (*bhikkhunī*). The Pāli
canon attributes to the Buddha the subordination of nuns to monks
and a narrative in which the lifespan of the sāsana is halved due
to the presence of nuns in the saṅgha. Problematic in terms of
Buddhism's perceived tolerance and egalitarianism, the texts are
analyzed for inconsistencies by feminist Buddhist scholars. They
attribute such passages to misogynistic forces that postdate the
Buddha and were retrospectively inserted into the texts as a result
of corrupting influences from varied sources, such as Hinduism and
unenlightened monks. More traditionalist scholars and practitioners, in response, attribute such relativist readings on the part of even
Asian feminists to the (corrupting) influence of twentieth-century
Western, secular conceptions of gender equality. Another example
is the sidelining of the Abhidhamma, which is treated by some
secular Buddhists as a later decline into scholasticism and taken
as an affront to notions of the Buddha's teaching as a simple message. The extent to which Theravāda modernism coincides in these
secularizing tendencies varies. As we have seen, the Burmese elite
emphasized the importance of the Abhidhamma, while the Thai
elite rejected it. However, both coincide in their rejection of the full
ordination of nuns, which remains illegal in both countries.[26] This
prohibition is seen by insiders as a means of protecting the sāsana,
by critical observers as reactionary misogyny. In Sri Lanka, the
late twentieth-century revival of bhikkhunī ordination was made

possible by those monastic lineages that had been most engaged with Theosophists and lay supporters back in the nineteenth and early twentieth centuries, even though those lineages stem from Burma, which now has the most punitive response to bhikkhunī ordination.

Although Burma and Thailand have followed different trajectories on the traditionalizing-secularizing spectrum, at points these trajectories meet, opening up news paths of development. The vacuum created by the sidelining of meditation in Thailand facilitated the spread there of Burmese vipassanā—and to a lesser extent Burmese Abhidhamma—in the mid-twentieth century.[27] The politics of meditation fashions in Thailand in turn influenced which meditation systems were taken up by Western Theravāda monastics and influential lay practitioners,[28] in turn influencing secularized practice. However, that same sidelining, coupled with the neglect of the Abhidhamma and the turn to Western sciences in Thailand, had already contributed to the loss of the family of meditation systems that once dominated Theravāda practice in Thailand, neighboring Laos, and Cambodia, and that had been exported to Sri Lanka as part of the earlier eighteenth-century Buddhist revival there.

The Loss of Meditation as a Physical Science

The nature of premodern Theravāda meditation, as we shall see, demonstrates that the relationship between meditation and science has gone back centuries, involving sciences now discarded. It also challenges the assumption that meditation is purely a mind science and one that, in a traditional Buddhist context, did not participate in the temporal or secular realm.

Although King Mongkut had been taught some of these premodern meditation practices as a monk, he had not taken to them. For him, they were among the "corruptions" that he needed to reform. Because, as king, Mongkut was the sole surviving autonomous royal Buddhist authority, he was sought out by revivalists of other Theravāda countries. This made his rejection of the meditation practice then prevalent in Thailand significant. The prioritization of administration and Pāli-based exams under the Thammayut also contributed to its disappearance, a process then exacerbated by the banning of local medicine under Mongkut's grandson Vajiravudh in the 1920s. When Thai scholar monks came to reexamine premodern Thai meditation texts in the 1930s, they labeled the practices as *boran*, "ancient" or "old," in contrast to the newer forms of meditation then available. Boran meditation was also suppressed in Cambodia under the influence of Thai reforms and, with its secularizing agenda, French administration. Nonetheless, boran meditation continued to thrive in rural areas in Cambodia and throughout Laos into the 1970s, at which point Marxist revolution dealt it its final blow.

Unlike Burmese vipassanā and meditations based on *sutta* texts and their commentaries, boran meditation was an enactment of the complex processes of transformation from an ordinary person to an enlightened being, as detailed in Abhidhamma commentaries from the fifth century C.E. onward. Taking seriously the possibility of the radical transformation that leads to enlightenment, boran meditation tries to bring that transformation about in a single lifetime, not unlike vipassanā in the later Burmese context. However, its underlying premises became unrecognizable in the modern period, in part because it assumed a full knowledge of the Abhidhamma principles of change and in part because it harnessed methods of transformation found in other, now displaced, sciences of premodern Asia.

Boran meditation is complex, contrary to modern expectations of meditation as a simple process. As a holistic system it sought to bring about not only the psychological and cognitive changes associated with the ridding of greed, hatred, and delusion but also the corresponding changes to the physical body that were understood to result. While later meditation systems were influenced by the Cartesian mind-body divide hegemonic in the colonial worldview, boran practices were not. Practitioners sought to transform the entire set of five aggregates (*khandha,* Sanskrit *skandha*) which make up the psychophysical continuum of individual existence.[29] They did this by internalizing the transformative experiences attained in meditation, drawing on methods used to bring about change in other sciences. For example, they used techniques employed in ayurvedic obstetrics to treat the fetus in the womb, with the transformative meditative attainments taking the place of the "pharmaceuticals" of ayurvedic medicine. So rather than generating and treating the desired child, the practitioner generates and treats the Buddha within. The practices also mirrored chemical processes employed in the purification of mercury to ensure the purification of the khandha through the catalyzing "chemicals"—again the attainments in meditation take the place of the catalyzing chemicals. These examples give some idea of the complexity of this system of meditation. It is also of a sequential nature, unlike the reiterative nature of modern, secular meditation.

Boran meditation was applied not only to spiritual transformation but also to other spheres now generally regarded as falling within the secular realm, including medicine, military prowess, and protection. The sidelining of the Abhidhamma meant that the framework for *boran* meditation ceased to be recognized. Changes in the dominant sciences also meant that the processes of transformation employed ceased to be understood. Some of the protective practices to which boran meditation was applied, such as the use of protective yantras and tattoos, have continued even without the meditation expertise that underlies them. However, such protective practices are now generally regarded as superstitious magic or popular religion, not part of Buddhism proper, because their origins in the Abhidhamma and displaced sciences are unrecognized.[30]

The history and disappearance of boran meditation undermines several assumptions about the secularization of Buddhism. Although Thailand seemed to be on a more secularizing trajectory in its reform of Buddhism, the lack of recognition of the Abhidhamma and the turn to Western sciences led to the loss of a meditation that was somatic, relevant to the physical realm, and connected with sciences, and so in some ways more "secular" than the solely mind-focused meditations that flourished as it disappeared.

Secularizing Tendencies in Burma

Above I have painted Burma as a relatively reactionary, conservative society, which nonetheless, through vipassanā, contributed significantly to the development of secular Buddhism and Buddhist-derived secular meditation practices. However, here I wish to return to the fate of the monks who left Burma for India in order to circumvent the restriction on their learning of English and secular subjects. This allows us to see a more nuanced picture of developments in Burma, and how the secularizing and traditionalizing tendencies influenced and affected individual monks.

One such monk was Shin Ukkaṭṭha (1897–1978), who, after his return from India in 1929, promulgated a Buddhism transformed by his seven years there. He went to India to learn English and stayed first at the Mahābodhi Society in Calcutta, then in various temples and Theosophists' homes. Erudite in traditional monastic subjects, he sought to understand global worldviews in order to defend the sāsana, writing an influential book on comparative religion—which naturally concluded that Buddhism surpassed all others. Recognizing the importance of secular subjects to uplift Burmese from the poverty and humiliation of colonial rule, he also set up a school with a combined syllabus. The defense of Buddhism and the relief of Burmese poverty seem to have been the primary driving forces in Ukkaṭṭha's life. He also had a reputation for challenging authority. These traits may be traced to the suffering of his own family, driven into poverty by the British after his parents provided the wherewithal for an abortive rebellion led by the grandfather of Aung San (great grandfather of current state counselor Aung San Suu Kyi).

Ukkaṭṭha's mentor in India was another Burmese monk, Ashin Ādiccavaṃsa (1881–1950). Ādiccavaṃsa's liberal and relativist views would influence Western views of Buddhism both during his own decade-long stay in London from the late 1920s and through his student Ashin Seṭṭhila, who—also flouting the pressure on monks not to learn English—went on to become a missionary in the United Kingdom during World War II, publishing English translations of the Abhidhamma for the Pali Text Society.[31] Ashin Ādiccavaṃsa's views foreshadow much now found within secular Buddhism. He was willing to question the authenticity of passages of the Pāli canon. In 1935, far ahead of those feminist writers who came two generations later, he published a book in favor of allowing the full bhikkhunī ordination for nuns, resulting in the most severe possible reprimand by the saṅgha hierarchy in Burma, headed by the monk U Ñeyya.[32]

During their joint travels in India, Ukkaṭṭha took part in various debates and competitions. Although defending Buddhism and winning were clearly very important to Ukkaṭṭha, he was nonetheless open to being persuaded by the others' arguments. For example, he won a victory in favor of meat-eating in a debate about vegetarianism, arguing that monks have a duty to avoid being a burden on laypeople, so should accept whatever food is given to them, while challenging his Hindu opponents on other forms of violence such as caste discrimination. Theravāda monks normally eat meat, on the premise that the meat is not being killed for them personally. However, that assumption was increasingly outdated both because of modern meat production and marketing and because of changes in how monks are supported, with meals for monks no longer begged leftovers but planned and prioritized. Ukkaṭṭha, realizing the logic of the nonviolence argument against meat-eating, became vegetarian, against Theravāda tradition, and later published a book advocating vegetarianism for Buddhists.[33] In this, he was more similar to many Western, more secularized Buddhists, who look to the logic of the first precept when considering animal-based foods rather than following Asian traditions. Despite warm relations with Muslims in India, Ukkaṭṭha's nonviolence did not extend to preventing his school pupils from participating in anti-Muslim riots in 1938. The motive of defending the sāsana, colonial narratives about how Buddhism disappeared in India, and resentment of economic strictures imposed by the British underlie this apparent inconsistency.

After his return from India, Shin Ukkaṭṭha's inclination to adapt Buddhist thought and practice on the basis of his own scrutiny would initially serve him well. In 1936, a Buddhist village headman and his Christian wife decided to host a debate between Buddhism and Christianity. Chief among the representatives on the Buddhist side would be U Ñeyya, the monk who had led the campaign against Ādiccavaṃsa for his support of the ordination of nuns. The traditionalist U Ñeyya had recently written a well-known anti-Christian work but failed to show up to the debate. Shin Ukkaṭṭha stepped in. Rather than use the arguments the Christian side had anticipated from U Ñeyya's work, Ukkaṭṭha—experienced in debating from his days in India—used the types of argument that had won the day back in the Pānadura debate of Sri Lanka over sixty years earlier. He compared the record of Buddha and God in terms of their compassion and nonviolence: that the Buddha had never been responsible for killing anyone, whereas God had. Further, when a Christian opponent pointed out the irrationality of some accounts of the Buddha's birth, Ukkaṭṭha had no problem in dismissing those accounts as later works, corruptions reflecting later superstitious beliefs. Ukkaṭṭha's victory and the subsequent conversion of Christian villagers to Buddhism was reported in the national press. His form of Buddhism with its relativist, secularizing traits had won the day, and he was a national hero.

Secularizing and Traditionalizing Tendencies in Conflict: Burma's Heresy Trials

Shin Ukkaṭṭha is no longer a national hero in Burmese history as it is told today. In 1982, four years after his death, he was convicted of heresy. How did this turn of fortunes come about? The focus of the court case was a doctrine that betrays the influence both of Darwinian Theosophy, significant in the development of secular Buddhism, and Indian debating methods. Ukkaṭṭha's doctrine, the "die human–born human" theory, posits that, in line with evolutionary theory, a living being who has reached human birth cannot then regress to a lower birth. If you die as a human, you'll be reborn as a human if reborn at all. He did not exclude rebirth in its entirety, but restricted the possibility to animals and humans, both included in Darwin's evolutionary theory. His reasoning relates to Indian rules of argumentation, which state that in a debate between opponents who do not share a scriptural authority, the highest criterion for assessing the truth of a statement must be direct observation. (Inference and analogy are the next two valid criteria.) Since Ukkaṭṭha had never directly perceived the heavens and hells, nor knew anyone who had, he concluded that there is no evidence for their existence.

Rather than take the mention of gods and hell dwellers in the Pāli canon and commentaries as an authority for the existence of heavens and hells, as Ledi Sayadaw had done a generation earlier, Shin Ukkaṭṭha regarded those passages as later corruptions. Moreover, the *Abhidhamma Piṭaka* is regarded as originating in heaven, where it was first taught by the Buddha to his deceased mother, now a deity. Since Ukkaṭṭha regarded heavens as nonexistent, he disregarded the entirety of the Abhidhamma. This is in stark contrast to its standing in the rest of Burma, where—as we have seen—it represents the ultimate truth, and the text that requires protecting most, since it will be the first to disappear. Invited to the prestigious sixth council, which in 1956 brought together the most learned monks of the Theravāda world to create the famous sixth council critical edition of the Pāli canon, Ukkaṭṭha walked out of the proceedings because the committee did not excise such texts from the canon. He thereby insulted the entire committee as well as U Nu, the first prime minister of independent Burma and the chief patron of the council.

Although his arguments align with a relativist, secularizing agenda, Ukkaṭṭha did not regard himself as such. He claimed, like Mongkut, to be even more traditionalist, seeking the original teachings of the Buddha. Ukkaṭṭha was initially brought to trial under U Nu, with the saṅgha hierarchy seeking the unity of the eighteenth century by bringing into line monks who, under the British policy of noninterference, had enjoyed a degree of autonomy in their religious teachings. These proceedings were interrupted when U Nu's

preferential treatment of Buddhists brought about unrest, with pro-
tests demanding that U Nu respect Aung San's "vision of united and
secular Burma."[34] The ensuing military coup, seeking to prevent the
disintegration of the country, led to an amnesty, and Ukkaṭṭha was
released. The military was initially secular. Its subsequent efforts to
demonstrate Buddhist piety in the 1990s came in response to Aung
San Suu Kyi's greater claim to Aung San's authority. However, in the
early 1980s, to control the saṅgha, the junta acted as if working for
the protection of Buddhism, by instituting the centralized registration of the saṅgha and setting up an ecclesiastical court system. This
court system was to try anyone caught promulgating teachings that
were *adhamma,* not the truth taught by the Buddha, or practices
that were *avinaya,* not in keeping with the monastic rules ascribed
to the Buddha. Ukkaṭṭha was posthumously tried and found guilty
at the second of these court cases, with his disciples representing
him. His teachings were banned and, for the next thirty-five years,
were only available on the black market.[35]

There have now been seventeen such heresy trials and three malpractice trials held at the national level in Myanmar. The verdict
was guilty or partially guilty in all of them. Noncompliance is pun-
ishable by a lengthy prison sentence and there is no opportunity
of appeal. A close scrutiny reveals that many of these cases revolve
around issues of cosmology, whether meditation teachings comply
with the Abhidhamma, the nature of the mind-body relationship,
or challenges to traditional interpretations of karma, rebirth, and
merit-making. One of the malpractice cases involved a woman who
had been ordained in Sri Lanka and was in Myanmar to look after
her father; while in Myanmar she was charged and imprisoned
for being a nun. None of the *adhamma, avinaya* positions would
raise an eyebrow among secular Buddhists, while most of the ver-
dicts would. As such, these trials, overseen by erudite judges and
meticulously documented with reference to the evidence of the Pāli
canon and its commentaries, represent the epitome of the potential tensions of the traditionalizing-secularizing dichotomy. Yet all
parties—the judges, the accused, and the secular Buddhists who

would find such proceedings unimaginable—often claim that they themselves are the ones to protect and promulgate the true dharma.

Shared Origins, Divergent Paths

In this essay I have drawn on a few case studies from the Theravāda world to examine how shared anxieties to protect Buddhism could lead to different trajectories, how conceptions of science and compassion have changed, and how these trajectories could both sit side by side and come into direct conflict. I have attempted to show how it is that these shared origins have also led to some of the stark contrasts between the reputation of Buddhism globally and its practice in Theravāda countries. Global and national politics and individual responses and life stories all played their part. The story of Shin Ukkaṭṭha and his contemporaries revealed how conjunctures of these factors might play out in just a single example, with changes that began in the colonial period continuing to shape how Buddhism is interpreted and practiced to this day. The history of these developments in Theravāda complicates the idea of a traditional-secular linear spectrum, with variation between and within Buddhist countries, and over different times. Secularization is also not a one-way trajectory. It can blossom then disappear. Features that may seem to go hand in hand in the West may not be bedfellows in Asia. Those who share an interest in the genuine teaching of the Buddha may be looking at mutually unrecognizable visions of the dharma.

BIBLIOGRAPHY

Ashin, Janaka. "Die-Human, Born Human: The Life and Posthumous Trial of Shin Ukkaṭṭha, a Pioneering Burmese Monk during a Tumultuous Period in a Nation's History." PhD diss., King's College, London, 2016.

Ashin, Janaka, and Kate Crosby. "Heresy and Monastic Malpractice in the Buddhist Court Cases (*Vinicchaya*) of Modern Burma (Myanmar). *Contemporary Buddhism* 1 (2017): 199-261.

Aung, Shwe Zan. "Buddhism and Science." *Journal of Burma Research Society* 8, no. 1 (1918): 99–106.

Azzopardi, David. "Religious Belief and Practice among Sri Lankan Buddhists in the U.K.," PhD dissertation. School of Oriental and African Studies, University of London, 2010.

Braun, Erik C. *The Birth of Insight: Meditation, Modern Buddhism, and the Burmese Monk Ledi Sayadaw*. Chicago and London: University of Chicago Press, 2013.

Charney, Michael W. *A History of Modern Burma*. Cambridge: Cambridge University Press, 2009.

Churton, Tobias. *Aleister Crowley in India: The Secret Influence of Eastern Mysticism on Magic and the Occult*. Rochester, VT: Inner Traditions, 2019.

Choompolpaisal, Phibul. "Reassessing Modern Thai Political Buddhism: A Critical Study of Sociological Literature from Weber to Keyes." PhD thesis. University of London, 2011.

Crosby, Kate. *Theravada Buddhism: Continuity, Diversity, Identity*. Oxford: Blackwell-Wiley, 2014.

——. "*Abhidhamma* and *Nimitta* in 18th-century Meditation Manuscripts from Sri Lanka: A Consideration of Orthodoxy and Heteropraxy in *boran kammaṭṭhāna*," in *Variety in Theravada Meditation*. Special Issue *Contemporary Buddhism* 20, no. 1-2 (2019): 111–51.

Crosby, Kate. *Esoteric Theravada. The Story of the Forgotten Meditation Tradition of Southeast Asia*. Boulder: Shambala Publications, 2020.

Crosby, Kate and Janaka Ashin. "All too Human: The Impact of International Buddhist Networks on the Life and Posthumous Conviction of the Burmese Nationalist Monk, Shin Ukkaṭṭha (1897-1978)." *Journal for the Irish Society for the Academic Study of Religions* 3 (2016): 219–35.

Dhammasami, Khammai. "Idealism and Pragmatism: A Dilemma in the Current Monastic Education Systems of Burma and Thailand." In *Buddhism, Power and Political Order*, edited by Ian Harris, 10-25. London and New York: Routledge, 2007.

Frasch, Tilman. 2012. "The Theravāda Buddhist Ecumene in the 15th Century: Intellectual Foundations and Material Representations." In *Buddhism across Asia: Networks of Material, Intellectual and Cultural Exchange* 1, edited by Tansen Sen, 291-311. Singapore: ISEAS, 2012.

Hansen, Anne Ruth. *How to Behave: Buddhism and Modernity in Colonial Cambodia, 1860-1930*. Honolulu: University of Hawai'i Press, 2007.

Hickey, Wakoh Shannon. *Mind Cure: How Meditation Became Medicine*. New York: Oxford University Press, 2019.

Karpiel, Frank J. "Theosophy, Culture, and Politics in Honolulu, 1890-1920. *Hawaiian Journal of History* 30 (1996): 169-194.

Kemper, Steven. *Rescued from the Nation: Anagarika Dharmapala and the Buddhist World.* Chicago and London: University of Chicago Press, 2015.

———. "Anagarika Dharmapala's Meditation." *Contemporary Buddhism* 20, no. 1 (2019): 223–46.

Kyaw, Pyi Phyo. "Paṭṭhāna in Burmese Buddhism." PhD thesis, King's College London, University of London, 2014.

Lopez, Donald S., Jr. *Prisoners of Shangri-La: Tibetan Buddhism and the West.* Chicago and London: The University of Chicago Press, 1998.

———. *Buddhism and Science: A Guide for the Perplexed.* Chicago and London: University of Chicago Press, 2008.

Malalgoda, Kitsiri. *Buddhism and Sinhalese Society 1750–1900.* Berkeley: University of California Press, 1976.

Naono, Atsuko. *State of Vaccination: The Fight Against Smallpox in Colonial Burma.* Hyderabad: Orient Blackswan, 2009.

Peebles, J. M. *The Great Debate: Buddhism and Christianity Face to Face. Being an Oral Debated Held at Panadura between The Rev. Migettuwatte Gunananda a Buddhist Priest and The Rev. David De Silva a Wesleyan Clergyman:* Colombo: P. K. W. Siriwardhana 1878.

Piyobhaso, Phramaha Bhatsakorn. "Abhidhamma in Contemporary Thailand." Unpublished paper.

Samuel, Geoffrey. "Between Buddhism and Science, between Mind and Body" *Religions* 5 (2014): 560–79.

Skilton, Andrew, Kate Crosby, and Pyi Phyo Kyaw. "Terms of Engagement: Text, Technique, and Experience in Scholarship on Theravada Meditation," in *Variety in Theravada Meditation,* Special Issue *Contemporary Buddhism* 20, no. 1-2, edited by Kate Crosby, Andrew Skilton, and Pyi Phyo Kyaw (2019): 1–35.

Turner, Alicia. *Saving Buddhism: Moral Community and the Impermanence of Colonial Religion.* Honolulu: University of Hawai'i Press, 2014.

Verkerk, Mark. *Buddha's Lost Children.* EMS Films, 2006.

7 | Manifesting the Buddha Dharma in a Secular Age

BHIKKHU BODHI

While Western interest in Buddhism may have blossomed during the 1960s, Westerners had been attracted to Buddhism even as far back as the late nineteenth century, when translations of authentic Buddhist texts started to appear. In the early decades of the twentieth century, before jet airliners made cross-continental travel easy, seekers from the West endured the hardship of journeying by sea to distant Asian lands, some to take ordination as Buddhist monks. In the United States, interest in Buddhism gradually grew in the 1950s, but it was only in the 1960s that attraction to Buddhism—and for many, a total commitment to the dharma—took off at an exponential rate. Why this sudden spurt of interest in Buddhism at just this time?

My concern here is not with historical specifics, but with the changes in consciousness that opened many Westerners to the dharma and eventually led them to embrace Buddhism. Among the factors responsible were the loss of faith in the established religions of the West, the breakdown of a unified narrative about the place of humankind in the cosmos, the spread of existentialist modes of thought into the general culture, the increasing interest in psychology as providing a scientific understanding of the mind, and the use of psychotherapy to deal with the tension, perplexity, and alienation of modern life.

Psychotherapy had undergone a process of evolution that took it from the psychoanalytical system of Sigmund Freud, with its mechanistic premises and dark pessimism, to more optimistic forms that affirmed the positive side of human nature. Humanistic psychologists encouraged clients to change their state of mind and behavior from compulsive reactions to healthier ones with more productive self-awareness. In the late 1960s humanistic psychology gave birth to transpersonal psychology, which endeavored to integrate the spiritual and transcendent dimensions of human experience into a scientific understanding of the mind. Psychedelic drugs, too, had opened up hidden dimensions of the mind and stimulated interest in Eastern spirituality.

Once those in the cultural vanguard came to see the mind as the ultimate source of meaning and purpose, of wellness and happiness, at least a few realized that to fully tap the mind's potentials a more radical method of inner transformation was needed than psychedelic drugs or psychotherapy could provide. Some explored meditation as the means of inner change, and as part of this Eastward turn interest in Buddhism expanded and gradually culminated in the appearance of Western manifestations of the dharma.

Three Contemporary Approaches to the Dharma

This brief survey of the factors behind the upsurge of Western interest in Buddhism during the 1960s shows us why Western Buddhism has taken on a largely secular shape focused on existential and psychological issues rather than the pursuit of liberation in the sense advocated in the texts of classical Buddhism. It has taken this shape, I would argue, because the Buddhist pioneers of the 1960s approached it from a predominantly secular orientation rather than as the solution to a religious quest. Buddhism could exercise this kind of appeal because its nontheistic teachings seemed to be exceptionally "secular" from the outset. It laid down a clear analysis of human suffering and a program of mental training that could be adopted independently of any belief system and could lead to such goals as self-knowledge, inner peace, happiness, and elevated states of consciousness.

As an increasing number of Westerners took up Buddhist practice, a complex tapestry began to appear among Western Buddhists that extended even beyond the divisions between the major Buddhist traditions into Theravāda, East Asian Mahāyāna, and Tibetan. The complicating factor was the introduction of various modernizing and secularizing strands into each of those traditions. Of course, modernized versions of the dharma were already being constructed by the intellectual elite among Asian Buddhists, who responded to the challenges posed by the West, especially Christian missionaries, by depicting Buddhism as scientific, rational, psychological, and socially progressive.[1] But there was still a significant difference between the roles that modernizing interpretations played in Asian Buddhism and in newly emergent Western Buddhism. In Asia, the modernizing trends were superimposed on a well-established foundation of Buddhist tradition, which served as the substratum for the modern interpretations. Modernized interpretations were partly a defensive maneuver intended to defend the dharma against external criticism, partly a way to make Buddhism an attractive alternative to seekers from the West disenchanted with both Christianity and secular materialism.

In the West, on the other hand, the substratum for the modernizing tendencies was a montage made up of various secular strains of thought, and the task faced by the young Western interpreters was to integrate the intellectual content of the dharma with the dominant secular worldview. In the initial stages the secularized approach probably occurred imperceptibly, as Westerners brought their own horizons of understanding into their encounters with the dharma, which perhaps appealed to many who were exposed to the more rationalized forms of Buddhism being offered by modern Asian interpreters. In time, however, a decisive breach with Buddhist tradition occurred when a version of the dharma emerged that called itself Secular Buddhism. This approach is perhaps most clearly articulated in Stephen Batchelor's works, as we will see below, but it is not confined to them.

I provisionally call the two camps "Traditional Buddhism" and "Secular Buddhism." Although there are problems with these expressions, I use them as terms of convenience, as representing not fixed and easily definable categories but as the end points of a spectrum of possibilities that may blend in any given person's relationship to the teachings. The two categories primarily diverge from each other over their different perspectives on the human condition. Traditional Buddhism sees human life as literally embedded in the beginningless chain of rebirths called *saṃsāra*, which includes not only past and future lives but multiple planes of existence above and below the human plane. Life in all realms is *dukkha*. The Buddha appeared in the world to discover the way out of this predicament, the way that leads to nirvana, which does not mean merely a state of sublime peace and bliss experienced in this life but a state of irreversible release from the beginningless round of rebirths.

Most practitioners in the traditional mode hope to make gradual progress from one life to the next until their faculties are mature enough to realize the final goal. Those with more mature faculties may aspire to cut the ties binding them to the round of rebirths and win the bliss of nirvana within this life itself. Followers of the bodhisattva vehicle, the traditional Mahāyāna path, seek to develop the *pāramitās*, or transcendent virtues, over many eons until they qualify to attain buddhahood. But what is common to all these practitioners is an acceptance of the classical Buddhist framework of rebirth and karma, understood as a moral force with consequences extending beyond the present life.

Secular Buddhists, in contrast, claim to begin with our immediate existential situation, without relying on beliefs about past and future lives. They generally do not accept the teachings of rebirth and karma or acknowledge any state of liberation other than a relative freedom from greed, hatred, and delusion that can be achieved through Buddhist practice. Most regard rebirth merely as a plank of ancient Indian metaphysics that has to be deleted in order to bring the dharma into accord with the naturalistic worldview of the present age.

I believe this dichotomy of Traditional Buddhism and Secular Buddhism conceals a third alternative that may actually be *the most prevalent expression* of Buddhism in the West today. This is what I will call "Immanent Buddhism," by which I mean an approach to the dharma that avoids doctrinal issues to focus almost entirely on existential and psychological aims. Those who fall within this category see in Buddhism a practical means of inner transformation, for recovering our connections with our own inner depths, with other people, and with the natural world. The dharma, as practiced in this mode, is essentially a set of tools for transforming the mind and healing our inner wounds.

While proponents of Secular Buddhism explicitly reject traditional Buddhist beliefs, those who adopt the "immanent" mode simply treat these beliefs as irrelevant. They see no need to reject them on rational grounds or to ponder whether they are true or false, valid or invalid. Whereas the secularists study the texts of classical Buddhism and try to interpret them in purely secular terms, those who follow the "immanent" approach seldom struggle to determine their relationship to formal Buddhist doctrine. Rather, they randomly draw from the canonical texts whatever teachings serve their purposes, often blending meditation with techniques derived from more humanistic models of psychotherapy.

Although I have given this approach a distinct designation, I must emphasize that *Immanent Buddhism is not a self-defined movement* but an orientation that operates below the threshold of conscious recognition. While this orientation may be shared to some extent by all forms of contemporary Western Buddhism, the focus on immanent concerns may be most apparent in the Western offshoot of the Theravāda tradition called Vipassana Buddhism.

The transmission of *vipassanā* meditation from East to West has led to something more than a simple repackaging of the practice in American cultural forms and language. It has brought about a change in the premises and the goal of the practice itself, transposing it from the sphere of transcendent realization to the domain of purely immanent aims and objectives.

One support for this approach, commonly cited by contemporary Western teachers, is the *Kālāma Sutta*,[2] a discourse in which the Buddha tells a group of inquirers not to rely on external authorities such as tradition, lineage, scriptures, and charismatic teachers but instead to determine for themselves which things are unwholesome and which are wholesome, which things lead to happiness and which to suffering. Such instructions could be read as justifying agnosticism about ideas in the canonical texts that do not match one's personal experience, particularly statements about karma and rebirth.

Another theme that lent itself to an immanent interpretation was the Buddha's insistence that what he teaches is not a speculative system but just suffering and the end of suffering, a program laid out in the four noble truths. While the four truths are promulgated against the background of a worldview that includes rebirth, modernist Western exponents of the dharma have given precedence to a psychological understanding of the truths, an approach that has resonated well with the pivotal role that psychology came to play in Western culture in the late twentieth century.

Traditional Theravāda aims at *vimutti*, liberation from the mind's defilements and from the cycle of repeated birth and death. In contrast, teachers of Immanent Buddhism emphasize the freedom to participate more actively, joyfully, and spontaneously *in the world*, to participate in the dance of life with calm and clear awareness. As Jack Kornfield puts it, with awakening "we are now truly alive, able to care, to work, to love, to enter life fully, with an open heart."[3]

It is likely that the basis for this shift from the transcendent orientation of Asian Buddhist tradition toward a Buddhism focused on immanent aims was the convergence of various secularizing trends in Western culture that occurred during the late 1960s. Even the language used by experimental psychology during this period seems to anticipate the kind of terminology the early Western teachers of insight meditation used to describe the practice they had learned in Asia. For instance, Fritz Perls, the founder of Gestalt Therapy, stressed the need to be fully aware of "the present moment" as a way to get "in touch with thoughts, feelings, and sensations as they occur from moment to moment."[4] Such styles of expression must have been picked up by the early Buddhist pioneers of the 1960s and then used to explain the Buddhist practices they learned from their Asian masters. It was in this way that the practice of meditation, particularly insight meditation, came to be seen primarily as a program for anchoring attention in the present, devoid of any religious basis or transcendent aim.

Since the naturalistic worldview rejects all beliefs in an objective moral order etched into the cosmos, it is quite understandable that those who subscribe to this worldview would be disposed toward a purely immanent approach to Buddhist teachings. This immanent disposition does not function primarily as an explicit conceptual ground for understanding and practicing the dharma. Rather, it is tacitly assumed, ticking in the background as an implicit "operating system" for the ways contemporary Westerners approach and appropriate the Buddhist teachings.

While the framework seems self-evident, impervious to questioning, it is actually the product of various strains of thought that came together in the middle and late sixties, molding the outlook and expectations of the pioneers of contemporary Western Buddhism. Thus, if Westerners who come to the dharma today find immediate rapport with a purely immanent interpretation, this is because they share the same modernist worldview as those who teach it. Approaching the Buddha's teachings with the premise that scientific naturalism holds the key to knowledge and truth, and that psychological transformation is the key to happiness, they see in the dharma a system of thought and practice that, with a few revisions, could easily be brought into alignment with those premises.

The above discussion shows that the division of contemporary Western Buddhists into two opposed camps, Traditional Buddhism and Secular Buddhism, is an oversimplification. What we find rather are three broad modalities that run largely parallel but often intersect or shade into each other, yielding great diversity. These three modalities constitute different life worlds in which Buddhist practitioners dwell, three ways in which they encounter the dharma and live their lives through its lens.

The three are not sealed off from one another, and people may casually migrate among them. In practice, all three modalities will largely be occupied with immanent concerns. Such concerns are not the unique preserve of those I am calling Immanent Buddhists— not by a long shot. Where they differ is in the background against which they pursue these ends and the ultimate purpose that guides their efforts. The traditionalist will see these practices as part of their long journey through *saṃsāra*, as stepping-stones toward a transcendent goal, whether conceived as nirvana or as buddha-hood. The secularist and immanent practitioner will pursue them against a naturalistic backdrop of understanding and focus on the immediate concrete benefits they yield.

Toward a Critical Assessment

Given these three modes of contemporary Buddhist practice, I now want to inquire whether they are equally viable as vehicles for carrying the Buddha's teaching forward into the modern world. Secular Buddhists certainly claim that their version of the dharma best meets the needs of modernity. Batchelor, for instance, is apprehensive that if we do not cast off the belief structure of Asian Buddhism "the dharma might find itself condemned to an increasingly marginal existence in mainstream culture, catering only to those who are willing to embrace the worldview of ancient India." He even argues that "the cultural divide that separates traditional Buddhism from modernity is so great" that it may not suffice merely to modify a traditional form of Buddhism to better meet the needs of contemporary practitioners. He sees all forms of traditional Buddhism, from Theravāda through Zen and Shin to Vajrayāna, as based on the same "operating system," the soteriology of ancient India, which he calls "Buddhism 1.0." He proposes replacing this with a new operating system, one based on a naturalistic worldview, which he calls "Buddhism 2.0."[5] Other secularists may not go as far as Batchelor, but virtually all hold that the doctrinal framework of Traditional Buddhism is no longer relevant to people struggling to make sense of their lives in our secular modern world.[6]

Gil Fronsdal may be taken to represent the approach of Immanent Buddhism. His position partly corresponds with that of the secularists but it avoids their polemical tone and drastic attempts at revision. Although he is an avid student of the Pāli *suttas*, he stresses that the benefits of Buddhist practice are accessible even without adherence to a framework of traditional beliefs.[7] He sees four key practices of Buddhist tradition as central to contemporary life: mindfulness (*sati*), loving-kindness (*mettā*), ethics (*sīla*), and generosity (*dāna*). Cast in this mold, he says, the dharma functions "as a form of therapy from which practitioners can benefit in their current lives."[8]

As a proponent of a more traditional point of view, I want to challenge the presuppositions that underlie the modernizing project of Secular Buddhism and the ambivalence toward classical Buddhist doctrine adopted by Immanent Buddhists. In insisting that certain core elements of Traditional Buddhism should be preserved, however, I don't want my position to be construed as a rigid conservatism. I believe that the course of historical development through which Buddhism has passed has been immensely fruitful, bringing to manifestation new facets of thought and practice that were not immediately apparent in the more ancient expressions of the dharma. These range from the analytical schemes of the Abhidharma to the contemplative techniques of the Vajrayāna.

Perhaps one can argue that Secular Buddhism is the next step in the evolution of the dharma, a step brought to light by the secular spirit of our era. However, I would seriously question this supposition. Against the assertion that Secular Buddhism marks a step forward in the evolution of the dharma, I would maintain that to the extent that it jettisons the underpinnings of the traditional Buddhist worldview, Secular Buddhism could be putting in jeopardy the future of the dharma as a genuine path to liberation.

I see the secularists as guilty of a double error. The *first* is that they discard too much that is central to the dharma as an organic whole, thereby tearing away the archaic root of the Buddhist heritage. Despite the arguments of some secularists, the ideas of *saṃsāra* as the round of birth and death, nirvana as an ultimate state of liberation, and karma and rebirth as fundamental dimensions of the human condition are not monastic fabrications but are all derived from the canonical texts, which are not at all ambiguous about their meanings. The *second* is that they place too much trust in the assumption that naturalistic science—science conducted according to materialistic premises—exhausts the methods for accessing verifiable truth. They take as indubitable a version of science that operates with a two-dimensional picture of reality, neglecting the multiple dimensions of reality and intricate intersections between these domains testified to by contemplatives from various traditions, Buddhist and non-Buddhist alike. I believe that if we are to preserve the dharma as an integral program for resolving the deepest problem at the heart of the human condition, we have to be extremely cautious about what we cast away. Otherwise, in our eagerness to enhance the contemporary relevance of Buddhism, we may actually cut off the bloodline that keeps the dharma alive.

In response to those disposed to an immanent approach to the dharma, I would say that if we are to responsibly represent the dharma in its fullness and its depth, it is not sufficient to extract the practice from its roots in Buddhist faith and formal doctrine and merely focus on the temporal benefits the practice is capable of delivering. Rather, we should strive to widen our perspectives toward those revealed by the Buddha on the basis of his supreme enlightenment. We must make an effort to clearly grasp the context in which the practice is situated, the underlying premises, and the ultimate aim of endeavor along the path. Certainly, as Buddhists, we can offer the secular world practices that help people better understand themselves, better relate to each other, and deal more skillfully with the problems of modern life. But it would be more prudent to offer this as a pragmatic program of training *derived from Buddhism*, not as a new and more highly evolved form of the dharma.

In regard to both contemporary approaches, secularist and immanent, we also have to be extremely careful not to fall into a subtle cultural arrogance that tells us that because we are Westerners— mostly white, middle-class, educated Westerners—we therefore understand the dharma better than those nurtured in a traditional Buddhist culture. We should not look down at them as mere "religious Buddhists" who seek from the dharma little more than "a belief system" and a source of "spiritual consolation."[9] If the dharma is to retain its integrity, it must at minimum preserve the doctrinal imprint that has been central to Buddhism's self-identity through the centuries.

Since scientific naturalism is now taken to be the one valid criterion for the assessment of truth claims and the determination of values, the question may be raised why contemporary Buddhists should adopt and disseminate ideas that don't easily fit into this paradigm. I would offer several answers to this question.

For me the most persuasive is the fact that the Buddha himself taught rebirth, taught it on the basis of his direct experience, and made it one of the pillars of his teaching. The texts of Early Buddhism consistently describe his enlightenment as involving the attainment of three "clear knowledges": of his own past births, of the rebirth of beings in accordance with their karma, and of the destruction of the *āsavas*, the primordial defilements that sustain the round of rebirths. After each breakthrough, the Buddha declares: "Darkness was dispelled and light arose, ignorance was dispelled and clear knowledge arose."[10] Attainment of this last knowledge culminated in the realization that rebirth has been ended and there is no coming back to any state of being.

The quest that the Buddha successfully completed serves as a model for others, and the texts report that numberless disciples also attained the threefold knowledge. Are we to dismiss these claims to supernormal knowledge as mere beliefs entertained by ancient Indian monks who subscribed to the presuppositions of Indian metaphysics? Or should we take them as the texts present them to us, as truthful assertions made by those who have reached the pinnacle of wisdom, the heights of realization? If we do take them to be truthful assertions, shouldn't they also influence our understanding and practice of the dharma?

A second reason for a professed follower of the dharma to accept the twin ideas of rebirth and karma is also related to claims made by and about the Buddha. In the canonical texts of all schools of Buddhism, the Buddha is said to possess ten "Tathāgata powers," powers of knowledge that entitle him "to claim the place of a chief bull, roar a lion's roar in the assemblies, and set rolling the supreme wheel."[11] At least six of these involve a grasp of the workings of karma and their relation to different spheres of rebirth. If we reject these knowledges because they do not resonate with the premises of a philosophical naturalism, we will wind up with a greatly diminished conception of the Buddha. He may emerge as a sage, even in some respects a holy man, but would fail to match the claims he makes about himself.

Still a third reason the ideas of rebirth and karma should be preserved in contemporary representations of the dharma is because they are essential to the unity of the Buddha's teaching as an integral path of understanding and practice. They are integral to right view, the forerunner of the path, which guides the development of the other factors. They underlie the four noble truths and the twelvefold formula of dependent origination. They give substance to the four stages of realization. Each of these stages is described in two ways, first by way of the particular cluster of defilements eliminated at that stage, and second by way of the number and sphere of rebirths that remain. Thus the very distinction among these four stages only makes sense when the idea of rebirth is taken into account.[12]

Still a fourth argument in support of the twin ideas of karma and rebirth hinges on moral reflection. Consider the following scenario involving two individuals. One is the CEO of a corporation that manufactures weapons of war that he knows will be used in devastating attacks against the civilian population of other countries.

The other is an American medical doctor who goes to serve in a war-torn country. While treating wounded civilians in a decrepit hospital there, she is killed in a bombing raid, falling victim to one of the bombs that the CEO's company had sold to the aggressor nation. Now on the premises of materialistic naturalism, at death both these individuals—the CEO of the weapons company and the self-sacrificing medical doctor—meet the same fate. From the materialist point of view, both are obliterated, snuffed out into eternal oblivion, a consequence that seems strongly counterintuitive.

Although such reflection cannot *compel* a belief in survival of death, it seems to me that the scenario I depicted flies in the face of the heart's yearning for some kind of moral order to prevail in the world. It may well be the case that tragedy has the final say, that our moral intuitions are purely subjective and do not have any foundation beyond our personal desires. But the contrary, affirmed in some way by most religions, may in fact be true. It could well be that our yearning for the cosmos to operate in accordance with certain norms of moral equilibrium actually reflects the way the cosmos does work. And it could be that our sense of moral justice is not a vain fantasy but a subjective reflection of this objective principle.

Now if it is the case that good and bad deeds produce results that correspond to their moral quality, as the doctrine of karma holds, consciousness must in some way continue beyond death; for it is obvious that in this present life people's fortunes do not usually correspond with the moral quality of their lives. The bad flourish; the good suffer. Wrongdoers escape the arm of the law; the innocent are subjected to the cruelest fate. If consciousness does survive death, it may do so in one of two ways: one is by reaping an eternal reward (perhaps after a temporary spell in purgatory) or eternal punishment for one's conduct; the other is by passing through a series of lives in which past deeds produce results that, like the deeds themselves, are of finite strength and duration. I would contend that since any morally significant deed, no matter how evil or how good, necessarily arises from a volition of finite psychological force, its fruition must also be finite, eventually due to end when it has exhausted the force of the original deed. In my view, the one framework that can reasonably accommodate such a relationship between deeds and their fruits is that provided by the tenets of karma and rebirth. And since deeds flow from volitions, from states of mind, this entails a view of the cosmos in which consciousness and material processes are bound together in a much more intimate relationship than that envisaged by the materialistic interpretation of modern science, by a "scientism" that sees the mind as a fluke of nature, a chance byproduct of bare material processes.

A final argument in favor of the twin principles of karma and rebirth hinges on the supposition that the spiritual life must aim at some kind of closure. Both the canonical collections of Early Buddhism and the Mahāyāna sūtras see the path as pointing toward a transcendent goal in which it reaches completion. For Early Buddhism this is arahantship and the attainment of nirvana; for Mahāyāna Buddhism, it is buddhahood. But both secular and immanent modes of Buddhism rule out the possibility of closure. It may be that this conception of closure to the spiritual life is "ancient Indian soteriology," but that does not undermine its validity. The ancient Indian Buddhists may have had it right. If the spiritual life reached culmination in the Buddha's time, then it would seem that such a culmination remains a valid possibility at any time, and that those who make sufficient effort in any age should be able to achieve it.

Central to the idea of closure in Early Buddhism is completion of the "four tasks." In his first discourse, the Buddha not only speaks of those four tasks as jobs to be done but declares that he himself had completed them. He has fully understood the truth of suffering, abandoned its origin, realized its cessation, and cultivated the path. And it was precisely this achievement—the completion of the four tasks—that entitled him to proclaim that he had achieved unsurpassed enlightenment. The same set of tasks that the Buddha himself completed are laid down as the duties for the disciples, and many of these declare in the texts that they succeeded: "Done is what had to be done." Yet for such a declaration to have any meaning, two conditions are necessary as grounds for its cogency. One is the state of bondage to the round of rebirths that the path is intended to overcome. The other is a state of liberation that is ever-present, always available to us, that has to be realized by the practice of the path.

In retrospect, the problem that I see with both Secular Buddhism and Immanent Buddhism is that they consider the purpose of Buddhist practice to be simply the achievement of a kind of human flourishing: stable happiness, inner peace, equanimity, greater awareness, and practical wisdom in dealing with the challenges of life. This flourishing is, of course, superior to the pursuit of wealth, sensual pleasures, high position, and other worldly goals. But it is still a flourishing of the empirical person within the bounds of contingency, a flourishing that can fit into our usual categories of understanding.

However, while the full cultivation of the Buddhist path in the traditionalist mode also leads to this type of flourishing, the latter is not its goal. The goal is *a state of holiness*, and that can only be achieved by breaking through the bounds of contingency in order to realize, experience, and dwell in a dimension that is not conditioned, not contingent, not perishable. Within the system of Early Buddhism, that dimension is nirvana, the deathless, and its full realization is arahantship. For Mahāyāna Buddhism, it is called suchness, emptiness, buddha-nature, or the peak of reality (*bhūta-koṭi*), the experience of which turns one into a true bodhisattva. In either case, the prospect of holiness is achieved by rising above and beyond the bounds of finitude and contingency and touching a reality that transforms us in a most fundamental way at the very base of our personal being.

The Buddha noted that our views influence our motivations, which in turn influence our conduct. If we adopt the views prescribed by the Buddha on the basis of his unsurpassed enlightenment, our motivation will be to attain the goal prescribed by his teaching: according to Early Buddhism, liberation from the cycle of repeated birth and death; according to the Mahāyāna, the enlightenment of a buddha. If we reject the idea of rebirth as a literal fact, its corollaries, liberation from the cycle of rebirths and buddhahood, become untenable, even unintelligible except perhaps as metaphors. In that case, we will turn to other aims as the mainstay of our practice: living with wisdom, clarity, and kindness; dwelling mindfully in the present; experiencing happiness, joy, and calm within the bounds of this present existence. As worthy as these goals may be in their own right, we should ask whether they are worthy of replacing the goals laid down for us in the canonical texts. To set them up in this role would, in my view, entail a serious impairment of the dharma.

A Wider Sense of Responsibility

I have sketched three broad orientations among contemporary Western Buddhists: the Traditional, the Secular, and the Immanent. While I distinguish Immanent Buddhism as a distinct modality, I also noted that Buddhists who fall into each of these three modalities can entertain immanent aims and may even give them precedence in their practice. Thus Buddhists following all three modes may give primacy to the "immanent" task of navigating their way through today's chaotic and perplexing world. In the West, however, those who adopt Buddhism as a spiritual path have tended to focus mainly on the enrichment and deepening of their personal life rather than on applying Buddhist values to the task of transforming the larger structures under which we live—the political, social, and economic structures responsible for the suffering of war, hunger and poverty, racism and ethnic hostility, ecological devastation, and sexual and gender-based violence.

This trend poses a risk that contemporary approaches to the dharma may foster a purely private type of spirituality pursued mainly by educated, upper-middle-class people in the tranquility of their meditation halls and dharma centers. While Socially Engaged Buddhism has served as an antidote to this tendency, coordinated projects of social engagement have won relatively limited support among Buddhists, whether in the East or the West. Though Buddhism elevates loving-kindness and compassion to the highest ranks in the moral life, we seldom see Buddhists undertaking the truly self-sacrificial risks on behalf of vulnerable populations that we see among conscientious Christians, Jews, and even nonreligious people.

It is here perhaps that Buddhists have much to learn from Christianity and Judaism. Christianity has enunciated a social gospel that calls on the faithful to serve the poor, the sick, the homeless, and the hungry—the wretched of the earth—to undertake not only deeds of charity but daring acts of political and social resistance on behalf of justice and human dignity. As manifestations of their faith, Christians have created impressive humanitarian organizations that save the lives of millions. Yet Buddhists have lagged behind in such undertakings. We do make our contributions, to be sure— for instance, through the Buddhist Peace Fellowship (based in the United States), the Tzuchi Foundation (based in Taiwan, with US branches), Sarvodaya (based in Sri Lanka), and Buddhist Global Relief (based in the United States), as well as an umbrella organization, the International Network of Engaged Buddhists, that brings together disparate Buddhists to share insights and engage in common projects. But these have been minority efforts, far outweighed by the offering of courses in mindfulness meditation as the cure for all the ills the world is facing.

The reason for this feeble responsiveness to collective suffering may be partly rooted in Buddhist doctrine. The Buddhist scriptures are filled with praise of kindness and compassion and exhortations to act for the good of all sentient beings, yet seldom do they advise Buddhists to actively strive for social justice, to resist tyranny, or to stand up against the degrading material and social conditions that afflict disadvantaged and marginalized communities. Through the centuries, Buddhists have largely pursued kindness and compassion as internal meditative states or as guidelines to personal ethics rather than as spurs to action aimed at wider dimensions of transformation. Yet I believe that if Buddhism is to fulfill its potential as a positive moral force in today's world, it must draw upon its ancient insights and ethical values as incentives to transformative action, even radical action in promoting a different kind of world. The need for such action has become especially urgent with the rise over the past few years of authoritarian regimes in Eastern Europe and the United States—regimes that attempt to consolidate their hold on power by inciting hatred, violence, and bigotry.

At present, the global community faces two overwhelming challenges, both of which must be tackled if we are to avoid horrific consequences. One is to preserve an ecologically safe space for humanity to survive and thrive—a space constantly under threat from chemical pollution, ocean acidification, diminishing sources of fresh water, soil erosion, biodiversity loss, and above all, escalating climate change. The other is to ensure that all people everywhere can obtain the basic requisites to live a dignified life, particularly adequate food, clean water, housing, health care, education, political rights, and a safe environment. These two challenges put our collective future at risk, yet instead of effectively addressing them, we have been thoughtlessly and even spitefully aggravating them.

While it may seem that the Buddhist emphasis on compassion and generosity would contribute to an ethic of active social concern, certain long-standing attitudes and ideas widespread among Buddhists may actually be hindering the manifestation of a cogent Buddhist program of social change. If Buddhism is to unleash its potential as a force for positive transformation, these attitudes and ideas may have to be critically reassessed.

One is Traditional Buddhism's overriding orientation toward transcendence of the mundane world, an orientation that, despite philosophic differences, is shared by virtually all schools of Buddhism. Once the supreme good is located in a state, dimension, or domain that lies beyond the limits of the phenomenal world, in a transcendent nirvana—or even at its heart, in the essence of mind, buddha-nature, or the emptiness of all phenomena—the need to secure the temporal welfare of living beings in this world of contingent events may tend to be overshadowed by the effort to realize the final aim of striving. This obstacle appears in different guises among Secular and Immanent Buddhists. While the latter do not recognize transcendent liberation, they still largely locate the aim of their practice in personal transformation to be achieved through an inward focus.

As a Traditional Buddhist, I do not wish to maintain that the dharma should discard its transcendent orientation in favor of an agenda of social and political reform. For Buddhism to be true to its origins, the experience and attainment of a transcendent state must be the final aim. However, I believe that to manifest the full breadth of the dharma as a liberative teaching, we have to strike a balance between transcendent and socially transformative goals.

It is possible too that the teaching of *anattā*, non-self, when extended beyond its proper context, may become an obstacle to transformative action. While this teaching definitely doesn't entail that persons as such do not exist, the denial of the substantial reality of human persons and their relegation to the sphere of conventional reality may have the unintended consequence of diminishing the claims they make on us as subjects meriting ultimate concern. A similar problem perhaps arises from the teaching of emptiness as expounded in the Mahāyāna sūtras and treatises. Although it is said that the truth of emptiness must be balanced by the conventional truth that affirms the phenomenal reality of sentient beings and conditioned dharmas—that it is only their inherent existence that is denied—it is possible that the rhetoric of emptiness undermines the claims of beings to an existential status sufficient to generate an ethic committed to promoting the good of people in the social and communal aspects of their lives.

It is true that the bodhisattva vows to deliver all sentient beings, and this could be taken as a ground for promoting social and economic policies that ameliorate the suffering of others. However, when beings and phenomena are said to be like magical illusions, like a mirage, like a flash of lightning, and so forth—when, it is said, a "being" or "person" or "dharma" is not to be apprehended—then, from one angle, it seems that the moral claims these beings make on us, claims that might motivate us to take action to address the structural causes of their very real suffering, are left without an adequately strong foothold. Mahāyāna Buddhism has the resources to avoid this pitfall through its stress on compassion and the altruistic vow, but historically, it seems, this vow has too often been eclipsed by the language of emptiness, which weakens its role as a motive for social engagement.

Still another historically obstructive factor that Buddhism must address if it is to become a positive force in promoting social justice is a passive and almost resigned interpretation of the doctrine of karma. While the workings of karma are not inevitable and thus an appeal to karma cannot be relied upon to validate violations of social justice, still, even in the suttas, the doctrine is used to explain glaring disparities in wealth, power, status, bodily health, and physical disabilities and so is not altogether innocent of rationalizing social injustices. Thus, even on a fairly liberal interpretation—one that avoids any kind of predetermination—the teaching of karma can still be seen as discouraging concerted efforts to abolish oppressive social systems and change toxic policies that today privilege some, especially in the North, while consigning millions, mainly in southern Asia, Africa, and the Middle East, to unbearable misery.

The persistence of poverty and the escalating climate crisis, along with war, militarism, racism, and other kinds of violence, should sound a call of conscience to Buddhists, no matter what orientation we may adopt. The dharma potentially provides us with tools for developing a critical diagnosis of the pressing problems we face as a global community. We know that the suffering we face in our personal life originates from the greed, aversion, and delusion that obsess the mind and propel us into harmful courses of conduct. Today, however, these mental defilements have spread beyond the confines of individual minds. They have infected institutions and social systems, driving reckless policies that bring short-term gain to a privileged few but spell calamity for billions of others. To emerge intact we must first clearly recognize the dangers inherent in these systemic embodiments of greed, aversion, and delusion; then, with insight and courage, we must come forward to tackle them, not only in the depths of our minds but also in the massive systems that are crushing the lives of millions of people around the globe.

To promote more just and benign alternatives is, I believe, a task that should unite Buddhists of all three geographical traditions—South Asian, East Asian, and Himalayan—a task that should also unite those of the three orientations, Traditional, Secular, and Immanent. But to succeed, we will have to look closely and critically at long-entrenched attitudes and a disposition to passive resignation. It is only by taking such steps, I believe, that we can best manifest the vital relevance of the dharma in this secular age.

BIBLIOGRAPHY

Anālayo, Bhikkhu. *Rebirth in Early Buddhism and Current Research*. Boston: Wisdom Publications, 2018.

Batchelor, Stephen. *Buddhism without Beliefs*. New York: Riverhead Books, 1997.

——. *Confessions of a Buddhist Atheist*. New York: Spiegel & Grau, 2010.

——. "A Secular Buddhism." *Journal of Global Buddhism* 13 (2012): 87–107.

Fronsdal, Gil. "Insight Meditation in the United States: Life, Liberty, and the Pursuit of Happiness." Insight Meditation Center website, https://www.insightmeditationcenter.org/books-articles/articles/insight-meditation-in-the-united-states-life-liberty-and-the-pursuit-of-happiness/. Originally published in Charles S. Prebish and Kenneth K. Tanaka. *The Faces of Buddhism in America*. Berkeley and Los Angeles: University of California Press, 1998, pp. 163–80.

——. "Should I Believe in Rebirth?" Insight Meditation Center website, https://www.insightmeditationcenter.org/books-articles/articles/should-i-believe-in-rebirth/.

Janov, Arthus. "Gestalt Therapy: Being Here Now, Keeping Unfinished Business Unfinished." Chapter 12 in his *Grand Delusions: Psychotherapies without Feeling*. http://primaltherapy.com/GrandDelusions/GD12.htm.

Kornfield, Jack. *The Wise Heart*. New York: Bantam Books, 2008.

McMahan, David L. *The Making of Buddhist Modernism*. New York: Oxford University Press, 2008.

Secular Buddhist Association. "Frequently Asked Questions on Secular Buddhism." http://secularbuddhism.org/faq/.

Smith, Doug. "A Secular Evaluation of Rebirth." Secular Buddhist Association (website). May 29, 2013. https://secularbuddhism.org/a-secular-evaluation -of-rebirth/.

8 | Buddhism without a View

A Friendly Conversation with Stephen Batchelor's Secular Buddhism

PHILIPPE TURENNE

Stephen Batchelor speaks with one of the loudest voices of contemporary secular Buddhism. His popular books and courses, in which he develops his interpretation of what dharma should mean in the contemporary world, have reached many readers and students, triggering strong reactions from representatives of existing Buddhist traditions.

I have a particular interest in his version of secular Buddhism, because a great deal of my own work consists in explaining the value and importance of the voice of Buddhist intellectual traditions for an open approach to Buddhist studies, with a particular focus on the Himalayan Buddhist tradition, which is a particular target of Batchelor's criticism. Batchelor's version of Buddhism as a secularized spirituality, which goes so far as to deny the viability of the most fundamental doctrines and practices of Mahāyāna Buddhism, calls for a response. So far, though, representatives of the Himalayan tradition have answered his critique more by denouncing and deriding it than by addressing his arguments in detail, giving the impression that they do not have good answers to his questions, or confirming the impression that their interpretation of Buddhism is dogmatic and incapable of engaging with modern critical thinking.

Those answers to his views are not very helpful. The arguments and positions he brings forward deserve to be taken seriously. Some elements of his critique of Buddhist tradition, although perhaps not altogether new, point to some serious shortcomings and risks that come out of refusing to engage with modernity, and they convey valuable advice on how to allow Buddhist intellectual practice to retain its vitality. Representatives of "religious," "traditional," or "classical" Buddhist traditions[1] have failed to appreciate the validity of some of Batchelor's criticism, but they would benefit by looking at his criticism honestly and recognizing its value. It would be a mistake for Buddhists to think that they can simply dismiss his views as being wrong or superficial without showing exactly how that is the case.

Buddhists, as followers of other religions, are unfortunately not immune from believing so much in the superiority of their view that they do not feel the need to engage with criticism they perceive to come from outside their religion or tradition. Buddhists need to recognize that people who do not identify as followers of their religion—or at least the institutions that represent Buddhists—do have a say in and an effect on how Buddhism is understood in the world; ignoring dissonant voices leads to isolation, dividing Buddhist communities and making it harder for a sincere discussion to take place between traditionalists and secularists.

Accepting the useful points of Batchelor's critique of Buddhist tradition, however, does not mean we need to accept uncritically his solution to the problems he identifies. Does his solution, secularized Buddhism, answer all issues? If not, what are the main problems with his interpretation? One of the most cited problems with Batchelor's secular Buddhism is that it "cherry-picks" among Buddhist doctrines in order to suit his own modern culture. Buddhists may be uncomfortable with the fact that he feels at liberty to adopt or reject doctrines that traditions consider essential, but the cherry-picking itself is hardly unusual enough to justify the outrage raised by his interpretation. After all, does the Tibetan tradition, for example, not cherry-pick in a similar way, focusing on two or three main points of doctrine as a key to interpret the whole of Buddhist ideas? I think there are other reasons explaining why Buddhists are uncomfortable with Batchelor's particular brand of secularized Buddhism, and that understanding those reasons can help us identify important issues Buddhism faces as it adapts itself to contemporary culture. In other words, finding out why Batchelor is so annoying to Buddhists can tell us something useful and important about Buddhism, modernity, and secular culture more generally. What is really the problem with Batchelor's secular Buddhism? Simply put, by proposing the view that Buddhism has nothing to say about the nature of reality, Batchelor ends up inserting non-Buddhist views about reality as important parts of buddhadharma. By extending that claim into a new form of exclusivist orthodoxy, Batchelor is presenting a version of dharma that not only fails to meet his own criteria for a nondogmatic, pragmatic form of spiritual practice but also makes it impossible for one to keep the very elements that give the practice of buddhadharma its intellectual vitality. If, in order to remain relevant to the modern world, buddhadharma has to accept all the assumptions of Buddhist modernism—such as rationalism and the belief that mental cultivation practices can be extracted from a religious worldview—that creep into Batchelor's secularized Buddhism, as well as give up all attempts at criticizing modern metaphysics, then it is no surprise Buddhists are afraid to live in modernity. Fortunately, buddhadharma can indeed adapt to modern culture, only not necessarily in the way proposed by Batchelor.

One of the weaknesses of Batchelor's critique of Himalayan Buddhism, I will argue below, is that it targets an artificial, often unfair representation of how certain doctrines and practices are held. In order to avoid the same pitfall, we must critique his interpretation not only piecemeal but also after having given a fair summary of the coherent system of interpretation he has developed over the years. Here are therefore some of the main features of Batchelor's Buddhism as a secular spirituality.

First, he explains the important concept of *nirvāṇa* not as the cessation of suffering or even craving but as the cessation of "reactivity"—the latter being his preferred translation for the Pāli *taṇha*, which is usually translated as thirst or craving.[2] Batchelor's overall approach to Buddhism is to avoid at all costs references to buddhadharma being otherwordly or transcendent. Any presentation of the goal of Buddhist practice as reaching beyond this life or as presenting a state of bliss or cessation of suffering is rejected as contradicting the historical Buddha's main message, which is limited to pragmatic approaches to dealing with the suffering encountered in this life. An extension of this attitude leads Batchelor to recast the doctrine of the four noble truths into the idea of the four noble *tasks*. The Buddha did not teach truths—he gave students wishing to follow his footsteps work to accomplish.[3] This emphasis on doing rather than knowing leads into reinterpretations of various Buddhist doctrines. Notably, not-self (*anattā*) does not mean that we do not have a self but, instead, that nothing we can find in our experience can be held as a self. Closely related to this kind of reinterpretation is Batchelor's utter rejection of the notion of two realities or two truths.[4] His overall empirical outlook goes against any attempt at pointing at a reality beyond the world experienced through our senses. The idea that liberation can be attained through knowledge or wisdom, which is found throughout Buddhist traditions of various times and places, is dismissed altogether, as is any assessment of reality that goes beyond what can be ascertained through our senses. These last points all fit into one of the most fundamental ideological orientations of Batchelor's secular Buddhism: the opposition between what he calls metaphysical thinking and an empirical, pragmatic disposition. Metaphysics does not include only theories about ultimate reality or the true nature of the self, samsara, and the like, but also any claims about things that we cannot perceive directly through our senses—an idea that extends, these days, to scientific observation. This distinction between a pragmatic philosophy, in his way of thinking, happened over the development of Buddhism. As he puts it, "In taking a metaphysical turn toward truth, Buddhists shifted away from an emphasis on know-how to an emphasis on knowledge. They became increasingly concerned with attaining a state of mind that could allow them to gain infallible knowledge of truth or reality."[5] Hence his famous agnostic stance on the question of rebirth, doubtless one of his positions that traditional Buddhists have the most trouble accepting.

From a scriptural point of view, Batchelor accepts the Pāli canon as representing the earliest, most original, and authentic source for the historical Buddha's teaching. He is aware of the Pāli canon's various layers, and even ventures into analyzing the canon according to the originality and authenticity of the many ideas we find in it. In terms of Buddhist practice, in brief, Batchelor's model gives a high level of importance to morality, and mental cultivation, in his writings, depends primarily on the cultivation of mindfulness. The latter, we must note, is itself interpreted not according to canonical explanations as found in Abhidharma literature, for example, but under the very modernist notion of bare awareness of the present moment: a state of mind where we pay attention to our sense feelings as a way to create a mental space where reaction to stimuli is slowed down so one can apply rational criteria to govern our actions and reactions rather than being carried off by unconscious impulses. (See David L. McMahan's essay in this volume for a discussion of two different ways in which mindfulness is used, one of which is a strengthening of the autonomous individual in a fashion similar to that described here.) The practice of mindfulness also gives us access to the "everyday sublime," a mystical experience embedded in direct sensory experience rather than in metaphysical, transcendent states of mind.[6] Mindfulness can thus be considered as being compatible with the cultivation of aesthetic experience as part of "meditation" and mental cultivation, with a focus on art and nature as spiritually conducive experiences. Underlying this model, implicitly, is the assumption that the biological conditions for our existence as samsaric beings—the material world that includes our bodily existence—are a given reality and not something we can impact through Buddhist cultivation. Liberation happens in this world and in this body, and it is primarily psychological in nature, a combination of mindfulness and rational thought guiding our behavior. As in other modern forms of mindfulness practice, the concept of meditative absorption (*samādhi*) is not important, if not rejected altogether.

Given the variety of doctrines and practices found in the Buddhist canonical collections, the accusation of cherry-picking, which is inevitable to any organization and systematization of buddhadharma, hardly explains the harsh reactions to Batchelor's particular take on the essence of Buddhism. What is the outrage and extreme annoyance with his views really about, then? A simple answer is that he draws the line between core, essential Buddhist doctrines and accessory, culturally determined doctrines in a way that goes against fundamental orientations taken by Buddhist traditions. I am not convinced, though, that this alone explains how strongly Buddhists have reacted to his interpretation. Traditional Buddhists may also be reacting to the fact that he points to their own failure at meeting the standards they set for themselves—for example, in making sure the study of views about reality does not fall into sectarian or dogmatic debates, using that failure as a reason to dismiss their tradition altogether, replacing it with his own newly created approach to dharma.

Batchelor's critique of the Tibetan scholastic tradition targets that tradition's tendency to be dogmatic, its strong emphasis on view as opposed to practice, and its strong adoption of what Batchelor considers to be purely metaphysical theses as necessary on the path to liberation. His long interaction with Tibetan Buddhism has left him convinced that Buddhists of the Tibetan tradition have become more interested in vindicating their tradition's philosophical and metaphysical theories than in applying them to their own life. Following his own account,

> Yet contrary to what the Buddha said in these texts, my Tibetan teachers insisted that if one did not accept that mind was different from the body and that one is reborn after death, then one could not even consider oneself a Buddhist. As the words of Siddhattha Gotama metamorphosed into the religion called

"Buddhism," I began to suspect that something might have gone awry.[7]

The Tibetan emphasis on debates about emptiness are, in Batchelor's assessment, purely metaphysical and go against the fundamentally pragmatic orientation of buddhadharma. Even fundamental concepts such as the thought of awakening, which depend on cosmological or metaphysical notions such as there being an infinite number of sentient beings in various forms of rebirth, violate Batchelor's basic precept of not making claims about reality.

As we will see below, this characterization of Buddhist doctrines such as emptiness is in many ways unfair. This line of criticism, though, has not been invented by Batchelor but has been hurled back and forth by Tibetan scholars since the foundation of Buddhism in Tibet. Himalayan Buddhists talk of a well-known and accepted risk of becoming a "dry scholar" in the course of intellectual pursuits—someone who is interested in such pursuits not as aids on the path to liberation but, rather, for their own sake or for reasons other than liberation, such as prestige or material gain. These motivations are judged as likely to make one arrogant or overconfident about the depth of one's own understanding.

Where Batchelor's approach differs from the traditional attack on dry scholars is in the solution he proposes. Tibetan sources usually encourage scholars to apply the teachings they study to their own life and to make sure their study fits a model of personal transformation—referencing, for example, the threefold model of study, reflection, and mental cultivation. Batchelor's solution to the epidemic of dry scholarship and the ensuing dogmatism that plagues Tibetan Buddhism in our time is to give up the study and debate of views of reality altogether. The problem his reaction poses to Buddhists is not only that he cherry-picks among doctrines but that he is overly picky in the way he picks the cherries: he rejects cherries altogether. The result of his purification of "metaphysics" from Buddhist practice and doctrine is that a majority of Buddhist doctrines and practices end up discarded as wrong.

He does, nevertheless, point at many serious problems in current Buddhist institutions. One such problem is an overemphasis on tenets and doctrines, often along the lines of sectarian affiliations. There is also a disconnect between intellectual study and speculation and transformative practice. Another problem is overreliance on traditional categories and dismissiveness of systems of knowledge or practice that do not come from a few Indian or Tibetan sources, including failure to engage with contemporary culture, especially intellectual culture. Also problematic is the lack of interest for seriously reading actual Buddhist scripture as opposed to relying on commentaries and summaries. Reliance on structures of authority and hierarchy can be seen as incompatible in many ways with the spirit of open intellectual inquiry officially adopted by Buddhist institutions. Also, an evident inability of Buddhist study and practice to challenge cultural or social habits of injustice, prejudice, or discrimination is a problem, as is the failure to take seriously moral precepts and their application. All of those are real issues threatening the vitality of Buddhist traditions. Each can be associated in some form or other with Batchelor's main point of contention with Buddhist tradition—namely, the reliance, under the guise of intellectual criticism, on rational practices that fail to provide the self-criticism and skepticism required to contribute to personal development in a Buddhist sense.

Batchelor can be included in the category of "British Buddhists"—a label that seems to include some academic scholars and historians of Buddhism as well as modern interpreters of dharma informed by the academic study of Buddhism. He could also, though, easily be associated with the likes of Gendun Chophel, Shākya Chokden, and the many Tibetan intellectuals who have criticized the Buddhist scholastic orthodoxy and have therefore been punished by Buddhist institutions in some form or other. What distinguishes Batchelor from these authors is not that he criticizes Buddhist tradition. It is his lack of success at proposing a solution acceptable to Buddhists as allowing a revitalization of Buddhist practice. That does not remove the accuracy of Batchelor's attacks on real and serious problems arising from how Buddhist institutions have come to portray a certain orthodoxy and orthopraxy, and which has prevented dharma from appealing to a certain number of modern students. The validity of his critique, though, does not mean we have to accept his solution uncritically.

The Problems with Batchelor's Reading of Buddhist Sources

Batchelor's cherry-picking among Buddhist doctrines and choosing only those that suit his preferences does not explain how strongly Buddhists react to his interpretation. More irritating than his critique or rejection of certain doctrines, I would propose, is how unsatisfactory the model he proposes as an alternative to traditional Buddhism turns out to be: his secularized Buddhism is deeply at odds with fundamental Buddhist orientations—not only of Buddhist doctrines but of the whole worldview into which those doctrines fit.

Because of his skeptical attitude toward tradition, Batchelor is sometimes accused of making things up on his own without any basis in Buddhist tradition. This is also somewhat misleading, because whatever faults we can find in his notion of secular Buddhism, it would not be fair to deny that he bases his interpretation on an engaged reading of Buddhist scripture. His main writings on secular Buddhism quote extensively from the Buddhist canon—almost exclusively, though, from the Pāli canon. Batchelor is either unaware of or unwilling to recognize how problematic the axiomatic association of the Pāli canon and "early Buddhism" is.[8] Even if we leave that consideration aside, though, it is not that he does not read Buddhist scripture or take it seriously but, rather, the way he uses Pāli canonical literature as a basis for his secularized Buddhism that is disappointing. In short, I see three main problems with his method: (1) he uses academic scholarship on Buddhism to give an appearance of legitimacy to his interpretation, but he does not take the same scholarship seriously; (2) he unnecessarily projects his philosophical interpretation of Buddhism into historical claims, leading to exclusivism, essentialism, and another kind of ortho- doxy; and (3) he sets the boundaries between dharma and modern culture in such a way as to make Buddhism incapable of criticizing modern culture and ideas.

First, although his writings target a nonspecialist audience, Batch- elor makes the occasional reference to academic literature on the history of Buddhism. This can give the reader the impression that his reading of the sources is informed by current academic research on the topic. Unfortunately, his use of academic research on Bud- dhism does not reflect a sincere wish to bend his interpretation to our latest and best understanding of how Buddhism has appeared and developed but rather the desire to give his reading an appear- ance of authority by correlating it with selected academic studies. A closer look at how he produces his interpretation of what Buddhism is and should be about and how that appeared historically shows that he does not base his reading on historical sources; instead, he goes the other way around and grounds his reading of history on his ideological or doctrinal interpretation of what he thinks Buddhism is about. He does make reference to historical scholarship on early Buddhism—for example, to Johannes Bronkhorst's work on the culture of the greater Magadha area[9]—but only insofar as it con- firms his reading of Buddhist sources. The arguments he produces for his own historical claims do not follow any kind of historical method. For example, he tries to identify canonical statements that are likely to have been spoken by the historical Buddha based on whether they could have been said by other teachers, based on whether followers of the Buddha may have had another motivation for inserting them into the canon,[10] or he rejects some because they simply represent the general culture of the time. His method follows a circular logic: How can you determine what is simply culture as opposed to "pure" dharma if not by a careful historical study? But his approach turns things around and distinguishes dharma from culture based on what he has already identified as pure dharma.

Second, the unhealthy connection between Batchelor's "theological" or philosophical position and historical arguments is problematic in many other ways. Batchelor is honest and explicit about the
fact that he is giving his own interpretation of Buddhist canonical
sources, and he is comfortable with being accused of reading those
sources creatively or in an innovative way. We cannot disagree with
him when he says that this is precisely what Buddhist traditions
have done for as long as we remember. Where his position is unconvincing, though, is in his tendency to translate his philosophical
or doctrinal arguments into historical claims, especially since he
often does that without convincing evidence. He participates in the
modern habit, especially found in Western academic sources on
Buddhism, to identify "right" Buddhism with *original* Buddhism.
This attitude participates in the Indological perspective (dating
from the eighteenth and nineteenth centuries) that, in the Indian
subcontinent, whatever is sophisticated must be old. It also shares
the association of early Buddhism with Protestant religion and associated modern features, such as rationalism, individualism, and
the rejection of ritual, mythology, and the religious organization
of society.

Not only does this approach inspire suspicion—how many times
have scholars found out that the original and authentic happens
to match what they themselves consider authentic and original in
their own culture?—but it also leads Buddhism into dark areas that
Batchelor is trying to escape: exclusivism and essentialism. Batchelor argues on two levels: first, he presents his reading simply as a
new interpretation that matches the cultural context of contemporary society in order for buddhadharma to retain its vitality; at the
same time, though, he cannot refrain from claiming that what the
Buddha originally taught must be the same thing that happens to
be relevant and popular nowadays. For him, the Buddha's original
pragmatic method of self-transformation has gradually lost its true
identity and purpose by becoming more and more interested in
metaphysical questions, to the point of dogmatism, and by suffering
the negative outside influence of Brahmanical culture, for example.

This is what Richard K. Payne labels the "rhetoric of decadence" in his contribution to this collection. As Batchelor puts it,

> As Brahmanism came to be accepted as normative, elements of its worldview started to be taken for granted even among non-Brahmanic communities....This was the environment in which Buddhism would have mutated from a pragmatic ethical philosophy to an Indian religion that competed with brahmins, Jains, and others for the allegiance and support of powerful, wealthy patrons.[11]

Batchelor's argument suggests that forms of Buddhist practice that emphasize the study of the view of emptiness or the cultivation of the thought of awakening, for example, are not only poorly suited to the modern mind, but they are not even Buddhist—instead they result from the influence of non-Buddhist culture. While it is not clear what his system gains by such claims—for the quality of his interpretation does not have to depend on historical arguments—what it loses is clear. First, because his historical claims are supported by arguments that are more theological than historical (and often very speculative) and because his desire to root his interpretation in history goes against the general principles of his interpretation—that is, that he is in the end only trying to produce an interpretation that makes sense in the contemporary world—his readings are unconvincing from a historical point of view.

Second, and more importantly, such a reading creates an exclusivist orthodoxy following which centuries of Buddhist doctrine and practice suddenly become not only inadequate for the modern world but also non-Buddhist in nature and presented as the result of unfortunate accidents of history. Of all the many kinds of Buddhist practice that have been developed over the centuries, according to Batchelor's reading only a very limited set are considered authentic and original. When Buddhism adapted to Indian Brahmanical culture, for example, it not only reshaped some of its doctrines to make sense to people of that place and time, but it also lost its essential identity as a pragmatic philosophy. Readers who share Batchelor's respect for skepticism will likely apply that same attitude to his suggestion that all others are wrong, and only his interpretation is "true." Buddhist tradition has indeed developed interpretive tools allowing us to consider some practices as more advanced or accurate than others, such as the distinction between provisional and definitive doctrines, the two truths, and the various vehicles or systems of practice. But Batchelor's secular Buddhism has only one vehicle and only one practice: the study and reflection on other doctrines, which he considers metaphysical and useless, are all to be abandoned. Most problematic here is not Batchelor's rejection of certain doctrines but that he gives up the fundamentally Buddhist attitude of open-mindedness, appreciation of diversity, and flexibility—not to mention the ancient preference for ortho-praxy over orthodoxy.

Although a tradition of exclusivism and wanting to reduce all practice to a simple and monolithic model has long existed within Buddhism, such a tradition seems unsuited to the contemporary world, where diversity and flexibility is generally valued. Batch-elor's exclusivism therefore undermines his emphasis on the contemporary—and furthermore, his argument in defense of his exclusivism—based on the premise that (unlike others) *his* inter-pretation captures the original and true meaning of the Buddha's teaching—is not likely to have credibility with anyone who has studied the history of religions.

Batchelor's position would be more coherent and convincing if he were able to recognize that his new, innovative interpretation does not have to be connected with original or early Buddhism to retain its relevance to the modern world. In so doing, he would also avoid the pitfall of creating a reductive interpretation of dharma that denies the validity of methods developed by Buddhists over the centuries. In short, by identifying the essence of dharma as a pragmatic, anti-metaphysical philosophy, he makes all other kinds of Buddhist practice non-dharma. One can disagree about the value of debating over interpretations of reality, but the essentialist opposition to views as metaphysics ends up labeling virtually all post-Abhidharma Buddhism as a misinterpretation and a degeneration of original Buddhism. In his reification of the theoretical and metaphysical assumptions behind the distinction between pragmatic philosophy and metaphysical beliefs, Batchelor ends up championing the very attitudes he wanted to reject in the first place.

Third, Batchelor's emphasis on the historical accuracy of his interpretation insinuates that traditional Buddhism is incapable of making a critical contribution to modern culture and ideology. If our ideas about what is original and authentic in Buddhism are determined strictly by what makes sense in the modern world—rationality, skepticism, and the rejection of metaphysical interpretations of reality—then elements of traditional Buddhism that might usefully challenge modern ideology have already been removed from the equation before we can even consider what they contribute. Batchelor asks us to assume that the only authentic features of Buddhism are those that support our current ideology; the rest are to be discarded as degenerations of Buddhism.

Surely not even the most traditional Buddhist in our time accepts, literally, the totality of Buddhist views and practices throughout history—but can we not at least give traditional elements of Buddhism a chance of encountering modernity, in order to see what they can contribute? Can we not actually learn from Buddhist ideas that are at odds with our modern ideologies—and that might therefore (helpfully) make us aware of ideas that we nonetheless take for granted as obvious or necessary? The dichotomy Batchelor creates between modern, secularized, rational thought and traditional, religious, dogmatic culture leaves traditional Buddhists with only one option: give up your traditional beliefs or be irrelevant to the modern world.

In fact, however, the dialogue between Buddhist thought and modern culture does not have to be that simplistic. A Buddhist perspective can help us see, for example, how science can be used to create a dogmatic worldview, as discussed by Shaw in her essay in this volume. A scientific perspective can help us redefine the boundaries of categories of knowledge—for example, by bringing some topics within the fold of things we can observe rather than speculate about through metaphysics. By determining that Buddhism can only be modern by accepting uncritically the main dogmas of modern culture, Batchelor does not allow it to fully participate in modernity. The latter assumption also implies, in a very problematic way, that modern Buddhists share a fixed set of expectations and assumptions. A successful interpretation of Buddhism in modernity rather needs to accommodate a variety of perspectives.

Is Batchelor Aware of His Own Metaphysical Assumptions?

As noted above, Batchelor's secularized Buddhism is in many ways also a naturalized Buddhism, combining pragmatic philosophy with empiricism. Batchelor then sets this combination of the pragmatic and empirical in opposition to metaphysics, which he defines as the pursuit of questions that have no practical relevance or that cannot be verified empirically. Buddhists should be concerned about ending suffering, not finding out the truth about reality or the world, he insists. Batchelor's association of the Buddha's insight on those matters and modern culture seems based on the similarity between ideas of the European Enlightenment, such as the opposition between science and nonempirical disciplines such as metaphysics and theology. Batchelor extends his love of empiricism to the teachings of early Buddhism. For example, he contrasts "truth" with "life," which he also calls "the all," noting that "awakening consists of a threefold reorientation to experience rather than the attainment of a single privileged insight into an ultimate truth such as the Unconditioned."[12] What is surprising with this assertion is how unaware he seems of the fact that this same belief rests on its own metaphysical presuppositions—for example, about how our senses work in relation to the physical world, consciousness relates to the body, and so forth. Batchelor seems to believe that empiricists are exempt from examining the worldview and assumptions on which they base their belief in that mode of knowledge. He does not seem to appreciate that modern people still hold metaphysical views, and calling them "scientific" does not automatically take away their tendency to reify claims about reality. In short, if Batchelor wants to reject metaphysics altogether, he should apply the same criteria to his own secularized Buddhism. Instead, he makes dharma fit into a modern interpretation of reality, as if that model were uniquely different from all other theories of reality. The view that consciousness is a by-product of the brain, for example, is not a scientific theory, and it can be used as a metaphysical doctrine in just the same way as the doctrine of emptiness. Knowing the biological expressions or determinants of emotions is a useful thing. But that does not mean we cannot look critically at the view of reality behind that model—namely, one according to which the body and the material world are real, and our mental processes are by-products of the real material body. This view is not only outdated and problematic scientifically, but it is clearly a metaphysical assumption put forward as a scientific theory—just another type of unconvincing metaphysics.

Batchelor's attitude toward religion shares a lot with what John Gray calls "new atheism," a nineteenth-century presumption that religious worldviews have been manifestly disproved and constructively replaced by a scientific worldview. But that way of seeing the relationship between religion and science is itself outdated. As Gray explains, "The idea that religion consists of a bunch of discredited theories is itself a discredited theory—a relic of the nineteenth-century philosophy of Positivism."[13] The idea that traditional or religious worldviews are obsolete is problematic, says Gray, because "science cannot replace a religious view of the world, since there is no such thing as 'the scientific worldview.'"[14] Thus, Batchelor's take on metaphysics and science brings him in the end to reifying a modern worldview as having replaced earlier metaphysical models. He cannot avoid proposing, in the end, his own metaphysics.

Finally, even if Batchelor makes short work of views about things we cannot observe through our senses, with frequent references to the analogy of the man who was injured by an arrow but wants to know everything about it before it is removed, he does not answer legitimate questions about the place views of reality have in our experience as deluded sentient beings. To dismiss views of reality as having no practical relevance for the problem of suffering assumes that views are not part of what Buddhists call samsara. Batchelor can try to reduce awakening to psychological factors, getting rid of the cognitive aspects of samsaric experience. But, by doing so, he bundles *all* views within the category of frivolous metaphysical questions. Any claim about reality is considered frivolous. He does not, though, disprove that certain views can be liberating, while some others can be alienating or delusional. That some views are practically irrelevant is not controversial; to consider all views as practically irrelevant is something that needs to be established, but Batchelor fails to do so.

A Caricature of the Mahāyāna

Issues of interpretation alone aren't sufficient to explain how harshly Buddhists have reacted to Batchelor's secularization of Buddhism. I would like to propose yet another reason for this reaction, which perhaps traditional Buddhists have not yet completely clearly identified. Simply put, Batchelor's empirical disposition together with his own personal experience with Buddhist tradition have shaped his understanding of what Buddhism is about, but he does not seem to appreciate that other people have other experiences— their own experiences—of what Buddhism is about. He extends his personal experience of dharma—or, shall we say, the failure of traditional Buddhists to satisfy his own epistemological and cultural expectations—into claims that other forms of practice are invalid or misleading. But why should Batchelor's experience of certain types of practice be used as a standard for all practice? The feeling traditional Buddhists can have when facing his interpretation is that of being deeply misunderstood or misrepresented—yet at the same time criticized as irrational, dogmatic, or missing the point of Buddhist practice altogether.

For example, Batchelor rejects the two-truth model, dismissing it as part of Buddhism's turn to metaphysics, ontology, and dogmatism.[15] He also writes that he has no interest in "letting my consciousness be absorbed in the transcendent perfection of the unconditioned,"[16] clearly making reference to the cultivation of emptiness, for example, as an object of meditation. Batchelor's description of the doctrine of emptiness and how it is cultivated is so squarely opposite the Buddhist understanding of emptiness as a practice of mental cultivation that he ends up criticizing a caricature, or at least a misunderstanding, of the view of emptiness rather than the doctrine itself.

It is true that Mahāyāna practitioners will usually not claim that they have attained direct understanding of emptiness. That does not mean, though, that emptiness is practically irrelevant or is useful merely as a theoretical possibility or a metaphysical doctrine. A fairer reading of emptiness would locate it in close relation to impermanence, dependent arising, and the practice of mental cultivation, where partial insight into the nature of reality can be glimpsed temporarily, giving rise to other types of inspiration and, yes, insight into how we construct our vision of reality. A fairer reading would acknowledge widely shared accounts of those insights being deeply transformative and making it possible to break one's attachment to negative mental states, the latter being more often than not inscribed in a particular understanding of reality, or at least of the reality of things as we construct them in our emotional experience. And a fairer reading would also consider how rational analysis in the context of Buddhist doctrine fits on a continuum of contemplative practices that include not only logical arguments but also reflections on life experiences and the cultivation of certain mental qualities as part of one's study and contemplation—all elements that point to emptiness, for example, not being a purely theoretical or metaphysical category.

To dismiss Buddhist practices involving rational analysis as being limited to practically irrelevant metaphysics betrays a lack of appreciation of how most individuals justify our emotional conditioning by associating it with certain narratives about right and wrong, truth and falsity, and notions of what will finally satisfy our deep-seated craving for more. How can we work with our habituation to those narratives if not by bouncing them against other rationally backed narratives? In other words, painting the critical, deconstructive function of reason as used in Buddhist practices that examine metaphysical notions such as emptiness as practically irrelevant shows that Batchelor's dislike of metaphysics is so strong that he is unwilling to entertain simple and obvious facts about how Buddhists use rational exercises.

But, Batchelor tells us, if we do experience the liberating effect of reflecting on emptiness, for example, we must be deluded or simply dogmatic. Not because he disagrees with the doctrine or has reasons to show it is harmful or irrational, but because simply believing that reality can be experienced other than as the object of our senses is, in his judgment, necessarily and automatically wrong. There are so many levels of assumption and misunderstanding in that judgment that it is no surprise traditional Buddhists have little interest in pursuing the conversation with such a version of secularized Buddhism. Despite his love of empiricism, Batchelor can easily be perceived as denying the experience of Buddhists, telling them that their empirically derived impression that emptiness was a useful category, for example, is wrong and mistaken, whereas his own empirical feeling of what is right is to be trusted.

That attitude leads Batchelor so far from the experience of traditional Buddhists as to create the impression that he really does not like Buddhism. For example, it is no surprise that his rejection of devotion as having any value on the Buddhist path alienates Buddhists. In Himalayan traditions, devotion, with compassion, is considered the most crucial and powerful thing to be cultivated on the Buddhist path. That someone may not want to follow that path is one thing, but to portray it as wrong and basically antithetical to liberation shows little interest in understanding the experience of Buddhists that cultivate devotion. Such an attitude shocks Buddhists much more than not believing in rebirth or emptiness.

Students of Madhyamaka and Yogācāra philosophy, for example, feel that they also have something to say about metaphysical views and how they are problematic. Many even describe their system of philosophy as being radical techniques for eliminating our attachment to such views. By being forced into Batchelor's distinction between metaphysics and pragmatic philosophy, though, they do not get a chance to enter the conversation. The disappointing impression gained by traditional Buddhists is that he rejected such systems and practices not after a careful consideration of their value but simply as the result of his own lack of interest in what they are about or his own failure at benefiting from them.

In his role as a sophisticated representative of secular Buddhism, Batchelor should be taken seriously as someone who is sincerely interested in a friendly conversation on what dharma means in the current world. His reading of dharma also can bring to traditional Buddhism many points of valid advice on how to preserve the vitality of Buddhist study and practice. I hope that traditional Buddhists will start taking his views more seriously and engage in a genuine conversation about what they mean for Buddhism. But Batchelor and other secularists also have their share of responsibility in allowing a healthy dialogue to take place between secular and traditional Buddhism. First, radical attachment to categories such as metaphysics and practical philosophy should not itself be held to the point of dogmatism and exclusivism. Batchelor's lament about not being taken seriously after he has rejected most of the history of Buddhism as non-Buddhist is simply ironic. In its rejection of the Buddhist experience of liberation based on understanding reality, Batchelor's secular Buddhism is not only Buddhism without a view; it is also Buddhism without awakening. For many traditional Buddhists, Batchelor's secular approach is not only a rejection of their view of the goal of Buddhist practice, but its very possibility.

Finally, for a good dialogue to take place, Batchelor might realize that his view of modernity and contemporary culture itself can be refined and relaxed. Modern culture does not have to be portrayed as an inevitable race toward secularism, mind-body dualism, and so forth. History does not necessarily evolve toward its natural end in rationalism and secularism, and Buddhists who are still interested in traditional or even religious aspects of their tradition do not necessarily have to be portrayed as anachronistic and irrational. I hope that secular Buddhism can become aware that it also faces the risk of becoming dogmatic, and therefore it can benefit from a sincere and friendly dialogue with traditional Buddhism. Secular Buddhism does not have to be monolithic and exclusivist. Perhaps it can also develop as an open-minded form of Buddhism.

BIBLIOGRAPHY

Batchelor, Stephen. *After Buddhism: Rethinking the Dharma for a Secular Age.* New Haven, CT: Yale University Press, 2015.
———. *Confession of a Buddhist Atheist.* New York: Spiegel & Grau, 2010.
Gray, John. *Seven Types of Atheism.* London: Allen Lane, 2018.
Skilling, Peter. "Scriptural Authenticity and the Śrāvaka Schools: An Essay towards and Indian Perspective." *The Eastern Buddhist* 41, no. 2 (2010).

9 | Secular Buddhism in a Neoliberal Age

RON PURSER

In making its way to the West and the modern world, Buddhism faces new challenges. Since the 1980s, neoliberalism has become the dominant economic and political philosophy of the Western ruling order. As a radical social philosophy of autonomy, a neoliberal ethos operates on both traditional and secular Buddhism, in that both have focused primarily on individual liberation. This chapter examines how mindfulness—a central meditation practice among secular Buddhists—has become infected and shaped by neoliberal cultural forces producing an entrepreneurial subjectivity and self-policing individuals. Mindfulness serves an ideological function in ensuring the reproduction of capitalist relations and, in effect, has become the new capitalist spirituality.

Whatever the benefits on the individual level, a restricted focus on the inner workings of the mind can shift attention away from the hard truths of contemporary society: the massive inequalities, harmful material conditions, and injustices that have become the bread and butter of our daily lives, not to mention a planet in crisis, nefarious corporate business practices, and political corruption. Secular Buddhists are not exempt. In fact, many practitioners have elevated mindfulness meditation as the path to individual liberation.

Secular Buddhism is situated within a neoliberal order. Mindfulness is promoted as an antidote to the neoliberal rat race—a way
of navigating more skillfully in a capitalist economy. By practicing
mindfulness, individuals can learn to manage their emotional reactions and impulses, racing thoughts, stresses and worries, providing
an oasis of relief. (Sarah Shaw, in this volume, argues for the value of
individual agency.) Posing no threat to the status quo, self-managing
individuals may serve to maintain it. But, as the Venerable Bhikku
Bodhi, an American-born Buddhist monk and social activist (and
also a contributor to this volume) warns, "Absent a sharp social
critique, Buddhist practices could easily be used to justify and
stabilize the status quo, becoming a reinforcement of consumer
capitalism."[1]

The Default Mode Network of Secular Buddhism: Neoliberalism

At its root, neoliberalism is a politically conservative movement, for
it valorizes the status quo; what is more, it argues that those who
enjoy power and wealth should be given free rein to accumulate
more power and more wealth if that is how market forces play out.
It should come as no surprise why mindfulness made such a splash
at the World Economic Forum in Davos the last several years.

Political thinkers such as Wendy Brown and Ilana Gershon have
argued that over the past few decades, neoliberalism has outgrown
its conservative origins to become widely accepted cultural dogma.
In fact, it has taken over our public discourse, so that today even
progressives think in neoliberal terms. Market values have invaded
every corner of human life. As the social geographer David Harvey
puts it, neoliberalism "has become incorporated into the common-
sense way many of us interpret, live in, and understand the world."[2]

So what, essentially, is neoliberalism? Probably the most straight-
forward response comes from Pierre Bourdieu, who says that neoliberalism is "a programme for destroying collective structures
which may impede the pure market logic."[3] And that program is

not merely a set of economic policies doled out by the elites at the World Bank or the International Monetary Fund. Rather, neoliberalism is a complex form of cultural hegemony—an insidious worldview that human beings are best understood as rational, economic actors—what Michel Foucault in a pioneering analysis referred to as *homo economicus*.[4] In effect, it sees individuals as entrepreneurs running their own enterprises—the business of Me, Inc.—in competition with others. It is a free market-based society that supposedly provides ample (but not equal) opportunities for increasing the value of one's own "human capital" and self-worth, and for fully actualizing one's personal freedom and human potential. In other words, neoliberal actors are hailed to maximize their own welfare, freedom, and happiness by deftly managing their internal resources to survive.

Since competition is central, the neoliberal ideology holds that all decisions about how society is run should be left to the workings of the marketplace, the most efficient mechanism for allowing competitors to maximize their own good. In sum, neoliberalism is "a theory of political economic practices that proposes that human well-being can best be advanced by liberating individual entrepreneurial freedoms and skills within an institutional framework characterized by strong private property rights, free markets, and free trade,"[5] as David Harvey puts it. In this light, other social actors, including the state, voluntary associations, and the like are viewed merely as obstacles to the smooth operation of marketplace capitalism, and they should be dismantled or disregarded.

The Slovene philosopher Slavoj Žižek has analyzed these developments with great acuity. As he sees it, Western Buddhism stands poised to become "the hegemonic ideology of global capitalism." Its meditative stance offers "the most efficient way…to fully participate in the capitalist dynamic while retaining the appearance of mental sanity."[6] By deflecting attention from the social, political, and economic structures—that is, the material conditions in a capitalist culture—secular Buddhism is perfectly suited to the formation of the ideal neoliberal self.

Turning inward to a private, interior, inner subjective activity carried out in isolation from wider social, political, and economic structures has dominated the popular imagination. Perhaps unwittingly, secular Buddhism, especially mindfulness meditation, has been portrayed in the media and understood as an individualizing activity among psychologists. As neoliberalism has deregulated markets and taken control of governments to ensure market-friendly policies, governance becomes the self-governance of "free" and autonomous individuals. The mandate is individuals must self-regulate by taking responsibility for their own "self-care," stress management, and well-being if they are to be employable and thrive in a precarious economy. However, this mandate is delivered with a velvet glove rather than an iron fist.

In his 1978-1979 Collège de France lectures, Foucault signaled this shift as the "neoliberal turn," in which neoliberal styles of government emerge—a dual concept that he calls "governmentality."[7] For Foucault, in the modern neoliberal period, government is understood not merely as a political activity but in a much broader sense—as a way of linking power relations to processes of subjectification—what he described as the "conduct of conduct." His critique and historical account focused on exposing how institutions shape, regulate, and inform the behaviors, attitudes, and affective sensibilities of individuals. Governmentality then is concerned with exploring how knowledge, expertise, and practices are developed to guide people's voluntary conduct. In other words, Foucault illustrated how neoliberalism operates at micro-levels of power, reformulating what it means to be a person, self, and identity.

Foucault distinguishes between two different modes of power: "techniques of domination" and "techniques of the self." Both modes of power are instrumental for formation of the selfhood. Foucault argues the processes for the formation of a neoliberal subject requires taking into account "the points where technologies of domination of individuals over one another have recourse to processes by which the individual acts upon himself. And conversely, he has to take into account the points where the techniques of the self are integrated into structures of coercion and domination. The contact point, where the way individuals are driven by others is tied to the way they conduct themselves, is what we can call government."[8]

The form of governmental power under neoliberalism is that of disciplinary power, which operates at professional-institutional levels, in contrast to previous forms of "sovereign" governmental power, which used harsh punishment to restrict forbidden behaviors. Sovereign power never reached down into the psyches of subjects. Disciplinary power, on the other hand, is productive as it operates through the subjectivity of free and enterprising individuals who can govern themselves. According to Foucault, it is this link between enterprise culture and individual well-being that is most instructive. As Jeff Sugerman argues, "This relation consists in the premises that the economy is optimized through the entrepreneurial activity of autonomous individuals and that human wellbeing is furthered if individuals are free to direct their lives as entrepreneurs."[9]

This presumed autonomy is very different from early forms of institutionalization that derived their authority from the church and organized religions, where the clergy served as intermediaries between church doctrine and cultural codes of conduct. The processes of secularization and detraditionalization have given way to the new scientifically authorized mindfulness priests, where remnants of the Catholic confessional still remain intact. As Foucault points out, "The obligation to confess is now relayed through so many different points...that we no longer perceive it as the effect of a power that constrains us."[10] Instead of confessing their cardinal sins, participants confess to Buddhist teachers how their mind wandered, or how they got lost in their thoughts and mental ruminations, or how they were carried away by an emotional reaction or judgment. In this respect, confession does not operate as a coercive, top-down power structure. Rather, mindful confessions work by presupposing a bandwidth of acceptable affects and styles of thought, deviations from which must be confessed. Through such confessions, participants shape themselves into dutiful mindful subjects who can monitor, care for, and govern themselves. It is in this respect that power relations in mindfulness courses, as Peter Fletcher argues, "gives to the authority demanding the confession a resource or tool by which the individual can be assessed and dealt with in accord with the wishes of those in authority."[11]

Similar to self-help modalities, secular Buddhism valorizes individual autonomy, freedom, choice, and authenticity. As Christopher Ziguras argues, "This ideology of autonomy allows for the penetration of power deep into the person, while disguising this as the expansion of personal freedom."[12] It is thus no coincidence that neoliberalism and secular Buddhism similarly conceive of well-being in individualistic and psychologized terms. The rhetoric of "self-mastery," "resilience," and "happiness" assumes that well-being is simply a matter of developing a skill.

Neoliberalism divides the world into winners and losers. It accomplishes this task through its ideological linchpin: the individualization of all social phenomena. Since the autonomous (and free) individual is the primary focal point for society, social change is achieved not through political protest, organizing, and collective action but via the free market and atomized actions of individuals. Collective structures and organized political reform are troublesome to the neoliberal order.

We have been duped that only individual action and individual responsibility is the vehicle for solving societal problems. Under the trance of neoliberalism, we are, as the critical education scholar Henry Giroux points out, entrapped in a "disimagination machine" that stifles critical and radical thinking.[13] Disimagination operates through the neoliberal imperative of individualization, where we are admonished to look to ourselves and turn inward as the only viable way to solve social problems. When we are disimagined, we lose the utopian impulse and remain stuck under the regime of capitalist realism. As Julie Wilson notes, disimagination then amounts to "a pernicious form of cultural discipline and social control; it strips us of an open future, of potentialities for creating different worlds."[14]

Neoliberal Individualism:
Does Changing Your Mind Change the World?

To change the world, we are told to change ourselves—that is, to change our minds by being more mindful, nonjudgmental, and accepting of our circumstances. In effect, such practices function as a disimagination machine, interpellating the self to make (or make over) a project out of its own identity, constantly monitoring its conduct, and refashioning it in ways that feed fantasies of unfettered agency, aspiring to be free from the constraints of social conditioning. Ilana Gershon makes this point when she writes that, for a neoliberal agent, "there is always already a presumed distance to oneself as an actor. One is never 'in the moment'; rather, one is always faced with one's self as a project."[15]

In a blog post titled "Buddhism under Capitalism: Understanding 'Neoliberalism,'" Richard K. Payne observes:

> Neoliberalism as a social philosophy of radical self-autonomy… informs much of the present-day rationale for Buddhist practice and mindfulness. The wide range of issues that meditation is supposed to be good for are represented as individual issues. The almost deliberately hazy term 'happiness' covers a lot, but is often used to both give primacy of value to one's emotional state, and to place responsibility for that with the individual."[16]
> He goes on to question the claim that social action is the sum total of individual actions. This faux revolution is achieved one mindful individual at a time, essentially "ignoring the massively entrenched power of capitalist institutions in favor of a mystical notion of all wisdom being inside oneself."[17]

This observation brings us to a key tenet of neoliberal mindfulness: that the source of problems is located inside the heads of individuals. This assumption is particularly accentuated by the neoliberal emphasis on pathologizing and medicalizing stress, which then requires a remedy and expert treatment. The ideological message is that if you cannot alter your circumstances, if you can't change the causes of your distress, just practice mindfulness meditation. Just change your reactions to your circumstances! The notion "as long as I am mindful, I'm OK," is a form of magical thinking. Because neoliberalism views stress as purely a maladaptive psychophysiological reaction, there is no need for critical inquiry into the systemic, institutional, and structural causes of stress.

Tim Newton, in his book *Managing Stress: Emotion and Power at Work*, traces how the stressed subject has been historically constituted and legitimized by academics, practitioners, and journalists. Newton reminds us that the "truth of stress" should be seen as an effect, intimately related to Foucault's notion of power, which "works through us by telling us about ourselves and our world through, say, the discourses of psychiatry, psychology, biology, medicine, economics which reveal the secret of our selves."[18] Despite the fact that this supposed secret will never be found, more important in this context is what Nikolas Rose has described as the "systems of truth" that are established, produced, and evaluated in relation to stress.[19] Most of us have come to understand stress through the discourse of science—namely, biomedicine, which presents an image of the "stressed subject as someone who is apolitical, ahistorical, individualized, decontextualized."[20]

The question as to how we explain and respond to human and social suffering is ultimately an ethical and political one. Buddhist practices, as they are currently conceived and taught, do not permit critique or debate of what is unjust, culturally toxic, and environmentally destructive. Rather, the imperatives to "accept things as they are" and the practice of "nonjudgmental, present-moment awareness" function as a social anesthesia, preserving the status quo.

Erasure of the Body Politic

Privatizing the causes of stress dovetails nicely with the assumptions of neoliberal discourse, which—argue thinkers such as Mark

Fisher and Wendy Brown—undermines the very concepts of the public and the body politic. In neoliberalism, public discourse gives way to private gain. Brown contends that depoliticized practices of self-care diminish our capacities for political citizenship, collective action, and civic virtues.[21] The risk is that these practices will encourage a potent form of political quietism.

The implicit political vision is one of retreat into the "authentic" private self as a way of celebrating the fully autonomous individual in pursuit of an elusive happiness free of the collective. As a member of the body politic, the neoliberal self is always being encouraged to "go a little deeper" into the interior, to care for the self. This is the version of mindfulness described by David L. McMahan in his essay in this volume as that which reinforces the self, rather than deconstructing the self. As this journey moves to the foreground, our collective and political lives disappear from view. It squares nicely with the neoliberal stories that, as Julie Wilson puts it, "prompt us to turn our disaffected consent inwards toward ourselves, to double down on the present in order to protect and secure ourselves against others."[22]

This doubling down on the present moment amounts to a sophisticated fetish. A fixation on the present moment is a practice that cultivates temporal myopia, repressing historical memory while atrophying the utopian imagination. This "present momentism" contributes to social amnesia, encouraging a collective forgetting. Present momentism effectively forecloses a creative and dynamic engagement with the future (there is no alternative), resulting in what the psychologist Herbert Rapaport calls "telepression," a defense of impending future anxiety, including our own death and imminent ecological destruction.[23]

Present momentism operates in resonance with what Eric Cazdyn, in his book *The Already Dead: The New Time of Politics, Culture and Illness*, characterizes as " the new chronic."[24] Present momentism appears, at least on the surface, as a therapeutic solvent for all our problems, making our present situation more bearable. But this bearability of the status quo amounts to a permanent retreat to the psychic bomb shelter of the present moment, extending the crisis, "permitting the present to fully colonize the future."[25] This bury-your-head-in-the-sand mindfulness is sanitized palliative care for neoliberal subjects who have lost hope for a curative treatment to capitalism. Present momentism allows for ongoing adaptation to an ongoing crisis but is morally and spiritually bankrupt for envisioning and mobilizing a genuine revolution.

Cazdyn explains that the new chronic "extends the present into the future, burying in the process the force of the terminal, making it seem as if the present will never end."[26] Just be in the present moment and all will supposedly be well. By living mindfully, we can continue our lives as neoliberal subjects deferring, evading, and repressing an ongoing crisis. Mindfulness operates in the new chronic mode—as Cazdyn points out, "If the system cannot be reformed...then the new chronic mode insists on maintaining the system and perpetually managing its constitutive crises, rather than confronting even a hint of the terminal."[27] Like a terminally ill patient whose life is prolonged through medical advances, mindfulness interventions provide a way of managing, coping, prolonging, and living through the ongoing crisis of capitalism.

These promissory notes on our future resonate with the false promises of neoliberalism, what Lauren Berlant calls "cruel optimism."[28] Such optimism is cruel in that one makes affective investments in what amount to fantasies that will never come to pass. We are promised that if we only practice mindfulness, and get our individual lives in order, our dreams of securing happiness, attaining security, stable employment, home ownership, social mobility, career success, and civic equality will naturally emerge. We are also promised that we can gain a self-mastery and full control over our mental and emotional lives that will allow us to thrive and flourish amid the vagaries of capitalism. We just have to sit in silence, watching our breath, and wait. It is doubly cruel because, one, these normative fantasies of the "good life" are crumbling under neoliberalism, and, two, this affective orientation and individualistic focus that we believe sustains our lives also works to diminish and endanger our lives by obfuscating our shared vulnerabilities and by disimagining our interdependent social and collective worlds. Despite the emptiness of these fantasies, we continue to cling to them. The cruelty is that neoliberalism's elevation of mindfulness naturalizes the ideology of free choice, espousing a vision of human flourishing that enables people to accept things as they are, mindfully enduring the ravages of capitalism.

The Political Closure of Mindfulness

As a cruel optimism, neoliberal mindfulness encourages settling for a resigned political passivity. Secular Buddhism, with its practice of mindfulness, is prescribed as a way of managing, naturalizing, and enduring toxic systems rather than turning effort toward a critical questioning of the historical, cultural, and political conditions that are responsible for social suffering. As a cruelly optimistic narrative of enchantment, mindfulness emulates idealism coupled with individualism. For capitalism to survive, as Nicole Ashoff points out in *The New Prophets of Capital*, "people must willingly participate in and reproduce its structures and norms," and in times of crisis, "capitalism must draw upon cultural ideas that exist outside of the circuits of profit-making."[29] Mindfulness is a new cultural idea serving this purpose.

What may have begun as an emancipatory spirit for radical change has become co-opted by elites colluding with, and acting on behalf of, institutional interests. The very success of the mindfulness movement and the appeal of secular Buddhism is also its downfall. The potential for a radical and truly revolutionary mindfulness movement was usurped by the elites who stood to benefit. As a means for legitimizing their roles as experts, the mindful elites have a personal stake in maintaining that distress is localized to the individual. Whether it be books, trainings, courses, interventions, or apps, the mindful elites have managed to hide their interests, allowing them to control the narrative—that the source of all human distress is to be found deep in the interiors of individuals.

In complicity with a neoliberal ethos, mindfulness practices lack the narrative and explanatory frameworks to focus collective attention on larger social-material systems. As William Davies explains, movements and practices become deeply conservative when "critique is turned inwards."[30] Captivated by the spell of neoliberal market-generated narratives of personal responsibility, flourishing, resilience, happiness, and the veneer of brain plasticity, the mindfulness pundits can only tell us that we only need to look deep within to find our authentic selves.

BIBLIOGRAPHY

Aschoff, Nicole. *The New Prophets of Capital.* New York: Verso Books, 2015.

Berlant, Lauren. *Cruel Optimism.* Durham: Duke University Press, 2011.

Bourdieu, Pierre. "The Essence of Neoliberalism." *Le Monde diplomatique,* December 1998. https://mondediplo.com/1998/12/08bourdieu.

Brown, Wendy. *Undoing the Demos: Neoliberalism's Stealth Revolution.* New York: Zone Books, 2005.

Cazdyn, Eric. *The Already Dead: The New Time of Politics, Culture and Illness.* Durham: Duke University Press, 2012.

Davies, William. *The Happiness Industry.* London: Verso Books, 2015.

Eaton, Joshua, "American Buddhism: Beyond the Search for Inner Peace." *Religion Dispatches* (blog), February 20, 2013. http://religiondispatches.org/american-buddhism-beyond-the-search-for-inner-peace/.

Fletcher, Peter. 2010. "Foucault on Confession." *Peter Fletcher* (blog). August 10, 2010. https://peterfletcher.com.au/2010/08/10/foucault-on-confession/.

Foucault, Michel. *The History of Sexuality Volume 1: An Introduction.* New York: Vintage Books, 1978.

——. *The Birth of Biopolitics: Lectures at the College de France, 1978-79.* Translated by G. Burchell. New York: Palgrave Macmillan, 2008.

Gershon, Ilana. "Neoliberal Agency." *Current Anthropology* 52, no. 4 (2011): 537-55.

Giroux, Henry. *The Violence of Organized Forgetting: Thinking Beyond America's Disimagination Machine.* San Francisco: City Lights Publishers, 2014.

Harvey, David. *A Brief History of Neoliberalism.* Oxford: Oxford University Press, 2007.

Newton, Timothy. *Managing Stress: Emotion and Power at Work.* London: Sage Publications, 1995.

Payne, Richard K. "Confusions Informing Secular Buddhism: Technology and Ideology." *Critical Reflections on Buddhist Thought: Contemporary and Classical* (blog), December 21, 2018. https://criticalreflectionsonbuddhistthought. org/category/buddhism-under-capitalism/.

Rappaport, Herbert. *Marking Time.* New York: Simon & Schuster, 2009.

Rose, Nikolas. *Inventing Ourselves: Psychology, Power, and Personhood.* Cambridge: Cambridge University Press, 1998.

Sugarman, Jeff. "Neoliberalism and Psychological Ethics." *Journal of Theoretical and Philosophical Psychology* 35, no. 2 (2015).

Wilson, Julie. *Neoliberalism.* London: Routledge, 2017.

Žižek, Slavoj. "From Western Marxism to Western Buddhism." *Cabinet Magazine*, Spring 2001. http://www.cabinetmagazine.org/issues/2/western.php.

10 | The Modern Mindfulness Movement and the Search for Psychological Redemption

Kathleen Gregory

That the discipline of psychology has been instrumental in both legitimizing and making accessible the practice of mindfulness outside of its Buddhist context is no surprise to most people. Mindfulness has come to make sense as a psychologically oriented practice, juxtaposed that is, with mindfulness as part of a spiritual or soteriological orientation in Buddhism. The secularizing of mindfulness in the West may be seen as a process of *psychologization*, which highlights an interesting issue for the contemporary understanding of secularization. One of the enduring motifs of secularization is the idea of emancipation from the constrictions of religious tradition, so that the individual is able to affirm themselves separately from any religious paradigm. However, in affirming the "psychological self," the modern mindfulness movement transposes the binary of "religious" versus "secular" with another binary, "religious" versus "psychological," as if these involve two diametrically opposed realms of human experience. This reflects the view many of us have that the religious requires a rejection of our mundane psychological experiences for some idealized "higher plane" of existence.

In contrast to this binary, in Buddhism there is a dynamic relationship between "religious" and "psychological," since spiritual development is practically oriented toward "building character."[1] Buddhist practice therefore includes engaging with the psychological reality of thoughts, emotions, attitudes, feelings, and so on, that each of us live within. Spiritual development or transformation cannot be separated from the development of a healthy "psychology." Western psychology suggests that our subjective well-being—the evaluation of how we experience our lives—is positively impacted by our sense of satisfaction related to spirituality or religiosity.[2] Having spiritual beliefs is itself good for our psychological health.

Here it is important to clarify the terms "religious" and "spiritual." I make the distinction that "religious" refers to the outer, observable practices a person undertakes as part of a religion; I use the term "spiritual" to refer to the internal subjective experiences that are generated on the basis of those practices. However, the psychological and spiritual are not simply the same. The distinction of mindfulness as either spiritual—that is, Buddhist—or psychological—that is, secular—provides an opportunity to help clarify both of these domains. The fact that Western secular mindfulness has become established in its own right means these two contexts for mindfulness practice—psychological and religious—can be brought into relationship, throwing light on our understanding of each.

This chapter is not an argument against the secular presentation of mindfulness or the role psychology and increasingly neuroscience have played in its development. Rather, I will explore how this process of psychologization, and more recently neurologization, within the secular mindfulness movement reflects something about our modern psychology and accustomed ways of thinking. This is relevant to mindfulness practice whether we consider ourselves secular or Buddhist practitioners, because we are by necessity engaging with our own psychological reality, which has been inevitably conditioned by contemporaneous cultural discourses.

It is evident that the psychological view dominates contemporary understandings of human experience. Knowing ourselves (and others) requires thinking "psychologically" to make sense of internal mental processes. The current magnitude of the popularity and penetration of the modern mindfulness movement across a range of disciplines and institutions indicates how accustomed we have become to relating to experience through a psychological lens.

In this context, it can be said that the secularizing—or more rightly, psychologizing—of mindfulness is a process of reconstituting this meditation practice in familiar ways of thinking about ourselves. Within the modern mindfulness movement, the aim of the practice can be described as psychological redemption, which includes the goals of feeling, thinking, and being *better*. When mindfulness is presented in familiar psychologized constructs, then familiar ways of knowing and being ourselves can show up in how we relate to the practice and our experiences in this process. As we shall see, mindfulness as a psychologically oriented practice has the potential to fortify our habitual critical and deficit orientation toward ourselves.

In the context of Buddhism, mindfulness practice is in the service of cultivating "another way of being ourselves."[3] This requires gaining insight into how habitual ways of seeing ourselves and behaving can root us in the conditions of suffering. On the basis of insight, familiar perspectives are challenged and ultimately transformed. What were initially unfamiliar ways of seeing ourselves and our experiences begin to become familiar, informing our behavior, including how we relate to our experience. This is the process emphasized in Buddhist practice. In contrast, when mindfulness is presented from a psychological orientation, familiar ways of relating to experience can in fact become assimilated into a person's practice.

Since I am both a counseling psychologist and a practicing Buddhist, I find myself in a unique position navigating the worlds of these two approaches to mindfulness. My aim in this essay is to bring forth what I have learned through both counseling and meditation practice, about how as contemporary people many of us are engaging—and sometimes struggling—with mindfulness practice. In this endeavor, I seek to bring into view the dynamic relationship between the religious, spiritual, and psychological.

The Psychologization of
the Modern Mindfulness Movement

The creation of modern, secularized mindfulness and the movement it has engendered is commonly attributed to the work of Jon
Kabat-Zinn, who first introduced mindfulness in a clinical setting
to help patients manage their stress and blood pressure.[4] Due to
Kabat-Zinn's exposure to Theravāda Buddhism, mindfulness in the
clinic was first characterized in terms of its Asian origins and in
relation to Buddhist concepts such as intention, compassion, and
acceptance. In 1979 Kabat-Zinn founded the Mindfulness-Based
Stress Reduction Clinic at the University of Massachusetts Medical
School and systematized his approach into a program of the same
name—commonly known by its acronym, MBSR.[5] Established in
definition and operationalized within a program, mindfulness took
on the status of an object of clinical research and a practical technique with real-world relevance.

In time, the research evidence began to mount affirming the ability of mindfulness to reduce clinical symptoms such as depression
and anxiety as well as enhance general psychological well-being.
Mindfulness as a distinctly Western and contemporary practice
began to take shape—as a practice that had not only been adopted
from its Asian Buddhist roots but, more compellingly, *adapted* to
the unique needs and conditions of modern Western people. This
resulted in the distinction of two kinds of mindfulness practice. First
was mindfulness as a psychologically oriented practice with significance clinically as well as in terms of general well-being. Second was
mindfulness in the context of the religious tradition of Buddhism,
as part of a system of soteriological practices in the service of spiritual transformation. This binary of secular and religious served
to locate mindfulness in Buddhism as *other* to the secular and its
accompanying constructs such as worldly, modern, contemporary,
relevant, and so on.

The secular definition refined over time by Kabat-Zinn remains
the most influential and generally accepted understanding of mind-

fulness as a psychologically oriented practice. That is, mindfulness is "cultivated by paying attention in a sustained and particular way: on purpose, in the present moment, and nonjudgmentally."[6] With the concept of "attention" front and center, researchers looked to determine the elemental cognitive factors within the scope of this definition. This shift in emphasis saw the research evidence affirm the view that mindfulness was not only a means to *feel better* but that it could also help you *do better* in whatever activities you undertook.

As a result, the reach of mindfulness began to extend out of the clinical realm to include application within educational, sports, corporate, and military contexts, contributing to the exponential growth in a mindfulness industry serving those fields. This development sparked controversy related to the ethics of teaching mindfulness to "produce," for example, more efficient workers or combat personnel.[7] However, the idea you could *do better* through mindfulness found broader legitimacy by dovetailing with the accumulating neuroscientific research. In fact, the notion that through mindfulness you can "change your brain"—the underlying neurological mechanisms of psychological or mental processes—is generally accepted as an accurate expression of the mechanics of the practice. We will consider the neurologization process of mindfulness below.

The subsequent commodification of mindfulness within the wellness and self-help industry has seen Western mindfulness developed as a means of combining *feeling* better and *doing* better, if not surpassing those with *being* better. A recent *Time* single-issue magazine titled "The New Mindfulness," subtitled "Living, Thinking, Being," reflects these domains.[8] These three domains correspond to the principal research areas mindfulness is shown to positively impact:

1. Clinical applications: mindfulness helps deal with problematic symptoms and behaviors (*feel better/living goals*)—for example, reduce anxiety, ameliorate depression, manage stress.

2. Cognitive enhancement: mindfulness changes how we process external and internal stimuli (*do better/thinking goals*)—for example, increase efficiency by improving attention and concentration.

3. Psychological mindedness: mindfulness allows us to better enact the goals of the self (*be better/being goals*)—for example, enhance self-awareness and self-expression to ensure alignment with who we want to be.[9]

Given the popular uptake of mindfulness consonant with these domains, it can be said that now not only do most people believe they know what mindfulness is and how to practice it, many now assert it as a kind of virtuous activity. That is, to practice mindfulness is part of the "package" of being a person committed to one's mental well-being and—potentially more importantly—being one's "best self" in whatever one does and aspires to be. This, as Richard K. Payne argues in this volume, has seen mindfulness take on the status of a "moral imperative."

Currently, a second generation of research confirms the view that the West has secured an operationalization of mindfulness amenable to clinical and neurological measure and manipulation independent of its Asian origins. In turn, this view has been realized in popular perception—as exemplified in the aforementioned *Time* magazine special edition. Here we find no image of a meditating Eastern monk (or nun) of the kind that had for some time served as a potent cultural image of the appearance of serenity that mindfulness continues to personify. There are only two short pictorially embedded quotes from "ancient Eastern sages," the text relying on the accounts of Western researchers and mindfulness teachers, as well as celebrities. Mindfulness as a distinctly Western phenomenon has, without a doubt, arrived.

Having been transformed from a foreign practice—in the sense of being both Asian and spiritually oriented—to a Western secular psychological practice, mindfulness necessarily had to go through an interpretive process via the disciplines of psychology and more recently neuroscience. In the first instance, it seems curious how the circumstance of psychology's role in this interpretative process has been received with little question. On the contrary, generally it is "recognizable" that psychology has the authority to explain human beings.[10] Thus it has been taken as a given that psychology is well positioned to adopt mindfulness away from its Buddhist context—the ways in which psychology has adapted mindfulness are "intelligible" and "acceptable" to most people. Mindfulness linked to psychology has easily been able to trump its Buddhist origins, while the association with neuroscience has only served to cultivate if not enhance its popularity.

If we compare this situation with the challenge Sigmund Freud faced well over a hundred years ago in introducing his ideas on the psychological nature of persons, it seems impossible to imagine from this historical standpoint how *psychological* we have become. In the middle of the last century, the backlash against behaviorism—which eschewed the "mind" of thoughts and emotions for environmental conditioning—may have suggested how unlikely it would be that *brain-based* explanations of human experience could garner such popular appeal. The pervasive acceptance of a psychologically oriented practice of mindfulness supported by neuroscientific research illustrates a shift over time in the Western worldview. Here a qualification is necessary. In the mainstream, secular mindfulness has been commodified in relation to neoliberal values that principally serve the aims and aspirations of those who are socially privileged—those being white, educated, and middle-class. This statement does not diminish the increasing presence of teachers and practitioners of color nor the active ways the modern mindfulness movement is seeking to address issues of diversity, or indeed, the global reach of the modern mindfulness movement. (Ron Purser's essay in this volume discusses the relation between neoliberalism and the secularizing of Buddhism.)

It is evident over the course of the last century that the discourses of the "psy" disciplines, which include psychology, psychiatry, psychoanalysis, and psychotherapy, have crossed the boundaries of their discipline and into society at large.[11] The growth in so-called pop psychology and the current boom of the wellness and self-help industry are manifestly evident in popular culture. The self-help industry functions as an important channel for the dissemination of the psy disciplines, and itself is testament to the extent of this boundary-crossing. The "therapeutic turn" as described by Madsen, can be understood as an historical development emerging as an outcome of the Enlightenment project. With the decline of the authority of religion and the ascent of science, the growing orientation was toward a secular worldview favoring rationalization.[12] It is in this context of modernism that the knowledge generated by the psy disciplines, and psychology in particular, began to penetrate society—the psychologization of society.[13] Here it is noted that in an increasingly global world, the current influence of psychology has gone beyond the confines of the West and resulted in a "global psychological" mentality with an emphasis on individuality as a result.[14]

The consequence is that psychology and, increasingly, neuroscience are instrumental in "inventing" many of the ways we as contemporary people generally understand and relate to ourselves and others. Psychologization also includes the knowledge generated via the range of channels such as pop psychology, popular science, new age spirituality, self-help and wellness mediums, and further reinforces the dominance of the "psychological lens."

The ease with which a psychologized presentation of mindfulness has been received as intelligible and acceptable can be seen as an indication of how familiar this way of understanding and knowing experience is to us. The familiarity may well be the result of such a closeness to this perspective that we do not, for the most part, recognize it as a *kind* of knowledge about human experience, since we ourselves are engaged in the processes of psychologization in relation to our own experience.

Psychologization of Experience

Given the psychologized context we live in as contemporary persons, we have all become psychologists to ourselves as Jan De Vos, who has been mapping the effects of psychologization, asserts.[15] Simply, we are accustomed to relating to our thoughts, feelings, emotions via the knowledge originated from within the psy disciplines. By "applying" that knowledge to our subjective experiences, we *think psychologically* and, on that basis, come to "know" ourselves (and others). To this end, we replicate the general orientation of the scientific-clinical method and make ourselves an "object of scrutiny" through engaging in processes of observation, categorization, and explanation of our internal experiences.[16] As in the clinic, formulating goals (outcomes) in relation to feeling, thinking, and doing *better* involves identifying factors of *impairment* amenable to evident and measurable *improvement* contingent on the application of a treatment intervention such as a daily mindfulness practice, for example.[17] Here we rely on the assertion that there are identifiable mental phenomena such as "calmness," and indeed "mindfulness," that can be isolated and differentiated as either present or absent, or described on a continuum of strong to weak.

This kind of differentiation of experience is pertinent when it comes to measuring an anticipated treatment effect to be observed, categorized, and explained. For instance, objectives such as the presence of calmness, absence of self-judgment, or stronger focused attention may be articulated. However, relating to experience premised on judgments of presence or absence, strength or weakness, is not the objective process we believe it to be—the presupposition being that engaging in mindfulness practice is to address what is "wrong" or "lacking" in our self. The emphasis then becomes creating the "right" kind of internal mental space to feel better and to effect doing and being better. This sets the condition for a person to relate to mindfulness from the view of differentiation and impairment. Holding a critical vigilance toward their own experience is familiar to many people. As a result, they may come to rely on this attitude in relation to the practice.

The potential for this to occur is compounded by the fact that psychologization can reinforce a deepening "split" in relation to our experiences. This is the case because psychologization acts to position us at once both as a subject that *is* (the observer, explainer, categorizer, and controller of experience) and—through the expert knowledge from which we are called upon to see ourselves—as the idealized subject that *could be*.[18] (See Sarah Shaw in this volume for an assertion of the value of individual agency, particularly in medical settings.) As a consequence, a gap can be perceived between the knowledge we have—for example, about mindfulness—and what we find ourselves to be when we apply that knowledge to our practice experience. Since knowledge shapes expectations of a treatment effect—an identified change in experience—a person can be vulnerable to judging any perceived "failing" to be a matter of personal "failure." I understand, from a narrative therapy perspective, that if a failure to experience "more calm"—as the stated goals for instance—occurs, then in likelihood this "failure" becomes construed as a matter of lack or as a failure of will, commitment, capacity, or competency.[19] The perception in this context is that it is a matter of *personal* failure that explains the absence or weakness of "treatment effect." This view is reinforced since we tend to anticipate exerting some control over elements of experience to meet our stated feeling, doing, or being *better* goals. As a consequence, when the expert knowledge employed "fails" to bring the anticipated effect, then a person (despite their efforts to help themselves) can end up feeling worse.

My emphasis here is not on the accuracy of the knowledge, although this may be a contributing factor. Rather I am concerned with how psychologizing this new object of knowledge—mindfulness—becomes reconstituted in the problematic ways by which we are accustomed to understanding and relating to our experiences. Although psychologically oriented mindfulness presents promises of "new experiences" or at least ones that are known only fleetingly or occasionally, the prevailing psychological framework remains intact.

If we return to the popular definition of mindfulness, we can see how this can be played out:

1. Mindfulness advocates nonjudgmentalism, while the broader context of psychologization supports the differentiation of experiences in terms of presence or absence, and strength to weakness. On the basis of differentiation, certain experiences can

become perceived as a threat or obstacle to "our mindfulness," including experiences of judgmentalism. As a result, the critical relationship to experience can become fortified.

2. Mindfulness involves "paying attention in a particular way, on purpose" but when the habit of observing, explaining, and categorizing is transferred to meditation experiences, it can lead to hypervigilance. When the inward gaze becomes exaggerated in this way, the habit of self-absorption is reinforced. Self-absorption can "weigh us down" both mentally and physically.[20]

3. Mindfulness is about "the present moment" while being oriented to the accomplishment of a future state premised on a perceived past-to-current lack or deficit. When the "result" is deemed a "failure" because of a judgment of absence or weakness of an anticipated treatment effect—for example, an isolated psychological state such as "calmness"—then a person is vulnerable to experiencing a sense of inadequacy, failure, or lack. This can lead a person to give up on mindfulness and potentially give up on themselves, experiencing a sense of defeat in relation to their aspirations.

Our psychology depends on external sources of knowledge to both understand and shape ourselves in relation to identified feeling, doing, and being goals. We must engage with our experiences to influence how we think, feel, and behave, to even transform ourselves in ways to which we aspire. However, when our efforts to bring forward new ways of being are understood through a familiar orientation to experience, this can only mire us further in the very conditions we were seeking to free ourselves from, even leading a person to judge themselves a "hopeless case"—as one client described themselves in response to their perceived "failure" at mindfulness.

Detaching from the Familiar

In Buddhism, to bring unaccustomed feelings, thoughts, and behaviors forward in the service of personal transformation, we are required to "detach ourselves from everything that is familiar."[21] This includes the habits of psychologization such as differentiating our experiences, self-vigilance, and self-judgment. To this end, we can rely on Buddhist teachings such as the three marks of existence—that there is pervasive suffering, that everything is impermanent, and that there is no fixed self, or "egolessness." The three marks reflect an understanding of our existence with which most of us are not yet familiar or perhaps at best "know" superficially but have not internalized.

Detaching from the familiar does not mean imposing an ideal or jettisoning certain experiences, as if that were possible. To detach or "liberate" ourselves from the underlying mental processes that perpetuate the samsaric condition, we need to bring the three marks of existence close to our experiences through reflection and contemplation.[22] This occurs in the practice of insight meditation (Pāli vipassanā, Skt. vipaśyanā), which is the companion practice to tranquility meditation (Pāli samatha, Skt. śamatha). Insight meditation is an active form of meditation using conceptual processes to investigate mind's construction of reality. Together tranquility and insight meditation help us gain understanding of what is beneficial or harmful to us.

For example, we can return to the three experiences outlined above in relation to the psychologization of mindfulness and see how the three marks of existence can bring insight to those experiences:

1. Usually when we suffer, we focus on the particularities of our specific suffering and how we might avoid or attenuate that experience. From the point of view of insight, all human endeavor is tinged with suffering. On this basis, we develop resilience around suffering in which we no longer reject it—or any experience—outright.

2. A hypervigilant state leads us to scan the environment of our experiences for signs of change which we perceive as deterioration. As a result, we make these the object of our dissatisfaction

or fear. From the point of view of insight, each experience of change reminds us of the nature of impermanence. Thus, this awareness promotes the view that is more in accord with reality as it is and stabilizes resilience in the face of change.

3. When viewing our experience and finding it deficient, we see our ego or self as weak and in need of support. From the point of view of insight, there is no intrinsic "self" to be found. Experiencing egolessness serves to "liberate" us from the project that has become "self-improvement."

Herein is how we develop the conviction that the habits of psychologization are the cause for becoming entangled with the "particularities" of our subjective experiences and mental states[23]—an entanglement that is characterized by the terms of a critical and vigilant relationship to experience that only "roots" us deeper into the familiar environment of self-absorption. The subsequent sense of being a self-divided person becomes reinforced as we cycle between attraction (hope that things will improve) and aversion (fear that things will get worse) in relation to our experiences. Thus, we see clearly how we perpetuate the habitual dissatisfaction of samsara through what can only be futile attempts to get ourselves "right," while a tendency to reify what we habitually pay attention to only causes us to view any perceived "lack" or "wrongness" as intrinsic to ourselves. As a result, it becomes evident that this is how we shore up our accustomed beliefs and further habituate the critical and vigilant relationship to our experiences. In this process we in fact only further solidify our taken-for-granted notions of "a self," fortifying the condition for our own suffering.

Fundamentally, we gain insight into how the force of our mental habit patterns propel us forward. Most tellingly, we gain insight into how we have mistaken this as a movement toward progress and improvement. We come to realize that habitually and without reflection, we return again and again to the same psychological reality, rather than seeing that this *is* the cycle of samsara.

At the same time, with insight, experiences of spaciousness and expansiveness may begin to permeate our feeling, thinking, and being. These experiences can undermine the speed and intensity of our habitual cognitive patterns. In these ways, spiritual awakening entails weakening the grasp of our habitual modes, such that unfamiliar or less-known ways of feeling, doing, and being can become manifest. Eventually the unfamiliar becomes the familiar. As such, the emphasis here is on the capacity of human beings to function beyond their current psychologized state.[24] This capacity, however, does not involve further reinforcement of a dualistic view of our experiences as good or bad.

Here we can return to the familiar mode of psychologization. As we have seen, many people approach mindfulness with the aim of creating the "right" mental state—characterized, for example, as calmer or more focused—in *contrast*, that is, to their "everyday mind." The assumption here is that this "calmer mental state" can *affect* our "everyday mind" to help us feel, think, or be better. This suggests a perceived duality of the "meditative mind" as opposed to the "everyday mind." On this basis we are more vulnerable to differentiate experiences and rely on the habit of rejection and grasping to meet our feeling, thinking, and being goals.

To put this observation in more context, we need to consider how the neuroscientific perspective has increasingly come to play an explanatory role in the presentation of psychologically oriented mindfulness and the impact of the "neurologization of persons."

The Neurologization of Persons

Neuroscience promotes and reinforces the view of physical materialism that contends our subjective experiences and psychological processes are reducible to physical brain function. The late twentieth century saw a surge in neuroscientific research. The dissemination and popular uptake of this view of human experience and functioning has been called the "neuroturn." Encompassing both scientific and popularized views, there has even been a suggestion of an ensuing "neuromania."[25]

"Neurologization" is a term that has been coined to capture the growing presence and consequential societal influence of this understanding of human beings.[26] Like psychologization, neurologization also refers to a way people come to understand and relate to themselves. Neurologization is defined succinctly by De Vos, who describes it as a movement away from the idea of "having a brain" to the idea of "being a brain."[27] When mindfulness is shaped by physical materialism, it reinforces this view of being a human, collapsing all experiences and ways of knowing ourselves into a matter of brain function. In the modern secular presentation of mindfulness, the idea of "being a brain" has been subsumed by the idea of "changing your brain."[28]

However, this idea that brain changes explain meditation experiences requires some interrogation. Does it mean the application of mindfulness unlocks the brain circuitry responsible for the experience of presence and calmness, for example? Does mindfulness "wash" the brain out so that it is "new" and "changed"? What is changed? How is it changed? What happens to old habits?

"Changing your brain" has for many people become a cogent rationalization to practice. The plethora of pop psychology, self-help, and new age mindfulness expressions have come to rely on a kind of naturalized neuroscientific view. However, since mindfulness is promoted primarily as a psychologically oriented practice concerned with the development of our subjective "internal life," this suggests a tension. To counter the reductionist view of human being implicit in the neuroscientific view, notions such as meaning, agency, choice, and subjectivity, De Vos argues, become emphasized within the research lab and beyond.[29] This is evident in the modern mindfulness movement, since psychological or subjective values and motivations related to living, doing, and being provide the context that makes doing the practice personally meaningful and intentionally acted.

The fact is both neuroscientific and psychological perspectives occur together, and indeed coexist in persons in their approach to, and understanding of, mindfulness. However, this blending raises interesting questions as it relates to the idea of "failing" at mindfulness, as we explored previously. "Failure" at mindfulness maybe perceived as a failure to change one's brain—evidenced in the absence of what may be *perceived* as brain-based experiences of calmness, for example. However, perceiving lack or failure of capacity, will, or commitment as the "cause" suggests an internal, subjective will*er* or committ*er*—a suggestion that raises some questions: Is this "willer" or "committer" perceived as a "self"? Is it understood as simply a brain-based phenomenon or is it separate? Can failure at mindfulness lead a person, on the basis of neurologization, to come to believe their brain is hardwired and can't be changed? Here the confluence of these two views—psychologization and neurologization—becomes evident. Potentially, this confluence solidifies a critical view of our capacity to experience the fruits of mindfulness, resulting in a sense of having been defeated.

In the spirit of insight meditation, the questions offered here are in the service of prompting interrogation and analysis of how any naturalization of neurologization of persons has taken hold in our understanding of ourselves. Because as we have seen, through the process of psychologization our beliefs and assumptions become operationalized in the kind of relationship we have to our experiences. This is a matter relevant both to our subjective well-being and our spiritual development.

Conclusion: Transforming Experience

Through the subject of mindfulness, this chapter has brought Buddhist and Western psychological approaches to knowing and relating to experiences into relationship, and it has explored how psychologization and neurologization have shaped the modern secular mindfulness movement. The emphasis has been on how these are not merely abstract ideologies but have become characteristic ways that we as contemporary persons understand and relate to our experiences. Whether we are practicing mindfulness in a secular context or a spiritual context, we are all working with the same "psychology."

On the level of practice, we have seen that our habitual relationship to our experiences can become entangled with our relationship to mindfulness. The habits of psychologization drive this entanglement, fortifying the familiar critical and vigilant relationship to experience. In seeking to feel, think, or be better through mindfulness, a person who judges themselves to have failed potentially becomes further entrenched in the conditions of suffering.

In Buddhism the application of reflection and contemplation through insight meditation is the practice of disentangling ourselves from the familiar and habitual. Spiritual development is an intimate process of exploring unaccustomed ways of knowing and relating to experiences. Eventually, experience and realization become integrated. Herein lies the radical awakening of the Buddhist path.

BIBLIOGRAPHY

De Vos, Jan. *Psychologization and the Subject of Late Modernity*. New York: Palgrave MacMillan, 2013.

———. *The Metamorphoses of the Brain: Neurologisation and Its Discontents*. New York: Palgrave MacMillan, 2016.

Illouz, Eva. *Saving the Modern Soul: Therapy, Emotions, and the Culture of Self-Help*. Berkeley: University of California Press, 2008.

Jha, Amisha P., Jason Krompinger, and Michael J. Baime. "Mindfulness Training Modifies Subsystems of Attention." *Cognitive, Affective and Behavioral Neuroscience* 7, no. 2 (2007): 109-19.

Kabat-Zinn, Jon. *Mindfulness for Beginners: Reclaiming the Present Moment— and your Life*. Boulder: Sounds True, 2012.

Kyabgon, Traleg. *The Essence of Buddhism*. Boston: Shambhala Publications, 2001.

———. *The Benevolent Mind: A Manual in Mind Training*. Auckland, NZ: Zhyisil Chokyi Ghatsal Publications, 2003.

———. *Mind at Ease: Self-liberation through Mahamudra Meditation*. Boston: Shambhala Publications, 2004.

———. *Desire: Why It Matters*. Ballarat, Australia: Shogam Publications, 2019.

Madsen, Ole Jacob. *The Therapeutic Turn: How Psychology Altered Western Culture*. East Sussex, UK: Routledge, 2014.

McAvoy, Jean. "Psy Disciplines." *Encyclopedia of Critical Psychology*. edited by T. Teo. New York: Springer, 2014. doi.org/10.1007/978-1-4614-5583-7_611.

Ostafin, Brian D., Michael D. Robinson, and Brian P. Meier, "Introduction: The Science of Mindfulness and Self-regulation." *Handbook of Mindfulness and Self-regulation*, edited by Brian D. Ostafin, Michael D. Robinson, and Brian P. Meier. New York: Springer, 2015.

Rose, Nikolas. *Power and Subjectivity: Psychology, Power and Personhood*. London: Cambridge University Press, 1998.

Tallis, Raymond. *Aping Mankind: Neuromanis, Darwinitis and the Misrepresentation of Humanity*. Oxford: Routledge, 2014.

Time. "The New Mindfulness: Living, Thinking, Being." Single-issue edition, November 28, 2018.

Villani, Daniela, Angela Sorgente, Paola Iannello, and Alessandro Antonietti, "The Role of Spirituality and Religiosity in Subjective Well-Being of Individuals with Different Religious Status," *Frontiers in Psychology* 10 (2019): 1525. doi.org/10.3389/fpsyg.2019.01525.

White, Michael. "Addressing Personal Failure." *International Journal of Narrative and Community Work*, no. 3 (2002): 33–76.

11 | Avoiding Rebirth

Modern Buddhist Views on Past and Future Lives

ROGER R. JACKSON

Did it matter? Does it now?
Stephen would answer if he only knew how.

ROBERT HUNTER, "St. Stephen"

Thurman v. Batchelor, 1997

If there is a signal moment in the articulation of "secular Buddhism," it may well be the publication, in 1997, of Stephen Batchelor's *Buddhism without Beliefs: A Contemporary Guide to Awakening*.[1] In his Buddhist modernist manifesto, which has served for over two decades as both a touchstone and a lightning rod, Batchelor lays out a vision of the Buddha, and of Buddhism, in which the key tenets of the dharma are regarded not as cosmological or metaphysical claims but, rather, as ontological, existential, psychological, and ethical guidelines for living. Batchelor does not dispute that the Buddha propounded a cosmology involving five or six realms of samsaric existence or a metaphysics entailing the precise operations of karma through a series of rebirths undergone by each sentient being, but he argues that these ideas were incidental to Śākyamuni's true purpose: to help us transcend anxiety and attain an authentic way of being that is informed by both a deep understanding of reality and compassion broad enough to encompass all beings.[2]

The chapter on "Rebirth" in *Buddhism without Beliefs* is brief,[3] but crucial to Batchelor's argument. He acknowledges that rebirth is difficult to accept for those, like him, who have been shaped by the scientific worldview, and he argues that the Buddha used the concept simply as an easily understandable scaffolding for his more important psychological and ethical teachings. He further argues that—the claims of Asian Buddhists notwithstanding—acceptance of rebirth is by no means crucial to those teachings' truth and effectiveness. Invoking the critical spirit he sees the Buddha encouraging in his followers, Batchelor says that we moderns need not accept the reality of rebirth simply on the tradition's say-so or because we fear that we will not be able to live ethically in the absence of an elaborate but unproven metaphysics. He himself does not reject rebirth—he declares himself agnostic on the matter—but he clearly thinks that the question is largely irrelevant to the practice of dharma and should be left in abeyance.

Batchelor's views on rebirth clearly would be anathema to many traditionalists—whose aim, after all, is to avoid *taking* rebirth rather than to avoid *discussing* it (see Bhikkhu Bodhi in this volume)— but they also met with criticism from many thoroughly modern Buddhists. Indeed, on the occasion of the publication of *Buddhism without Beliefs*, *Tricycle* magazine, a bellwether of modern North American Buddhism, staged a debate on the question of rebirth between Batchelor and Robert Thurman, a renowned scholar of Tibetan Buddhism who is also a proponent of his own distinctive vision of modern dharma.[4] Even two-plus decades later, the exchange crackles with intelligence, as two scholar-practitioners grapple honestly—and often quite subtly—with difficult questions of history, culture, and philosophy. The lively back-and-forth of the conversation only can be appreciated by reading the transcript,[5] but it is worthwhile to identify the key questions debated by Batchelor and Thurman (and the stances taken by each), because, arguably, they remain questions that sooner or later all modern Buddhists must face.

The central question animating the debate is, quite simply, can we be Buddhist without believing in rebirth? Batchelor argues that we can—that the Buddha's teachings on ethics, meditation, emptiness, and the nature and workings of the mind all can "work" perfectly well even in the absence of a metaphysics of karma-influenced personal mental continuity—that is, rebirth. For Thurman, the abandonment of such a metaphysics, with its implication that we only live once, undercuts our motivation to behave ethically—let alone to try to attain Buddhahood in order to free all sentient beings from suffering, the stated goal of most Mahāyāna Buddhists. What's more, Thurman argues, there is ample empirical evidence for rebirth, both in the experiences of the Buddha and his awakened followers and in more recent scientific investigations of past-life reports, most notably those of Ian Stevenson.[6] Batchelor is skeptical about the evidentiary power of claims based on the alleged super-knowledges attributed to or even claimed by long-dead humans, and he finds the cases studied by Stevenson intriguing but far from convincing proof of the universality and operations of the Buddhist system of rebirth.

Batchelor and Thurman do agree on the definitive truth—and centrality—of the Mahāyāna Buddhist doctrine of emptiness, but to say that two Mahāyānists agree on emptiness as the deepest and most definitive truth of their tradition is akin to observing that two Christian theologians agree on the existence of God: the complications and controversies emerge from the ways they use "emptiness" or "God," which in turn are shaped by (among other things) their varying conceptions of the relation between ontology on the one hand and cosmology and metaphysics on the other. Thus, for Thurman, the fact that the Buddha taught the definitive truth of emptiness serves as a basis for confidence in his key provisional teachings, including the metaphysics of karma and rebirth, while according to Batchelor taking emptiness literally on an onto-logical level does *not* vouchsafe other, more provisional, Buddhist teachings, least of all those on karma and rebirth.[7] Such ideas, he believes, must be either eschewed entirely or, if retained, must be read existentially, psychologically, or metaphorically—in effect, as myths that inspire us to live authentically within a cosmos of which we know precious little. For his part, Thurman finds it hard to take inspiration from a vision we don't take more or less literally; a corollary is that it is impossible to take our bodhisattva vows seriously without believing in a multiplicity of lives in which we might work for others. Batchelor brings the discussion to a close by admitting that, in the absence of certainty, the best he could do would be to "try to behave as if there were infinite lifetimes in which I would be committed to saving beings."[8] In short, for Batchelor, it doesn't matter in the end whether there is rebirth or not, while for Thurman, it matters a great deal.

Tradition

While modern Buddhists like Batchelor and Thurman may debate whether acceptance of rebirth is central or peripheral to their own way of seeing the world and living within it, it is well-nigh impossible to dispute that Śākyamuni Buddha taught rebirth, and liberation from it, to his followers in ancient India, and it is nearly as difficult to deny that the idea was a crucial component of his understanding of the cosmos and our place within it.[9] Nor is there any real doubt that the concept of rebirth, interlinked with that of karma, is a key part of the worldview adopted by hundreds of millions of Buddhists in a wide range of Asian cultures over the past two-plus millennia. Of course, there were many particular expressions of this worldview, linked to time and place and intellectual and practical concerns, but in the premodern Buddhist world there was broad agreement on the saṃsāra-nirvāṇa cosmology, in which sentient beings travel from life to unsatisfactory life impelled by their delusions and karma, and only achieve nirvāṇa through living virtuously, mastering meditation, and seeing the nature of the self and the world to be impermanent, interdependent, selfless, and empty. Buddhist cosmology and metaphysics were ideologically influential wherever they spread in Asia, and Buddhist masters "on the ground" became renowned for their knowledge of and control over the processes of death and rebirth—from Indian reflections on the unsatisfactoriness of even the most blissful heaven, to Sri Lankan recitations of stories of the Buddha's previous lives, to Thai temple murals depicting next-life punishments for bad karma, to Chinese prayers aimed at rebirth in the pure land of Amitābha, to complex Tibetan practices for mastering the death-process and directing one's rebirth, to Japanese funerary rites.

Most of the Buddha's early followers probably accepted the samsāra-nirvāna cosmology (and rebirth as a component of it) unquestioningly, on the basis of the Master's charisma and reputation and on the authority of his teachings as collected in the canonical Tripiṭaka. But to the degree that they cared to argue for the reality of rebirth rather than simply accept it a priori, they could (and sometimes did) adopt a range of strategies, from refutations of materialist "science"; to evidence based on advanced meditative experiences, especially those of the Buddha; to appeals to explanatory analogies; to moral arguments rooted in appeals to causal regularity and cosmic justice; to faith-based assertions that if the Buddha is trustworthy on matters evident to the senses, he must be reliable on metaphysical matters as well. It was really only in the seventh century C.E., in an era marked by Indian philosophers' rising confidence in the reliability of formal rational argument, that a Buddhist attempted to prove systematically the key elements of the Buddhist worldview, including rebirth. The author of that proof is Dharmakīrti, who in the "proof of epistemic authority" (*pramāṇasiddhi*) chapter of his early and influential verse treatise, the *Pramāṇavārttika* (Commentary on Valid Cognition), lays out a detailed demonstration that the Buddha is an epistemically reliable person (*pramāṇabhūta*), on the grounds that (1) he was able, over the course of time, to develop the perfect qualities attributed to an awakened being, and (2) what he teaches—in this case, the four noble truths—is demonstrably true. It is in the discussion of the Buddha's development of perfect qualities that Dharmakīrti undertakes his proof of rebirth. He recognizes that if the Buddha, as claimed by tradition, attained *infinite* compassion, or knowledge, or skill, he could not possibly have done so in the course of one life but must have taken many lives to reach perfection. That, of course, requires that he had lived before, and that, more generally, all of us have lived before and, unless we are liberated, may live again—in other words, that rebirth is real. For there to be rebirth, there must be something that survives the death of the material body, and to demonstrate that there is "something" that survives, we must consider the question of the relation between mind and body.

Dharmakīrti's arguments have been analyzed elsewhere,[10] so I will not rehearse them in detail here, merely noting that they are built on both (1) a rejection of materialist metaphysics—with its assertion that "mind" is simply a function or epiphenomenon of the body—on the grounds that it leads to various logical absurdities, and (2) a demonstration that while body may *affect* mind by serving as a cooperative condition, it cannot *effect* mind by serving as its substantial cause or indispensable condition—on the grounds that the body, like matter in general, is coarse, insentient, and physical, while the mind is clear, knowing, and immaterial. While both body and mind are subject to moment-to-moment causation, each can be brought into existence only by causes of the same type (*sabhāga-hetu*). Thus, because mind exists as part of a causal continuum that is not, in the end, dependent on matter, the first mental moment of this life can only have been preceded by the final mental moment associated with the body of the previous life, and by the same token, the final mental moment of this life will—assuming we have not been liberated—be followed by the first mental moment of the next life, in association with a different body. Further, because of the mind's subtle nature, its qualities may be expanded to the nth degree, in ways that matter cannot; thus, the Buddha was capable of developing the infinite wisdom, compassion, and other virtues attributed to him. Dharmakīrti's argument received a great deal of attention, first in India and then, starting in the eleventh century, in Tibet and other parts of inner Asia, where it became the standard response whenever the reality of rebirth or other elements of the Buddhist worldview were questioned. It was less well known or influential in the Theravāda world of South and Southeast Asia, or in Mahāyāna East Asia. We will consider its place in modern Buddhist discourse in the next section of the essay.

Of course, not all Buddhist traditions consider rebirth and its avoidance to be the keys to liberation. Certain radical meditative traditions—including some Theravāda approaches to attaining mental serenity (*samatha*) or insight (*vipassanā*); Tibetan methods for directly realizing the pure, empty, and luminous nature of mind, such as the Great Seal (*mahāmudrā*) or the Great Perfection (*rdzogs chen*); or the present-moment-focused contemplations encouraged in the East Asian "Zen" schools—at times consign cosmological, metaphysical, and eschatological concerns to the margins. Furthermore, in general we find that individual Buddhists in many places and times are actually motivated less by fear of rebirth and hope of spiritual liberation than by this-worldly concerns—and that people generally, even in "traditional" societies, tend to be less driven by eschatological anxiety than the guardians of normativity or the champions of modernity would have us believe. Nevertheless, it is fair to assert that premodern Asian Buddhists overwhelmingly operated with the assumption that rebirth was real and important, and ought to be mastered by any means available.

Modernity

Modernity, Religion, and Buddhism

There is much debate about precisely what "modernity" is, where and when it begins, and how it relates to its supposed antonym, "tradition." I will not enter those debates here but simply affirm the broadly consensual view that modernity is a social and intellectual condition introduced into a given cultural setting by direct or indirect contact with ideologies and technologies originating primarily in the post-Enlightenment West. It cannot easily be separated from the West's colonial or neocolonial modality, with its accompanying promotion, or imposition, of corporate capitalism or socialism (or both), ideals of social equality, employment of high-intensity technologies, and use of science as a touchstone for questioning, understanding, and mastering physical reality. One significant by-product of the onset of modernity, of course, is its challenge to traditional religious ideas, institutions, and practices. The cosmologies propounded by traditional religions are challenged by the scientific worldview; religious institutions are challenged by new sources of political and social authority, such as the nation-state; and religious practices are increasingly viewed as optional acts that may be psychologically effective but are irrelevant to the actual operations of the world. This being so, we might expect that religion would simply disappear from cultures that have entered modernity, and early social scientists like Karl Marx and Sigmund Freud predicted exactly that. It has not worked out that way, however, for it turns out that, as Clifford Geertz memorably observed, the question for religious people in most modernizing societies "is less a matter of what to believe as how to believe it."[11]

This is no less true for Buddhists. Whether in Asia or the West, modernity has challenged their traditional ideas, institutions, and practices. Intellectually, the metaphysical materialism, epistemological skepticism, and fallibilist view of human nature generally assumed in the Western sciences and social sciences tend to cast doubt on many elements of the saṃsāra-nirvāṇa cosmology underlying traditional Buddhism. Thus, while rebirth may have been axiomatic for many traditional Asian Buddhists, it is far from a given for modern Buddhists, especially in the West. At the same time, because rebirth has been part of Buddhism's ideological apparatus since the beginning, it cannot easily be dismissed out of hand; contemporary Buddhists must confront it as surely as their Christian counterparts must confront traditional ideas of God, heaven, hell, and final judgment. As we saw in the Batchelor-Thurman debate, there is room for honest disagreement as to whether acceptance of a traditional presentation of rebirth is essential to being a "good Buddhist" or not, but—to revert to Geertz's perspective—it is for most Buddhists not so much a question of *whether* to believe in rebirth, since it is part of the conceptual framework of Buddhism, but *how* to believe it: whether to take it literally or figuratively.

Just as Christians, Muslims, and other religious people have responded to the challenges of modernity in a variety of ways, so have Buddhists. Indeed, just as in other religions, it is easy to discern in modern Buddhism a spectrum of approaches that runs from literalism, through neotraditionalism and modernism, all the way to self-conscious secularism. In terms of rebirth, literalists tend to assume that the karma-rebirth cosmology is real, the arguments for it persuasive, and the details of its operations more or less as described in traditional texts. Neotraditionalists accept the reality of the system and many of the traditional arguments in its favor, but they seek to understand its operation through an admixture of traditional and modern ways of approaching the world. Modernists tend to think the traditional cosmology may or may not be literally true but that arguments in its favor are unpersuasive, and that it is best understood in symbolic, psychological, or existential terms. Secularists often assert that the concept of rebirth was not essential to the Buddha and should not preoccupy us, for the dharma is a non-metaphysics-based way of life and of seeing the world that is psychological and ethical: in effect, secular humanism with a Buddhist lexicon. With the exception of literalists, all other types on the spectrum agree that the traditional cosmology requires some reinterpretation, and with the exception of secularists, all others agree that rebirth is an idea that must be accounted for—even if they disagree on how central it is to one's identity as a Buddhist. Modernists and secularists tend to agree that, whether one thinks rebirth is more likely or less likely to be the case, or more or less central to the dharma, some degree of agnosticism on the matter is probably warranted.[12]

Modern Philosophical Discussions

An historical survey of modern Buddhist perspectives on rebirth is, unfortunately, beyond the scope of this essay,[13] but a brief, general observation may be in order. When we read the works of the many Asian and Western teachers and writers who have shaped Buddhist ideology since 1800—from highly educated Asian monks, nuns, and laypeople addressing Asian or Western audiences, to Western Transcendentalists, Theosophists, Beat poets, explorers, scholars, feminists, social activists, and promulgators of Zen, Theravāda, Pure Land, and Tibetan Buddhism[14]—it becomes clear that they evince a wide range of positions on the reality and meaning of past and future lives, ranging from deliberate silence, to outright rejection, to symbolic or psychological reinterpretation, to acceptance of the doctrine on metaphysical, empirical, religious, or other grounds.[15] I will illustrate this by turning briefly to the writings of philosophically inclined scholars and teachers of Buddhism published in the past several decades.

Some writers who wish to place Buddhism in dialogue with contemporary philosophy and science make a point of leaving traditional cosmology and metaphysics—especially the notion of rebirth—in abeyance. Thus, the philosopher and neuroscientist Owen Flanagan writes, in *The Bodhisattva's Brain*, of his desire to "naturalize" Buddhism within modern philosophical discourse, in part by bracketing such unproven and likely unprovable notions as rebirth, karmic causation, nirvāṇa, magical powers, heavens and hells, and nonphysical states of mind.[16] In his best-selling *Why Buddhism Is True,* journalist Robert Wright specifies that the Buddhism he claims is "true" is *not* "the 'supernatural' or more exotically metaphysical parts of Buddhism—reincarnation, for example—but rather...the naturalistic parts: ideas that fall squarely within modern psychology and philosophy."[17] Even the philosopher and Buddhism scholar Jay Garfield specifies, at the outset of his *Engaging Buddhism: Why It Matters to Philosophers,* that he will "not discuss Buddhist theories of rebirth, of karma, or approaches to meditation...not because I take these to be unimportant...[but] because I do not see them as principal sites of engagement with Western philosophy."[18] Along similar lines, we will look in vain for significant discussions of rebirth in the presentations of Buddhism by such significant and philosophically astute Asian writers as D. T. Suzuki, Walpola Rahula, and Thich Nhat Hanh—and we find in the works of the great Indian Buddhist convert B. R. Ambedkar a stark denial that the Buddha ever taught past and future lives. Similar attitudes are evinced by Western Buddhist scholar-practitioners intent on aligning the tradition with modern culture. Stephen Batchelor, for instance, surveys a range of Buddhist rational, empirical, and ethical justifications for rebirth, finds them unpersuasive, and concludes that:

> All the pictures I entertain of heaven and hell, or cycles of rebirth, merely serve to replace the overwhelming reality of the unknown with what is known and acceptable.... [T]o cling to the idea of rebirth...can be spiritually suffocating...[and] we will only gain by releasing our grip on such notions.[19]

Instead, says Batchelor, we should treat rebirth as "a useful symbol or hypothesis." Similarly, and even more pointedly, Richard Hayes asserts that the potential of Buddhism in the West "will never be realized...[until it] is purged of some of the Asian habits it has acquired down through the millennia," and he goes on to specify that the first of the teachings that should be discarded "are the obstructive doctrines of...of rebirth and karma...[reflection on which] dulls the mind and impairs the faculty of reasoning"[20]— though he does concede later that the traditional cosmology might serve as a suggestive myth or useful fiction. These attitudes were presaged by teachers of an earlier era, such as Alan Watts, who saw Buddhist discourse on rebirth as a symbolic way of discussing the multiple social roles we assume in our one and only life, and Chögyam Trungpa Rinpoche, who interpreted both the six realms of samsara and the stages of the dying process as psychological states—though not reductively so. For all these thinkers, the implicit or explicit assumption seems to be that contemporary philosophy and science will not countenance nonphysicalist accounts of the operations of mind, let alone belief in life after death in general and rebirth in particular—and that Buddhists would be wise to either let these notions go or reinterpret them along less culturally objectionable lines.

As we saw earlier, a standard argument for rebirth in Indian and Tibetan Buddhist philosophical circles was that of Dharmakīrti, and while notoriously complex, it has not gone unstudied or unanalyzed by university-educated scholars—most of whom find his reasoning less persuasive than do Tibetans, for whom Dharmakīrti's *Pramāṇavārttika* (Commentary on Valid Cognition) is a text central to monastic education. The first such scholar to express a view on the argument in print, Martin Willson, adduced a number of criticisms, which boil down to the claim that (1) nonmaterialist explanations of sentient beings' birth processes proffered by Dharmakīrti and his followers are based on outdated science and insufficient evidence, and (2) Dharmakīrti's attempts to argue against materialist presentations of the mind-body problem do not decisively refute the possibility that mind is, as materialists claim, actually a function of the body (or, in modern terms, the brain).[21] I raised similar points in my 1993 translation and analysis of a fifteenth-century Tibetan commentary on Dharmakīrti, and further observed that the supposedly clinching argument—that mind cannot arise from body because the former is coarse, insentient, and physical, while the latter is clear, knowing, and immaterial—appears to beg the question by defining terms in such a way that the desired philosophical outcome is unavoidable.[22] Around the same time, Richard Hayes summarized and partially translated a number of Dharmakīrti's arguments against materialism and in favor of rebirth, concluding that, ingenious as they are, they do not fully succeed in dismantling materialist claims about the physical basis of mind or in establishing mind as ultimately independent of physical causes.[23] In a recent study of the problem of intentionality in Buddhist and contemporary philosophies of mind, Dan Arnold faults Dharmakīrti for discussing mental causation in terms that actually are based on the model of *physical* causation that we observe in the world, pointing out that modern cognitive philosophers frequently eschew such classic causal language when attempting to make sense of how the mind works—and that doing so would have made a case like Dharmakīrti's easier rather than more difficult to argue.[24] More recently, Evan Thompson has observed that Dharmakīrti's arguments would fail to convince a modern philosopher of mind because they are based on definitions of matter and consciousness that set them apart as mutually exclusive and foreclose the possibility that matter could ever be the basis of what we call "the mental"; for his part, Thompson suggests that we need "to work our way to a new understanding of what it means for something to be physical, in which 'physical' no longer means essentially nonmental or nonexperiential."[25]

Thompson, like Flanagan, Arnold, and a number of other recent writers concerned with the mind-body problem in Buddhism and contemporary philosophy, is prompted to reflection by the writings of the Fourteenth Dalai Lama, who has repeatedly paraphrased Dharmakīrti's arguments for rebirth, most notably in his book-length discussion of Buddhism vis-à-vis science, *The Universe in a Single Atom*. The Dalai Lama has famously declared that if a Buddhist doctrine is contradicted by irrefutable scientific evidence, then the doctrine ought to be discarded, and in the case of the traditional flat-earth theory, he has proposed just that. When it comes to rebirth, however, he argues that because absence of evidence does not constitute evidence of absence, he cannot accept that the doctrine has been refuted. He continues to present Dharmakīrti's arguments, at least in a general way, and to insist that although there may be a stronger connection between neurological events and *ordinary* mental states than traditional Buddhists believe, there remains the possibility that there are *extraordinary* mental states that do not depend on the neurological system—namely, the meditative experiences of advanced tantric yogis, especially those who have entered the postmortem concentration on the clear-light nature of the mind known as *thukdam*.[26] The Dalai Lama has encouraged neuroscientific studies of meditators in thukdam, and a few have been carried out, though whether these will provide support for either the materialist or Buddhist position on mind and body remains to be seen: the discovery of subtle neural activity in such contemplatives might prompt revision of current biomedical definitions of death, but it cannot determine whether, at the conclusion of thukdam, the consciousness of a yogi passes into another realm—or not.[27]

Other contemporary thinkers seek to justify rebirth, and Buddhist mind-body metaphysics, not by reframing Dharmakīrti's arguments but by embracing alternative scientific cosmologies that make the mind or consciousness, rather than matter, the driving force in the universe—hence its passage from one life to another less problematic. Robert Thurman, for instance, has sought to reinterpret evolutionary biology along Buddhist lines by giving pride of place in the process to mind, rather than matter, and finding in the traditional samsara-nirvana cosmology a perfect explanation of the way in which mind-directed cosmos may be understood as teleologically oriented toward spiritual awakening, or buddhahood.[28] Alan Wallace has argued that science's prejudice against "first-person" subjective experiences as a source of knowledge both overestimates the reliability of science's "third-person," publicly observable methods and underestimates the role and reliability of what is often dismissed as "mere subjectivity." This is especially true at the quantum level, where on some interpretations it seems that mind plays an active role in shaping so-called external reality. Indeed, says Wallace, an important implication of cutting-edge research in quantum mechanics is that the universe is properly conceived not—as classical physics insisted—as a physical system but as "fundamentally an information-processing system, from which the appearance of matter emerges at a higher level of reality."[29] On such a view, the independence of mind from body is easier to maintain, and rebirth easier to defend. Similarly, David Loy has proposed a "new evolutionary myth," inspired by the work of the cosmologist Thomas Berry, which sees the universe as an organism and "evolution as the creative groping of a self-organizing cosmos that is becoming more self-aware."[30] If, as suggested by such a scenario, "consciousness is basic—if there might be rudimentary awareness even at the quantum level…then there may be some plausibility to the notion of [karmic formations] persisting after death."[31] Indeed, because according to Buddhist ontology there is no self that is reborn and emptiness (or infinity) is the nature of all things, "there is *only* rebirth"—the real seeking and taking form—but such "rebirth" is not individual immortality as traditionally conceived.[32] Incidentally, the stances taken by Thurman, Wallace, and Loy, while influenced by radical interpretations of contemporary biology, physics, and cosmology, are also deeply redolent of both the Madhyamaka school's perspective on the doctrine of emptiness and the Yogācāra school's idealism or phenomenalism—and compatible in a number of ways with such Mahāyāna contemplative traditions as tantra, the great perfection, and Zen. They seem considerably less compatible with current mainstream thinking in evolutionary biology, cosmology, or subatomic physics, but we would do well to remember that science itself, as Thomas Kuhn has shown, is subject to regular "paradigm shifts," such that what seems implausible, indemonstrable, or speculative today may be the conventional wisdom of the future.

Descending from the realm of metaphysics, we find that a number of contemporary Buddhist thinkers are intent on demonstrating rebirth by appealing to "empirical" evidence, stemming from either scientific investigation or meditative experience. Thus, the French-born Tibetan Buddhist monk Matthieu Ricard finds that "the certainty arising from a life of contemplative practice, or a life lived with a spiritual teacher, is just as powerful as that arising from the demonstration of a theorem" and hence must be granted real epistemic value.[33] Alan Wallace, with his insistence on the importance of "first-person" evidence for knowledge about reality, argues that the experiences of advanced contemplatives give us real information about the mind and the world, and that the memories of past lives often unearthed by such yogis may therefore be reliable—hence evidence of the possibility of rebirth.[34] In support of his claim, Wallace mentions not just the experiences of yogis but also the work of Ian Stevenson, who, as noted earlier, researched a large number of twentieth-century cases "suggestive of reincarnation."[35] Modern Buddhists intent on providing empirical arguments for rebirth commonly cite Stevenson's case histories. Thus, Martin Willson, despite his dismissal of Dharmakīrti's rational arguments for rebirth, seems quite receptive to the evidentiary value of spontaneous recollections like those reported by Stevenson, and he also is willing to entertain the reliability of other ways people remember past lives, such as focused training, hypnotic regression, or psychic readings.[36] More recently, Bhikkhu Anālayo has examined a number of modern grounds for accepting rebirth, including near-death experiences and past-life regression analysis, both of which he finds unreliable. He also delves into Stevenson's research—agreeing that there are a small number of cases that truly seem inexplicable without the notion of rebirth—and investigating in particular detail a case with which he is personally familiar, that of a Sri Lankan boy whose style of reciting Pāli texts was completely unknown early in his life but turns out, on the basis of more recent research, to have been prevalent in an earlier era, of which he claimed to have memories.[37] These cases are, as Stevenson himself concedes, *suggestive* of rebirth, but hardly conclusive. As Evan Thompson notes, Stevenson's studies may be faulted on a number of methodological grounds, particularly as relates to the time lag between a child's first report of a past-life memory and the time they were interviewed, leaving "a large amount of room for false memory and after-the-fact reconstruction."[38] And Stephen Batchelor observes that even if some such reports are reliable, and that certain people have undergone rebirth, "this in itself would not furnish any proof...that they themselves would experience rebirth again or that anyone else was reborn in the past or will be in the future."[39] In other words, even an "empirical" proof of rebirth—were there one—would not necessarily confirm the *Buddhist* theory of rebirth, either in its broad strokes or fine details. Further, any Buddhist claims about metaphysical truths, such as rebirth, that are based solely on extrasensory or other special yogic perceptions must inevitably face comparison with similar claims in other traditions, which may point to a very different way of "seeing" the cosmos—and in the absence of third-person, publicly available evidence, there is no way to give priority to one claim or the other, except on purely dogmatic grounds.

Did It Matter? Does It Now? Concluding Retrospect and Prospect

To recapitulate, some modern Buddhists simply refuse to talk about rebirth, but those who do have typically done so by adopting one of the four possible approaches outlined earlier.

1. Among literalists—who accept traditional descriptions of the karma-rebirth cosmology and arguments for it either unquestioningly or on the basis of their own analysis—the most common constituency is Asian Buddhists. These would include many traditionally trained Theravāda monks or nuns, East Asian masters, and Tibetan lamas who have taught in Asia and the West, and who in many cases have published books that present traditional teachings. Although too numerous to name, these teachers and their presentations have produced a significant proportion of modern Buddhist literature. These teachers' Western disciples often have adopted a literalist idea of rebirth—in line with the beliefs of the teachers' Asian followers—but these followers do not often write about their views, and what they do write is sometimes difficult to find outside of small, narrowly targeted dharma publications.

2. Neotraditionalists—who seek to justify traditional cosmology and metaphysics in more "up-to-date" terms—comprise a large and diverse group. Among them, we might count Robert Thurman, who has asserted the truth and importance of the classical notion of rebirth but reframed it in evolutionary terms; Alan Wallace, who has argued on the basis of quantum physics that the mind is a more prominent factor in the cosmos than materialist science will allow and that first-person experience is more

reliable as a source of knowledge than philosophers will admit; Martin Willson, who is unpersuaded by rational arguments for rebirth but finds several types of empirical evidence very promising; and the Fourteenth Dalai Lama, who accepts many of the premises and conclusions of Dharmakīrti's argument but limits its true applicability to the very subtlest level of the operations of mind and body, conceding that ordinary consciousness may indeed be impossible without neural activity.

3. Modernists—who in some cases doubt the literal truth of traditional cosmology and metaphysics and are unpersuaded by arguments for it—seek in various ways to maintain the language and imagery of karma, rebirth, and the realms of saṃsāra—but to recast it in symbolic, psychological, or existential terms that are more amenable to modern sensibilities. Stephen Batchelor, with his "existential" interpretation of Buddhism, is the most prominent Western exponent of such an approach, but there are many others. As noted, Alan Watts understood claims about past and future lives as a way of describing the multiple social roles we adopt in our present life, while Chögyam Trungpa Rinpoche seemed (at times, at least) to favor a largely psychological explanation of the six realms of rebirth and traditional ideas about death. David Loy recasts notions of rebirth within a new cosmological myth that effectively removes them from the standard individual-survival framework. Richard Hayes considers the classic cosmology a useful fiction, at best.

4. Like those in the other groups, secularists vary in their motives and arguments but tend to agree that rebirth just doesn't matter that much. Even if it was taught by the Buddha and his followers over the past two millennia, it is actually superfluous to the real meaning of the dharma, today as in BCE India: as a way to understand reality and live wisely, compassionately, and meaningfully within our present lives and in the world we share. Thus, writers like Owen Flanagan, Robert Wright, and Jay Garfield deliberately leave rebirth aside when attempting to engage Buddhism with modern philosophy or psychology.

Engaged Buddhists usually reject the idea outright, as B. R. Ambedkar did, or simply ignore it, as have Thich Nhat Hanh and many others. And for the many modern people who do not identify as Buddhists but wish to draw on Buddhist insights and meditation techniques for specific purposes in their daily lives, rebirth is irrelevant at best, a distraction at worst, and in any case hardly worth worrying about.

These categories must be taken with a grain of salt: the lines between one and the other are not always evident. For instance, the difference between literalism and neotraditionalism is not always clear, nor that between modernism and secularism. By the same token, many of the thinkers discussed here are too complex to assign solely to one category. Thus, in various contexts, the Dalai Lama may be read as a literalist, a neotraditionalist, or a modernist— and he even has propounded a secular ethics that might align him with the fourth camp. Batchelor and Hayes may be classified as modernists but show strong secularist tendencies; indeed, Batchelor describes his as a Secular Buddhism, even though he presents Buddhist doctrines, including rebirth, symbolically and existentially, as a modernist would. And a figure like Thich Nhat Hanh, who eschews discussion of rebirth and hence appears "secularist," clearly has both traditional and modern elements at work in his public ministry—and perhaps in his private convictions as well.

Further, while most of the thinkers we have surveyed attempt in one way or another to align traditional Buddhist cosmology and metaphysics with modern Western ideas and practices—whether simply to make Buddhism comprehensible, to defend it, to reject it, or to reinterpret it along less traditionally "religious" lines—it might be urged that such efforts stem from a failure to recognize that traditional Buddhism is largely incommensurable with modern science, psychology, and aesthetics. This is the stance taken by Donald Lopez in his analysis of "the Scientific Buddha"—the Buddha imagined by moderns as perfectly consonant in his life and teachings with the scientific perspective and procedures developed in the past several centuries in the West. Lopez finds that to posit such a Buddha is to do serious violence to the way Buddhists have usually understood their master and his teaching, for the Buddha and the tradition he founded—with their focus escaping rebirth through a life of renunciation—are largely incompatible with modern, Western ideas and values, and must be acknowledged as such. Indeed, Lopez says,

> The Old Buddha, not the Scientific Buddha, presented a radical challenge to the way we see the world, both the world that was seen two millennia ago and the world that is seen today. What he taught is not different, it is not an alternative, it is the opposite. A certain value lies in remembering that challenge from time to time.[40]

Lopez says, in effect: don't try to align Buddhism with science, psychology, or contemporary philosophy, don't try to justify it, don't try to reimagine it; rather, understand it as a counterpoint to modernity and its complacencies. Perhaps this is a fifth approach: literalism as radical cultural critique.[41]

Lopez's approach is highly demanding, for it forces modern Buddhists to continually hold in mind opposing ways of understanding the world, an exercise only sustainable by a few. The vast majority, I expect, will opt for one of the four approaches to rebirth outlined above, or some combination of them. Each has a role to play in the ongoing conversation among Buddhists as to how the tradition ought to be imagined and enacted in the modern world: literalists remind us of the classical Buddhist outlook, so different from our own; neotraditionalists provide ways to argue for the traditional cosmology and metaphysics, or something akin to it; modernists either suspend or reject the classical paradigm but find new, non-metaphysical ways of making it meaningful; while secularists raise vital questions about just how much of tradition can be jettisoned in the process of finding a place for Buddhism in our dis-enchanted world.

My own view—certainly debatable—is that one or another form of modernism best points the way forward. I am particularly drawn to the various forms of "Buddhist agnosticism" that have been articulated in recent decades. The term was coined by Stephen Batchelor but may appropriately be applied to any thinker who finds traditional rational, empirical, or faith-based arguments in favor of rebirth problematic but does not reject the idea outright, admitting that—with our present limitations—we simply do not know whether past and future lives are real. One intriguing agnostic argument comes from an unexpected source, the late Tibetan lama Lati Rimpoche, who in a 1986 conversation with Richard Hayes suggested that Westerners uncertain about karma and rebirth (which Rimpoche concedes are "beyond absolute proof") should remain open to the possibility that the traditional cosmology and metaphysics are true, and in any case *behave* as if they were true by living ethically and compassionately. In that way, they will generate happiness for themselves and others in this life, and if there are future lives, they will be happy ones; conversely, if they behave negatively, they will bring misery to themselves and others in this life, and face a sorrowful rebirth, if rebirths there are.[42] As Hayes rightly notes, this argument is akin to Blaise Pascal's famous "wager" regarding the existence of God and the reality of final judgment. Leaving aside the question whether so tentative an acceptance of religious claims might itself be problematic in the eyes of God or amid the subtleties of karma, we may agree with Hayes that:

> [Rinpoche] seems to place these doctrines in a mythical space, as opposed to a historical or scientific framework. Access to this mythical space can be gained, not by logical proof or through a methodical empirical investigation of the sensible world, but by exercising one's imagination and then having the courage of one's imaginings.[43]

For Hayes, reading traditional cosmology and metaphysics as mythical—as "fictional" rather than "factual" or empirically verifiable—allows modern people to imagine ways of living quite different from their own, the way a good novel does; just as a novel or other work of art may widen our perspective and ennoble our lives without being taken as "literally" true, so engaging with the traditional Buddhist imaginary allows modern Buddhists to enter more meaningfully into the streams of Buddhist life and provide meaning within their own lives.[44]

Along similar lines, Batchelor opts for a "middle way" agnosticism in which one "does not have either to assert [rebirth] dogmatically or deny it; one neither has to adopt the literal versions presented by tradition nor fall into the other extreme of believing that death is the final annihilation."[45] This, he asserts, does not mire us in indecision. Rather, it allows us (as in Zen) to confront with ruthless honesty "the Great Matter of Life and Death," and "is a powerful catalyst for action, since in shifting concern away from a hypothetical future life, to the dilemmas of the present, it demands...a compassion-centered ethic" that will bring joy to our lives and the lives of others.[46] In his writings, Batchelor seems ambivalent about entertaining traditional cosmology and metaphysics even at the symbolic level; he often implies that we simply ought to dispense with these outmoded conceptions. Recall, however, that at the conclusion of the debate with Thurman with which I began this essay, he says that *if* he were to utilize the traditional Buddhist vision, "I would try to behave as if there were infinite lifetimes in which I would be committed to saving beings."[47]

I myself would argue without ambivalence for what I call "As-If Agnosticism." My stance is agnostic because, like Hayes and Batchelor (and many others), I do not find traditional descriptions of karma and rebirth literally credible, nor am I fully persuaded by arguments in their favor, whether rational, empirical, or faith-based; on the other hand, I cannot rule out the possibility that such descriptions (or something like them) may be true. The universe, after all, is passingly strange. In the spirit of Wallace Stevens's gnomic but suggestive assertion that in the modern world, our only choice is to "believe without belief, beyond belief,"[48] I propose that we live *as if* such descriptions were true. I am not suggesting we simply take up wishful thinking: *if only* there were past and future lives, *if only* karma works the ways tradition says it does, *if only* glorious and perfect buddhahood awaited us all. Maybe they do, maybe they don't. But, as humanists long have argued, and scientists have begun to recognize, the world is actually built far more on our ideas, aspirations, and speculations—the As-If —than we suppose, and the solid foundation we presume to lie beneath us—the "As-Is"—is far more difficult to find than we believe. It's not, therefore, that by living *as if* certain doctrines were true we really are in flight from some bedrock, objective reality, because that reality—though it certainly imposes limitations on us, most notably at the time if death—turns out to be far more a matter of convention, and far less "just the way things are" than we had thought. Freed from the illusion of perfect objectivity, therefore, why *not* think and live as if Buddhism were true? In doing so, we empower ourselves to enter, as fully as is possible in a skeptical age, into the ongoing, ever-changing life of the dharma, adopting Buddhist ideals, telling Buddhist stories, articulating Buddhist doctrines, performing Buddhist rituals, and embodying Buddhist virtues in ways that make meaning for ourselves, provide help to others, and perhaps contribute in some small way to the betterment of the imperfect and imperiled world in which we all live. And if there is a buddha field at the end of the rainbow, so much the better.[49]

BIBLIOGRAPHY

Anālayo, Bhikkhu. *Rebirth in Early Buddhism and Current Research*. Boston: Wisdom Publications, 2017.

Arnold. Dan. *Brains, Buddhas, and Believing: The Problem of Intentionality in Classical Buddhist and Cognitive-Scientific Philosophy of Mind*. New York: Columbia University Press, 2012.

Batchelor, Stephen. *After Buddhism: Rethinking the Dharma for a Secular Age*. New Haven, CT: Yale University Press, 2015.

———. *Alone with Others: An Existential Approach to Buddhism*. New York: Grove Press, 1984.

———. *The Awakening of the West: The Encounter of Buddhism and Western Culture*. London: Aquarian, 1994.

———. *Buddhism without Beliefs: A Contemporary Guide to Awakening*. New York: Riverhead Books, 1997.

———. *Secular Buddhism: Imagining the Dharma in an Uncertain World*. New Haven, CT: Yale University Press, 2017.

Cho, Francesca, and Richard K. Squier. *Religion and Science in the Mirror of Buddhism*. New York and London: Routledge, 2016.

Dalai Lama, the Fourteenth. *The Universe in a Single Atom: The Convergence of Science and Spirituality*. New York: Morgan Road Books, 2005.

Fields, Rick. *How the Swans Came to the Lake: A Narrative History of Buddhism in America*. 3rd ed. Boston and London: Shambhala, 1992.

Flanagan, Owen. *The Bodhisattva's Brain: Buddhism Naturalized*. Cambridge, MA: MIT Press, 2011.

Franco, Eli. *Dharmakīrti on Compassion and Rebirth*. Vienna: Arbeitskreis für tibetische und buddhistische Studien Universität Wien, 1997.

Garfield, Jay L. *Engaging Buddhism: Why It Matters to Philosophy*. Oxford and New York: Oxford University Press, 2015.

Geertz, Clifford. *Islam Observed: Religious Development in Morocco and Indonesia*. Chicago: University of Chicago Press, 1968.

Goff, Philip. *Galileo's Error: Foundations for a New Science of Consciousness*. New York: Pantheon Books, 2019.

Hayes, Richard P. "Dharmakīrti on *Punarbhava*." In *Studies in Original Buddhism and Mahāyāna Buddhism*. Edited by Egaku Maeda. Kyōto: Nagata Bunshodo, 1993.

———. *Land of No Buddha: Reflections of a Sceptical Buddhist*. Birmingham, UK: Windhorse Publications, 1998.

Jackson, Roger R. "As Is/As If: The Anxious First-Year's Guide to Argument and Inquiry." Unpublished lecture. Carleton College Argument and Inquiry Convocation, September 23, 2016.

———. "For Whom Emptiness Prevails: An Analysis of the Religious Implications of Nāgārjuna's *Vigrahavyavartanī* 70." *Religious Studies* 21 (September 1985): 407-14.

———. "In Search of a Postmodern Middle." In *Buddhist Theology: Critical Reflections by Contemporary Buddhist Scholars*. Edited by Roger R. Jackson and John J. Makransky, 215-46. Richmond, Surrey, UK: Curzon Press, 2000.

———. "Indo-Tibetan Buddhist Responses to Darwinism." In *Religious Responses to Darwinism*. Edited by Mackenzie Brown. London: Springer, 2020, 209-39.

———. *Is Enlightenment Possible? Dharmakīrti and rGyal tshab rje on Knowledge, Rebirth, No-Self and Liberation*. Ithaca, NY: Snow Lion Publications, 1993.

———. Review of *After Buddhism: Rethinking the Dharma for a Secular Age*, by Stephen Batchelor. *Buddhadharma* (Winter 2016): 73–77.

Liebenrood, Mark. "Do Buddhists Believe in Rebirth?" *Windhorse*, March 5, 2015. https://www.windhorsepublications.com/do-buddhists-believe-in-rebirth/.

Lopez, Donald S., Jr, ed. *A Modern Buddhist Bible: Essential Readings from East and West*. Boston: Beacon Press, 2002.

———. *The Scientific Buddha: His Short and Happy Life*. New Haven, CT: Yale University Press, 2012.

Loy, David R. *A New Buddhist Path: Enlightenment, Evolution, and Ethics in the Modern World*. Boston: Wisdom Publications, 2015.

McMahan, David L. *The Making of Modern Buddhism*. Oxford and New York: Oxford University Press, 2008.

Obeyeskere, Gananath. *Imagining Karma: Ethical Transformation in Amerindian, Buddhist, and Greek Rebirth*. Berkeley and Los Angeles: University of California Press, 2002.

"Reincarnation: A Debate: Batchelor v. Thurman." *Tricycle*, Summer 1997. https://tricycle.org/magazine/reincarnation-debate/.

Revel, Jean-François, and Matthieu Ricard. *The Monk and the Philosopher: A Father and Son Discuss the Meaning of Life*. New York: Schocken Books, 1998.

Stevens, Wallace. *Collected Poems*. New York: Alfred A. Knopf, 1971 [1954].

Stevenson, Ian. *Cases of the Reincarnation Type, Volume 2: Ten Cases in Sri Lanka*. Charlottesville: University of Virginia Press, 1977.

Story, Francis. *Rebirth as Doctrine and Experience: Essays and Case Studies*. Kandy: Buddhist Publication Society, 1975.

Thompson, Evan. *Waking, Dreaming, Being: Self and Consciousness in Neuroscience, Meditation, and Philosophy*. New York: Columbia University Press, 2015.

Thurman, Robert A. F. *Inner Revolution: Life, Liberty, and the Pursuit of Real Happiness*. New York: Riverhead Books, 1999.

Wallace, B. Alan. *Meditations of a Buddhist Skeptic: A Manifesto for the Mind Sciences and Contemplative Practice*. New York: Columbia University Press, 2012.

Willson, Martin. *Rebirth and the Western Buddhist*. London: Wisdom Publications, 1987.

Wright, Robert. *Why Buddhism Is True: The Science and Philosophy of Meditation and Enlightenment*. New York: Simon and Schuster, 2017.

12|Naturalistic Buddhism

GIL FRONSDAL

This essay is an expanded version of a paper titled "Natural Buddhism" that appeared in the 2014 issue of *Insight Journal*. That original paper was first developed from one of twenty presentations made at the Barre Center for Buddhist Studies conference on secular Buddhism held in March 2013.

As a Buddhist teacher, I am often asked to identify the form of Buddhism with which I am associated. While, most broadly, I identify myself with Theravāda Buddhism, different contexts prompt me to answer in any one of many possible ways, including declining to answer. Within the many subdivisions of Theravāda Buddhism, I might explain that I am a Vipassana teacher in the lineage of the twentieth-century Burmese teacher Mahasi Sayadaw. To be more specific, I might further state that I am part of the Western network of insight meditation teachers associated with the Insight Meditation Society in Massachusetts and the Spirit Rock Meditation Center in California whose teachers have adapted Asian Theravāda *vipassanā* teachings for a Western audience. Within this network of insight meditation teachers, further distinctions sometimes become relevant. In some contexts, it might be appropriate to identify myself as belonging to the first generation of Western insight meditation teachers who had a unique social context that influenced the way we teach Buddhism. And within this first-generation group of teachers I might distinguish myself as having teachings influenced by years of Zen training. Or I might indicate that while I have some leanings toward "Secular Buddhism" my preference is to view my Buddhist orientation as "naturalistic" and therefore to identify it as a Theravāda form of "Naturalistic Buddhism."

I shy away from actually identifying myself with the designation "Secular Buddhism" because I understand the term to be oxymoronic. In ordinary English "secular" is commonly contrasted with "religious" or "spiritual"; as I view Buddhism as a religion and my involvement with Buddhism as deeply religious, I am disinclined to describe myself as a "secular Buddhist."

Through the label "Naturalistic Buddhism" I refer to Buddhist teachings that rely on what can be observed in this very life through our natural senses. It does not require any beliefs, agency, entities, or experiences that are supernatural—that is, that fall outside of the laws of nature as we know them or outside of what we can know for ourselves through our ordinary, natural senses. By using the term "naturalistic," I am associating but not equating my form of Buddhism with the fields of "philosophical naturalism" (also known as metaphysical naturalism) and "religious naturalism," both of which posit that only natural laws operate in this world.

While the idiosyncratic label "Naturalistic Buddhism" may be applicable only to myself, I use it because I believe it useful to have identifying labels for where one is situated within the context of Buddhism as a whole. It can quickly provide others with a general understanding of what teachings, orientation, and values a teacher is associated with. More importantly, when Buddhist teachers explicitly identify themselves with a particular tradition, school, sect, or type of Buddhism, they are providing their audience with a reference to which they can be held accountable—that is, teachers can then be asked how and why they may differ from or resemble the form of Buddhism they say they represent. Such accountability can prompt teachers to explain some of their assumptions, preferences, and reasoning, as well as the background for their particular formulation of Buddhism.

For example, by identifying myself as a Naturalistic Buddhist within the Theravāda Buddhist tradition, I am letting people know that, while my teachings are based on and accountable to the ancient scriptures of Theravāda Buddhism, I have a naturalistic perspective, orientation, or interpretation of these scriptures—that is, the Pāli *suttas*. When I teach, I don't represent all of what is found in these texts; I don't claim to represent the actual teachings of the Buddha as presented in them—a task that no discerning person can confidently do given the complicated historical origin of the surviving records. Rather, by identifying my naturalistic leanings, I am indicating that I have a particular perspective for interpreting and selecting teachings from the ancient texts. How accurately I am representing what the Buddha may have taught is itself a matter of interpretation, as is the case for anyone who bases their teachings on these scriptures. And if my Buddhist teachings differ from traditional Theravāda Buddhist teachings, my intention is to be aware of and responsible for these differences. From the historical records I have seen, it appears that every generation of Buddhist teachers adapts and interprets Buddhism in new ways. When I studied with senior Theravāda meditation teachers in Burma, I had the impression that they represented classical and orthodox Theravāda Buddhist teachings; certainly, they presented themselves as definitively representing the original teachings of the Buddha. Later I discovered that decades earlier they had been radical reformers who had broken away from the orthodoxy of their youth. While I am clearly not trying to reform Theravāda orthodoxy, I do believe it is honest and helpful for me to provide my audience with an understanding of the orientation I have toward the Buddhism I teach.

By relying on a naturalistic approach to Buddhism, I am not asserting that what could be called supernatural is not real or true. While some day we may have natural explanations for such phenomena, for now, I simply see no need to include them in the Buddhism I practice.

Beliefs found in Buddhism that could be called supernatural include rebirth, the working of karma over multiple lifetimes, heavens and hells, devas and *māras*, miracles, merit and merit transfer, and many of the psychic powers mentioned in Buddhist texts (for example, walking through walls, flying, talking with gods, and stroking the moon). I also include as supernatural any ideas of a self or consciousness that exists in a permanent and uncreated fashion, a view that both contradicts the principle of impermanence that lies at the foundation of the Buddha's teachings and falls outside the natural laws known to science. More controversially, I also include concepts of nirvāṇa as a transcendent, unconditioned dimension of reality as a supernatural belief.

I have a naturalistic orientation to Buddhism partly as a consequence of having studied with Buddhist teachers in the West and in Asia who did not require me to have faith in unverified beliefs. Instead, they instructed me to be deeply aware of my experience, including what beliefs I was holding. In fact, I suspect the deep questioning and skepticism of views and beliefs that they expected of me would have been inhibited by believing in anything that might be called supernatural.

Precursors to Naturalistic Buddhism

While the label "Naturalistic Buddhism" may be new, this orientation is not unique in the history of Buddhism; in addition to the modern appearance of "Secular Buddhism," other forms of Buddhism share a family resemblance. Particularly noteworthy are the modern Chinese and Taiwanese movements known in English as "Humanistic Buddhism" and in Chinese (in English translation) as "Buddhism for human life" (*rénshēng fójiào*) and "human world Buddhism." (*rénjiān fójiào*). In his essay in this collection, Charles B. Jones discusses the work of a key figure in the early-twentieth-century origins of "Humanistic Buddhism," the Venerable Taixu (1890–1947). In modern Theravāda Buddhism, perhaps the most prominent teacher with a naturalistic worldview was the twentieth-century Thai monk Buddhadasa, who rejected the literal idea of rebirth and the teachings of karma associated with it. His teachings also ignored any literal concepts of hells, heavens, and deities.

Perhaps the most significant precursor to Naturalistic Buddhism is found in some of the central teachings associated with the Buddha in the early Pāli scriptures (suttas). Because the earliest surviving texts of Indian Buddhism include many examples of teachings free of supernatural ideas, I believe that "Naturalistic Buddhism" can be considered as an equally valid form of Buddhism as "Supernatural Buddhism," the predominant form in existence today (see Bhikkhu Bodhi, who in this volume identifies his form as "Traditional"). An early text that supports a naturalistic approach to Buddhism is *The Book of Eights* (*Aṭṭhakavagga*), a text some scholars consider composed earlier than most of the other texts contained in the sutta collections (*nikāyas*). As the fourth book of the *Sutta Nipāta* in the *Khuddaka Nikāya*, *The Book of Eights* provides a foundation for teachings that do not rely on any ideology or supernatural beliefs; in fact, depending on doctrines of any type is seen as problematic in this Buddhist text. For example, not only is belief in rebirth not required, but the text discourages any concern with future lives or the wish for any future state of being. Accordingly, *The Book of Eights* also has nothing to say about ending the cycles of rebirth as a goal of practice.

Because having faith is often central to having supernatural religious beliefs, it is noteworthy that the word faith (*saddhā*) appears only once in *The Book of Eights* and then only in a passage stating that someone who has attained peace is without "faith"—that is, the person has no need for faith. While some form of faith may be implied in the teachings of *The Book of Eights*, no role for faith is mentioned. What is emphasized is having insight into what one can see for oneself, especially into the many forms of clinging and the benefits of letting go of these clingings.

In the hopes of demonstrating that the idea of a naturalistic Buddhism is not a far-fetched idea, I would like to present an overview of the main teachings of *The Book of Eights*.

Personal Peace through Not Clinging

Rather than a transcendent, supernatural reality to be attained, *The Book of Eights* focuses on a mental state accessible within the life that people actually live. The text champions a direct and simple approach for attaining peace (*santi*). The possibility of peace guides the teachings and practices the text advocates. Rather than a doctrine to be simply believed, these teachings describe means or practices for directly realizing peace.

Clinging is explained as the primary reason a person is not peaceful. Accordingly, the release of clinging is the primary means to peace. The value of these teachings is not found in philosophy, logic, or external religious authorities but, rather, in the results they bring to those who live by them. The goal emphasized in this text is described both by the states of mind attained and by the mental activities that have been pacified or abandoned. The most common terms used to refer to what is attained are peace, calmness, tranquility, and equanimity. In sharp contrast, clinging, craving, entrenchment, and quarreling are the most frequently mentioned activities that are to be abandoned. The relationship between these two sets—the states to be attained and what is to be abandoned—is that to personally attain peace for oneself, one must abandon the clinging that prevents it.

There are three primary themes in the text that elaborate on the message that peace comes from not clinging. These themes are letting go of views, the qualities of a sage, and the training to become a sage.

Letting Go of Views

In keeping with *The Book of Eights'* emphasis on peace and non-clinging, the main teaching on views is the importance of not clinging to philosophies, religious teachings, or views of any kind. This would include ideas about what happens after death, the nature of the "self," or whether or not it is possible to fly unassisted. The text teaches that someone should shake off every view without embracing or rejecting anything. In addition, a number of verses are critical of any judgment that one's own religious beliefs are the truest or best while others are inferior.

For many readers, this seeming no-view teaching is a radical message. It undermines the importance of religious doctrines that some people base their lives on. The teachings in *The Book of Eights* provide no support for the idea that one should believe in supernatural teachings just because they are found in other Buddhist texts.

The Book of Eights includes plenty of examples of the problems that arise if one clings to views: attachment to concepts leads to the person swinging between feeling high and low; debating others, one can become anxious for praise and bewildered when refuted; and if clinging to views brings a type of peace, it is an unstable peace. In addition, *The Book of Eights* frequently mentions that clinging to views leads to quarrels with others, which of course does not lead to peace.

Finally, the goal of practice is described in terms of letting go of views. Those who have realized the goal—the sages—are not attached to views and so avoid debates, quarrels, and any conceit that their views are better than those of others.

Letting go of their attachments, sages have no need for any doctrine and so do not oppose the doctrine of anyone else. According to one of the verses,

> They are not enemies of any doctrine
> seen, heard or thought out.
> Not making up theories,
> not closed down, not desirous,
> they are sages, wise,
> who have laid down their burden.[1]

The idea that a wise person would not be an enemy of any religious doctrine suggests that those who adhere to a naturalistic form of Buddhism and those who adhere to a supernatural Buddhism do not need to be opposed to each other's doctrines. They can coexist, with each being a valid form of Buddhism, especially if they both lead to "laying down the burden," a synonym for liberation.

The Sage Described

A second theme in *The Book of Eights* is the descriptions of the sage (*muni*). The text does not refer to those who have attained the goal of practice by using words that are common in other, probably later, Buddhist texts. For example, the terms *arahant*, Stream-Enterer, Once Returner, and Non-Returner are absent. In that rebirth has no role in the teachings of *The Book of Eights*, it is not surprising to find no reference to accomplished practitioners who return to be reborn once more or who will no longer return to rebirth.

Due to the sage's proficiency in realizing peace, the sage is often described as *kusalo*, meaning a skilled person or expert. In that sages are wise, they are also referred to as "the wise one" (*dhiro*), "the learned one" (*pandito*), and "one of much wisdom" (*bhuri pañño*). With the shedding of attachment this person is called "the cleansed one" (*dhono*).

The most common attribute associated with a sage is peace (*santi*). Such a person is peaceful, sees and knows peace, and advocates peace. Using related words, the text describes the sage as tranquil, still and unmoving, unshakable, and equanimous. Though peace is clearly an attribute of sages, they do not depend on peace or intentionally take it up. This is because sages do not depend on anything or take up anything; rather they are characterized as letting go.

These designations and descriptions of the adept suggest qualities that can be discerned in oneself and that are directly relevant for how one lives one's life. They do not suggest the sage has psychic or supernormal powers or has attained transcendent realities removed from this world. Rather, the sage has attained experiences, such as tranquility, equanimity, and peace, that are natural enough for humans to attain, at least in brief dosages.

What Sages Know and See

A significant attribute of skillful sages is their ability to know and see—sometimes they are called the "ones who know." What is interesting is what they do and do not see. They do not see transcendent, otherworldly realities or supernatural events. They do not see the nature of ultimate reality or some form of ultimate consciousness.

Rather, sages know and see ways in which people struggle. They know what is dangerous, what is dependent, and what is not harmonious. They know the problems that come from pride and holding to opinions. They see how people selfishly thrash about, get elated and deflated in their disputes, speak with arrogance, and cling to teachings. By such knowing, a wise person knows not to get involved with afflicted states and knows to let go of them.

The second thing a sage knows and sees is an inner peace realized through not clinging. Being at peace and having overcome cravings, sages become, according to *The Book of Eights*, independent in knowing the dharma. This means they know the peace of nonclinging through their own direct insight and experience.

In this way, rather than seeing ultimate, transcendent realities, their past lives, heaven or hells, or miraculous occurrences, sages see peace and what needs to be abandoned to attain this peace.

Training

A third theme of *The Book of Eights* is that of training—that is, doing practices conducive to peace and becoming a sage. While all the chapters of *The Book of Eights* discuss the ideal and nonideal behavior of someone who is on the path to peace, there are six chapters that give the most attention to this theme. These chapters describe the qualities and behaviors of someone who has attained peace, the peace taught by the Buddha.

The Book of Eights focuses on fundamental, personal, and inner transformations in which individuals are responsible for themselves: "Each person must train for one's own release"[2] and "not seek peace from others."[3] The text does not assume any helping role from the gods or external forces. To some modern, secular-oriented readers this would be less of a revolutionary message than it probably was at the time of the Buddha.

In many passages describing the goal, *The Book of Eights* emphasizes how skillful sages behave rather than describing an attainment distinct from how they live. For example, the text does not mention any transcendent and extraordinary states of consciousness. No mention is made of psychic powers such as the divine eye or the divine ear. Rather, the text enumerates the ethical behaviors such people would or would not do and the qualities of inner virtue or character they would have. In this way, the religious goal is always described in ordinary human terms rather than in mystical, transcendent, or metaphysical language.

In focusing on cultivating behaviors and virtues that are aligned with the goal, *The Book of Eights* has little mention of specific techniques or practices. Stated differently, the text not only does not put focus on religious practices that can be seen as steps toward attaining the qualities of the ideal person, it explicitly and provocatively says that religious observances and such practices in themselves are not adequate for becoming a person at peace. Rather, it encourages people to directly emulate the behavior of the ideal sage.

The Book of Eights avoids making a sharp distinction between the means and the goal. That is, the personal qualities that characterize someone who has already attained the goal are the same qualities one is to cultivate when training for that goal.

One is to train in being what one is to become. If the goal is to be peaceful, the way there is to be peaceful. If the goal is to be released from craving, the way there is a "training to subdue one's inner craving."[4] In this way the achievement of the goal is not radically different from what led to the goal; the naturalistic goal is attained through naturalistic means. This is in sharp contrast to the attainment of supernatural states that are distinct from the training that led to their achievement.

As a conclusion to this discussion of *The Book of Eights*, I would like to repeat the idea that just as the teachings of *The Book of Eights* instruct one to avoid opposing or debating religious doctrines, so too, in my understanding, Naturalistic Buddhism is not opposed to supernatural forms of Buddhism. And, as the teachings of *The Book of Eights* discourages positing any doctrine as ultimate, Naturalistic Buddhism does not need to see its approach to liberation as better than other approaches. Rather, for those not inclined to believe in the supernatural, Naturalistic Buddhism points to a practice and an awakening that does not require believing in rebirth, ultimate realities, miracles, heavens, and hells, but instead teaches about the value of peace and letting go. While supernatural beliefs may be useful for some people, for those who cannot believe in them, both Naturalistic Buddhism and *The Book of Eights* teach that to be at peace, one must let go of all clinging, including clinging to both natural and supernatural Buddhism.

> One who is attached gets into disputes over doctrines;
> But how and with what would one dispute with someone
>   unattached?
> By not embracing or rejecting anything
> A person has shaken off every view, right here.[5]

Further Naturalistic Tendencies in the Early Buddhist Teachings

Because *The Book of Eights* is a minor anthology in the vast corpus of Theravāda Buddhist scriptures, and because it appears to be something of an anomaly in this literature, it can be easy to dismiss its naturalistic teachings as not representative of early Buddhism. However, it is relatively easy to find this same orientation in significant portions of other Theravāda scriptures. One important set of passages are those that refer to the teachings emphasized in the early Buddhist tradition, that the monastics should memorize, chant, and teach others. Not coincidentally, these are all in verse, perhaps because poetry was more conducive to memorization and recitation. Rather than relying on modern interpretations of what may have been important teachings of the early tradition, we can read these verses, which give voice to something the early Buddhists gave priority to themselves.

The Book of Eights is one of these memorized and recited texts. The ancient scriptures contain a story of the Buddha asking a monk named Soṇa to recite the dharma. Soṇa does this by reciting *The Book of Eights*. That the monk chooses this text to recite the dharma for the Buddha suggests it was a valued formulation of the teachings.

A number of suttas contain a poem called "An Auspicious Day" that was also used for memorization, recitation, and teaching. The teachings here are similar enough to those in *The Book of Eights* to suggest a common understanding of what comprises the dharma. "An Auspicious Day" is found in the *Middle Length Discourses*, one of the five large anthologies of scriptures attributed to the Buddha and his immediate disciples. The popularity of the poem is indicated by the fact that it occurs nine times in four different suttas, two of which contain commentaries on it. The poem reads as follows:

Don't chase the past
  Or long for the future.
  The past is left behind;
  The future is not yet reached.

Have insight into whatever phenomenon is present,
  Right where it is;
  Not faltering and not agitated,
  By knowing whatever is present
  One develops the mind.

Ardently do what should be done today—
  Who knows, death may come tomorrow.
  There is no bargaining with Mortality
  And his great army.

Whoever dwells thus ardently,
  —active day and night—
  Is, says the peaceful sage,
  One who has an auspicious day.[6]

Except perhaps for the reference to Mortality's great army (which could, of course, be taken as a metaphor), the teachings in this poem are remarkably naturalistic. The poem contains no references to transcendent, divine, or supernatural realities. Its message that one should not focus on the future discourages concern with rebirth and future lives. Instead it emphasizes attaining insight into the immediacy of one's present experience, an activity that gives one an "auspicious day." The reference to a "peaceful sage" also suggests that peace is the desired attainment, as it is in *The Book of Eights*.

Because "An Auspicious Day" is a single short poem, we shouldn't use this alone to draw conclusions about early Buddhist teachings. However, together with *The Book of Eights*, the poem begins to reveal a pattern in the kind of teachings the early Buddhists memorized, recited, and taught one another.

This pattern is also seen in *The Book of the Way to the Other Shore*, another collection of poems found in the *Sutta Nipāta*. The early scriptures provide evidence that this text was also memorized and recited by both monastics and laypeople. The simplicity, directness, and naturalistic quality of this anthology of sixteen poems are represented by the following verses:

> Subdue greed for sensual pleasure.
> See renunciation as peace.
>> Let there be nothing
>> You take up or reject.

> Let what was in the past fade away,
>> Make nothing of the future.
>> If you don't cling to what is in the present,
>> You can wander about calm.[7]

Here too we come across the instruction not to be concerned with the future, an instruction that suggests not thinking about rebirth. The goal of attaining calm is a thoroughly naturalistic goal that is something attainable in one's own lifetime.

Rather than *The Book of Eights,* "An Auspicious Day," and *The Book of the Way to the Other Shore* being anomalies in the vast anthologies of early Buddhist scriptures, the fact that other scriptures refer to these texts as having been used for memorization, recitation, and teaching suggests that these teachings may well have laid at the heart of the earliest Buddhist community, and perhaps even constituted the core of the Buddha's original message. If the core of these early teachings was naturalistic, this would certainly appear to support a naturalistic approach to practicing the dharma.

The Naturalistic Dharma of the Buddha

The Dhamma well proclaimed by me is clear,
open, evident, and free of patchwork.

THE BUDDHA, *Middle Length Discourses*

Putting aside *The Book of Eights,* "An Auspicious Day," and *The Book of the Way to the Other Shore,* a survey of the Buddha's teachings in the vast corpus of Theravāda suttas repeatedly suggests that his core teachings are thoroughly naturalistic.

The teachings of the Buddha are often referred to as the "dharma." This word is closely associated with "truth"—a truth that one can know for oneself—and is sometimes treated as a synonym of the English word "nature." When he taught the essence of his dharma, the Buddha consistently avoided metaphysical, supernatural, and speculative ideas in favor of practical teachings that serve to make available the path of liberation. In being practical, he put emphasis on perspectives and practices that lead to the end of suffering. In referring to his teachings, he himself explicitly said, "I teach suffering and the end of suffering." His dharma is also empirical in that it is something that can be experienced for oneself. He expressed this clearly by referring to the dharma as "directly visible," as well as by his frequent emphasis on *knowing* and *seeing* as integral to the path he taught. *Believing*, something generally required for supernatural doctrines, does not stand out as having a significant role in the Buddha's core teachings.

In fact, when it comes to beliefs—at least those that could be called speculative views—the primary instruction the Buddha gave was to remove and uproot them. In a discussion where he contrasts his teaching with the speculative views others hold about the self, the world, and what happens after death, the Buddha stated, "The Buddha or a disciple of the Buddha [teaches] the Dhamma for the elimination of all speculative views, determinations, biases, adherences, and underlying tendencies, for the stilling of all mental constructs, for the relinquishing of all attachments, for the destruction of craving, for dispassion, for cessation, for Nibbāna."[8]

Elsewhere he claims that he does not take any position on similar speculative views, because doing so "is not beneficial, does not belong to the basics of the holy life, does not lead to disenchantment, to dispassion, to cessation, to peace, to direct knowledge, to enlightenment, to Nibbāna."[9] What this means is that his teachings are pragmatically connected to a practice leading to the end of suffering, as well as something personally accessible and verifiable by our natural senses.

While the Buddha taught the dharma in many different ways, we can get a clear sense of his primary teachings through the various brief summaries he gave. For example, the *Dhammapada* (Dhp) contains two verses in which he encapsulates "the teachings of the Buddhas." The first states:

> Doing no evil,
>   Engaging in what's skillful,
> And purifying one's mind:
>   This is the teaching of the Buddhas.[10]

Though it lacks details, this verse gives a general overview of the teachings in terms of what "Buddhas" encourage people to actually do. Rather than referring to religious tenets that one must learn, this verse underscores ethical actions one should or shouldn't engage in. The important role of ethics—that is, principles of conduct—is also represented by a second verse from the *Dhammapada*:

> Not disparaging others, not causing injury,
> Practicing restraint by the training rules,
> Knowing moderation in food,

Dwelling in solitude,
And pursuing the higher states of mind,
This is the teaching of the Buddhas.[11]

Both verses end with an instruction to develop the mind. The Buddha's teachings here are more than instructions in how to live in the world; they include teachings on cultivating qualities and states of mind that are beneficial for the ending of suffering.

This focus on mental development is seen in a teaching the Buddha is said to have given to his foster mother, Mahāpajāpatī (the woman who raised him), when she asked him to teach the dharma in brief. The Buddha replied:

As for those qualities of which you may know, "These dharmas lead to dispassion, not to passion; to being unfettered, not to being fettered; to simplifying, not to accumulating; to modesty, not to self-aggrandizement; to contentment, not to discontent; to independence, not to entanglement; to aroused persistence, not to laziness, to being unburdensome, not to being burdensome": you may definitely hold, "This is the Dharma, this is the Discipline, this is the Teacher's instruction."[12]

In this passage the word "dharma" is used in two ways. In the first line "dharma" refers to qualities of mind and to practices one undertakes. In the last line it refers to the Buddha's teachings, which is why the word is capitalized. This means that in the original language, the word "dharma" is easily associated with "teachings" that are concerned with developing the mind. The Buddha's teachings to Mahāpajāpatī can thus be paraphrased as follows: "The Buddha's teaching (*dharma*) and discipline (*vinaya*) are those things that lead to dispassion, being unfettered, simplicity, modesty, contentment, independence, persistence, and not being burdensome." While this can be seen as a form of ethical teaching, it is also a teaching about doing those things that support the cultivation of a peaceful and liberated mind.

On another occasion, when a confrontational person wishing to debate the Buddha asked him what he "proclaims," the Buddha answered: "I assert and proclaim in such a way that one does not quarrel with anyone in the world…in such a way that concepts no longer underlie a person who abides free of sensual desire, perplexity, worry, and craving for any kind of identity."[13]

In saying this, the Buddha makes it clear that he will not engage in a debate over teachings. Instead, his teachings focus on the possibility of freedom from concepts, desire, perplexity, worry, and craving. Not finding the Buddha's statement a suitable topic for a debate, the aspiring disputant left.

The Buddha's dharma is something available for people to see for themselves. This is expressed succinctly and powerfully in a quote that has become a standard part of Buddhist liturgy: "The Dharma is well proclaimed by the Blessed One; it is visible here and now, immediate, inviting to be seen for oneself, onward leading, and to be personally realized by the wise."[14]

In the same discourse the Buddha explains that the way to gain unwavering confidence in the dharma is by seeing in one's own mind the presence of such afflictive states as covetousness, greed, ill will, anger, contempt, envy, and arrogance and then abandoning them. Knowing the mind that is free of these states is a direct validation of what the dharma is. This idea is also expressed in the following teaching of the Buddha:

> When you know there is greed, hatred, or delusion within you and when you know there is no greed, hatred, or delusion within you, then you know the dharma is visible here and now, immediate, inviting to be seen for oneself, onward leading, and to be personally realized by the wise.[15]

This suggests that writings about the dharma, including this very essay, only point to the dharma; to really know the dharma we must know our own minds. Knowing something about external realities that can be considered supernatural is never mentioned in these brief summaries of the essence of the dharma. It is as if they are simply not relevant for walking the path of liberation.

Because *nibbāna* (nirvāṇa) is often presented as the ultimate goal of Buddhist practice, it's interesting to consider one of the most naturalistic explanations of nibbāna found in the suttas, given in the words of the Buddha's disciple Sāriputta: "The destruction of greed, hatred, and delusion: this, friend, is called Nibbāna."[16]

Here there is no claim of understanding the ultimate nature of reality or having some privileged knowledge about transcendent states of consciousness or supernatural dimensions of reality. While the full destruction of the very human tendencies of greed, hatred, and delusion may seem difficult to accomplish, any diminishment or temporary cessation of these states is something we can know for ourselves; it is the dharma visible here and now.

That the ultimate goal of the dharma is indeed seen in the ending of these inner forces of greed, hatred, and delusion is reinforced by the variations the Buddha provided to the quote by Sāriputta above: "The destruction of greed, hatred, and delusion: this is called the final goal of the holy life."[17] "The destruction of greed, hatred, and delusion: this is called the unconditioned."[18] "The destruction of greed, hatred, and delusion: this is called the deathless."[19]

Here we see that concepts such as "the unconditioned" and "the deathless" that lend themselves to mystical and even transcendental interpretations are clearly defined in naturalistic terms. There is nothing mysterious or supernatural about this dharma.

In studying the teachings of the Buddha we should keep in mind these core principles of his teaching of the dharma. To be the dharma, teachings must be something that we can know for ourselves, accessible through our natural senses, albeit refined through the powers of concentration and mindfulness. The dharma is realized through practices connected to the destruction of greed, hatred, and delusion, and it culminates in the attainment of peace.

A Final Word on Naturalistic Buddhism

The label "Naturalistic Buddhism" is not a radically new or strange designation—on the contrary, it reflects one meaning of *dhamma*, one of the key terms used to designate the Buddha's teachings. While the Pāli word *dhamma* (Sanskrit: *dharma*) has a multitude of meanings, in addition to signifying "doctrine" and, more specifically, the doctrine of the Buddha, the *Concise Pali-English Dictionary* provides "nature" as one of its meanings. Similarly, the Pāli Text Society's *Pali-English Dictionary* offers "natural law" as an applied meaning. The dictionary associations of dhamma with nature make it a short step to adopting the adjective "naturalistic" as a descriptive quality of the Buddha's teaching.

Certainly, in the Pāli suttas, the Buddha is depicted describing and discussing many supernatural elements. Prominent are the concepts of rebirth, heavens and hells, and deities. Even if the Buddha actually accepted and taught these ideas—something that is impossible to know for sure, based on the sources available to us—this does not mean that these are central aspects of his core liberation teaching. For example, in the many passages where he explicitly teaches the "dharma in brief," rebirth, heavens and hells, and deities are not mentioned.

The Buddha is depicted in a few places as performing supernatural feats, such as both walking and talking within minutes of his birth. He is also reported to have visited heaven realms. Textual analysis of these and other suttas containing supernatural events suggests that they were composed well after the Buddha's death, at a time when the stories of the Buddha were becoming more like pious legends than actual historical records.

In the discussion above, I do not intend to claim that what I refer to as Naturalistic Buddhism faithfully represents the teachings of the Buddha. Rather, I view Naturalistic Buddhism as a valid and effective way of selecting, interpreting, and adapting Theravāda teachings for people with a naturalistic orientation. The vast amount of naturalistic teachings in the early scriptural discourses provides a rich source of inspiration, information, instruction, and insight for the naturalistic practice of Buddhism. At the same time, the abundant presence of the supernatural in these early texts encourages any of us with this orientation to not insist that Naturalistic Buddhism is truer or better than other forms of Buddhism. The presence of these supernatural elements can serve as a reminder to be open to possibilities that fall outside the views of those of us who have naturalistic inclinations.

BIBLIOGRAPHY

Fronsdal, Gil. *The Buddha before Buddhism: Wisdom from the Early Teachings.* Boulder: Shambhala Publications, 2016.

13 | Conscious and Unconscious Dynamics in the Secularizing Discourse

RICHARD K. PAYNE

In this final essay, we step back in order to look at how the secularizing discourse itself works. Conversations about the secularizing of Buddhism employ several concepts, categories, and concerns that are closely integrated and mutually supportive of one another. The mutually supportive concepts, categories, and concerns cluster together as a convincing way of talking about Buddhism, that is, a discourse. This discourse provides an effectively invisible framework grounded upon preexisting understandings of our own existence as humans, our relations with one another, and our relations with the natural world we inhabit. Unless consciously attended to, discourse naturalizes certain beliefs and values, meaning that those are then taken for granted, as obvious and natural. The intent of this collection is to interrogate the discourse, rather than simply using it. To reverse a trope commonly used in contemporary Buddhist teachings, this collection is saying that what is important is to "look at the finger, not the moon!" That is, these essays should help the reader attend to how the finger is directing your attention, instead of just looking at the moon that the person pointing the finger wants you to pay attention to.

"Discourse" identifies something much broader and more diffuse than an argument, although specific arguments may be deployed as part of a discourse. In some cases these arguments are repeated so frequently that they are abbreviated, their conclusions alone remaining. Then, what were conclusions to arguments have become simply claims considered to be true, and these claims become accepted as part of the common knowledge, shared so widely that it becomes difficult to question their truth because, well, everyone knows that they're true. Being reduced further, they become slogans that, along with frequently repeated images, metaphors, and rhetorical strategies lead thought to certain conclusions without explicit argumentation, contributing to the effectiveness of a discourse.

Here, I'd like to propose that the secularizing discourse regarding contemporary Buddhism contributes to constructing a "Secular Buddhist" identity through opposition to a "Traditional Buddhist" identity. These terms are capitalized here so as to indicate that what is being examined are the two concepts and their rhetorical significance, rather than Buddhism as modified by two different adjectives. This Secular Buddhist identity is represented by well-known contemporary Western authors and thinkers—many who formerly considered themselves to be Buddhists—such as Stephen Batchelor and Sam Harris, as well as institutional bodies that overtly advocate secular Buddhist views such the Secular Buddhist Association. In order to avoid reifying Secular Buddhism, however, this essay does not focus on individuals and groups as such but rather on the secularizing discourse that employs both Secular Buddhism and Traditional Buddhism as rhetorical objects. As David L. McMahan has put it, "The very categories of religious and secular are modern and co-constitutive, and do not simply refer to natural, unambiguous species of phenomena."[1] In other words, the secular constitutes its own opposite, one that is asserted to actually exist as "traditional" Buddhism. That is, the two conceptual categories are constructed by their opposition to one another.[2]

The dynamic by which "secular" and "traditional" are constructed by opposition to one another becomes clearer when we consider the role of additional, complementary, concepts. In addition to "secular" and "traditional" are "modern" and "religious." By creating a flexible set of relations that allow for characteristics to be implied rather than demonstrated, the four together are stronger than each pairing:

> symbolically,
> religious is the opposite of secular
> and
> traditional is the opposite of modern
> allowing
> religious to be identified with traditional
> and
> secular to be identified with modern

In this way "religion" comes to be characterized as "not modern," and "secular" to be characterized as "not traditional." This double pairing gives meaning to each term at the same time it reinforces the structural relation between all four of them.

The characterization of traditional Buddhism is often applied not only to Buddhism in Asia but also to various Buddhist groups in the United States, Europe, and Australia. In the present context of secular versus traditional, this use of "traditional" reformulates the older dichotomy of immigrant and convert.[3] These categories are not neutral, sociological ones, but instead constitute another polarized identity. The ambiguities of the rhetoric are such that in some usages "traditional" is another act of "othering," one that can encode "not white" into the category. If we think of the secularizing discourse as a network, then immigrant/convert join traditional/modern and religious/secular, creating three semiotically paired opposites with several possible links between the various members. As additional concepts in the form of paired opposites are added into the discourse, the more effective it becomes—by further expanding the network, additional concepts strengthen the rhetorical power of the secularizing discourse, allowing it to expand into a too easily deployed polarization, one that becomes an all-encompassing way of thinking about Buddhism. The realities of Buddhism as a lived religion also mean that these kinds of category systems, whether deployed in the secularizing rhetoric or in the putatively secular rhetoric of the academic study of Buddhism, are not only artificial but always a distortion of a changing reality. Ann Gleig's recent research shows that "significant demographic shifts are occurring within meditation-based convert lineages that disrupt the immigrant/convert distinction."[4]

The Secularizing Discourse

In the secularizing discourse Traditional Buddhism has come to be characterized as authoritarian, hierarchical, irrational, ritualistic, rigid. On the other hand, Secular Buddhism is represented as characterized by the opposites of these—democratic, egalitarian, rational, free of ritualism, flexible, adaptable. The attitude informing this dichotomous portrayal is itself part of "high modernism," an attitude that claims inherent superiority because it has surpassed the old. "New is better" is the rhetoric of progress—each phase of human development being represented as an improvement over earlier phases. In the high modernist logic, however, progress is not uniform.

The imperialist dichotomy between colonialist and colonized employs this notion of uneven progress, and in some cases it justified colonialism by enacting a duty to assist those who had not progressed as far. This logic of progress allows the colonialist to assert superiority over the colonized because they are represented as "less developed"—that is, inferior. This self-image as superior then justifies rejection, suppression, and exploitation. Creating representations of "traditional Buddhism" is enabled by this claim to superiority: "I know both what true Buddhism is and what traditional Buddhism is." Having projected the rejected characteristics of one's own self-identity onto this "traditional" Other, allows not just dismissing this straw-man, but freely abusing it for its supposed inferiority.

Implicitly present in the secularizing discourse, the logics of progress and of colonialist superiority are foundational to the way that Secular Buddhism is represented as modern and therefore superior to outdated forms practiced by culturally inferior peoples. Yet, some of the specific concepts employed in the secularizing discourse originate in the Protestant Reformation.

Origins: Protestant Foundations of the Secularizing Rhetoric

Much of the rhetorical dynamics of the secularizing discourse draws on the structures of Protestant thought that originate during the Protestant Reformation (mid-sixteenth to early seventeenth century). These ideas about religion have become dislocated from their origins in Protestant theology, and so in this fragmented form do not represent the living tradition of Protestant thought. Ideas about the historical trajectory of religion as an institution, the subjectivity of adherents, why ritual is not a meaningful form of practice, how only some texts are considered authentic, and the authority of a supposedly original teaching all play key roles in contemporary popular religious culture in the West. Despite originating in Reformation-era discourses, these ideas are now considered universally true of all religions, a neocolonialism of religious culture. Because they are not explicit, these presumptions support the claims of the secularizing discourse.

A general thematic guiding the secularizing discourse is what I've called the "rhetoric of decadence"[5] —a view of religious history in which the original, pure, rational system of ethics and self-development taught by the founder decays over time. This view then justifies the imagery of a return to an original purity, which in Christian terms means the early church, or in Buddhist terms is the sangha as it existed at the very start—in both cases a kind of institutional virginity. The rhetoric of progress allows one to not only portray a religious tradition as having fallen into decadence but to then also claim superior knowledge regarding how it should be purified. Stephen Batchelor has employed the rhetoric of decadence in claiming the superiority of his own teachings. Batchelor describes the history of Christianity and Buddhism as paralleling one another, treating the rhetoric of decadence as a universal historical trajectory for religions. He says that "the history of both traditions is marked by critical moments when the gap between the ordinary person and her religious ideal becomes so vast that it can no longer be sustained. There then follows a collapse of the old order, which allows the possibility of something new being born." Consistent with the rhetoric of decadence, he portrays this as an inevitable cycle, saying that:

> No matter how radical the reform of a religious tradition, over time the new and vibrant school tends to coalesce into yet another orthodoxy and hierarchic institution. As power becomes concentrated into the hands of an elite body of priests, the gap between the unenlightened and the enlightened starts opening up again, thus repeating the old pattern of disempowerment and alienation.[6]

In addition to the rhetoric of decadence, there are several other themes that the secularizing discourse draws from Protestant views of religion. Four key themes are the "priesthood of all believers," opposition to ritual, textual fundamentalism, and the quest for the purity of origins.

The Priesthood of All Believers

The "priesthood of all believers" is the idea that any baptized Christian has the requisite religious status needed to proclaim the Gospel, forgive sins in Jesus's name, and offer prayers for others.[7] This challenged the claim that only ordained priests could validly perform rituals. Central to much of Mahāyāna is the claim that awakening is available to anyone, known as "buddha-nature" and other related terms (for example, *tathāgatagarbha*). And although lay practice groups were known, but uncommon earlier in Buddhist history, Buddhist modernism promotes meditative practice as fundamental—appropriate for laymen and laywomen, and not restricted to monastics. And, while there are instances of nonmonastic teachers in both tantric history and the history of Pure Land Buddhism, the modern secularizing extension of this idea that everyone can be awakened is the belief that meditation teachers need not have received Buddhist initiations of any kind, either lay or monastic. Though many meditation teachers today have received ordination, they do not necessarily represent themselves as having authority by virtue of their initiations. Instead of initiation or seniority in a monastic system, personal meditative experience, including in Asian monastic settings, is the basis upon which authority to teach is claimed.[8] Personal meditative experience displaces institutional authority and initiatory status. While the content of Protestant and the Buddhist ideas of what constitutes liberation and associated methods differ, the rhetorical structure of rejecting monastic ordination as establishing a higher spiritual status is directly parallel.

Opposition to Ritual

A negative view of established religion is not infrequently accompanied by a negative attitude toward ritual. The Protestant Reformers had a mix of different attitudes toward the rituals of the Christian church—that is, the sacraments. Some of them wanted to retain some as having biblical precedent, while others were more critical, leaning toward eliminating ritual more generally. Despite this variety, the conception of ritual in popular religious culture in the West is largely that it is not actually effective in any way, that it doesn't actually do anything. This is sometimes expressed as the claim that ritual is based on a mistaken understanding of causality. This attitude is reinforced by the symbolic opposition between ritual and meditation, in which ritual is understood to consist of physical actions done mindlessly and meditation is represented as mental activity done attentively. In many cases the secularizing rhetoric equates ritual with superstition. In an overview exploring how various North American practitioners define "secular Buddhism," Justin Whitaker quotes Stephen Batchelor, who rejects "traditional Buddhism" because of the way it operates "within the soteriological worldview of ancient India." In opposition to this soteriology, Whitaker says,

> "Secular Buddhism" refers to a Buddhism that rejects the supernatural, most prominently in doctrines such as rebirth, or many interpretations of karma, or beliefs in spirits or gods. Other aspects of Buddhism rejected by secular Buddhists include strong emphasis on ritual, belief in the power of amulets or relics, and notions of extraordinarily powerful teacher-student relationships.[9]

However, in light of understanding that ritualized activity is integral to human religiosity, some Buddhist teachers have more nuanced views. Gil Fronsdal, a contributor to this volume, has written that "often enough Western Buddhists have seen rituals as superficial and as a distraction from the 'real' work of practice. This view overlooks the way in which rituals are a practice as much as meditation."[10] Recently the Secular Buddhist Association has suggested that some practitioners may find it beneficial to integrate rituals and images into their secular Buddhist practice.[11]

Textual Fundamentalism

One way in which the Protestant Reformation dramatically changed Western religious culture was to place the individual believer in a direct relation with God—that is, without a priest acting as mediator between God and the individual. Given that direct relation, the individual was thought to need direct access to the word of God— that is, the Bible—and this has motivated the projects of translating the Bible into ordinary language—the idea being that thereby any individual believer, without the skills required to understand the text in Latin, Hebrew, or Greek, could know God's intent. This also contributes to the belief that it is not necessary to understand religious texts in their historical and cultural context—that by definition religious texts convey a "timeless" message of absolute truth, a characterization not infrequently attributed to Buddhist texts as well.

The secularizing discourse has developed a canon of its own. Texts, almost exclusively from the Pāli canon, are considered authoritative, in large part because they accord with the views being promoted in the secularizing discourse—in much the same way that the formation of the Pāli canon was a politicized process to begin with, as is common in canon formation generally.[12] Contemporary textual selectivity is circular: the texts selected as authoritative are those that are perceived to meet present-day standards of rationality, and then those texts are used to support a rationalistic representation of the dharma at large. Texts that do not meet secular expectations of rationality are dismissed or ignored.

Another example of the way in which textual selectivity is employed in the secularizing discourse is the emphasis on the merely human nature of the founder Śākyamuni, despite frequent descriptions of Śākyamuni's superhuman status in the suttas. While the secularizing rhetoric may claim to have discovered a Śākyamuni Buddha who is "a human who faced confusions, got sick with bloody diarrhea, and died,"[13] such an assertion is itself dependent on textual selectivity. At the same time this recreates in Buddhist language the modern Protestant insistence on the actual existence of "the historical Jesus." The centrality of a human founder as the originator of each tradition is another direct parallel between modern Protestant theology and the secularizing of Buddhism.

This "merely human" person is not the sole representation of the Buddha found in the suttas. In many of the Pāli suttas the Buddha displays a variety of supernatural powers. One exemplary instance is the *Aṅgulimāla Sutta*, in which the Buddha purposely takes a path that will lead past the dwelling place of Aṅgulimāla, a serial killer who wore a garland of the fingers taken from people he has slain.

Seeing the Buddha pass, Aṅgulimāla decides to kill him as well. Taking up his sword and shield, his arrows and bow, Aṅgulimāla sets off behind the Buddha. "Then the Blessed One willed a feat of psychic power such that Aṅgulimāla, though running with all his might, could not catch up with the Blessed One walking at normal pace."[14] By this miraculous act, Aṅgulimāla is eventually led not only to become a member of the sangha, but ultimately to become an arhat capable of his own miraculous feats.

To say that the Buddha is presented as merely human in the suttas is to argue from the authority of specifically selected suttas, which raises the question of the criteria for selection. Why are only the suttas that portray a merely human Buddha the ones that constitute a proper understanding of the Buddha? Is it on the grounds that these meet our own modern standards of what is rational, realistic, or natural, while those that represent a supernatural Buddha capable of miraculous psychic feats are obviously not to be accepted because they are irrational or supernatural and only appeal to crude superstition? If that is the case, then not only is the argument circular, but the authority is not the texts as such, but rather the modern judgment of rationality—or maybe just personal preference. Responding to a critique by Alan Wallace, who asserts textual authority for the claim that the Buddha had direct experience of rebirth at the time of his awakening, Stephen Batchelor replies "As to the Buddha's awakening, it is hardly surprising that you select a Pāli text that describes it in terms of remembering past lives, while I prefer to cite the accounts that don't."[15] The only rationale he gives for selecting one particular sutta as more accurately representative of what the Buddha taught regarding rebirth is that in his view it provides "the most economic and compelling account."[16] Claiming that it is the texts of the Pāli canon that are the foundation for an understanding of the dhamma is textual fundamentalism. This fundamentalism allows for the exclusion of both later commentarial literature—trending toward textual literalism—and also Mahāyāna sūtras, commentaries, and the tantras. Pāli textual fundamentalism is, however, further qualified by the selectivity involved in only accepting as authoritative those texts from the Pāli canon that meet modern standards of rationality. In this way the image of the "merely human" Buddha is a mythic creation based on the Pāli texts (textual fundamentalism), without recourse to commentaries (textual literalism), and limiting texts accepted as authoritative to those that reinforce one's own preexisting expectations (textual selectivity).

Quest for the Purity of Origins

Key to the rhetoric of the Protestant Reformation was the ideal of a return to the purity of the early church. The church was said to have become corrupted over the millennium and a half since the time of Jesus and needed to be purified of those corruptions—this is the rhetoric of decadence. The early church was held as the model to guide the reformers, allowing them to identify corruptions in need of purification. This narrative about the history of Christianity, the rhetoric of decadence, has been generalized as a view of the history of all religions, including Buddhism.[17]

One of the most common rhetorical forms employed for distinguishing Secular Buddhism from its Traditional opposite is the claim to be representing the original, pure, essential, and authentic teachings of Śākyamuni Buddha in contrast to what are dismissed as merely cultural accretions. As Sam Harris put it, "The wisdom of the Buddha is currently trapped within the religion of Buddhism."[18] Similarly, in the mission statement for his podcast, *The Secular Buddhist*, Ted Meissner gives two of the rationales for the program: "1. With the qualities of a philosophy and a religion, Buddhism's empirical practice can be hidden by trappings not part of the actual teaching. 2. In the same way that religious practices can obscure a teaching, cultural manifestations can also be confused for that teaching."[19]

The claim that such a distinction exists implies that the individual making that claim has the authority to make the distinction. In the case of the secularizing discourse, the distinction between the "pure, original" teachings and later "merely cultural" accretions is not argued for. It is instead dialectically simply asserted and simply accepted as an accurate representation of Buddhist history—an understanding that at the same time reinforces the authority of those making the claims to make those claims. Further, the claims that practice is "hidden by trappings" of philosophy and religion, or confused with "cultural manifestations" constitute a central tenet of the Perennialist view, a specific system of religious thought discussed below.

Two rhetorical strategies are used for the claim that there is a distinction between the essential teachings regarding practice, and the forms of religion, philosophy, and custom that are merely cultural: authenticity and transcendence. What Meissner calls "Buddhism's empirical practice" is in other words asserted to be the authentic dharma, and the authentic dharma transcends any particular cultural location. Possessing the authentic, transcendent dharma, particularly in the form of practice-based experience, is then in turn the basis for claims to authority. The idea that the dharma is somehow transcendent, that it exists in some location other than a cultural one, is a commonplace of the metaphysics of the secularizing of Buddhism. Ann Gleig quotes Lenore Friedman as saying, "In what unique and perfect form would the Dharma flourish *here, now*? In some places, there has already been a shaking-free from Asian forms and a collective searching for more authentic, indigenous ones."[20]

The equation of transcendent, authentic, and authoritative is the same set of ideas that allowed the Reformers to claim authority outside the structures of the Catholic Church, authority that was personal in basis rather than institutional. Because it allowed for purifying later corruptions from the religion, it constituted a return to "the primitive church" of Jesus and his disciples. While corollaries to this complex of ideas—authentic = transcendent = authoritative—can be found in the history of Buddhism, the structure is part of Western religious culture's Protestant heritage. Found in both Buddhist thought and Western popular religious culture, the constructed nature of this compound of claims equating transcendent, authentic, and authoritative largely goes unnoticed, and equating the three characteristics seems to be only natural.

All of these characteristics of the secularizing discourse—the primacy of personal meditative experience, the futility of ritual, the authority of selected texts, and the transcendent character of the essence of the tradition—are presumptions deriving from the Protestant roots of American popular religious culture. Because they selectively highlight particular aspects of the Buddhist tradition, they can operate at the level of what is taken as simply true, and control how Buddhism is thought about in the West.

Conceptual Polarities: Dynamics of the Secularizing Discourse

The secularizing discourse about Buddhism can be analyzed into two dynamics, one conscious, while the other is unconscious. One dynamic of the secularizing discourse is the conscious rejection of values, beliefs, and practices that are identified as "traditionally religious," while consciously embracing their opposites.[21] And in this way, the secularizing discourse does not simply establish itself in opposition, but doing so simultaenously defines that which it is in opposition to: "traditional religion" is created as a category. In other words, the dialectic of rejection creates Traditional Buddhism as the negatively valued mirror image—and that very image may come to be embraced positively by those rejecting a secularized Buddhism. The second dynamic is the unconscious reproduction of beliefs and values—cultural presumptions—found in the society in which the secularizing discourse operates.

The conscious dichotomies that we will examine here are dogmatism and superstition versus empiricism and reason, elitism versus democratic anticlericalism, and conservative versus progressive.

Dogmatism and Superstition versus Empiricism and Reason

Religion is characterized in the secularizing discourse as depending on dogmatic assertions, that is, irrational beliefs unsupported by empirical evidence. This emphasis on empiricism is also discussed by Phillipe Turenne in his contribution to this collection. For example, characterizing the opposite of his own secular approach, Stephen Batchelor defines institutionalized religion as "a revealed belief system valid for all time, controlled by an elite body of priests."[22] This quote also evidences the anticlerical attitude prominent in the secularizing discourse.

An oppositional relation between reason and dogma as characterizing the difference between secular and religious underlies the way that Batchelor goes beyond the specifics of belief in heaven or belief in karmic reincarnation to create a general characterization of all religions, saying,

> Religions are united not by belief in God but by belief in life after death. According to religious Buddhism we will be reborn in a form of life that accords with the ethical quality of actions committed in this or a previous life....Yet while religions may agree that life continues in some form after death, this does not indicate the claim to be true.[23]

And another instance of this polarity is found on the Frequently Asked Questions page of the Secular Buddhist Association website, which includes the following FAQ phrased in a way that establishes an oppositional relation between secular and traditional Buddhism: "How does Secular Buddhism differ from traditional Buddhism, such as Theravāda or Zen?"[24]

The answer goes on to describe traditional Buddhism as holding to unverifiable beliefs. The FAQ asserts,

> The primary difference is that Secular Buddhism has no dependency on assertions not in evidence, it is based solely on that which can be verified in the natural world. It does not rule out such claims, but merely recognizes that such assertions (like literal rebirth) have not been able to provide any externally verifiable or convincing evidence. And, like the claims of other religions which cannot be verified by any known means, can be set aside.[25]

One of the central tendencies of the secularizing rhetoric is this strong emphasis on empirical evidence as the sole measure of truth, reflecting a modern construction that polarizes the category of religion as primarily a matter of belief in opposition to science as primarily a matter of knowledge. Specifically, in this case, belief in the unverifiable is placed at the center of the secularizing image of Traditional Buddhism.

Beyond this naive epistemology, however, is another issue, which is the unnuanced characterization of such strains as Zen and Theravāda as Traditional. This simplistic dichotomy (purposely?) obscures the fact that in both Asia and the West there are modernizing forms not only of Zen and Theravāda, but of Chinese (see Charles B. Jones in this collection) and other Buddhist traditions that have themselves moved to reform Buddhism in accord with their perceptions of the changes of modernity.

Elitism versus Democratic Anticlericalism

The secularizing discourse treats Traditional Buddhism as hierarchical, patriarchal, and authoritarian—in other words, elitist. Batchelor claims that such elitism is what Secular Buddhism is rejecting: "Exotic names, robes, insignia of office, titles—the trappings of religion—confuse as much as they help. They endorse the assumption of the existence of an elite whose explicit commitment grants them implicit extraordinariness."[26] The secularizing rhetoric is, in other words, "anticlerical." Priestly elites are portrayed as attempting to exercise power over believers by means of "priestcraft"—that is, mystification and ritual—as well as dogmatism and superstition. In the secularizing rhetoric regarding Buddhism this anticlerical attitude is evident in portrayals of monks and priests as simply maintaining their position and institutional power by ritual and doctrinal rationales such as the karmic benefits of *dana*—offerings made by lay members to monastics.

In contrast, Secular Buddhism characteristically asserts that awakening is attainable by anyone, whether they self-identify as a Buddhist or not, much less whether they have monastic status or formal initiation into a lineage. A consequence of the rhetoric of decadence is that it allows for a short-circuiting of the tradition, claiming a direct connection to the founder and eliminating the entire history and lineal transmission between then and the present.

A consequence of promoting the idea that awakening in this life is universally available is a reinterpretation of awakening in secular, pragmatic, and experiential terms. Thus, for example, Vincent Horn describes one of the principal tenets of the program of what he labels "Pragmatic Dharma" as "awakening is possible," saying:

> At the center of this whole approach is the shining gem of Awakening. Awakening is often experienced as a process, sometimes rapid and sometimes more progressive, by which the sense of personal identity is radically transformed. Identity begins as a small, separate, and localized phenomenon that is always in reference to my body, my emotions, my perception, and my self. Through questioning the very assumptions this sense of identity rests upon it transforms to a more expansive, open-ended, and constantly changing situation, one that can simultaneously include us, but which goes beyond us as well. This shift brings an incredible sense of internal freedom, expansiveness, and well-being.[27]

This understanding of awakening presents it as a set of psychological characteristics—a beneficial change in one's sense of self-identity. At the same time it suggests that awakening is actually much easier than traditionally taught—that awakening does not require many thousands of lifetimes during which one gradually accomplishes vast numbers of meritorious actions, intense and extended practice, and deep study.

Some important streams of Buddhist praxis teach parallel understandings of a universal potential for awakening. One such understanding involves an analysis of the workings of consciousness as being grounded on a fundamental level (*ālayavijñāna*) that is either inherently pure or can be purified. Another concept involves the idea that each of us has an inherent potential for awakening (*tathāgatagarbha*). A third concept is the existence in all sentient beings of an element enabling awakening (*buddhadhātu*). In the transmission to East Asia these tended to be identified with one another using a single designation, *foxing*, generally rendered into English as "buddha-nature." That claims to the universal potential for awakening as somehow inherent are presented in the secularizing discourse as simply true reflects first the idea of individual religious authority found in popular religious culture, which derives from the idea of the priesthood of all believers. It also, however, demonstrates how the secularizing rhetoric draws widely from the rich resources of the entire Buddhist tradition, despite its claim of adhering solely to the original and pure teachings of Śākyamuni Buddha as found in selected texts from the Pāli canon.

Conservative versus Progressive

The Orientalist "othering" of nonwhite communities, both in Asia and in the West, is evident in the dichotomy of immigrant and convert (as introduced above) but also ramifies into a dichotomy of conservative and progressive. Summarizing the issues raised by Natalie Quli in relation to immigrant communities, Ann Gleig has highlighted that "a problematic consequence of the immigrant/convert split is the positioning of immigrant communities as a static, conservative, traditional 'other' against which progressive, innovative, modern American Buddhism is defined and celebrated."[28]

For example, Stephen Batchelor has talked about "the traditional forms of Buddhism inherited from Asia," which he says appear to be stagnating (an issue discussed by Turenne in this volume). When "even a liberal and modernized church such as that of Anglicanism struggles to come to terms with women bishops and homosexual relations," says Batchelor, "there seems little prospect that conservative Buddhist institutions will change their patriarchal stances in the foreseeable future."[29] The question here is not whether this is true or not, or even how true it might be, but to highlight the rhetorical function of the claim—as if of necessity a secularized Buddhism could not be conservative, authoritarian, hierarchical, and patriarchal, as if those characteristics are somehow inherently "traditional" and "religious."

The conscious embrace of characteristics such as rational and empirical, democratic and anticlerical, and progressive and liberal, creates a particular image of Secular Buddhism. Simultaneously the opposites of those characteristics—dogmatism and superstition, hierarchical and authoritarian, and stagnant and conservative—are consciously rejected. Those characteristics are then projected onto Secular Buddhism's polar opposite, Traditional Buddhism. Both Secular Buddhism and Traditional Buddhism are rhetorical objects created by the dynamics of the discourse itself, ones that do not exist as objective entities in the world.

Unconsciously Reproducing Cultural Presumptions

The secularizing discourse simultaneously creates Secular Buddhism and Traditional Buddhism as discursive objects by a dynamics of polarization in which specific characteristics are consciously embraced and rejected. That discourse, however, exists in a wider cultural field. Already introduced are the religious themes that derive from the Protestant Reformation pervading the popular religious culture and that structure the values and beliefs expressed in the secularizing discourse. We turn now to other strains of thought in popular culture more widely, which the secularizing discourse unconsciously reproduces: Orientalist disdain, Perennialism, neoliberal ideology, technological conceptions of practice, and rhetorics of inevitability.

Orientalist Disdain: The Invisibility of Whiteness

As an attitude, Orientalism privileges the experience and beliefs of members of the dominant social order in colonial and postcolonial contexts—classically, British imperialists and in the present, American techno-elites. Dominance is not simply an established matter, but rather needs to be constantly reasserted, and race and religion are central to the ongoing project of domination. As Michael Altman explains,

> Race and religion both functioned as categories through which the West made sense of, dominated, and represented the East. Both race and religion worked as plastic categories through which Europeans and Americans constructed the difference between themselves and the Oriental other, rendering those categories differently in different historical moments and under varying historical circumstances. Orientalism, then, provides an example of how "religion" and "race" lack any stable definitions but are constantly reimagined and reconstructed as social agents and groups define the boundaries between "us" and "them."[30]

Like the relation between secular and its created opposite, traditional, Orientalism is a discourse that is an exercise of power over the object constructed by that discourse. It is not that knowledge is power, but that control of the discourse is power over knowledge.

One of the most effective rhetorical devices of the secularizing discourse is the expression of Orientalist disdain: elite representatives of secularized Buddhism express disdain for "Asians" (itself a socially constructed category) whose Buddhism is somehow inferior to the "pure and sincere Buddhist practice" of American practitioners. One reason this kind of disdain is such a powerful rhetorical tool is that it simultaneously creates a sharp division between two seemingly clear groups, a rhetoric of "us" versus "them." The two groups are (1) the despised Others pointed to by the speaker and (2) those who self-identify with the speaker and thus reflexively experience themselves as superior too. In addition to creating a simple and seemingly clear opposition, this rhetoric panders to the audience, making them part of the superior class of those who are in the know—in this case, those who understand what Buddhism really is. Three instances are offered as examples of Orientalist disdain.

In a 2016 interview Chade-Meng Tan, famously the Google engineer who founded Google's in-house meditation program, claimed that when he was growing up in Asia, the Buddhism that he experienced consisted of going to temple to make offerings, and it was "extremely *uncool*." However, after coming to the United States, he says, he discovered Vipassana:

> When I started learning Vipassana, everything changed. I became a real Buddhist. The dharma you see in America is pure, as opposed to Asian Buddhism in which you go to a temple and there's nothing else. I have credibility in saying that because I've seen both sides. Not that American Buddhism is free of problems, but it's the purest Buddhism.[31]

Here, from his privileged Orientalist position as part of the American techno-elite, Tan is defining "real Buddhism" as meditation, and claiming that this is what makes American Buddhism "pure." By implicit contrast Asian Buddhism is not pure, it is impure.

Similarly, in an interview published in the popular Buddhist magazine *Lion's Roar*, Trudy Goodman, a founding teacher of InsightLA,[32] was asked about criticisms that secularized mindfulness is "watered-down Buddhism." In response she declared:

> I think these critiques come from more fundamentalist Buddhists. I mean, if you want to see watered-down Buddhism, travel to the beautiful Zen temples of Korea, a country where Buddhism is still alive and well, and you'll see all the ladies in the temples working their malas, chatting about their kids, sometimes shucking peas; the temples are very much village and urban gathering places. How many people are deeply practicing? I don't know, but I think in any center, it's always the minority who are doing what dyed-in-the-wool Buddhists would recognize as pure practice.[33]

Along with the disdainful attitude toward "ladies in the temple," Goodman's us/them rhetoric implies that her audience, like herself, are the experts on "pure practice"—that they are the ones who actually are true Buddhists, as opposed to those who merely use the temple for socializing. This works rhetorically because many members of Goodman's audience—readers of the interview—will want to see themselves as included in this knowledgeable, committed group of "dyed-in-the-wool Buddhists."

A final example of Orientalist disdain is Stephen Batchelor's portrayal of Tibetan lamas as not only ignorant of the modern world but also constrained by outdated dogmas:

> Educated in the monasteries of old Tibet, they were ignorant of the findings of the natural sciences. They knew nothing of the modern disciplines of cosmology, physics, or biology. Nor did they have any knowledge of the literary, philosophical, and religious traditions that flourished outside their homeland. For them, all that human beings needed to know had been worked out centuries before by the Buddha and his followers and was preserved in the Kangyur and Tengyur (the Tibetan Buddhist canon). There you would learn that the earth was a triangular continent in a vast ocean dominated by mighty Mount Sumeru, around which the sun, moon, and planets revolved.[34]

The point here is not to claim that Tan's or Goodman's or Batchelor's descriptions are actually wrong. Buddhists in Taiwan do offer incense, ladies in Korea do gather at local temples, and Tibetan lamas can be ignorant of modern science. Instead, the issue is the role that such representations of Traditional Buddhism play in the secularizing discourse—particularly the disdain these descriptions convey toward both monastics and laity who do not participate in the same religious culture as these authors, and can therefore be dismissed because they are not "real Buddhists." Since they are not "real Buddhists" they also cannot challenge, even by example, the authority of the image of real Buddhism or the authority of those who offer that image. And, as alluded to above, these characterizations are applied not only to native practitioners of Buddhism in Asia but to immigrant and sectarian convert groups in the United States as well.

Perennialism: The Essential Ideology

The ideology of Perennialism pervades popular Western religious culture and has played a key role in the secularizing discourse regarding Buddhism. Perennialism has two central ideological claims that influence the interpretation of Buddhism: the first is that the true, spiritual core of all religions is "ultimately" the same, and the second is that the true spiritual core of every tradition transcends the cultural and historical particularities of that tradition. The word "ultimately" is given quotation marks to indicate the problematic character of the claim. What "ultimate" means is either never defined or at best is "explained" as something beyond language. If something is beyond language, then no claim about it can be shown to be true—or false. Despite this, the claim of an ultimate unity informs much of the secularizing discourse.

The second claim is that the essence of any religious tradition is separate from any particular cultural setting in which it might exist. In many cases it is Western or Westernized teachers, or teachers speaking to Western audiences, who claim to be able to know the essence of Buddhism separate from any cultural accretions—and who apparently fail to recognize that this rhetoric is itself a construction of the culture in which they are located. Discussing the homogenization of views in a collection of essays on mindfulness by a wide variety of contributors writing from different backgrounds, Ann Gleig notes that the harmony "was achieved primarily by separating Buddhism as a religious and cultural particularity, and dharma as the universal truth underlying and ultimately separate from that historic particularity."[35]

However, this way of thinking about Buddhism—as essentially, universally, timelessly a meditative practice without doctrinal commitments, or a universal teaching without cultural location ("the dharma")—is itself a cultural construct. For many people, including teachers promoting various forms of secularized Buddhism (as well as academics and editors of collections of essays about secularized Buddhism), unless confronted by a different cultural context their own remains effectively invisible. They do not see the cultural character of their own belief system—and so do not see that the claim of what constitutes the essence of Buddhism, and the claim to a privileged position from which they know that essence, is itself culturally constructed. Asserting that one knows the essence of Buddhism is the first step toward claiming the authority to identify "true Buddhism," the authority to distinguish it from that which is not true, and ultimately the authority to not only make but to enforce that judgment.

Neoliberal Ideology

Being stripped of preexisting institutional structures, Secular Buddhism is itself being formed by the organizing principles of late capitalism. This despite most of the proponents apparently being unreflective about the relation between the secularity that they claim and the structuring function of the neoliberal ideology of late capitalism—the recent historical period when capitalism has become not simply a means of organizing production and exchange, but a widespread system of beliefs and values determining political and social relations as well.

Although secular society is represented as a neutral context, a container within which different religious traditions have the opportunity to promote themselves in a competitive fashion, the society within which the secularizing of Buddhism is taking place is itself far from an ideologically neutral one. Because it is so widely taken for granted neoliberal ideology has become "naturalized"— that is, treated as simply describing the conditions and goals of human existence—rather than an ideology that gives form to our understanding of the conditions and goals of the life of individuals in society.

The cultural heritage of the United States divides every member of that society into two. One is personal and private, the other is interpersonal and public. It is the public self that operates in the social space of secular society—such as economic, community, and political activities. In contrast the private self operates in domestic spaces, such as the home, which is where religious identity is active.[36] The ethical ideology of neoliberal capitalism simultaneously employs and reinforces this twofold schema. Economic action in the public sphere is secularized as a purely rational pursuit of profit, and profit is the measure of success in that rationale. Other applications of values are not considered rational in this limited sense of rationality promoted by neoliberal thought and are only considered appropriate in the private sphere along with religious beliefs.

Equally central to private, individual autonomy in the neoliberal worldview is the idea of competition, which is not only used to understand economic relations, but is extended metaphorically throughout the conceptual framework that neoliberal ideology establishes for human existence. In this view society is a marketplace in which different religious, spiritual, self-help, and secularized practices are free to compete with one another. This transforms adherents into customers whose choices of what they purchase are constituted as the appropriate arbiter of what teachings survive in the marketplace and how they are marketed there. It is not some intrinsic value in teachings and practices that determines which of them survive in the marketplace, but rather what adherents as customers consume that makes that determination.

A Mental Technology: The Divorce of Practice and Belief

Also common in the secularizing rhetoric is the assumption that meditative practices are mental technologies that can be employed without accepting any belief system. This in turn reflects a wider social belief that technology is context-neutral and value-free. In other words, it is commonly believed that technology is just the same no matter what the cultural context is, and that technology in itself carries no values.

This idea has played a key role in the rise of mindfulness as a practice that can be separated from Buddhism. Crudely, the metaphor at work here is something like the image of a hammer, which can be used to drive nails or to flatten tin cans. The hammer remains "the same" no matter what use it is put to (context-neutral), and that its value derives solely from the use to which someone puts it (value-free). The metaphor, however, is profoundly misleading. Not only is mindfulness itself a social construct, but it is transmitted in particular social settings each of which has its own value system and rationale for engaging in mindfulness. To claim that it is just the same as a hammer in being context-neutral and value-free is simply a rhetorical strategy—one that is, however, a key part of the secularizing discourse.

It is this rhetorical strategy that one hears in the declaratives of Barry Boyce's explanation of mindfulness: "It can be practiced equally by people of any religious faith and those who have no religious faith, based as it is on fundamental mental and physical capabilities that all human beings have, irrespective of any ideological views they may hold."[37] Thus, we have mindfulness being practiced to benefit one's productivity at work or to improve one's golf game, as if mindfulness itself is value-free and can be applied to any endeavor chosen by the individual—or the corporation sponsoring it. (See Ron Purser's essay in this volume for further inquiry into the relation between corporations and secularized mindfulness.)

The Rhetoric of Inevitability

The last rhetorical strategy that we will examine here is the claim that the rise of Secular Buddhism is inevitable. Turning again to the FAQ page of the Secular Buddhist Association's website we find the following question: "Why do we need Secular Buddhism when we already have many different Buddhist traditions?"

The first part of the response claims that like all religious traditions, Buddhism necessarily evolves "to suit the culture in which it finds itself." Two aspects of this are worth noting. First, that the container-contained metaphor, in which "culture" is the container and "Buddhism" is the contained, employs the modernist understanding of society as a field of competing organizations. Second, note that Buddhism is personified, "in which it finds itself," effectively implying that the secularizing trends are being enacted by some agency that is Buddhism itself. The next sentence adds another nuance to this representation by claiming that because contemporary "Western" society tends toward secular views, "the growth of Secular Buddhism is an inevitable manifestation of these attitudes." Claiming inevitability makes questioning a secularizing of Buddhism irrelevant, such questions do not need to be asked—to secularize Buddhism is somehow a natural, inevitable process, one simply in response to cultural conditions, and not a consequence of decisions made by individual people for which they are responsible.

The secularizing discourse emerges from a particular culture, and unconsciously instantiates specific beliefs and values of that culture. No doubt a different analysis would identify a different set of unconsciously reproduced cultural presumptions from the five we have explored above: Orientalist disdain for other ways of practicing Buddhism, Perennialist artifice of the separability of practice and belief, neoliberal ideology of the individual consumer in a marketplace, the treatment of meditation as a value-free mental technology, and the rhetoric of inevitability.

Dynamics of the Secularizing Discourse

Secular Buddhism roots itself in a fundamental dichotomy between the religious and the secular. This dichotomy is not something that is justified, but it is instead simply presumed as given. Indeed, this reflects popular religious culture—the sea in which Secular Buddhist fish swim—and the foundational role of the religious/secular dichotomy in that culture. The dichotomy is not, however, in any way a natural one. It is instead a social construct with a specific cultural history, a history in which the construction of the dichotomy is enmeshed with contestation over political and economic power from the Protestant Reformation and the Wars of Religion (of the sixteenth to early eighteenth centuries), right up to the present-day debates about the appropriate role of Christianity in modern society.

Further, the dichotomy is not a simple opposition between equals. Instead it is structured so that the secular is the naturalized framework within which the religious exists as a particular instance—a set of social institutions located in the field of the secular along with other social institutions, such as business, manufacturing, agriculture, the military, media, and so on.

What gets carried into contemporary usage of the distinction is a set of oppositional characterizations. These include such things as

secular = rational, traditional = superstitious
secular = empirical, traditional = metaphysical
secular = psychological, traditional = mythological[38]

and so on.

Again, however, such oppositions are not between two equals. The cultural structure that makes secular the norm applies to these characteristics as well.[39] Not only are value judgments entailed, but those judgments reinforce what is considered normal in contrast to what is deviant. Thus, rational—that is, secular—is normal, and superstitious—that is, religious—is deviant. Similarly, psychological understandings are normal, and metaphysical ones are deviant.

The secularizing discourse tends to emphasize an understanding of Buddhism that is individual, rational, and mental—a form of what in an earlier era in American popular religious history would have been called "mental hygiene," or "mind cure."[40] It is instrumental and pragmatic, promoting itself on the basis of values such as "well-being," "happiness," or "human flourishing." This complex of ways of thinking about a secularized Buddhism both accepts and reinforces the neoliberal subject. The neoliberal subject is a person who is wholly autonomous, someone who makes their own decisions, creates the conditions for their own well-being and happiness—including by practicing meditation. It is a view that conceals the social construction of its conceptions of human existence, our relations with one another, and our relations with the natural world, treating those conceptions as if they are simply the way things are, just given, unquestionable, and inevitable.

The secularizing discourse creates both Secular Buddhism and its opposite, Traditional Buddhism. That discourse employs concepts, categories, and concerns from popular religious culture that derive from the Protestant Reformation, were conveyed by the neo-Romanticism of 1960s new-age religiosity, and were given new value in the saga of self-discovery that is embraced by many white upper-middle-class Americans. Some characteristics are consciously embraced as true of Secular Buddhism, and others are simultaneously consciously rejected and projected in such a fashion as to construct Traditional Buddhism. And lastly there are themes in popular religious culture that are unconsciously reproduced—Orientalist disdain, Perennialism, the neoliberal subject, meditation as mental technology, and the rhetoric of inevitability. The goal of this essay has been to bring into focus the dynamics of the secularizing discourse itself—to raise consciousness of how the finger is directing our attention, rather than just looking at the moon.

BIBLIOGRAPHY

Altman, Michael J. "Orientalism in Nineteenth-Century America." *The Oxford Handbook of Religion and Race in American History*, edited by Paul Harvey and Kathryn Gin Lum, 123–137. Oxford and New York: Oxford University Press, 2018.

Batchelor, Stephen. *After Buddhism: Rethinking the Dharma for a Secular Age.* New York: HarperCollins, 2016.

——. *Buddhism without Beliefs: A Contemporary Guide to Awakening.* New York: Riverhead Books, 1997.

——. *Confession of a Buddhist Atheist.* New York: Random House, 2010.

——. "Dropping the Bodhisattva Gods." *Tricycle*, June 13, 2018. https://tricycle.org/trikedaily/stephen-batchelor-secular-buddhism/.

——. "An Open Letter to B. Alan Wallace." *Mandala*, January 2011. https://fpmt.org/mandala/archives/mandala-issues-for-2011/january/an-open-letter-to-b-alan-wallace/.

Boyce, Barry, ed. *The Mindfulness Revolution: Leading Psychologists, Scientists, Artists, and Meditation Teachers on the Power of Mindfulness in Daily Life.* Boston and London: Shambhala Publications, 2011.

Chidester, David. *Savage Systems: Colonialism and Comparative Religion in Southern Africa.* Charlottesville: University of Virginia Press, 1996.

Fitzgerald, Timothy. *Discourse on Civlity and Barbarity: A Critical History of Religion and Related Categories.* Oxford and New York: Oxford University Press, 2007.

——. *The Ideology of Religious Studies.* Oxford and New York: Oxford University Press, 2000.

Fronsdal, Gil. "Rituals in Buddhism," Insight Meditation Center website, accessed June 30, 2020. https://www.insightmeditationcenter.org/books-arti cles/rituals-in-buddhism/.

Gleig, Ann. *American Dharma: Buddhism beyond Modernity.* New Haven, CT, and London: Yale University Press, 2019.

Harris, Sam. "Killing the Buddha." *Shambhala Sun*, March 19, 2006, reprinted at https://samharris.org/killing-the-buddha/.

Helderman, Ira P. "Drawing the Boundaries between 'Religion' and 'Secular' in Psychotherapists' Approaches to Buddhist Traditions in the United States." *Journal of the American Academy of Religion* 84, no. 4 (December 2016): 937-72.

——. *Prescribing the Dharma: Psychotherapists, Buddhist Traditions, and Defining Religion.* Chapel Hill: University of North Carolina Press, 2019.

Hickey, Wakoh Shannon. *Mind Cure: How Meditation Became Medicine.* Oxford and New York: Oxford University Press, 2019.

——. "Two Buddhisms, Three Buddhisms, and Racism." *Journal of Global Buddhism* 11 (2010): 1-25.

Horn, Vincent. "The Core Features of Pragmatic Dharma." *Buddhist Geeks* (blog), October 18, 2018. https://www.pragmaticdharma.training/blog/core -features-pragmatic-dharma.

Kruse, Kevin M. *One Nation under God: How Corporate America Invented Christian America.* New York: Basic Books, 2015.

Lion's Roar. "What Does Mindfulness Mean for Buddhism?" Staff forum. May 5, 2015. https://www.lionsroar.com/forum-what-does-mindfulness-mean-for -buddhism.

McMahan, David. "Buddhism and Global Secularisms." *Journal of Global Buddhism* 18 (2017): 112-28.

Meissner, Ted. "About: Mission." The Secular Buddhist (website). http://www. thesecularbuddhist.com/about_mission.php.

Payne, Richard K. "Introduction." In *Re-Visioning "Kamakura" Buddhism*, edited by Richard K. Payne. Honolulu: University of Hawai'i Press, 1998.

———. "Introduction." In *Tantric Buddhism in East Asia*, edited by Richard K. Payne. Boston: Wisdom Publications, 2005.

———. *Language in the Buddhist Tantra of Japan: Indian Roots of Mantra.* London: Bloomsbury Academic, 2018.

———. "Lethal Fire: The Shingon Yamāntaka Abhicāra Homa." *Journal of Religion and Violence* 6.1 (2018): 11–31.

———. "Study of Buddhist Tantra: An Impressionistic Overview." *Pacific World: Journal of the Institute of Buddhist Studies.* Third series, no. 20 (2018): 25–53.

Quli, Natalie. "On Authenticity: Scholarship, the Insight Movement, and White Authority." In *Methods in Buddhist Studies: Essays in Honor of Richard K. Payne*, edited by Scott A. Mitchell and Natalie Fisk Quli, 154–72. London and New York: Bloomsbury Academic, 2019.

———. "Western Self, Asian Other: Modernity, Authenticity, and Nostalgia for 'Tradition' in Buddhist Studies." *Journal of Buddhist Ethics* 16 (2009): 1–38.

Smith, Doug. "Secular Practice with Images and Rituals." Secular Buddhist Association (website), April 30, 2018. https://secularbuddhism.org/secular-practice-with-images-and-rituals/.

Strohl, Jane E. "The Framework for Christian Living: Luther on the Christian's Callings." In *The Oxford Handbook of Martin Luther's Theology*, edited by Robert Kokb, Irene Dingel, and L'uobmír Batka, 365–69. Oxford and New York: Oxford University Press, 2014.

Talbott, Chris. "New Rivers, New Rafts: The Secular Buddhism Conference." *Insight Journal* 2013. https://www.buddhistinquiry.org/article/new-rivers-new-rafts-the-secular-buddhism-conference/.

Ṭhānissaro Bhikkhu, trans. "About Aṅgulimāla: *Aṅgulimāla Sutta* (MN 86)." www.dhammatalks.org/suttas/MN/MN86.html.

Whitaker, Justin. "Secular Buddhism in North America." Buddhistdoor (website). July 21, 2017. www.buddhistdoor.net/features/secular-buddhism-in-north-america.

Zahn, Max. "'Even the Rich Suffer': An Interview with Google's Jolly Good Fellow Chade-Meng Tan." *Religion Dispatches.* April 26, 2016. http://religiondispatches.org/rich-people-need-inner-peace-too-an-interview-with-googles-jolly-good-fellow-chade-meng-tan/.

Notes

Editor's Introduction

1. Natalie Quli, "Western Self, Asian Other: Modernity, Authenticity, and Nostalgia for 'Tradition' in Buddhist Studies," *Journal of Buddhist Ethics* 16 (2009): 5.

2. Chad Seales, "Spatial Constructions of the American Secular," *Oxford Research Encyclopedia of Religion* (Oxford and New York: Oxford University Press, 2018), 4.

3. See more at https://secularbuddhism.org/ and https://secularbuddhism.com/.

4. See more at https://bodhi-college.org/secular-dharma-by-stephen-batchelor/.

5. See more at http://www.pragmaticbuddhism.org/.

6. See more at https://www.pragmaticdharma.training/blog/core-features-pragmatic-dharma.

7. Roger R. Jackson and John Makransky, eds., *Buddhist Theology: Critical Reflections by Contemporary Buddhist Scholars* (London: Routledge, Taylor & Francis, 2016).

8. Tomoko Masuzawa, *The Invention of World Religions; or, How European Universalism Was Preserved in the Language of Pluralism* (Chicago: University of Chicago Press, 2005).

9. David L. McMahan, "Modernity and the Early Discourse of Scientific Buddhism," *Journal of the American Academy of Religion* 72, no. 4 (December 2004): 897–933.

10. Timothy Fitzgerald, *Discourse on Civility and Barbarity: A Critical History of Religion and Related Categories* (Oxford: Oxford University Press, 2007), 10.

11. Ann Gleig, *American Dharma* (New Haven, CT, and London: Yale University Press, 2019), 3.

12. Quli, "Western Self, Asian Other," 11.

13. Jens Reinke, "Sacred Secularities: Ritual and Social Engagement in a Global

Buddhist China," in *Religiosity, Secularity and Pluralism in the Global East,* eds. Fenggang Yang, Francis Jae-ryong Song, and Sakurai Yoshihide (Basel: MDPI, 2019), 135.

14. Reinke, "Sacred Secularities," 135.

15. Donald S. Lopez Jr., discussed this dynamic in his insightful and still important essay "Foreigner at the Lama's Feet," in *Curators of the Buddha: The Study of Buddhism under Colonialism,* Donald S. Lopez Jr., ed., 251-95 (Chicago: University of Chicago Press, 1995).

16. See Gil Fronsdal, *The Buddha before Buddhism: Wisdom from the Early Teachings* (Boulder: Shambhala Publications, 2016).

17. Quli, "Western Self, Asian Other," 1-38.

1. Has Secularism Become a Religion? by SARAH SHAW

1. Twelfth Major Rock Edict, Dineschandra C. Sircar, *Inscriptions of Aśoka* (Calcutta: Indian Publication Society, 1956), 50-51.

2. Ancient histories, such as the fifth-century *Mahāvaṃsa,* include much later legends and accounts, compiled centuries after Aśoka's rule.

3. George J. Holyoake, *English Secularism: A Confession of Belief* (Chicago: Open Court, 1896), 60.

4. Definition from *Shorter Oxford English Dictionary on Historical Principles* (Oxford: Clarendon Press, 1973).

5. Definition from Cambridge Dictionary Online.

6. Definition from *Collins English Dictionary and Thesaurus,* 5th edition.

7. Definition from Merriam-Webster Online.

8. Robert Bluck, *British Buddhism: Teachings, Practice and Development* (London and New York: Routledge, 2006); L. S. Cousins, "Theravāda Buddhism in England," in *Buddhism into the Year 2000: International Conference Proceedings* (Bangkok and Los Angeles: Dhammakaya Foundation, 1994), 141-50.

9. See Peter Harvey, *An Introduction to Buddhism: Teachings, History and Practices,* second edition, (Cambridge, MA: Cambridge University Press, 2013), 419-58.

10. Alexandra David-Neel, *Magic and Mystery in Tibet* (London: Souvenir Press, 2007); Harvey, *Introduction to Buddhism,* 415-56.

11. Bluck, *British Buddhism,* 3-24.

12. Peter Skilling, "The Buddhist Cosmopolis: Universal Welfare, Universal Outreach Universal Message," *Journal of Buddhist Studies* 15 (2018): 72.

13. L. S. Cousins, "Theravāda Buddhism in England," 141-50.

14. Kemala Tiyavanich, *Forest Recollections: Wandering Monks in Twentieth-Century Thailand* (Honolulu: University of Hawai'i Press, 1997), 29-31; J. L.

Taylor, *Forest Monks and the Nation State: An Anthropological and Historical Study in Northeast Thailand* (Institute of Southeast Asian Studies, 1993).

15. Tiyavanich, *Forest Recollections*, 29-31; Andrew Skilton and Phibul Choompolpaisal, "The Old Meditation (boran kammatthan), Pre-reform Theravāda Meditation System from Wat Ratchasittaram; The Piti Section of the kammatthan matchima baep lamdap," *Aseanie* no. 33 (2014), 83-116.

16. Cousins, "Theravāda Buddhism in England."

17. Kate Crosby, *Traditional Theravāda Meditation and Its Modern-Era Suppression* (Hong Kong: Buddha-Dharma Centre of Hong Kong, 2013), and Kate Crosby, *Esoteric Theravada: The Story of the Forgotten Meditation Tradition of Southeast Asia* (Boulder: Shambhala Publications, 2020).

18. L. S. Cousins, "*Samatha-yāna* and *Vipassanā-yāna*," in *Buddhist Studies in Honour of Hammalava Saddhātissa*, edited by Gatārē Dhammapāla, Richard Francis Gombrich, and Kenneth Roy Norman (Nugegoda, Sri Lanka: Hammalava Saddhātissa Felicitation Volume Committee, University of Jayewardenepura, 1984), 56-68; Cousins, "Theravāda Buddhism in England."

19. Stephen Batchelor, *Secular Buddhism: Imagining the Dharma in an Uncertain World* (New Haven, CT: Yale University Press, 2017).

20. Jack Kornfield, *A Path with Heart: The Classic Guide through the Perils and Pitfalls of Spiritual Life.* Revised and updated edition (London: Rider, 2002).

21. Sarah Shaw, *Introduction to Buddhist Meditation* (London: Routledge, 2009), 257-275.

22. Robert H. Sharf, "Mindfulness and Mindlessness in Early Chan," in *Meditation and Culture: The Interplay of Practice and Context*, ed. Halvor Eifring (London: Bloomsbury, 2015), 55-75.

23. David Brazier, "Mindfulness: Traditional and Utilitarian," *Handbook of Mindfulness*, edited by Ronald E. Purser, David Forbes, and Adam Burke (Cham: Springer International, 2016), 63-74.

24. Geoffrey Samuel, "Mindfulness Within the Full Range of Buddhist and Asian Meditative Practices," in *Handbook of Mindfulness*, ed. Ronald E. Purser, David Forbes, and Adam Burke (Cham: Springer International, 2016), 47-62; Sarah Shaw, *Mindfulness: Where It Comes From and What It Means* (Boulder: Shambhala Publications, 2020).

25. Mark Williams, John D. Teasdale, Jon Kabat-Zinn, and Zindel V. Segal, *The Mindful Way through Depression: Freeing Yourself from Chronic Unhappiness* (New York: Guilford Press, 2007); Tamara A. Russell and Gerson Siegmund, "What and Who? Mindfulness in the Mental Health Setting," *BJPsych Bulletin* 40, no 6 (2016): 333-340.

26. Nigela Ahemaitijiang, Xiaoyi Hu, Xuan Yang, and Zhuo Rachel Han, "Effects of Meditation on the Soles of the Feet on the Aggressive and Destructive

Behaviors of Chinese Adolescents with Autism Spectrum Disorders," *Mindfulness* 11 (2020): 230-240.

27. Eric B. Loucks, Zev Schuman-Olivier, Willoughby B. Britton, David M. Fresco, Gaelle Desbordes, Judson A., Brewer, and Carl Fulwiler, "Mindfulness and Cardiovascular Disease Risk: State of the Evidence, Plausible Mechanisms, and Theoretical Framework," *Current Cardiology Reports* 17, no. 12 (2015): 112.

28. Jack Kornfield, *Living Buddhist Masters* (Santa Cruz, CA: Unity Press, 1977), 13.

29. Bhikkhu Bodhi, "What Does Mindfulness Really Mean? A Canonical Perspective." *Contemporary Buddhism* 12, no. 1 (2011): 19-39; "The Transformations of Mindfulness," *Handbook of Mindfulness*, ed. Ronald E. Purser, David Forbes, and Adam Burke (Cham: Springer International, 2016), 3-14; Rupert Gethin, "On Some Definitions of Mindfulness," *Contemporary Buddhism* 12, no. 1 (2011): 263-79; M. T. Greenberg and J. L. Mitra, "From Mindfulness to Right Mindfulness: The Intersection of Awareness and Ethics," *Mindfulness* 6, no. 1 (2015): 74-78; Peter Harvey, "Mindfulness in Theravāda Samatha and Vipassanā Meditations, and in Secular Mindfulness," in *Buddhist Foundations of Mindfulness*, ed. Edo Shonin, William Van Gordon, and Nirbhay N. Singh (Cham: Springer International Publishing, 2015), 115-37; Shaw, *Mindfulness*, 141-46.

30. T. W. Rhys Davids, *Dialogues of the Buddha*, vol. 2, Sacred Books of the Buddhists (London: Froude, 1910), 323; Shaw, *Mindfulness*, 34-36, 42-45, 75-76.

31. Discussed, for example, by Mark Williams et al., *The Mindful Way*; "Mindfulness," NHS (website).

32. Graham Dixon, "Assertion and Restraint in Dhamma Transmission in Early Pāli Sources," *Buddhist Studies Review* 32, no. 1 (2015), 100.

33. *Majjhima Nikāya* (Oxford: Pali Text Society, 1993) 2.12-15; Sarah Shaw, *Buddhist Meditation: An Anthology of Texts* (London: Routledge, 2006), 86-96.

34. Shaw, *Buddhist Meditation*, 129-34.

35. Ud 34-37; Shaw, *Buddhist Meditation*, 24-28.

36. MN 1.420-6; Mv 1.277-80; Shaw, *Buddhist Meditation*, 189-93.

37. Richard Gombrich, *How Buddhism Began: The Conditioned Genesis of the Early Teachings* (London and Atlantic Highlands, NJ: Athlone, 1996), 29-31.

38. The situation is complex and needs further research. For a benchmark I take Patrick Olivelle's translation of *smṛti* in early Sanskrit literature as "tradition" or a "textualized form of memory;" Olivelle, *Language, Texts, and Society: Explorations in Ancient Indian Culture and Religion* (New York: Anthem Press, 2011), 168. After the time of the Buddha the word is most

commonly in Sanskrit non-Buddhist literature in this way too. Konrad Klaus argues, however, that those earlier than the Buddha also used *smṛti* as a selective adverting of the mind to events *in the present*; Klaus, "On the Meaning of the Root *Smṛ* in Vedic Literature," *Wiener Zeitschrift für die Kunde Südasiens* 36 (1992): 77–86. He concludes, nonetheless, that there is a radical difference of orientation within the Buddhist tradition. The Buddha "recognise[s] the importance of this mental factor, to determine how it works and how we can get control over it" (Klaus, "On the Meaning," 86). While Olivelle's understanding of the pre-Buddhist use of the term is more widely accepted, even if one takes Klaus's position, one should still go further than he does regarding the Buddha's adaptation and usage of the term. The *Abidharmakośa* does take *smṛti* as a simple "noting," capable of being tainted or not. The Pāli tradition, however, seems to take it as an ongoing, intuitive discriminatory factor that accompanies a particular state of alertness to the helpful and the ethical (Shaw, *Mindfulness*). The word changes its very nature from a simple remembering or adverting of attention to a discernment in regard to ethical appropriateness and skillful attention. Such a transformation would certainly be characteristic of the way Buddhism changes early Sanskrit terms (Gombrich, *How Buddhism Began*, 29, 129). In the Pāli Abhidhamma, mindfulness is a determinant of skillful consciousness: it is, thereby, always ethically positive, always associated with self-respect and regard for consequences, and always associated with the presence of one or other of the divine abidings. "Wrong mindfulness," and hence the possible presence of *sati* as a noting factor with negative connotations, is mentioned in the Abhidhamma on a couple of occasions. Such a "mindfulness," however, does not occur as an unskillful factor in the lists of states in unskillful consciousness. Nor is "mindfulness" of any kind listed, even in a neutral way, in the factors present in neutral consciousnesses. It is simply not a universal factor, as it becomes in the *Abhidharmakośa*. The Pāli Abhidhamma states clearly that mindfulness is only really present when it is skillful, otherwise it is not mindfulness—in the same way, one could say, as fool's gold is not real gold. This positive aspect is suggested in suttas: living in a continued state of loving-kindness, for instance, is described as a *sati*. In Buddhism, mindfulness is a path factor, with the right mindfulness of the eightfold path described as an adverting to the domains of body, feelings, mind, and dhamma, in a sustained and ongoing part of following the path (DN 2.290–315). Even if one is not inclined to favor the Abhidhamma approach, and some do not, an evaluative, ethical, and skillful attention needs to be linked to the Buddha's use of the term "mindfulness" in early Pāli Buddhism. It appears the Buddha did not just reemphasize *smṛti* but changed the word's meaning and scope. More research is needed to investigate how and in what senses he did this. For further discussion see Rhys Davids, *Dialogues of the Buddha*, 322-23; Gethin, "Definitions of Mindfulness"; Harvey, "Mindfulness in Theravāda"; Shaw, *Mindfulness*.

39. AN 4.111.

40. For example, AN 5.206-11, AN 5.332-34; see Harvey, "Mindfulness in Theravāda"; Gethin, "Definitions of Mindfulness"; Shaw, *Buddhist Meditation*, 109-62.

41. Vism VII.

42. Sn 151.

43. Bhikkhu Bodhi, *The Numerical Discourses of the Buddha: A Translation of the Aṅguttara Nikāya* (Somerville, MA: Wisdom Publications, 2012), 281; AN 1.190.

44. MN 2.12-15; Shaw, *Buddhist Meditation*, 6-20.

45. MN 3.25; Shaw, *Buddhist Meditation*, 97.

46. AN 4.85-8, Ud 39-40; Shaw, *Buddhist Meditation*, 36-38, 56-58.

47. SN 2.155-7; Shaw, *Buddhist Meditation*, 35-36.

48. We discussed this in a conversation shortly before his death in 2015.

49. Christmas Humphreys, "Zen Comes West." *Middle Way* 32, no. 4 (1958), 126.

50. DN 2.169-199.

51. Sn 285; K. R. Norman, *The Group of Discourses (Sutta-Nipāta)* II (Oxford: Pali Text Society 1995), 32; *Brahmacariyañ ca sīlañ ca ajjavaṃ maddavaṃ tapaṃ soraccaṃ avihiṃsañ ca khantiñ cāpi avaṇṇayuṃ* (Sn 292).

52. J 1.14-25; Shaw, *The Jatakas: Birth Stories of the Bodhistta* (New Delhi: Penguin, 2006), 1-5.

53. J 463.

54. J 1. According to the Pāli Buddhist tradition, Buddhas and their dispensations come and go (DN 2.1-54). Jātakas are mostly located in times when there is no Buddha. Individual jātakas here are cited by their numerical placing in the whole collection.

55. J 546; Naomi Appleton and Sarah Shaw, *The Ten Great Birth Stories of the Buddha: The Mahānipāta of the Jātakatthavaṇṇanā*, 2 vols. (Chiang Mai, Thailand: Silkworm Publications, 2015), 1.187-201.

56. The list of the ten (*dasavidha rājadhamma*), found as a series only in jātaka literature, is cited in commentarial prose in Jātakas 396, 482, 483, 520, 521, 530. All ten appear in canonical verse, usually considered the oldest layer of the text, in Jātaka 534 (J 5.378).

57. See Patrick Olivelle, *Dharmasūtras: The Law Codes of Ancient India* (Oxford: Oxford University Press, 1999), xxxviii-xxxix.

58. DhS 1340.

59. Vbh 87.

60. MN 2.105.

61. Margaret Cone, ed., *Dictionary of Pāli*, vol. 2 (Bristol: Pali Text Society, 2010), 3.

62. Vism VII 1-100.

63. I would like to thank Michael Smerconish Jr., Paul Baker, and Tod Olsen for helpful comments on this subject.

64. Rodney Smith, *Touching the Infinite: A New Perspective on the Buddha's Four Foundations of Mindfulness* (Boulder: Shambhala Publications, 2017), 247-59.

65. Sn 1133-49; Shaw, *Buddhist Meditation*, 117-18.

66. It 90-92.

67. Gombrich, *How Buddhism Began*.

68. Skilling, *The Buddhist Cosmopolis*.

69. AN 3.285-6; MN 1.37-38; Vism VII 82-88

70. Vism VII 85.

2. Buddhism and Secular Subjectivities by DAVID L. McMAHAN

1. You can find photos of the exhibit here: https://www.lamag.com/culturefiles/first-look-go-behind-scenes-broads-yayoi-kusama-exhibition/.

2. Charles Taylor, *A Secular Age* (Cambridge, MA: Harvard University Press), 2007. See also Charles Taylor, "Buffered and Porous Selves," The Immanent Frame (website), September 2, 2008, https://tif.ssrc.org/2008/09/02/buffered-and-porous-selves/.

3. Anthony Giddens, *Modernity and Self-Identity: Self and Society in the Late Modern Age* (Cambridge, UK: Polity Press, 1991), 32-33.

4. Giddens, *Modernity and Self-Identity*, 186.

5. Zygmunt Bauman, *Liquid Life* (Cambridge, UK: Polity Press, 2005), 6.

6. Baumann, *Liquid Life*, 24.

7. Baumann, *Liquid Life*, 26.

8. Kenneth Gergen, *The Saturated Self: Dilemmas of Identity in Contemporary Life* (New York: Basic Books, 2000), 7.

9. Gergen, *Saturated Self*, 7.

10. Gergen, *Saturated Self*, 15-16.

11. Gergen, *Saturated Self*, 16.

12. Gergen, *Saturated Self*, 73-74.

13. Michael Venables, "Review: 'Yayoi Kusama: Infinity Mirrors'—Of Dots and Emptiness," *Medium*, July 25, 2017, https://medium.com/future-technology-and-society/review-yayoi-kusama-infinity-mirrors-dots-and-a-sense-of-emptiness-f6ebf8bf363e.

14. Thich Nhat Hanh, *The Heart of Understanding: Commentaries on the Pra-jñaparamita Heart Sutra* (Berkeley, CA: Parallax Press), 1988; Thich Nhat Hanh, *Peace Is Every Step: The Path of Mindfulness in Everyday Life* (New York: Bantam), 1991.

15. Thomas Cleary, trans., *The Flower Ornament Scripture: A Translation of The Avatamsaka Sutra* (Boulder: Shambhala, 1984–1987).

16. See, for example, David Loy, *Ecodharma: Buddhist Teachings for the Ecological Crisis* (Somerville, MA: Wisdom Publications, 2019); Stephanie Kaza, *Green Buddhism: Practice and Compassionate Action in Uncertain Times* (Boulder: Shambhala, 2019); Joanna Macy, *World as Lover, World as Self* (Berkeley, CA: Parallax Press, 1991).

17. Richard Rorty, *Philosophy and the Mirror of Nature* (Princeton, NJ: Princeton University Press), 1979.

3. American Cultural Baggage by FUNIE HSU

1. Chenxing Han, "We're Not Who You Think We Are," *Lion's Roar*, May 15, 2017, https://www.lionsroar.com/were-not-who-you-think-we-are/.

2. Aaron J. Lee, "We're Not Who You Think We Are," *Angry Asian Buddhist* (blog), July 6, 2016, http://www.angryasianbuddhist.com/2016/07/were-not-who-you-think-we-are/.

3. Aaron J. Lee, "Don't Forget Vincent Chin," *Angry Asian Buddhist* (blog), June 23, 2012, http://www.angryasianbuddhist.com/2012/06/dont-forget-vincent-chin/.

4. Duncan Ryuken Williams, *American Sutra: A Story of Faith and Freedom in the Second World War* (Cambridge, MA: Harvard University Press, 2019).

5. Jane Naomi Iwamura, *Virtual Orientalism: Asian Religions and American Popular Culture* (New York: Oxford University Press, 2011).

6. Joseph Cheah, *Race and Religion in American Buddhism: White Supremacy and Immigrant Adaptation* (New York: Oxford University Press, 2011).

7. Vincent W. Lloyd, "Introduction: Managing Race, Managing Religion," in *Race and Secularism in America*, eds. Jonathon S. Kahn and Vincent W. Lloyd (New York: Columbia University Press, 2016), 4.

8. Cheah, *Race and Religion*, 78.

9. Carolyn Jones, "California Schools Turn to Mindfulness to Help Students Cope with Stress," EdSource, June 22, 2020, https://edsource.org/2020/california-schools-turn-to-mindfulness-to-help-students-cope-with-stress/633956.

10. Jones, "California Schools."

11. Barry Boyce, "The Mindful Politician: Why Tim Ryan is Promoting Mindfulness in Washington," *Mindful*, April 3, 2019, https://www.mindful.

org/the-mindful-politician-why-tim-ryan-is-promoting-mindfulness-in
-washington/.

12. Elizabeth A. Harris, "Under Stress, Students in New York Schools Find Calm
in Meditation," *New York Times*, October 23, 2015, https://www.nytimes.
com/2015/10/24/nyregion/under-stress-students-in-new-york-schools-find
-calm-in-meditation.html.

13. Lindsey I. Black, Patricia M. Barnes, Tainya C. Clarke, Barbara J. Stussman,
and Richard L. Nahin, "Use of Yoga, Meditation, and Chiropractors Among
U.S. Children Aged 4–17 Years," US Department of Health and Human Services, Centers for Disease Control and Prevention, National Center for
Health Statistics Data Brief, no. 324 (November 2018), 1–2, https://www.
cdc.gov/nchs/data/databriefs/db324-h.pdf.

14. Candy Gunther Brown, *Debating Yoga and Mindfulness in Public Schools:
Reforming Secular Education or Reestablishing Religion?* (Chapel Hill: University of North Carolina Press, 2019).

15. Oren Ergas and Linor L. Hadar, "Mindfulness in and as Education: A Map of
a Developing Academic Discourse from 2002 to 2017." *Review of Education*
7, no. 3 (2019): 19.

16. As cited in Ergas and Hadar, "Mindfulness in and as Education," 19.

17. Iwamura, *Virtual Orientalism*.

18. Scott Mitchell, "Yes, Buddhism Is a Religion," *Lion's Roar*, November 19,
2017, https://www.lionsroar.com/yes-buddhism-is-a-religion/.

19. Funie Hsu, "What Is the Sound of One Invisible Hand Clapping? Neoliberalism, the Invisibility of Asian and Asian American Buddhists, and Secular
Mindfulness in Education," in *Handbook of Mindfulness: Culture, Context,
and Social Engagement*, eds. Ronald E. Purser, David Forbes, Adam Burke
(New York: Springer, 2016), 374.

20. Mitchell, "Yes, Buddhism Is a Religion."

21. Hsu, "What is the Sound," 373.

22. "About Yoga 4 Classrooms," Yoga 4 Classrooms, http://www.yoga4classrooms
.com/about-yoga-4-classrooms.

23. "Funding Yoga, Mindfulness and SEL Using ESSA and Title IV Grants,"
Yoga 4 Classrooms (blog), August 29, 2018, http://www.yoga4classrooms.com
/yoga-4-classrooms-blog/funding-yoga-mindfulness-sel-essa-and-title-iv
-grants.

24. David L. McMahan and Erik Braun, "From Colonialism to Brainscans: Modern Transformations of Buddhist Meditation," in *Meditation, Buddhism,
and Science*, eds. David L. McMahan and Erik Braun (New York: Oxford
University Press, 2017), 5.

25. Brown, *Debating Yoga and Mindfulness*, 5.

26. Angela Davis, "Angela Davis in Conversation with Astra Taylor: Their

Democracy and Ours," interview by Astra Taylor, Jacobin, October 13, 2020, video, 1:12:49, https://www.youtube.com/watch?v=6ScF2GeTUsY.

27. Akira S. Gutierrez, Sara B. Krachman, Ethan Scherer, Martin R. West, and John D. E. Gabrieli, "Mindfulness in the Classroom: Learning from a School-based Mindfulness Intervention Through the Boston Charter Research Collaborative," *Transforming Education* 11 (January 2019), https://www.transformingeducation.org/wp-content/uploads/2019/01/2019-BCRC-Mindfulness-Brief.pdf.

28. Leah Lakshmi Piepzna-Samarasinha, "small island: on being a decolonial sri lankan buddhist for a just peace," Buddhist Peace Fellowship, October 8, 2013, http://www.buddhistpeacefellowship.org/small-island-on-being-a-decolonial-sri-lankan-buddhist-for-a-just-peace/.

29. William Barber, II and Jonathan Wilson-Hartgrove, "The Unveiling of Christian Nationalism," *Herald Sun*, January 27, 2018, https://www.heraldsun.com/opinion/article196961234.html.

30. Hsu, "What Is the Sound," 376.

31. Hsu, "What Is the sound," 370.

32. "Funding Yoga, Mindfulness, and SEL," *Yoga 4 Classrooms* (blog).

33. David Forbes, "Mindfulness and Neoliberal Education: Accommodation or Transformation?" in *Weaving Complementary Knowledge Systems and Mindfulness to Educate a Literate Citizenry for Sustainable and Healthy Lives*, eds. Malgorzata Powietrzynska and Kenneth Tobin (Leiden, Netherlands: Brill Sense, 2017), 148.

34. Forbes, "Mindfulness and Neoliberal Education," 148.

35. Forbes, "Mindfulness and Neoliberal Education," 148–49.

4. Curating Culture by PAMELA WINFIELD

1. For more on this process, see Jason Ananda Josephson, *Inventing Religion in Japan* (Chicago: University of Chicago Press, 2012), and Junichiro Isomae, "Deconstructing 'Japanese Religion': A Historical Survey," *Japanese Journal of Religious Studies* 32, no. 2 (2005): 235–48.

2. The Japanese phrase, which literally translates as "Buddhism for the pacification and protection of the state-family," is *chingo kokka bukkyō*. The "state-family" (Jpn. *kokka*) two-character compound derives from the Confucian social order that was modeled on the hierarchical and patriarchal family unit. According to Confucian ideology, the ruler should reign over the ruled like a father beneficently looks after his son.

3. Robert Sharf and Elizabeth Horton Sharf, eds., *Living Images: Japanese Buddhist Icons in Context* (Palo Alto, CA: Stanford University Press, 2002).

4. Yoshito Hakeda, *Kūkai Major Works* (New York: Columbia University Press, 1972), 141.

5. For more on this modern bifurcation, see Mircea Eliade, *The Sacred and Profane: The Nature of Religion* (New York: Houghton Mifflin Harcourt Press, 1959), and Charles Taylor, *A Secular Age* (Cambridge, MA: Harvard University Press, 2007).

6. The Meiji government issued "secret directives" against Tenrikyō in 1896, for example, and destroyed the Omotokyō headquarters in Kyoto in 1935. For a complete translation of directive no. 12 issued by Home Secretary (Jpn. *naimu daijin*) Yoshikawa Akimasa on April 6, 1896, see *Tenrikyology*, "The Life of the Honseki Izo Iburi, Part Twelve, The Final Osashizu," December 17, 2007, http://tenrikyology.com/96/the-life-of-the-honseki-izo-iburi-part-twelve/#fn-96-1. For more on Omotokyō, see Sheldon M. Garon, "State and Religion in Imperial Japan, 1912–1945," *Journal of Japanese Studies* 12, no. 2 (1986): 273–302.

7. Andrew Bernstein, *Modern Passings: Death Rites, Politics and Social Change in Imperial Japan* (Honolulu: University of Hawai'i Press, 2006).

8. Richard Gombrich and Gananath Obeysekere, *Buddhism Transformed: Religious Change in Sri Lanka* (Princeton, NJ: Princeton University Press, 1990), 202–41.

9. Bernard Faure, "The Buddhist Icon and the Modern Gaze," *Critical Inquiry* 24, no. 3 (1998): 768–813.

10. James C. Dobbins, *Behold the Buddha: Religious Meanings of Japanese Buddhist Icons* (Honolulu: University of Hawai'i Press, 2020), 5.

11. Calvin Thomkins, *Merchants and Masterpieces: The Story of the Metropolitan Museum of Art* (New York: Henry Holt, 1989).

12. Patricia J. Graham, *Faith and Power in Japanese Buddhist Art 1600–2005* (Honolulu: University of Hawai'i Press, 2007), 177, who says the number has been estimated at some eighteen thousand temples.

13. Graham, *Faith and Power*, 199–200.

14. Michael F. Marra, "The Creation of the Vocabulary of Aesthetics in Meiji Japan," in *Since Meiji: Perspectives in the Visual Arts of Japan 1868–2000*, ed. J. Thomas Rimer (Honolulu: University of Hawai'i Press, 2016).

15. Sonya S. Lee, ed. *Journal of the History of Collections: Special Edition: Ideas of Asian in the Museum* 28, no. 3 (November 2016).

16. According to the history of the museum provided at the Musée Guimet website,http://www.guimet.fr/francais/a-propos-du-musee/histoire-du-musee-guimet/.

17. This feedback loop of reenculturation is reminiscent of the "pizza effect," a term coined by the anthropologist Agehananda Bharati in 1970 to describe how host cultures may popularize new cultural forms that are then fed back into the home culture as indigenous. In this analogy, like pizza toppings that became popular in Italy only after Italian immigrants popularized them in America, Japan embraced its "Buddhist art" heritage only after it became

popular in overseas museum collections. Agehananda Bharati, "The Hindu Renaissance and Its Apologetic Patterns," *Journal of Asian Studies* 29, no. 2 (1970): 267-87.

18. Angus Lockyer, "Japan and International Exhibitions, 1862-1910," in *Commerce and Culture at the 1910 Japan-British Exhibition: Centenary Perspectives* (Leiden, Netherlands: Global Oriental/Brill, 2013), 27-34.

19. Interestingly, according to the art historian Carole Paul (University of California-Santa Barbara) the prototypical first public art museum in Europe was the Capitoline Museum in Rome (est. 1734), not the Louvre (est. 1793) as is often believed. Andrea Estrada, "Art for the Masses," *University of California News*, July 24, 2014, https://www.universityofcalifornia.edu/news/origins-public-art-museum.

20. Graham, *Faith and Power*, 200.

21. Graham, *Faith and Power*, 202.

22. Julie Christ Oakes, "Japan's National Treasure System and the Commodification of Art," in *Looking Modern: East Asian Visual Culture from the Treaty Ports to World War II*, ed. Jennifer Purdle and Hans Bjarne Thomsen (Chicago: Center for the Art of East Asia, University of Chicago, with Art Media Resources, 2009), 220-42.

23. Gregory Levine, *Daitokuji: The Visual Cultures of a Zen Monastery* (Seattle, WA: University of Washington Press, 2006), and Ikumi Kaminishi, *Explaining Pictures: Buddhist Propaganda and Etoki Storytelling in Japan* (Honolulu: University of Hawai'i Press, 2006).

24. Fabio Rambelli and Eric Reinders, *Buddhism and Iconoclasm in East Asia: A History* (London and New York: Bloomsbury Academic, 2012), 147-50.

25. For more on *shōgon*, see Andrew M. Watsky, *Chikubushima: Deploying the Sacred Arts of Momoyama Japan* (Seattle: University of Washington Press, 2003), 36, 196.

26. Matthew Mitchell, "Beyond the Convent Walls: The Local and Japan-Wide Activities of Daihongan's Nuns in the Early Modern Period (c. 1550-1868)," (PhD diss., Duke University, 2016).

27. Lindsay Jones, *The Hermeneutics of Sacred Architecture: Experience, Interpretation, Comparison, Vol. 2: Hermeneutical Calisthenics: A Morphology of Ritual-Architectural Priorities* (Cambridge, MA: Harvard University Center for the Study of World Religions, Harvard University Press, 2000), 315.

28. Catherine Bell, *Ritual Theory, Ritual Practice* (New York: Oxford University Press, 1992), 99.

29. Sally Promey, *Sensational Religion: Sensory Cultures in Material Practice*, ed. Sally M. Promey (New Haven, CT: Yale University Press, 2014), 651.

30. Rambelli and Reinders, *Buddhism and Iconoclasm*, 130.

31. Graham, *Faith and Power*, 248.

32. Jeff Wilson, *Mindful America: Meditation and the Mutual Transformation of Buddhism and American Culture* (New York: Oxford University Press, 2014), 87.

33. After the schism of 1938, Risshō Kōseikai soon eclipsed its parent group. According to 1992 statistics, Rishhō Koseikai claimed 6.47 million members and Reiyūkai claimed only 3.2 million members. Roy Tetsuo Forbes, *Schism, Orthodoxy and Heresy in the History of Tenrikyō: Three Case Studies* (MA thesis, University of Hawai'i, 2005), 3n5.

5. Establishing the Pure Land in the Human Realm
by Charles B. Jones

1. Holmes Welch, *The Buddhist Revival in China*. Harvard East Asian Series, 33 (Cambridge, MA: Harvard University Press, 1968), 51.

2. Interested readers may find a complete English translation of the essay in Charles B. Jones, *Taixu's "On the Establishment of the Pure Land in the Human Realm": A Translation and Study* (New York: Bloomsbury Academic, 2021).

3. All page numbers refer to Taixu, "Jianshe renjian jingtu lun" ("On the Establishment of the Pure Land in the Human Realm"), in *Taixu dashi quanshu* 24 (Taipei: Shandao Temple Sutra Distribution Center, 1956), 349-430.

4. *Fo shuo qishi yinben jing*, T. 24.1: 314a-317a. In premodern Buddhist cosmology, our world consists of four triangular continents that radiate in the four cardinal directions from a massive central mountain called Sumeru. We live on the southern continent of Jambudvīpa ("Rose-apple Island"), while Uttarakuru is located to the north. Human beings also dwell on Uttarakuru, but in conditions vastly more ideal than here. They live for one thousand years, enjoy hedonistic lives, and their environment provides everything they need naturally and without effort.

5. *Fo shuo wuliangshou jing*, T. 360.12: 270a-272c; English in Hisao Inagaki, and Harold Stewart, trans., *The Three Pure Land Sutras*, 2nd ed. (Berkeley, CA: Numata Center for Buddhist Translation and Research, 2003), 24-36.

6. *Xiandai renjian zhi kunao*.

7. Taixu, "On the Establishment of the Pure Land," 383.

8. The "five evils" and "five virtues" are detailed in a long citation from the *Larger Sukhāvatī-vyūha-sūtra* that Taixu provides in this section of the essay. The five evils are (1) commission of wrongdoing, (2) arrogance and lack of principles, (3) heresy and hedonism, (4) inciting others to practice evil, and (5) laziness and lack of resolve. Despite the mention of "five virtues" at the head of this quotation, they are not enumerated and must be assumed to be either the opposite of the evil with which each is paired or the Five Lay Precepts. The sutra passage runs from T. 360.12:275c-277c.

9. Taixu, "On the Establishment of the Pure Land," 384.

10. *Foshuo Amituo jing*, T. 360.12: 275c–277c; English in Inagaki and Stewart, 46–56.

11. See Lionel Giles, trans. *Taoist Teachings from the Book of Lieh-Tzu* (London: Murray, 1912), 48–50.

12. Taixu, "On the Establishment of the Pure Land," 394.

13. *Renjian jingtu zhi jianshe.*

14. Taixu, "On the Establishment of the Pure Land," 397.

15. *Baochi shenming zichan zhi anquanfa.*

16. Taixu, "On the Establishment of the Pure Land," 398–99.

17. *Juti zhi jianshe.*

18. These are precepts that laypeople take in a formal ceremony; they consist of vows not to kill, steal, engage in illicit sex, lie, or take intoxicants.

19. The ten virtuous deeds (*shi shan*) include not killing, not stealing, not committing sexual improprieties, not lying, not speaking harshly, not speaking hypocritically, not indulging in idle chatter, not being greedy, refraining from anger, and eschewing wrong views.

20. *Pubian zhi shehua.*

21. *Renjian jingtu yu yongsheng jile.*

22. Taixu, "On the Establishment of the Pure Land," 404–5.

23. *Foshuo guan Mile Pusa shangsheng doushuaitian jing*, T. 452.

24. *You benren fa dabeiyuan shishe wei shi.*

25. *Chuangzao renjian jingtu.*

26. This term is also sometimes rendered "five defilements" in English. They are (1) the decline of the present age, (2) the prevalence of heterodox views, (3) an increase in afflictions, (4) the defilement of sentient beings which increases misery, and (5) a decrease in lifespans.

27. Taixu, "On the Establishment of the Pure Land," 427.

28. Taixu's essay is long (about thirty thousand words), rambles, follows many threads of thought, and challenges any attempt at succinct recapitulation. Previous attempts to present its contents, such as those of Don Pittman and Justin Ritzinger, do not present the complexity of this text. I have provided a more detailed description of its contents here in order to give the reader the opportunity to see the extent to which Taixu mixes the modern with the traditional. Don A. Pittman, *Toward a Modern Chinese Buddhism: Taixu's Reforms* (Honolulu: University of Hawai'i Press, 2001), 221–29; Justin Ritzinger, *Anarchy in the Pure Land: Reinventing the Cult of Maitreya in Modern Chinese Buddhism* (New York: Oxford University Press, 2017), 195–97.

29. Karl Ludwig Reichelt, *The Transformed Abbot,* trans. G. M. Reichelt and A. P. Rose (London: Lutterworth, 1954), 80–81.

30. Reichelt, *Transformed Abbot,* 152–57.

31. Frank R. Millican, "T'ai-hsü and Modern Buddhism," *The Chinese Recorder* 54, no. 6 (1923): 331.

32. Clarence H. Hamilton, "An Hour with T'ai Shu, Master of the Law," *Open Court* 42 (1928): 165.

33. Paul Callahan quotes this phrase directly from the English version of a speech that Taixu delivered to the Far Eastern Buddhist Conference held in Tokyo in 1925. See Taixu, "A Statement to Asiatic Buddhists," in *The Young East* 1 (1925): 181.

34. Paul E. Callahan, "T'ai Hsü and the New Buddhist Movement," *Harvard University Papers on China*, no. 6, (1952): 156.

35. Callahan, "T'ai Hsü and the New Buddhist Movement," 158-59.

36. Welch, *Buddhist Revival*, 51-71.

37. Welch, *Buddhist Revival*, 68.

38. Pittman, *Toward a Modern Chinese Buddhism*, 294.

39. Eric Goodell, "Taixu's (1890-1947) Creation of Humanistic Buddhism" (PhD diss., University of Virginia, 2012), 20.

40. Goodell, "Taixu's Creation," 82.

41. Goodell, "Taixu's Creation," 207ff.

42. Goodell, "Taixu's Creation," 198.

43. Ritzinger, *Anarchy in the Pure Land*. See especially chapters 3 and 4.

44. Richard Madsen, *Democracy's Dharma: Religious Renaissance and Political Development in Taiwan* (Berkeley: University of California Press, 2007), 23.

45. In Muzhu Xu, Jinhua Chen, and Lori Meeks, eds., *Development and Practice of Humanitarian Buddhism: Interdisciplinary Perspectives* (Hualien, Taiwan: Tzu Chi University, 2007), 202-3.

46. Brooks Jessup, "The Householder Elite: Buddhist Activism in Shanghai, 1920-1956," chap. 1 (PhD diss., University of California-Berkeley, 2010).

47. The passage is cited with some abridgement in *Fo shuo wuliangshou jing*, T. 360.12:270a-272c; English in Inagaki and Stewart, 24-36.

48. *Fo shuo wuliangshou jing*, T. 360.12: 275c-277c; English in Inagaki and Stewart, 46-56.

49. *Fo shuo guan Mile Pusa shangsheng doushuaitian jing*, T. 452.14:418c-420c.

50. *Fo shuo Amituo jing*, T. 366.12: 346c-347b; English in Inagaki and Stewart, 91-93.

51. *Chan, tai, xian liugui jingtu xing.*

52. Taixu, *Collected Works*, 2:718.

53. This is the most prevalent English rendering of what in this chapter has been called "Buddhism for the human realm."

54. Scott Pacey, "Taixu, Yogācāra, and the Buddhist Approach to Modernity," in *Transforming Consciousness: Yogācāra Thought in Modern China*, ed. John Makeham (New York: Oxford University Press, 2014), 161.

6. The Shared Origins of Traditionalism and Secularism in Theravāda Buddhism by KATE CROSBY

1. On claims and misattributions relating to Buddhism and science, see Donald S. Lopez Jr., *Buddhism and Science: A Guide for the Perplexed* (Chicago and London: University of Chicago Press, 2008).

2. Geoffrey Samuel, "Between Buddhism and Science, between Mind and Body" *Religions* 5 (2014): 560-79.

3. On the current state of the Buddhism-science dialogue, looking at the Dalai Lama and the Mind and Life Institute, see Geoffrey Samuel, "Buddhism and Science," 560-79.

4. On Buddhaghosa's mention of meditation by laypeople in his commentary on the *Mahāsatipaṭṭhānasutta* as a possible influence on nineteenth-century expansion of meditation among laypeople, see Andrew Skilton, Kate Crosby, and Pyi Phyo Kyaw, "Terms of Engagement: Text, Technique, and Experience in Scholarship on Theravada Meditation," in *Variety in Theravada Meditation*, special issue of *Contemporary Buddhism* 20, no. 1-2 (2019): 19. On responses to previous crises in Theravāda history, and the resulting councils, many of which are not counted in the standard list of six that has become familiar as a result of the Burmese sixth council in 1956, see Tilman Frasch, "The Theravāda Buddhist Ecumene in the 15th Century: Intellectual Foundations and Material Representations," in *Buddhism across Asia: Networks of Material, Intellectual and Cultural Exchange* 1, (Singapore: ISEAS, 2012), 291-311. On meditation as part of the earlier eighteenth-century reform in Sri Lanka, see Kate Crosby, "*Abhidhamma* and *Nimitta* in 18th-century Meditation Manuscripts from Sri Lanka: A Consideration of Orthodoxy and Heteropraxy in *boran kammaṭṭhāna*," in *Variety in Theravada Meditation*, special issue of *Contemporary Buddhism* 20, no. 1-2 (2019): 111-51.

5. On the relationship between early texts and modern practices, and the way this obscures the history and diversity of Theravāda meditation, see Skilton, Crosby, and Kyaw, "Terms of Engagement."

6. On the impact of French colonialism on Buddhism in Cambodia, see Anne Ruth Hansen, *How to Behave: Buddhism and Modernity in Colonial Cambodia, 1860-1930* (Honolulu: University of Hawai'i Press, 2007).

7. On the fear of the decline of the sāsana in response to the devastation of colonialism, see Alicia Turner, *Saving Buddhism: Moral Community and the Impermanence of Colonial Religion* (Honolulu: University of Hawai'i Press, 2014).

8. For a discussion at ongoing attempts at medical reform throughout the colonial period, see Atsuko Naono, *State of Vaccination: The Fight Against*

Smallpox in Colonial Burma (Hyderabad: Orient Blackswan, 2009). For the situation in Thailand, see Kate Crosby, *Esoteric Theravada: The Story of the Forgotten Meditation Tradition of Southeast Asia* (Boulder: Shambhala Publications, 2020), 169-70.

9. Khammai Dhammasami, "Idealism and Pragmatism. A dilemma in the current monastic education systems of Burma and Thailand," in *Buddhism, Power and Political* Order, edited by Ian Harris (London and New York: Routledge, 2007), 12.

10. On the development of closer relations between lowland monks and laypeople in Sri Lanka, which began before the loss of the last king in the interior in 1815, see Kitsiri Malalgoda, *Buddhism and Sinhalese Society 1750-1900* (Berkeley: University of California Press, 1976). For the Burmese reaction to attempts to use the saṅgha to impart secular knowledge, as well as how the Burmese increasingly used the colonial policy on noninterference in religion to use religion as a sphere of anticolonial activity, see Turner, *Saving Buddhism*, who also provides a useful analysis of contrasting understandings of religion as individual versus communal.

11. J. M. Peebles, *The Great Debate: Buddhism and Christianity Face to Face, Being an Oral Debated Held at Panadura between the Rev. Migettuwatte Gunananda, a Buddhist Priest, and the Rev. David De Silva, a Wesleyan Clergyman* (Colombo: P. K. W. Siriwardhana, 1878), 165.

12. For a discussion of the relationship between Buddhist meditation and scientific explorations in the West in the early twentieth century, see Wakoh Shannon Hickey, *Mind Cure: How Meditation Became Medicine* (New York: Oxford University Press, 2019).

13. Peebles, *The Great Debate*, 165.

14. Donald S. Lopez Jr., *Prisoners of Shangri-La: Tibetan Buddhism and the West* (Chicago and London: The University of Chicago Press, 1998), 69.

15. Frank J. Karpiel, "Theosophy, Culture, and Politics in Honolulu, 1890-1920," *Hawaiian Journal of History* 30 (1996): 183.

16. Tobias Churton, *Aleister Crowley in India: The Secret Influence of Eastern Mysticism on Magic and the Occult* (Rochester, VT: Inner Traditions, 2019), 17.

17. Peebles, *The Great Debate*, 13-14.

18. Steven Kemper, *Rescued from the Nation: Anagarika Dharmapala and the Buddhist World* (Chicago and London: University of Chicago Press, 2015), 22.

19. See David Azzopardi, "Religious Belief and Practice among Sri Lankan Buddhists in the U.K.," chap. 7 and 8 (PhD diss., University of London, 2010). On the influence of modern discourse against the worship of gods as part of Sinhalese chauvinism, which leads to a convergence between

neotraditionalism and secular Buddhism, see Azzopardi, "Religious Belief and Practice," 130. Azzopardi's study provides a detailed exploration of the nuances of traditionalizing and secularizing tendencies among Sri Lankan Buddhists in the United Kingdom, with some surprising challenges to their perceived linear opposition. Despite this association of a more secular form of Buddhism with Angararika Dharmapala, Kemper has shown that his personal religion throughout his life was influenced by the Theosophical esotericism of Blavatsky. See Steven Kemper, "Anagarika Dharmapala's Meditation," *Contemporary Buddhism* 20, no. 1 (2019).

20. Dhammasami, "Idealism and Pragmatism," 12; Turner, *Saving Buddhism*, 56.

21. Monasteries in mainland Southeast Asia were, and in some cases in Thailand continue to be, places to learn martial arts. See, for example, the importance of training in traditional Thai boxing for novices in the Golden Triangle recorded in the 2006 film *Buddha's Lost Children* by Mark Verkerk. In Cambodia, Wat Preak Brang, one of the few remaining monasteries that still teaches the type of meditation described in this chapter, is closely associated with the military; see Crosby, *Esoteric Theravada*, 224.

22. Pyi Phyo Kyaw, "Paṭṭhāna in Burmese Buddhism," PhD thesis, King's College London (University of London, 2014); Erik C. Braun, *The Birth of Insight: Meditation, Modern Buddhism, and the Burmese Monk Ledi Sayadaw* (Chicago and London: University of Chicago Press, 2013).

23. Crosby, "*Abhidhamma* and *Nimitta*," 124.

24. Aung, "Buddhism and Science,"102-3.

25. On the attitudes of Mongkut and subsequent generations to meditation see Skilton, Crosby, and Kyaw, "Terms of Engagement." As Phibul Choompolpaisal points out, Mongkut's return to canonical orthodoxy was not applied in all aspects of his life. Unlike reform Buddhists in Bengal at this time, for example, he still sponsored large-scale animal sacrifice in his palace (Choompolpaisal, "Reassessing Modern Thai Political Buddhism," 198-199.). On the place of the Abhidhamma in Thailand in the modern period, including a revival under Burmese influence at the same time as the introduction of Burmese *vipassanā* there, see Piyobhaso (unpublished).

26. On the disputes over the full ordination of women and alternatives to full ordination in Theravāda countries that do not allow it, see Kate Crosby, *Theravada Buddhism: Continuity, Diversity, Identity* (Oxford: Blackwell-Wiley, 2014), chap. 9.

27. Piyobhaso, unpublished.

28. Skilton, Crosby, Shaw, "Terms of Engagement."

29. As I have written elsewhere, "These five aggregates (*khandha*) are (1) *rūpa*, materiality; (2) *vedanā*, sensation; (3) *saññā*, apperception; (4) *saṅkhārā*,

volitional responses; and (5) *viññāṇa*, consciousness. This list can be further analyzed under three main headings. The first is still *rūpa*, materiality, the first of the five *khandha*, which consists of the material elements and matter derived from them. The other four *khandha* are divided into two, aspects of consciousness, *cetasika*, and states of consciousness, *citta*. An important function of Abhidhamma…was to explain how these different categories combine and mutually cause one another. The result is a highly complex analysis of the human condition." See Crosby, *Esoteric Theravada*, 17.

30. On the history, practice, and disappearance of boran meditation, see Crosby, *Esoteric Theravada*.

31. Janaka Ashin, "Die-Human, Born Human: The Life and Posthumous Trial of Shin Ukkaṭṭha, a Pioneering Burmese Monk during a Tumultuous Period in a Nation's History," PhD diss. (King's College, London, 2016), 108. Khammai Dhammasami observes, "In the 1930s, Ashin Titthila (Seṭṭhila)…was asked by his benefactor in Mandalay never to come to his house for alms again because he had heard that Ashin Thitthila was studying English." (Dhammasami, "Idealism and Pragmatism," 18).

32. Ashin, "Die-Human, Born Human," 26, 109, 138.

33. Ashin, "Die-Human, Born Human," 151–52.

34. Michael Charney, *A History of Modern Burma* (Cambridge, MA: Cambridge University Press, 2009), 103.

35. On the life and trial of Shin Ukkaṭṭha, see Janaka Ashin and Kate Crosby, "Heresy and Monastic Malpractice in the Buddhist Court Cases (*Vinicchaya*) of Modern Burma (Myanmar)," *Contemporary Buddhism* 1 (2017): 199-261. For more in-depth study of Shin Ukkaṭṭha, see Ashin, "Die-Human, Born Human." For details of the seventeen cases and how these courts were organized, see Ashin and Crosby, "Heresy and Monastic Malpractice, 199-261.

7. Manifesting the Buddha Dharma in a Secular Age
by BHIKKHU BODHI

1. On this, see in particular David L. McMahan, *The Making of Buddhist Modernism* (New York: Oxford University Press, 2008), 61-116.

2. *Aṅguttara Nikāya* I 188-93. References to Pāli texts are to the editions of the Pali Text Society.

3. Jack Kornfield, *The Wise Heart* (New York: Bantam Books, 2008), 395.

4. Arthur Janov, "Gestalt Therapy: Being Here Now, Keeping Unfinished Business Unfinished," in *Grand Delusions: Psychotherapies Without Feeling* posted at http://primaltherapy.com/GrandDelusions/GD12.htm. Janov here quotes from Fritz Perls, *Ego, Hunger, and Aggression* (New York: Vintage Books, 1947).

5. Stephen Batchelor, "A Secular Buddhism." *Journal of Global Buddhism* 13 (2012): 90.

6. An example of a more conservative approach to Early Buddhism that still suspends belief in rebirth is that proposed by Doug Smith, Study Director of the Secular Buddhist Association, in his online essay, "A Secular Evaluation of Rebirth."

7. See Gil Fronsdal, "Should I Believe in Rebirth?" Insight Meditation Center (website), https://www.insightmeditationcenter.org/books-articles/articles /should-i-believe-in-rebirth/.

8. Gil Fronsdal, Insight Meditation Center (website), "Insight Meditation in the United States: Life, Liberty, and the Pursuit of Happiness," https://www. insightmeditationcenter.org/books-articles/articles/insight-meditation-in -the-united-states-life-liberty-and-the-pursuit-of-happiness/. (The essay originally appeared as chapter 9 in Prebish and Tanaka, *Faces of Buddhism*.)

9. For examples of this, see Stephen Batchelor, *Buddhism without Beliefs* (New York: Riverhead Books, 1997), 18-19, 81.

10. *Majjhima Nikāya* I 23.

11. *Majjhima Nikāya* I 69-71.

12. For a more detailed account of the relationship between the teaching of rebirth and other crucial teachings of Early Buddhism, see chapter 1 in Bhikkhu Anālayo, *Rebirth in Early Buddhism and Current Research* (Boston: Wisdom Publications, 2018).

8. Buddhism without a View by PHILIPPE TURENNE

1. There is no general agreement on what term to use to reflect the opposite of secular Buddhism. As Batchelor himself uses the term "traditional Buddhism," I will use it here to refer to forms of dharma that do not explicitly or self-consciously present themselves as being free of religion.

2. Stephen Batchelor, *After Buddhism: Rethinking the Dharma for a Secular Age* (New Haven, CT: Yale University Press, 2015), 74.

3. See Batchelor, *After Buddhism*, chapter 3.

4. Batchelor, *After Buddhism*, 129-32.

5. Batchelor, *After Buddhism*, 128.

6. See Batchelor, *After Buddhism*, chapter 9. Batchelor does not answer critiques (such as stated by Thanissaro Bhikkhu, Georges Dreyfus) of that interpretation of mindfulness but assumes the modern interpretation to be valid without the need for explanation.

7 . Stephen Batchelor, *Confession of a Buddhist Atheist* (New York: Spiegel & Grau, 2010), 100.

8. Peter Skilling, for example, tells us that "the idea that Pāli texts are the oldest

and most authentic is modern; it is a product of Western philological and text-comparative methodologies." Skilling, "Scriptural Authenticity and the Śrāvaka Schools: An Essay towards an Indian Perspective," *Eastern Buddhist* 41, no. 2 (2010): 5.

9. Batchelor, *After Buddhism*, 31.

10. For example, he writes of a certain passage, "It looks oddly out of place. For that very reason, it is probably original: It would have been in no orthodox tradition's interest to have added it later." "Stephen Batchelor in *Insight Journal*: 'You don't have to believe in rebirth to be a Buddhist,'" *Tricycle*, June 23, 2010, https://tricycle.org/trikedaily/stephen-batchelor-insight-journal -you-dont-have-believe-rebirth-be-buddhist/.

11. Batchelor, *After Buddhism*, 117.

12. Batchelor, *After Buddhism*, 147.

13. John Gray, *Seven Types of Atheism* (London: Allen Lane, 2018), 9.

14. Gray, *Seven Types*, 12.

15. Batchelor, *After Buddhism*, 115.

16. Batchelor, *After Buddhism*, 231.

9. Secular Buddhism in a Neoliberal Age by RON PURSER

1. Joshua Eaton, "American Buddhism: Beyond the Search for Inner Peace," *Religion Dispatches*, February 20, 2013, http://religiondispatches.org/american -buddhism-beyond-the-search-for-inner-peace/.

2. David Harvey, *A Brief History of Neoliberalism* (Oxford University Press, 2007), 3.

3. Pierre Bourdieu, The essence of neoliberalism. *Le Monde diplomatique*, December 1998, https://mondediplo.com/1998/12/08bourdieu.

4. Michel Foucault, *The Birth of Biopolitics: Lectures at the College de France, 1978-79*. Translated by G. Burchell. (New York: Palgrave Macmillan, 2008), 12.

5. Harvey, *Brief History of Neoliberalism*, 2.

6. Slavoj Zizek, "From Western Marxism to Western Buddhism," Spring 2001, *Cabinet Magazine*. http://www.cabinetmagazine.org/issues/2/western.php

7. Foucault, *The Birth of Biopolitics*, 43.

8. Foucault, *The Birth of Biopolitics*, 16.

9. Jeff Sugarman, "Neoliberalism and Psychological Ethics," *Journal of Theoretical and Philosophical Psychology* 35, no. 2 (2015): 105.

10. Michel Foucault, *The History of Sexuality Volume 1: An Introduction*. (New York: Vintage Books, 1978), 60.

11. Peter Fletcher, "Foucault on Confession," *Peter Fletcher* (blog), August 10, 2010, https://peterfletcher.com.au/2010/08/10/foucault-on-confession/.

12. Christopher Ziguras, *Self-Care: Embodiment, Personal Autonomy and the Shaping of Health Consciousness* (London: Routledge, 2013), 134.

13. Henry Giroux, *The Violence of Organized Forgetting: Thinking Beyond America's Disimagination Machine* (San Francisco: City Lights, 2014), 26-27.

14. Julie Wilson, *Neoliberalism* (London: Routledge, 2017), 220.

15. Ilana Gershon, "Neoliberal Agency," *Current Anthropology* 52, no. 4 (2011), 537-55.

16. Richard K. Payne, "Buddhism under Capitalism: Understanding 'Neoliberalism,'" *Critical Reflections on Buddhist Thought: Contemporary and Classical,* August 5, 2018, https://criticalreflectionsonbuddhistthought.org/2018/08/05/buddhism-under-capitalism-understanding-neoliberalism/.

17. Payne, "Buddhism under Capitalism."

18. Timothy Newton, *Managing Stress: Emotion and Power at Work* (London: Sage Publications, 1995), 11-12.

19. Nikolas Rose, *Inventing Ourselves: Psychology, Power, and Personhood* (Cambridge University Press, 1998), 160.

20. Newton, *Managing Stress*, 10.

21. Wendy Brown, *Undoing the Demos: Neoliberalism's Stealth Revolution* (New York: Zone Books, 2005), 34-35.

22. Julie Wilson, *Neoliberalism*, 212.

23. Herbert Rappaport, *Marking Time* (New York: Simon & Schuster), 191-92.

24. Eric Cazdyn, *The Already Dead: The New Time of Politics, Culture and Illness* (Durham: Duke University Press, 2012), 13.

25. Cazdyn, *The Already Dead*, 47.

26. Cazdyn, *The Already Dead*, 7-8.

27. Cazdyn, *The Already Dead*, 5.

28. Lauren Berlant, *Cruel Optimism* (Duke University Press, 2011), 1.

29. Nicole Aschoff, *The New Prophets of Capital* (London: Verso Books, 2015), 11.

30. William Davies, *The Happiness Industry* (London: Verso Books, 2015), 11.

10. The Modern Mindfulness Movement and the Search for Psychological Redemption by Kathleen Gregory

1. Traleg Kyabgon, *Desire: Why It Matters* (Ballarat, Australia: Shogam Publications, 2019), 141.

2. Daniela Villani, et al., "The Role of Spirituality and Religiosity in Subjective Well-Being of Individuals with Different Religious Status," *Frontiers in Psychology* 10 (2019): 1525. https://doi.org/10.3389/fpsyg.2019.01525.

3. Traleg Kyabgon, *Mind at Ease: Self-Liberation through Mahamudra Meditation* (Boston: Shambhala Publications, 2004), 54.

4. Jon Kabat-Zinn, "Some Reflections on the Origins of MBSR, Skillful Means, and the Trouble with Maps," *Contemporary Buddhism* 12, no.1 (2011): 281–306.

5. See "Guided Mindfulness Meditation Practices with Jon Kabat-Zinn," https://www.mindfulnesscds.com/.

6. Jon Kabat-Zinn, *Mindfulness for Beginners: Reclaiming the Present Moment – And Your Life* (Boulder: Sounds True, 2012), 1.

7. Alex Caring-Lobel, "Corporate Mindfulness and the Pathologization of Workplace Stress," *Handbook of Mindfulness and Self-Regulation*, eds. Brian D. Ostafin, Michael D. Robinson, and Brian P. Meier (New York: Springer, 2015), 195–214.

8. *Time*, "The New Mindfulness: Living, Thinking, Being," single-issue edition, November 28, 2018.

9. Brian D. Ostafin et al., "Introduction: The Science of Mindfulness and Self-Regulation" in *Handbook of Mindfulness and Self-regulation*, eds. Brian D. Ostafin, Michael D. Robinson, and Brian P. Meier (New York: Springer, 2015): 6.

10. Nikolas Rose, *Power and Subjectivity: Psychology, Power and Personhood* (London: Cambridge University Press, 1998), 2.

11. Jean McAvoy, "Psy Disciplines," *Encyclopedia of Critical Psychology,* ed. Thomas Teo (New York: Springer, 2014). https://doi.org/10.1007/978-1-4614 -5583-7_611.

12. Ole Jacob Madsen, *The Therapeutic Turn: How Psychology Altered Western Culture* (East Sussex, UK: Routledge, 2014), 29.

13. Jan De Vos, *Psychologization and the Subject of Late Modernity* (New York: Palgrave MacMillan, 2013).

14. Eva Illouz, *Saving the Modern Soul: Therapy, Emotions, and the Culture of Self-help* (Oakland: University of California Press, 2008), 188.

15. De Vos, *Psychologization*, 3.

16. Illouz, *Saving the Modern Soul*, 138.

17. Amisha P. Jha, Jason Krompinger, and Michael J. Baime, "Mindfulness Training Modifies Subsystems of Attention." *Cognitive, Affective and Behavioral Neuroscience* 7, no. 2 (2007): 109–119.

18. De Vos, *Psychologization*.

19. Michael White, "Addressing Personal Failure," *International Journal of Narrative and Community Work*, no. 3, (2002): 33–76.

20. Traleg Kyabgon, *The Benevolent Mind: A Manual in Mind Training* (Auckland, NZ: Zhyisil Chokyi Ghatsal Publications, 2003), 97.

21. Traleg Kyabgon, *Mind at Ease*, 69.

22. Traleg Kyabgon, *The Essence of Buddhism* (Boston: Shambhala Publications, 2001), 70.

23. Traleg Kyabgon, *Benevolent Mind*, 96.

24. Traleg Kyabgon, *Mind at Ease*, 61.

25. Raymond Tallis, *Aping Mankind: Neuromania, Darwinitis and the Misrepresentation of Humanity* (Oxford: Routledge, 2011).

26. Jan De Vos, *Metamorphoses of the Brain: Neurologisation and Its Discontents* (New York: Palgrave MacMillan, 2016), 16.

27. De Vos, *Metamorphoses of the Brain*, 2.

28. For example, the work of Richard J. Davidson and colleagues at the Center for Healthy Minds at the University of Wisconsin–Madison has been instrumental in forging the study into the neural basis of meditation. See their work at https://centerhealthyminds.org/science/overview.

29. De Vos, *The Metamorphoses of the Brain*, 54.

11. Avoiding Rebirth by ROGER R. JACKSON

1. Stephen Batchelor, *Buddhism without Beliefs: A Contemporary Guide to Awakening* (New York: Riverhead Books, 1997). An even earlier foray into the topic, first published in 1992, is reprinted in Batchelor, *Secular Buddhism: Imagining the Dharma in an Uncertain World* (New Haven, CT: Yale University Press, 2017), 111–25.

2. Batchelor first makes the case for an "existential approach to Buddhism" in *Alone with Others: An Existential Approach to Buddhism* (New York: Grove Press, 1984), but it was *Buddhism without Beliefs*, more than a decade later, that captured the attention of a broader public. See also the magisterial analysis in Gananath Obeyesekere, *Imagining Karma: Ethical Transformation in Amerindian, Buddhist, and Greek Rebirth* (Berkeley and Los Angeles: University of California Press, 2002), especially chaps. 1, 3–4.

3. Batchelor, *Secular Buddhism*, 34–38.

4. See, for example, Robert Thurman, *Inner Revolution: Life, Liberty, and the Pursuit of Real Happiness* (New York: Riverhead Books, 1999).

5 "Reincarnation: A Debate: Batchelor v. Thurman," *Tricycle,* Summer 1997, https://tricycle.org/magazine/reincarnation-debate/.

6. See, for example, Ian Stevenson, *Cases of the Reincarnation Type, Volume 2: Ten Cases in Sri Lanka* (Charlottesville: University of Virginia Press, 1977), and the renewed investigation of Stevenson's research in Bhikkhu Anālayo, *Rebirth in Early Buddhism and Current Research* (Boston: Wisdom Publications, 2017).

7. I have argued along similar lines in "For Whom Emptiness Prevails: An Analysis of the Religious Implications of Nāgārjuna's *Vigrahavyavartanī* 70," *Religious Studies* 21 (September 1985): 407–14.

8. *Tricycle,* "Reincarnation: A Debate."

9. On this question, see, for example, Stephen Batchelor, *After Buddhism: Rethinking the Dharma for a Secular Age* (New Haven, CT: Yale University Press, 2015); Roger R. Jackson, review of *After Buddhism*, by Stephen Batchelor, *Buddhadharma* (Winter 2016): 73-77; Anālayo, *Rebirth in Early Buddhism and Current Research*.

10. See, for example, Roger R. Jackson, *Is Enlightenment Possible? Dharmakīrti and rGyal tshab rje on Knowledge, Rebirth, No-Self and Liberation* (Ithaca, NY: Snow Lion, 1993); Eli Franco, *Dharmakīrti on Compassion and Rebirth* (Vienna: Arbeitskreis für tibetische und buddhistische Studien Universität Wien, 1997).

11. Clifford Geertz, *Islam Observed: Religious Development in Morocco and Indonesia* (Chicago: University of Chicago Press, 1968), 16.

12. For an interesting survey of the range of views to be found in a single Buddhist organization, the Triratna Buddhist Community, see Mark Liebenrood "Do Buddhists Believe in Rebirth?" *Windhorse*, March 5, 2015, https://www.windhorsepublications.com/do-buddhists-believe-in-rebirth/.

13. I plan to provide such a survey in a forthcoming book on rebirth in Buddhism to be published by Shambhala Publications.

14. For overviews of Buddhism in the modern world, especially the West, see, for example, Stephen Batchelor, *The Awakening of the West: The Encounter of Buddhism and Western Culture* (London: Aquarian, 1994); Rick Fields, *How the Swans Came to the Lake: A Narrative History of Buddhism in America*, 3rd ed. (Boston and London: Shambhala, 1992); and David L. McMahan, *The Making of Modern Buddhism* (Oxford and New York: Oxford University Press, 2008).

15. For a useful illustration of this in a single source, see Liebenrood, "Do Buddhists Believe in Rebirth?"

16. Owen Flanagan, *The Bodhisattva's Brain: Buddhism Naturalized* (Cambridge, MA: MIT Press, 2011), 3; see also his discussion of matter and consciousness in *Bodhisattva's Brain*, 70-90.

17. Robert Wright, *Why Buddhism Is True: The Science and Philosophy of Meditation and Enlightenment* (New York: Simon and Schuster, 2017), xi.

18. Jay L. Garfield, *Engaging Buddhism: Why It Matters to Philosophy* (Oxford and New York: Oxford University Press, 2015), 4.

19. Batchelor, *Secular Buddhism*, 125.

20. Richard P. Hayes, *Land of No Buddha: Reflections of a Sceptical Buddhist* (Birmingham, UK: Windhorse Publications, 1998), 59, 61, 62, 80.

21. Martin Willson, *Rebirth and the Western Buddhist* (London: Wisdom Publications, 1987), 39-46. Willson is actually commenting on a text by a modern Geluk lama, the late Losang Gyatso, but the arguments Gyatso cites are mostly Dharmakīrti's.

22. Roger R. Jackson, *Is Enlightenment Possible? Dharmakīrti and rGyal tshab rje on Knowledge, Rebirth, No-Self and Liberation* (Ithaca, NY: Snow Lion, 1993), 128–39, 366n36. More recently, I have come to appreciate that there is a sense in which Dharmakīrti is articulating what in Western philosophy of mind is called the "really hard problem": how to account for subjective experience from a materialist standpoint. I'm not sure that Dharmakīrti's dualism is the best solution, but I'm no longer sure I would simply say that he is begging the question.

23. Richard P. Hayes, "Dharmakīrti on Punarbhava," in *Studies in Original Buddhism and Mahāyāna Buddhism*, ed. Egaku Maeda (Kyōto: Nagata Bunshodo, 1993).

24. Dan Arnold, *Brains, Buddhas, and Believing: The Problem of Intentionality in Classical Buddhist and Cognitive-Scientific Philosophy of Mind* (New York: Columbia University Press, 2012), 40–47.

25. Evan Thompson, *Waking, Dreaming, Being: Self and Consciousness in Neuroscience, Meditation, and Philosophy* (New York: Columbia University Press, 2015), 82, 105. For a somewhat similar discussion, see Flanagan, *The Bodhisattva's Brain*, 70–90. For a panpsychist approach to these issues that nevertheless remains materialist, see Philip Goff, *Galileo's Error: Foundations for a New Science of Consciousness* (New York: Pantheon Books, 2019).

26. See the Fourteenth Dalai Lama, *The Universe in a Single Atom: The Convergence of Science and Spirituality* (New York: Morgan Road Books, 2005), 117–61.

27. See, for example, Thompson, *Waking, Dreaming, Being*, 293–99.

28. See *Tricycle*, "Reincarnation: A Debate"; Thurman, *Inner Revolution*. For a detailed analysis of Darwinian evolution vis-à-vis traditional Buddhist metaphysics, see Roger R. Jackson, "Indo-Tibetan Buddhist Responses to Darwinism," in *Religious Responses to Darwinism*, ed. Mackenzie Brown (London: Springer, 2020), 209–39.

29. See B. Alan Wallace, *Meditations of a Buddhist Skeptic: A Manifesto for the Mind Sciences and Contemplative Practice* (New York: Columbia University Press, 2012), 84.

30. David R. Loy, *A New Buddhist Path: Enlightenment, Evolution, and Ethics in the Modern World* (Boston: Wisdom Publications, 2015), 85.

31. Loy, *A New Buddhist Path*, 139.

32. Loy *A New Buddhist Path*, 142.

33. Jean-François Revel and Matthieu Ricard, *The Monk and the Philosopher: A Father and Son Discuss the Meaning of Life* (New York: Schocken Books, 1998), 78.

34. Wallace, *Meditations of a Buddhist Skeptic*, 149.

35. See, for example, Stevenson, *Cases of the Reincarnation Type*. A number of Stevenson's Buddhist cases are also discussed in Francis Story, *Rebirth*

as Doctrine and Experience: Essays and Case Studies (Kandy: Buddhist Publication Society, 1975), part two.

36. Willson, *Rebirth and the Western Buddhist*, 17–32.

37. Anālayo *Rebirth in Early Buddhism and Current Research*, part 3.3–4, and part 4.

38. Thompson, *Waking, Dreaming, Being*, 290.

39. Batchelor, *Secular Buddhism*, 121.

40. Donald S. Lopez Jr., *The Scientific Buddha: His Short and Happy Life* (New Haven, CT: Yale University Press, 2012), 131–32.

41. For another take on this question, see Francesca Cho and Richard K. Squier, *Religion and Science in the Mirror of Buddhism* (New York and London: Routledge, 2016), especially 140–58.

42. Hayes, *Land of No Buddha*, 78–79.

43. Hayes, *Land of No Buddha*, 79–80.

44. Hayes, *Land of No Buddha*, 80–81.

45. Batchelor, *Secular Buddhism*, 123.

46. Batchelor, *Secular Buddhism*, 125.

47. "Reincarnation: A Debate," 18.

48. Wallace Stevens, *Collected Poems* (New York: Alfred A. Knopf, 1971), 336.

49. I gestured at such an approach to Buddhism—terming it "aesthetic"—in Roger R. Jackson, "In Search of a Postmodern Middle," in *Buddhist Theology: Critical Reflections by Contemporary Buddhist Scholars*, edited by Roger R. Jackson and John J. Makransky (Richmond, Surrey, UK: Curzon Press, 2000), 223–27. For a seminal version of my as-if/as-is analysis (which will be expanded to book length in the future), see Roger R. Jackson, "As Is/As If: The Anxious First-Year's Guide to Argument and Inquiry" (Unpublished lecture, Carleton College Argument and Inquiry Convocation, September 23, 2016).

12. Naturalistic Buddhism by GIL FRONSDAL

1. Gil Fronsdal, *The Buddha before Buddhism* (Boulder: Shambhala Publications, 2016).

2. Fronsdal, *Buddha before Buddhism* v. 940.

3. Fronsdal, *Buddha before Buddhism* v. 919.

4. Fronsdal, *Buddha before Buddhism* v. 919; Sn 4.14.

5. Fronsdal, *Buddha before Buddhism* v 787; Sn 4.3.

6. *Majjhima Nikāya* 131–34; MN iii 187.

7. *Pārāyana Vagga* v. 1098–99; Sn 5.11.

8. *Majjhima Nikāya* 22; MN I 136.

9. *Majjhima Nikāya* 63; MN I 431.

10. *Dhammapada* v. 183.

11. *Dhammapada* v. 185.
12. *Aṅguttara Nikāya* 8.53; AN iv 280.
13. *Majjhima Nikāya* 18; MN I 108.
14. *Majjhima Nikāya* 7; MN i 37.
15. *Aṅguttara Nikāya* 6.47; AN iii 357
16. *Saṃyutta Nikāya* 38.1; SN iv 251.
17. *Saṃyutta Nikāya* 45.6; SN v 8.
18. *Saṃyutta Nikāya* 43.a; SN iv 359.
19. *Saṃyutta Nikāya* 45.7; SN v 8.

13. Conscious and Unconscious Dynamics in the Secularizing Discourse by RICHARD K. PAYNE

1. David L. McMahan, "Buddhism and Global Secularisms," *Journal of Global Buddhism* 18 (2017): 112–28, 113.
2. As Timothy Fitzgerald puts it, "The very powerful dominant notion that religion is essentially about personal belief in some unseen supernatural power separated from the public rationality of the secular objective standpoint... by being implicitly or explicitly assumed, is actually being constructed." Timothy Fitzgerald, *Discourse on Civility and Barbarity: A Critical History of Religion and Related Categories* (Oxford and New York: Oxford University Press, 2007), 11.
3. See Wakoh Shannon Hickey, "Two Buddhisms, Three Buddhisms, and Racism," *Journal of Global Buddhism* 11 (2020): 1–25.
4. Ann Gleig, *American Dharma: Buddhism beyond Modernity* (New Haven, CT, and London: Yale University Press, 2019), 36.
5. Richard K. Payne, *Language in the Buddhist Tantra of Japan: Indian Roots of Mantra* (London: Bloomsbury Academic, 2018), 16.
6. Stephen Batchelor, "Dropping the Bodhisattva Gods," *Tricycle,* June 13, 2018, https://tricycle.org/trikedaily/stephen-batchelor-secular-buddhism/.
7. Jane E. Strohl, "The Framework for Christian Living: Luther on the Christian's Callings," in *The Oxford Handbook of Martin Luther's Theology*, ed. Robert Kokb, Irene Dingel, and Ľuobmír Batka (Oxford and New York: Oxford University Press, 2014), 367.
8. Another ramification of this change from monastic authority is secular for-fee training programs that now provide certification in therapies such as mindfulness and reiki.
9. Justin Whitaker, "Secular Buddhism in America," *Buddhistdoor* (website), July 21, 2017, https://www.buddhistdoor.net/features/secular-buddhism-in-north-america.
10. Gil Fronsdal, "Rituals in Buddhism," Insight Meditation Center (web-

site), accessed June 30, 2020, https://www.insightmeditationcenter.org /books-articles/rituals-in-buddhism/.

11. Doug Smith, "Secular Practice with Images and Rituals," Secular Buddhist Association (website), April 30, 2018, https://secularbuddhism.org /secular-practice-with-images-and-rituals/.

12. Natalie Quli, "On Authenticity: Scholarship, the Insight Movement, and White Authority," in *Methods in Buddhist Studies: Essays in Honor of Richard K. Payne*, ed. Scott A. Mitchell and Natalie Quli (London and New York: Bloomsbury Academic, 2019), 165.

13. Chris Talbott, "New Rivers, New Rafts: The Secular Buddhism Conference," *Insight Journal* 2013, https://www.buddhistinquiry.org/article /new-rivers-new-rafts-the-secular-buddhism-conference/.

14. Ṭhānissaro Bhikkhu, trans., "About Aṅgulimāla: *Aṅgulimāla Sutta* (MN 86)," https://www.dhammatalks.org/suttas/MN/MN86.html, accessed June 30, 2020.

15. Stephen Batchelor, "An Open Letter to B. Alan Wallace," *Mandala*, January 2011, https://fpmt.org/mandala/archives/mandala-issues-for-2011/january /an-open-letter-to-b-alan-wallace.

16. Batchelor, "An Open Letter to B. Alan Wallace."

17. Richard K. Payne, "Introduction," in *Re-Visioning "Kamakura" Buddhism* (Honolulu: University of Hawai'i Press, 1998), 9–11; Richard K. Payne, "Introduction," in *Tantric Buddhism in East Asia*, ed. Richard K. Payne (Boston: Wisdom Publications, 2005), 1; Richard K. Payne, "Lethal Fire: The Shingon Yamāntaka Abhicāra Homa," *Journal of Religion and Violence* 6, no. 1 (2018): 14; and Richard K. Payne, "Study of Buddhist Tantra: An Impressionistic Overview," *Pacific World: Journal of the Institute of Buddhist Studies*, 3rd series, no. 20 (2018): 27.

18. Sam Harris, "Killing the Buddha," *Shambhala Sun* (now *Lion's Roar*), March 19, 2006, reprinted at https://samharris.org/killing-the-buddha/.

19. Ted Meissner, "About: Mission," *The Secular Buddhist* (website), accessed June 2, 2019, http://www.thesecularbuddhist.com/about_mission.php.

20. Gleig, *American Dharma*, 40.

21. The problematics of these oppositions is not simply that they are not descriptively accurate, or that they are rooted in the long history of European and American imperialism (that is, "the white man's burden"), but that they reinforce a framework of values having real world consequences. See Natalie Quli, "Western Self, Asian Other: Modernity, Authenticity, and Nostalgia for 'Tradition' in Buddhist Studies," *Journal of Buddhist Ethics* 16 (2009): 1–38.

22. Stephen Batchelor, *Buddhism without Beliefs: A Contemporary Guide to Awakening* (New York: Riverhead Books, 1997), 16.

23. Batchelor, *Buddhism without Beliefs*, 34–35.

24. *Secular Buddhist*, https://secularbuddhism.org/faq/.

25. *Secular Buddhist*, https://secularbuddhism.org/faq/.

26. Batchelor, *Buddhism without Beliefs*, 53.

27. Vincent Horn, "The Core Features of Pragmatic Dharma," *Buddhist Geeks* (blog), October 18, 2018, https://www.pragmaticdharma.training/blog/core-features-pragmatic-dharma.

28. Gleig, *American Dharma*, 36.

29. Stephen Batchelor, *After Buddhism: Rethinking the Dharma for a Secular Age* (New York: HarperCollins, 2016), 14.

30. Michael J. Altman, "Orientalism in Nineteenth-Century America," in *The Oxford Handbook of Religion and Race in American History*, ed. Paul Harvey and Kathryn Gin Lum (Oxford and New York: Oxford University Press, 2018), 125. One of the most important discussions of the plasticity of the categories of religion and race—and human—is David Chidester, *Savage Systems: Colonialism and Comparative Religion in Southern Africa* (Charlottesville: University of Virginia Press, 1996).

31. Max Zahn, "'Even the Rich Suffer': An Interview with Google's Jolly Good Fellow Chade-Meng Tan," *Religion Dispatches*, April 26, 2016, http://religiondispatches.org/rich-people-need-inner-peace-too-an-interview-with-googles-jolly-good-fellow-chade-meng-tan/.

32. See Goodman's bio at the InsightLA Meditation website, https://insightla.org/teacher/trudy-goodman/.

33. *Lion's Roar*, "What Does Mindfulness Mean for Buddhism?" Staff forum, May 5, 2015, https://www.lionsroar.com/forum-what-does-mindfulness-mean-for-buddhism/.

34. Stephen Batchelor, *Confession of a Buddhist Atheist* (New York: Random House, 2010), 6.

35. Gleig, *American Dharma*, 52. The work in question is Barry Boyce, ed., *The Mindfulness Revolution: Leading Psychologists, Scientists, Artists, and Meditation Teachers on the Power of Mindfulness in Daily Life* (Boston and London: Shambhala Publications, 2011).

36. This view, dating from the Enlightenment, while fundamental to the formation of the United States, is increasingly under assault by Christian nationalists who privilege the religious tradition over all others, and their own religious identity over their status as citizens. Indeed, one of the factors adding to the imposition of an individual "religious identity" is the pervasive belief in popular culture that morality—which is socially valued—is dependent upon religion. See Kevin M. Kruse, *One Nation under God: How Corporate America Invented Christian America* (New York: Basic Books, 2015).

37. Barry Boyce, "Introduction: Anyone Can Do It and It Changes Everything,"

in *The Mindfulness Revolution: Leading Psychologists, Scientists, Artists, and Meditation Teachers on the Power of Mindfulness in Daily Life*, ed. Barry Boyce (Boston and London: Shambhala Publications, 2011), xii.

38. Ira P. Helderman, "Drawing the Boundaries between 'Religion' and 'Secular' in Psychotherapists' Approaches to Buddhist Traditions in the United States," *Journal of the American Academy of Religion* 84, no. 4 (December 2016), 937–72; Ira P. Helderman, *Prescribing the Dharma: Psychotherapists, Buddhist Traditions, and Defining Religion* (Chapel Hill: University of North Carolina Press, 2019).

39. Timothy Fitzgerald, *The Ideology of Religious Studies* (Oxford and New York: Oxford University Press, 2000).

40. Wakoh Shannon Hickey, *Mind Cure: How Meditation Became Medicine* (Oxford and New York: Oxford University Press, 2019).

About the Contributors

VEN. BHIKKHU BODHI is an American Buddhist monk originally from New York City. He holds a PhD in philosophy from Claremont Graduate University (1972). After completing his university studies, he traveled to Sri Lanka, where he received novice ordination in 1972 and full ordination in 1973, both under the Sri Lankan scholar-monk Ven. Balangoda Ananda Maitreya (1896-1998). From 1984 until 2002 he was the editor for the Buddhist Publication Society in Kandy, and its president from 1988 until 2010.

Ven. Bodhi has many important publications to his credit, either as author, translator, or editor. These include *The Middle Length Discourses of the Buddha* (Majjhima Nikaya, 1995), *The Connected Discourses of the Buddha* (Samyutta Nikaya, 2000), *The Numerical Discourses of the Buddha* (Anguttara Nikaya, 2012), *The Buddha's Teachings on Social and Communal Harmony* (2015), and the *Suttanipāta: An Ancient Collection of the Buddha's Discourses* (2017).

Ven. Bodhi lives and teaches at Chuang Yen Monastery in upstate New York. In 2008, together with several of his students, he founded Buddhist Global Relief, a nonprofit supporting hunger and poverty relief for communities suffering from chronic hunger and malnutrition.

KATE CROSBY is professor of Buddhist Studies at King's College London. Her work focuses on Sanskrit, Pāli, and Pāli-vernacular literature and on Theravāda practice in the pre-modern and modern periods. Her other publications include *Theravada Buddhism: Continuity, Diversity, Identity*; *The Bodhicaryavatara*; and *Esoteric Theravada: The Story of the Forgotten Meditation Tradition of Southeast Asia*.

GIL FRONSDAL is the primary Buddhist teacher for the Insight Meditation Center in Redwood City, California. He has practiced Zen since 1975 and Vipassana since 1984. He received a PhD in religious studies from Stanford University with a dissertation on early Mahāyana Buddhism. He is the author of *The Issue at*

Hand: Essays on Mindfulness Practice and *The Book of Eights*, a translation of the *Aṭṭhakavagga*, which is a subject of this essay.

KATHLEEN GREGORY, PhD, is an Australian psychologist and academic. She has taught in graduate counseling programs both in Australia and the US. Recently, she served as Dean of the Graduate School of Counseling and Psychology at Naropa University in Boulder, Colorado. She has been a student of the late Traleg Kyabgon Rinpoche IX for over twenty-five years. She has taught regularly on Buddhism and psychotherapy at the E-Vam Institute in Melbourne and related international centers. She is published in the areas of contemporary Buddhism, ethics in counseling, and cross-cultural counseling.

FUNIE HSU is an assistant professor of American studies at San Jose State University. She received her PhD in education from the University of California Berkeley. Funie was a former University of California President's Postdoctoral Fellow as well as a former elementary school teacher. Her research broadly investigates knowledge construction and American empire. One area of her work examines American Buddhism, Asian Americans, race, and secular mindfulness. She was raised in a working-class Taiwanese–American Buddhist household and maintains her family practice alongside the study of Shin Buddhism.

ROGER R. JACKSON is Professor Emeritus of Asian studies and religion at Carleton College. He specializes in Indian and Tibetan Buddhist philosophy, meditation, and ritual. He has also written extensively on Buddhist religious poetry, mysticism, and contemporary Buddhist thought. His current research focuses on the Indian tantric adept Saraha. He is the author of *Is Enlightenment Possible?*, *Tantric Treasures*, and *Mind Seeing Mind: Mahāmudrā and the Geluk Tradition of Tibetan Buddhism*; co-author of *The Wheel of Time: Kalachakra in Context*, editor of *The Crystal Mirror of Philosophical Systems*, and co-editor of *Tibetan Literature: Studies in Genre*, *Buddhist Theology*, *Mahāmudrā and the Bka' brgyud Tradition*, and *Mahāmudrā in India and Tibet*.

CHARLES B. JONES is associate professor and director of the religion and culture graduate program in the School of Theology and Religious Studies at the Catholic University of America, Washington, DC. He earned a PhD in history of religions from the University of Virginia in 1996 with an emphasis on East Asian Buddhism. In 1999 he published his first book, *Buddhism in Taiwan: Religion and the State 1660–1990*, the first history of its type to be published in any language. Since then, he has focused primarily on the study of Chinese Pure Land Buddhism in the late imperial period. He has also published books and articles on the Jesuit missions in late Ming dynasty China, late Ming gentry Buddhism, and interreligious dialogue. He was a Fulbright scholar in Taiwan during the 2004–2005 academic year.

DAVID L. MCMAHAN is the Charles A. Dana Professor of Religious Studies at Franklin & Marshall College in Pennsylvania. He is the author of *The Making of Buddhist Modernism* (Oxford University Press, 2008), *Empty Vision: Metaphor and Visionary Imagery in Mahāyāna Buddhism* (Routledge Curzon, 2002), and several articles on Mahāyāna Buddhism in South Asia and Buddhism in the modern world. He is also the co-editor of *Buddhism, Meditation and Science* (Oxford University Press, 2017) and the editor of *Buddhism in the Modern World* (Routledge 2012).

RICHARD K. PAYNE is the Yehan Numata Professor of Japanese Buddhist Studies at the Institute of Buddhist Studies in Berkeley, California. Richard is active in the fields of Japanese Buddhist studies and ritual studies. He also serves as editor-in-chief of the institute's annual journal, *Pacific World*, and is chair of the Editorial Committee of the Pure Land Buddhist Studies Series.

RONALD PURSER is a professor of management at San Francisco State University and co-host of the *Mindful Cranks* podcast. His recent book is *McMindfulness: How Mindfulness Became the New Capitalist Spirituality* (Repeater Books, 2019).

SARAH SHAW attended Manchester University, where she read Greek and English and did her doctorate on English literature. She now works on early Buddhist texts and has published a number of translations and books on meditation and Buddhist narrative. She is the Khyentse Foundation Reader in Buddhist Studies, University of South Wales, UK, a fellow of the Oxford Centre for Buddhist Studies, and a member of the Faculty of Oriental Studies, University of Oxford.

PHILIPPE TURENNE has practice and studied Buddhism since 1995. He has received a BA and PhD degree from McGill University in Buddhist studies. In 2011, he joined the faculty at the Rangjung Yeshe Institute in Kathmandu, Nepal, where he is now serving as Principal.

PAMELA D. WINFIELD is associate professor of religious studies at Elon University, NC. She is the author of *Icons and Iconoclasm in Japanese Buddhism: Kūkai and Dōgen on the Art of Enlightenment* (Oxford University Press, 2013; AAS-SEC Book Prize 2015) and the lead co-editor (with Steven Heine) of *Zen and*

Material Culture (Oxford University Press, 2017). She has edited several special issues of *CrossCurrents Journal* (Wiley), and her scholarship has appeared in publications by Oxford, Columbia, Brill, Routledge, Springer, *The Japanese Journal of Religious Studies*, *Material Religion*, and *Religion Compass*, among others. Her research has been supported by grants notably from the American Academy of Religion, the Association of Asian Studies, and the Asian Cultural Council. She is currently the president of the Society for the Study of Japanese Religions (SSJR) and co-chair of the Arts, Literature and Religion Unit at the American Academy of Religion.